WHITECHAPEL AT WAR
ISAAC ROSENBERG & HIS CIRCLE

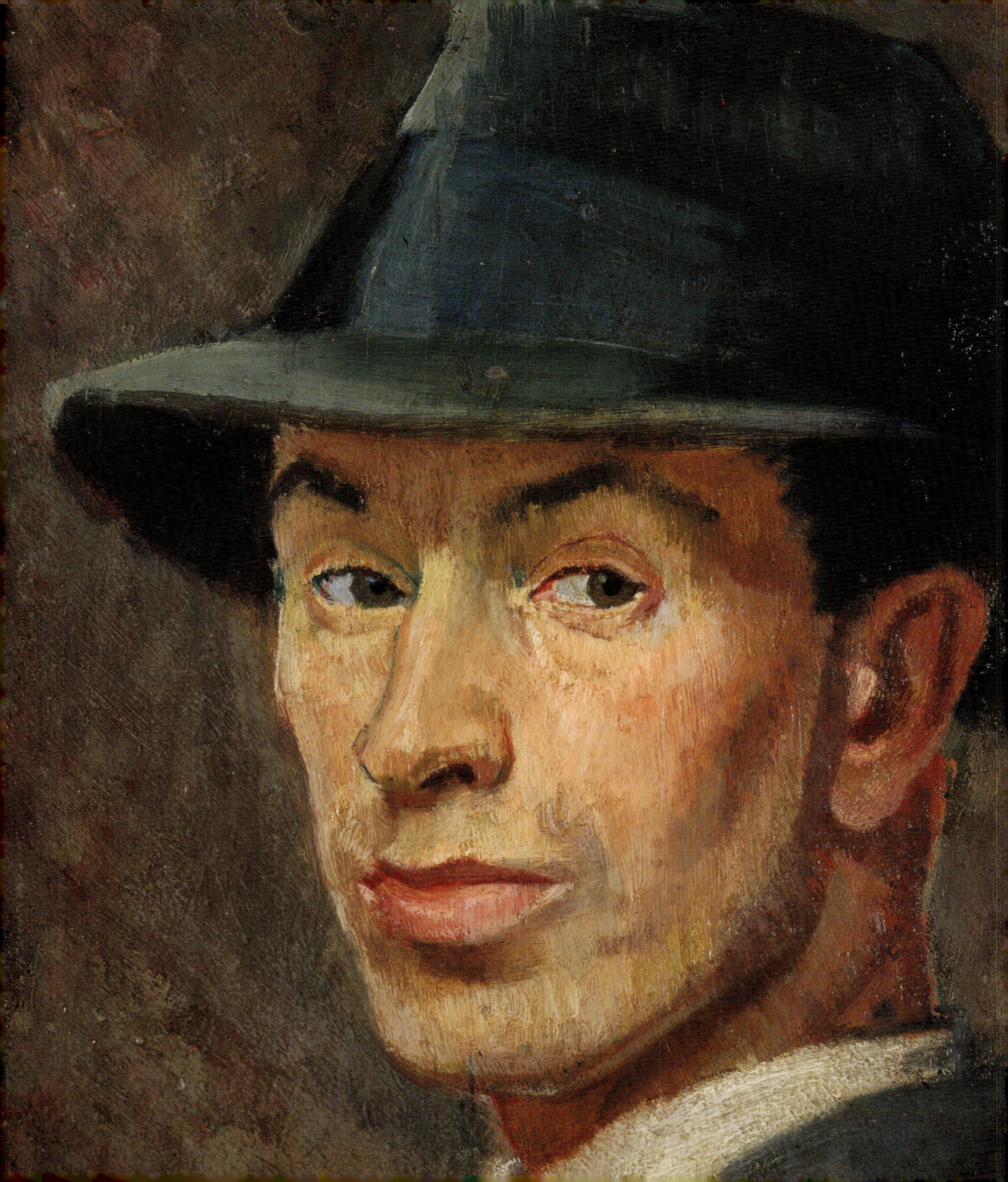

WHITECHAPEL AT WAR
ISAAC ROSENBERG & HIS CIRCLE

BEN URI GALLERY,
THE LONDON JEWISH MUSEUM OF ART
02 APRIL–08 JUNE 2008

THE STANLEY & AUDREY BURTON GALLERY,
LEEDS UNIVERSITY,
16 JUNE–05 SEPTEMBER 2008

The London Jewish Museum of Art
A Museum for Everyone Bridging Communities through Art

Ben Uri

The London Jewish Museum of Art

A Museum for Everyone Bridging Communities through Art

SHORT HISTORY AND MISSION STATEMENT

Ben Uri Gallery is Britain's oldest Jewish cultural organisation. It was founded by Lazar Berson in 1915 in London's East End as an art society to provide support for Jewish artists and crafts people who were working in the face of poverty, anti-semitism and isolation from the mainstream. It was named after Bezalel Ben Uri the craftsman who designed and built the Ark of the Covenant in biblical times.

It is Europe's only dedicated Jewish Museum of Art, working in partnership with secular and Jewish Museums in the UK and internationally.

The gallery and museum is an educational institution dedicated to enhancing the quality of life of all whom it impacts. It embraces a new broad and fully inclusive role for museums in today's society and addresses contemporary issues through art and its social history.

By fostering easy access, greater appreciation and both social and academic enjoyment of the visual arts, there is an ongoing opportunity to demonstrate its value as a robust and unique bridge between the cultural, religious, political differences and beliefs of our fellow citizens.

Its purpose is to enable the largest possible audience, drawn from the widest possible communities from both home and abroad, to explore for inspiration, learning and enjoyment, the work, lives and contribution of British and European artists of Jewish descent, placed where relevant alongside their non-Jewish contemporaries, within the artistic and social context of the national cultural heritage. Through this wide and open outreach 'A Museum for Everyone Bridging Communities through Art' is achieved.

Its principal route to achieving this is by enabling broad, easy and straightforward physical and visual access – through location, publication, Internet and outreach – to the following:

- THE PERMANENT COLLECTION: the largest of its kind in the world, accessed physically or virtually via continued exhibition, research, conservation and acquisition.
- TEMPORARY EXHIBITIONS: curating, touring and hosting important internationally-focused exhibitions of the widest artistic appeal that, without the museum's focus, would not be seen in the UK. Kids always Free!
- PUBLICATIONS: commissioning new academic research on the artists and their historical context to accompany the museum's exhibitions.
- LIBRARY AND ARCHIVE: a resource dating from the turn of the 20th century, documenting and tracing in parallel the artistic and social development of the Ben Uri and Jewish artists working or exhibiting in Britain as part of the evolving British historical landscape.
- EDUCATION PROGRAMMES: for adults, students, school children and artists, through symposia, lectures, student teaching packs, visits, after school art clubs, free family art days.
- ARTISTS: Monthly artist peer group programmes, Ben Uri International Jewish Artists of the Year Awards competition, guidance and affiliation benefits.
- CARE IN THE COMMUNITY: through the pioneering pilot project between the Ben Uri and the British Association of Art Therapists.
- WEBSITE: providing an on-line educational and access tool, to function as a virtual gallery and artists' reference resource for students, collectors and scholars.

To continue our objectives and fulfill the museum's potential Ben Uri desperately needs to relocate to the heart of Central London and is currently seeking *c*2000 sq m. to establish a permanent museum and exhibition space that will be both an international centre of scholarship and an exciting hub of activity for our local communities.

CHAIRMAN'S INTRODUCTION

As the 90th anniversary of the end of the First World War approaches and barely a handful of survivors remain, it is both timely and fitting for the Ben Uri to mark this occasion with the exhibition *Whitechapel at War: Isaac Rosenberg and his Circle.* The sixth in the Ben Uri's ongoing series, 'The Whitechapel Boys', it is the first exhibition for almost 20 years to focus on the British-born, Jewish poet-painter Isaac Rosenberg, who died at the Front on April Fool's Day 1918, aged just 27. It is also the first to critically examine his position as an artist rather than as a poet, located within the wider context of the emergence of British modernism in Whitechapel and set against the backdrop of the First World War.

Although Rosenberg is less well-known as a painter, his substantial literary reputation continues to grow, as the ever-expanding body of international academic work demonstrates. To this end, we are delighted that the opening reception of this exhibition coincides with the publication of Dr. Jean Moorcroft Wilson's new biography of Rosenberg (Weidenfeld & Nicolson, April 2008), its launch co-hosted by the Ben Uri.

The exhibition features more than 50 paintings, drawings and works on paper, as well as selected manuscripts, photographs and ephemera, drawn from public and private collections both here and abroad. In this endeavour, we are delighted to have support of so many national institutions, both those who have supported the Ben Uri in previous exhibitions: Tate, British Museum, National Portrait Gallery, Strang Collection at UCL and the Victoria and Albert Museum, and of those who are lending to us for the first time: the British Library, Imperial War Museum, Tullie House Museum & Art Gallery, Carlisle, and Special Collections at Southampton University. Works have also been lent from The Joseph Cohen Collection of World War I Literature/The Joseph M. Bruccoli Great War Collection, Thomas Cooper Library, University of South Carolina, where thanks are due to Dr Patrick Scott and Jeffrey Makala. We are delighted once again to extend our links within the USA. Thanks are also due to Sotheby's and Christie's for their enthusiastic help in tracing 'lost' works.

We also take this opportunity to thank all the private collectors who have assisted us so generously, in particular Joan Rodker, who has lent the portrait of her mother Sonia, prior to her kind donation of this wonderful painting to the Ben Uri Collection. We also thank all Rosenberg's relatives for their fantastic support in loaning works and archival material, and in giving so freely of their time and knowledge, especially Mr and Mrs Bernard Wynick, Mrs Betty Silver, Mrs Gerda Horvitch, Mrs Nina Canal and Dr Doron Swade. We extend out thanks to Jonathan Rosenthall and to those private lenders who prefer to remain anonymous.

Thanks are also due to all our catalogue contributors: to Joan Rodker who has provided a fascinating and personal link to the Whitechapel Boys with extracts from her mother's (previously unpublished) biography; to the Rosenberg biographers, chroniclers and literary critics: Dr. Jean Moorcroft Wilson, Dr. Joseph Cohen (USA) and Jean Liddiard, who have all contributed in many different ways to the exhibition and to the catalogue; and to Dr Dominic Williams for his essay on John Rodker and Isaac Rosenberg.

We are delighted that the newly re-opened Stanley & Audrey Burton Gallery, Leeds University, will host the exhibition during summer 2008, as touring continues to be one of our core objectives. As host, almost 50 years ago, of the 1959 *Isaac Rosenberg* exhibition, co-curated by Jon Silkin (Gregory Fellow in Poetry at the University, 1958–60) and repository of the Silkin archive, Leeds University is a most fitting second venue. We are most grateful to Hilary Diaper, Chris Sheppard and Layla Bloom for enabling the exhibition to be accessible to a wider audience.

We are indebted to all our sponsors, including many private supporters, and we pay particular tribute to The Paul Mellon Centre for Studies in British Art and The Dorset Foundation. Without their support the research and overall scale of the exhibition and this substantial accompanying catalogue could not have been possible. We also remain indebted to our growing band of Ben Uri Berson Patrons for their ongoing support of the BU Exhibition and Education programme.

Finally, we pay tribute to Suzanne Lewis who, as Director of Operations, ensures that the exhibition matches the curators' vision, ably assisted by her small expert team: Natasha Beckman, Marion Cohen and Bonnie Unger, and to the dedication, energy and scholarship of our curators, Rachel Dickson and Sarah MacDougall.

We do hope that this exhibition, three years in the making, will be long remembered by those who have the opportunity to travel to London and Leeds to see it, and that it will be referred to longer still by students, scholars and newly interested parties, as a significant reference point within the body of academic reference material relating to this extraordinary individual.

David J Glasser, CHAIRMAN

CURATORS' FOREWORD: LONDON

Upon his death in 1918, less than six months before the declaration of the Armistice, Rosenberg left behind a small but fascinating body of work, whose rarity evokes a keen poignancy for his lost talent. This re-examination of his art, timed to coincide with the 90th anniversary of his death and that of the ending of the First World War, draws upon the full range of Rosenberg's artistic output, from the earliest schoolboy compositions to the last hurried sketches, executed at the Front under extreme conditions. Focusing on Rosenberg 'the painter', within the larger context of early British modernism, the exhibition includes much of his most mature work, largely created against the backdrop of this conflict. Among these works, highlights include Rosenberg's highly accomplished *Self-Portrait* (1915), now in the National Portrait Gallery, whose bravura confidence contrasts with the fragile yet resilient subject of the *Self-Portrait with Steel Helmet* (1916), completed in the trenches only a year later. A number of masterful and rarely-seen early drawings are also exhibited, including his prize-winning *Head of a Monk* (1908-11) and *Head of a Barrister* (1910), as well as a small number of never previously exhibited works: *Self-Portrait* (1906), his three-quarter length *Self-Portrait* (1911) and *The Wharf*, the last published in a rare 1912 catalogue (Special Collections, Parkes Library, University of Southampton).

The exhibition also provides the opportunity to see the single greatest run of Rosenberg *Self-Portraits* ever exhibited together, with over a dozen images in a variety of media. A number of intimate reciprocal portraits of Rosenberg and the 'Whitechapel girl' Clare Winsten (Clara Birnberg) are also being shown, alongside the tender oil of Sonia Cohen, probably Rosenberg's best female portrait.

In reviewing Rosenberg's contribution to British modernism within the context of his Whitechapel peers, we are showing a range of works by his Jewish contemporaries (including David Bomberg, Mark Gertler, Jacob Kramer, Bernard Meninsky and Horace Brodzky), as well as by associates such as Henri Gaudier-Brzeska, drawn from across the period. Particular focus is given to Rosenberg's crucial relationship with his close friends, the Whitechapel writers John Rodker, Joseph Leftwich and Stephen Winsten, for whom the term 'Whitechapel Boys' was initially coined, and with the only female member of the group, the artist Clare Winsten.

The exhibition examines the range of the Whitechapel Boys' individual war experiences, from conscientious objector (Gertler, Rodker), 'alien' non-combatant (Kramer), Official War Artist (Meninsky), to frontline soldier (Rosenberg and Bomberg). It also throws light on the numerous literary and artistic 'little magazines', which characterised this period, and to which all the Whitechapel Boys so energetically contributed.

In researching this wide ranging contextual material, we are very grateful for the assistance of Dr Wendy Baron, Richard Cork, David Mazower and Martin Lloyd, who have all provided valuable insight and support for the catalogue essays. We also echo our Chairman's list of thanks, particularly to Rosenberg family members and to Joan Rodker, whose personal insights and access to material have been invaluable. We also thank Raymond Francis for his help in providing ephemera relating to his late father, the painter Morris Goldstein.

We are extremely grateful to the Paul Mellon Centre for the Study of British Art, whose catalogue grant has enabled us to explore a number of different facets for this exhibition, and to produce an extended publication in this important anniversary year.

Finally, we would also like to extend our warmest thanks to the Ben Uri team including Suzanne Lewis, Marion Cohen, Natasha Beckman and Bonnie Unger, without whom this exhibition and its associated events would not have been possible.

Sarah MacDougall & Rachel Dickson

CURATOR'S FOREWORD: LEEDS

In 2003, the University Gallery Leeds was delighted to collaborate with the Ben Uri Gallery and the curators in their preparation of *William Roberts and Jacob Kramer: The Tortoise and the Hare*, the third in their acclaimed series of exhibitions about the 'Whitechapel Boys' – and privileged to act as host for the first leg of a two-venue event. The Leeds connection was self-evident, Jacob Kramer being a Leeds boy as much as a Whitechapel one. Moreover, the University Library holds much of Kramer's correspondence. When we were asked to participate in this exhibition – the sixth of the same series – we were more than happy to agree. Once again, there is a Leeds connection; less self-evident perhaps, but nevertheless a compelling one.

Jon Silkin, Gregory Fellow in Poetry at the University from 1958–59, was deeply interested in Isaac Rosenberg's work, making him the subject of various essays and articles, as well as including some of his verse in his later critical work on poetry of the First World War, *Out of Battle* (1972) and in *The Penguin Book of First World War Poetry*, which he edited in 1979. It was during his time at Leeds that Silkin, together with the first Head of Fine Art, Maurice de Sausmarez, organised an Isaac Rosenberg exhibition. Held in the University in May 1959 and opened by Herbert Read, himself Kramer's mentor during the First World War, the exhibition included manuscripts, printed works, letters and photographs, as well as drawings and paintings. Rosenberg's sister, Annie Wynick, was also involved in organising the loan of materials to the University for the exhibition, and extensive letters from her to Silkin are amongst the Silkin archive held in the University Library. Interestingly, Silkin himself also had links with the Ben Uri Gallery, being involved in a 'Literary Circle' there in the 1950s, where he met poets including Philip Hobsbaum and Emanuel Litvinoff.

Rosenberg was also an influence on the work of Geoffrey Hill, who taught at Leeds University from 1954–80. Indeed, one of Hill's first published poems was 'For Isaac Rosenberg,' appearing in Oxford University's literary journal, *Isis*, in June 1952. The campaign to persuade the GLC to erect a blue plaque for Rosenberg in the East End of London was instigated by Hill in 1983. Silkin was also involved in the campaign, which resulted in the plaque being placed outside Whitechapel Public Library in November 1987.

Silkin and Hill both feature prominently in a current University project, *Leeds Poetry 1950–1980*, on which the Library and the School of English are working jointly to bring together online information about archival collections relating to poets working at the University of Leeds between 1950–80. I am particularly grateful to the project's Research Officer, Kathryn Jenner, who has researched in detail the Rosenberg connection and shared her findings with me.

The University is delighted to pay tribute once again to Isaac Rosenberg, by hosting the first significant exhibition of his work since 1991. It is fitting that it should find its way to Leeds.

Hilary Diaper, KEEPER OF THE ART COLLECTION AND THE STANLEY & AUDREY BURTON GALLERY, UNIVERSITY OF LEEDS

GOODBYE TO ALL THAT AND HELLO TO ALL THIS: THE BEAT GOES ON

I am exceedingly happy to express my appreciation to co-curators Sarah MacDougall and Rachel Dickson and the officers of the Ben Uri Gallery for inviting me to join in this new celebration of Isaac Rosenberg's life and work. It provides those of us who have toiled long in this labour of love a renewed opportunity to see how far we have come and envision how far we have yet to go to gain for Rosenberg his rightful place among the great poets of the twentieth century and among the great anti-war poets of all time. It is, moreover, an opportunity to welcome a new generation of admirers, students and scholars to our ranks. Their interpretations, insights and discoveries are already enriching our understanding and respect for Rosenberg.

Now in my early eighties, I like to think foremost how happy and fulfilled Rosenberg's sister and literary executrix, Annie Wynick would have been to have witnessed the developments of the last 35 years. How fortunate I was to have known and worked with her in 1959–60 when as a young professor Newcomb College of Tulane University gave me the opportunity to spend the year in London in charge of our 30 junior-year abroad students. That autumn was propitious: the Slade Exhibition of Rosenberg's works opened at the University of London and I not only got to view the poet-artist's work gathered there but also to meet the principal surviving players in Rosenberg's life. In the months following I talked with all of them, gleaning and noting everything a biographer could wish to know. Annie even convinced Rosenberg's brother, David Burton, still wary and sensitive about his own experiences on the Western Front to break his silence. Together, with Annie and a growing number of well-wishers, we became happy co-conspirators in advancing Isaac's cause.

So many helped. I think foremost of Dannie and Joan Abse in whose home much of my book was written on subsequent visits to London. A plethora of administrative assignments delayed my finishing the work, and by 1970 it had become a now or never necessity. Warm, funny and loving, Dannie in those years became my big brother, and he taught me much I needed to learn. It was he who gave my book its title but the sum of his contributions to my literary maturation was much greater than that one gift.

If Dannie Abse was my big brother, Ian Parsons was a wise mentoring uncle. I remember him too with great fondness and acknowledge with gratitude my indebtedness to him and his monumental 1979 edition of Rosenberg's *Collected Works.*

In 1975 the National Book League's Rosenberg exhibition took place, preceded just weeks before by the almost simultaneous publication of the three new biographies. Jean Liddiard's, Jean Moorcroft Wilson's and mine together constituted a unique send-off to that exciting and memorable occasion. In my quieter moments during the opening ceremonies I was saddened that Annie was no longer alive, but comforted and gratified that all she wished for was coming true

That exhibition included several of the artifacts from my Rosenberg Collection and those treasures and several others are present here again. This time, however, there is a difference. Along with my entire World War I literature collection these artifacts have found the perfect location in an ideally appropriate setting at the University of South Carolina where they form a separate and distinctly complimentary archive attached to the Joseph M Bruccoli Great War Collection. I never thought of my holdings as a private preserve; rather, its contents were simply vouchsafed to me to care for lovingly until the best permanent repository could be found for them. It gives me enormous satisfaction that I have been blessed with the opportunity to leave this legacy in a warm, engaging, knowledgeable and empathetic home for the use of future generations of students and scholars.

As pivotal as the 1975 exhibition was, in retrospect it seems to me now that it was more a beginning than an ending, Not only has a new generation of students, scholars and admirers come into being, this one has arrived armed with the awareness of the communicative power of the new Internet technology. I found this out early. As the Internet grew my number of annual enquiries about Rosenberg doubled and then trebled and my *Journey to the Trenches* gained a whole new audience and a whole new life.

I learned about new books, theses and dissertations being undertaken. Vivien Noakes's work became known to me, and on my last visit to London we had a chance to meet and talk. Books by Deborah Maccoby and Harold Finch came to my attention. Jean Moorcroft Wilson sent me news of her intention to revise and re-issue her biography.

The most exciting news came from Atlanta when Tara M Christie wrote to me about her forthcoming dissertation at Emory University on Rosenberg and T S Eliot. Her work is filled with significant promise. It may well change the twentieth century's perception of Eliot's sources for his 're-discovery' of John Donne's relevance to the spirit and thrust of modern literature. Eliot's deep but restrained and polite appreciation for Rosenberg is now more widely known but the restraint may be more peripheral than we previously thought. Obviously, on this matter, there is more yet to come. Other new voices are constantly announcing themselves on Internet sites and blogs. Oxford University has an Internet site on Rosenberg with a section of Tara Christie's work and 'a virtual seminar on 'Break of Day in the trenches''. A selection of my Rosenberg correspondence is now online as 'Rosenberg's Early Poetry and Related Documents at the University of South Carolina Library's Digital Collections'. And, most gratifying of all, is the recent recovery of a cache of Rosenberg's letters to Laurence Binyon and Gordon Bottomley at the British Museum. Annie knew about those letters, it was troubling to her that they seemed irretrievably lost.

So much is happening. So much more is going to happen!

With that in mind, I would 'modestly' observe that in the nature of things it isn't likely that I'll attend in my present persona the next major Rosenberg exhibition several decades hence. It will surely come. Nonetheless, look for me. You can be certain I'll be hovering around, smiling broadly.

Dr Joseph Cohen, New Orleans, 2007

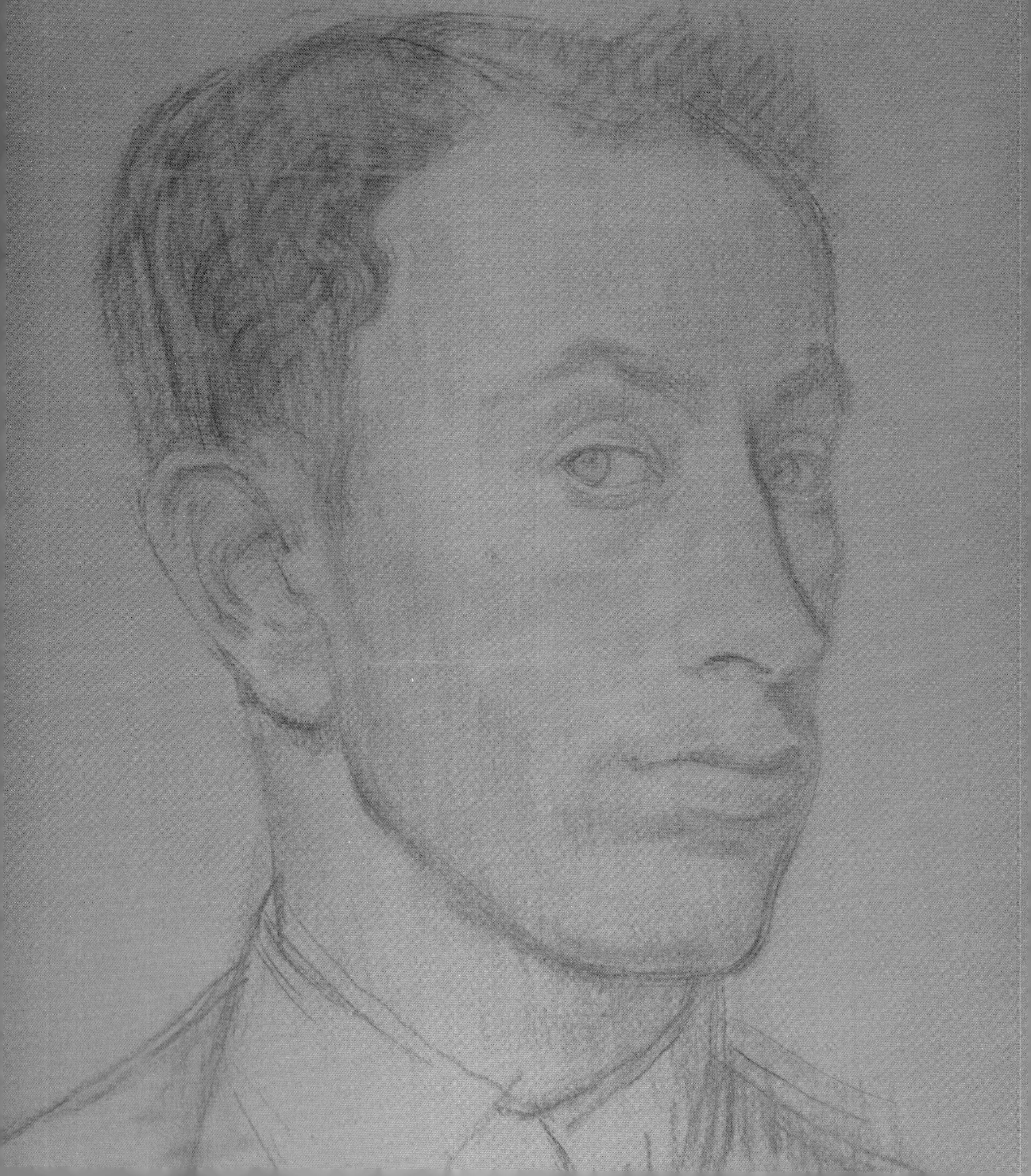

ESSAYS

1

ISAAC ROSENBERG THE PAINTER
PART I: 'ART IS NOT A PLAYTHING'

'Art is not a plaything, it is blood and tears, it must grow up with one; and I believe I have begun too late.'
ISAAC ROSENBERG TO MRS HERBERT COHEN, OCTOBER 1912[1]

15 *previous page*
ISAAC ROSENBERG
Self-Portrait, 1912

Rosenberg's current reputation as one of the finest war poets of his generation rests on a small body of literature. During his lifetime he published only two collections, *Night and Day* (1912, cat no. 55) and *Youth* (1915, cat no. 56), together with the play *Moses* (1916, cat no. 48), all at his own expense. 'His true vocation was poetry', wrote the poet Laurence Binyon, 'and he thought of himself as a poet rather than as a painter'.[2] This exhibition demonstrates that Rosenberg's talent as a painter deserves greater consideration than this statement suggests, for in painting as well as in poetry he sought to articulate the ongoing struggle between modernism and tradition, then at the heart of contemporary debate. The fact that he never resolved this struggle, or the contradictions it threw up, in no way undermines his contribution.

In contrast to his literary oeuvre, Rosenberg's artistic legacy has been little explored. He was included in the now much-debated 'Jewish Section' of the exhibition *Twentieth Century Art: A Review of Modern Movements* at the Whitechapel Art Gallery in 1914, and his art, like his poetry, attracted the patronage of Edward Marsh, but no solo exhibition of his work was held until the memorial show at the Whitechapel Art Gallery in 1937, almost 20 years after his death. Since then, despite three important Rosenberg exhibitions (Leeds University Gallery, 1959; National Book League, 1975; and the Imperial War Museum, 1990–91), all interweaving his art with his poetry, his reputation as a painter has remained low. Although his iconic *Self-Portrait* (1915, cat no. 24) was admired by artists and art historians, including William Coldstream, Andrew Forge, Eric Newton and Herbert Read,[3] Rosenberg was mentioned neither in Charles Harrison's important examination of *English Art and Modernism 1900–1939* (1981, 1994) nor in the two main survey exhibitions, *British Art in the 20th Century* at the Royal Academy (1987) and *Chagall to Kitaj: Jewish Experience in 20th Century Art* at the Barbican Art Gallery (1990–91). Richard Cork included Rosenberg in his comprehensive assessment *A Bitter Truth: Avant-Garde Art and the Great War* (Barbican Art Gallery, 1994) but, since the exhibition concentrated on avant-garde work, he was represented by only one picture – his final, haunting self-portrait, executed in chalk and gouache on crumpled brown wrapping paper (cat no. 30). It is therefore timely that this reassessment of Rosenberg's contribution as a painter, the first to concentrate solely on his work as a visual artist, should take place on the 90th anniversary of both his death and the end of the First World War.

Isaac Rosenberg was the second child and eldest son of Russian and Yiddish-speaking Jewish émigrés from Lithuania, who first settled in the Leeds ghetto in 1881 (almost a decade before Jacob Kramer and his family arrived there from the Ukraine), fleeing anti-Semitism and, in the case of Rosenberg's father, Barnett,[4] forced conscription. Towards the end of the 1880s Barnett moved to Bristol, where he was later joined by his wife Hacha and their daughter Minnie. Isaac was born in Bristol in 1890 and three further siblings (Annie, Rachel and David) followed before, in 1897, the family moved to Stepney in London's East End, 'the heart of the "Ghetto"',[5] where Barnett hoped it would be easier to find work. But, as his nephew points out, he was 'untrained and had no business aptitude.' Despite the birth of another son, Elkon, two years later, Barnett 'failed to find any work, and ended up pulling a barrow around London.'[6] Hacha was forced to sell embroidery to help the family survive and this added to the tensions within an already unhappy marriage.

Barnett Rosenberg (like Kramer's father, Max) was a pious and cultured man, from a family of rabbis and scholars, well versed in Yiddish and Talmudic studies. This traditional background was at odds both with the lure of a life beyond the prescribed rules of Orthodoxy and its restraints, and with the emerging modernity of the new century. Raised within a Orthodox Jewish household, where Judaism and its cultural traditions struggled to survive amidst conditions of overcrowding and extreme poverty, Rosenberg's early years closely mirror those of his Whitechapel contemporaries Mark Gertler and David Bomberg.

In his autobiography, Selig Brodetsky (1888–1954), the mathematician, Zionist and Rosenberg's Whitechapel contemporary, described the East End of the older generation as: 'religious. It was religious in the way of the ghetto, with many ghetto customs brought from Russia. There was much talk of Russia, of the troubles there and the pogroms, and there was a great deal of nostalgia for the "old home", for the intensely Jewish life of the Russian Pale of Settlement.'[7] As Bomberg's biographer Richard Cork has observed, the frustration of the Whitechapel Boys 'centred not only on economic deprivation but also on their ambiguous status as the children of Jewish immigrants. Torn between loyalty to family tradition and the ambition to move outside these limits and participate in the artistic or political life of Britain as a whole, these energetic friends constantly found themselves fighting contradictory impulses.'[8] For Rosenberg, the pull between painting and writing, as well as – in his painting – between modernism and tradition, was never resolved.

From his earliest years, Rosenberg 'lean[ed] towards the artistic',[9] and when he began school at Baker Street, Stepney, in 1899, he soon took 'little interest in anything but drawing.'[10] Even at playtime, oblivious to other pleasures – and to the other children – he remained inside the classroom, still drawing. In this, he resembled his fellow Whitechapel Boy, Mark Gertler (1891–1939), who so amazed his fellow pupils with his 'extraordinary' drawings that they voted him the most popular boy in the class. But for Rosenberg drawing was a solitary occupation and his teacher noted that Isaac 'didn't make friends with any of the other children and seemed too serious for his age.'[11] Out of school, however, when Rosenberg (again like Gertler) chalked pictures on the pavements, he regularly attracted crowds.[12]

Rosenberg was always able to attract allies to his cause and the first of these, his headmaster Mr Usherwood, was so supportive that he allowed Rosenberg to concentrate exclusively on drawing and writing, even entering his precocious schoolboy watercolour, *Caxton and Edward IV* (1901, cat no. 1), captioned 'Standard VII, 18.12.01, Baker Street', in an external competition of children's art. By the age of 12, his sister Annie recalled, Rosenberg was 'full of zeal & energy in the pursuit of his Art which he always held dear to himself. On one occasion he made a mental vision of an old gentleman in the street – a passer-by, and so struck was he with his finely moulded head that he immediately reproduced it on paper on his arrival home.'[13] Instinctively, Rosenberg seemed to realise that portraiture would become his strength.

Usherwood also arranged for Rosenberg to begin special afternoon classes at the Stepney Green Art School in 1902–03, where he became friends with another student, Morris Goldstein (1892–1970), a fellow Jewish boy from Whitechapel, whose family attended the same synagogue and whose early career for a time shadowed Rosenberg's own. Five years later Goldstein encouraged Rosenberg to join him at The London County Council School of Photo-Engraving and Lithography at Bolt Court, Fleet Street, and afterwards they studied together at the Slade School of Art.[14] In the meantime, following the Rosenbergs' move to 58 Jubilee Street, Isaac often accompanied his mother to the nearby home of the Amshewitz family, who were regular customers for her embroidery. There Rosenberg formed another crucial early friendship with the painter J(ohn) H(enry) Amshewitz (1882–1942).[15]

Amshewitz was to have a profound influence on Rosenberg's early work and development, despite the awkwardness of their first meeting: Rosenberg sought the older artist's opinion of one of his drawings but when Amshewitz offered him half a crown for it, Rosenberg fled from the room in tears. 'He did not want charity', Rosenberg's biographer Joseph Cohen explains, 'he wanted instruction'.[16] Afterwards, Amshewitz helped Rosenberg obtain a permit to draw in the National Gallery and this, as his friend Stephen Winsten later observed, became the younger artist's 'temple'. He spent days there; 'bulging from his pockets were his lunch and a book of poems; the latter he devoured and the former was forgotten.'[17] Rosenberg later dedicated a poem to Amshewitz in gratitude,[18] as well as presenting the older artist with an illustrated copy of his poem 'In the Heart of the Forest'.[19] Amshewitz later helped Rosenberg publish his first piece of art criticism, 'Romance at the Baillie Galleries' – appropriately, a review of an exhibition of work by Amshewitz and another émigré artist, Henry Ospovat (1877–1909), in the *Jewish Chronicle* (24 May 1912).

Seven years Rosenberg's senior and already on his way to becoming a prominent portrait painter, muralist, etcher, cartoonist and illustrator, Amshewitz

1
ISAAC ROSENBERG
Caxton and Edward IV, 1901

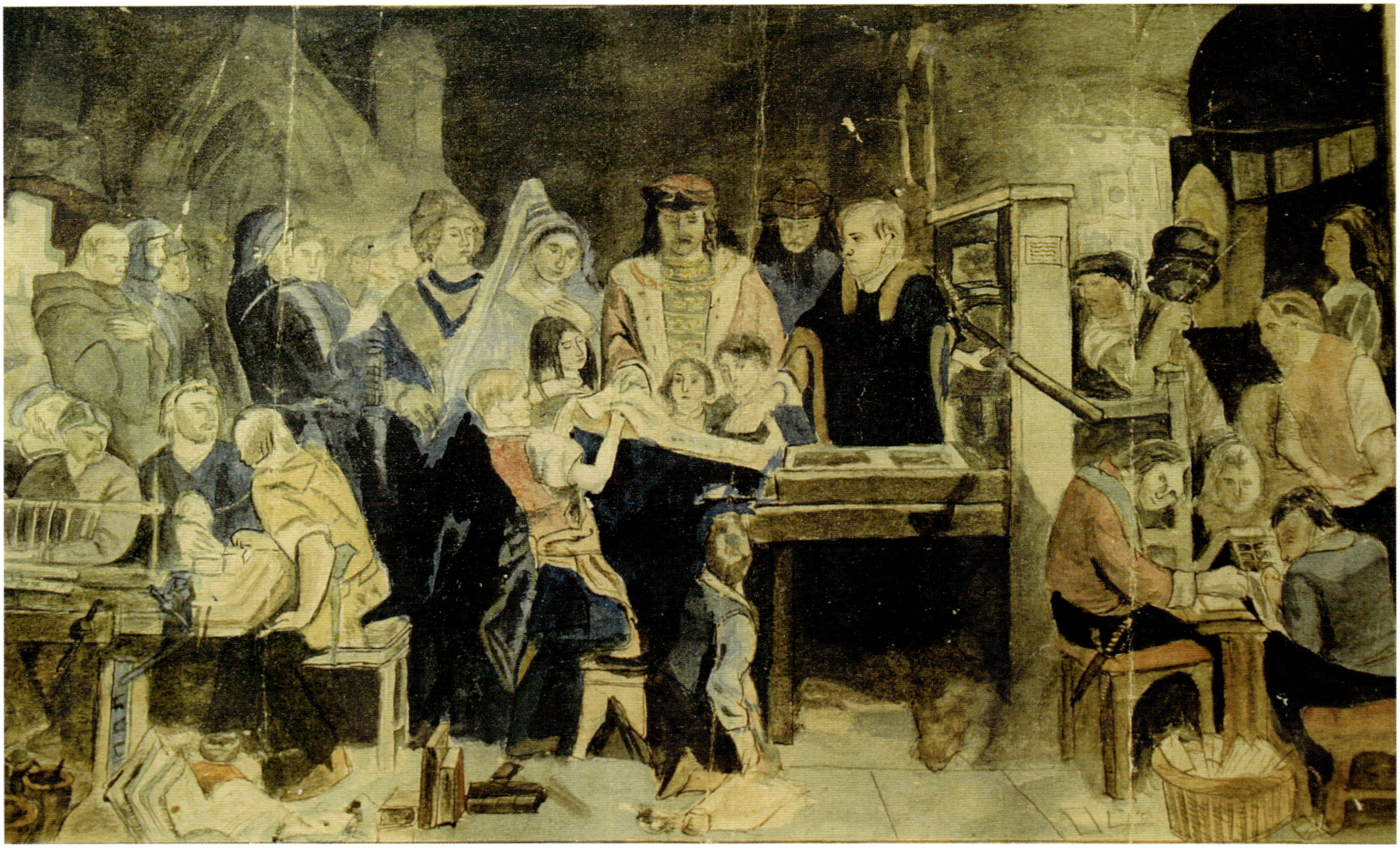

had trained at Birkbeck and the Royal Academy Schools, and received critical acclaim with his controversial scheme for the Liverpool Town Hall lunettes in 1908–09.[20] Two years earlier, he had executed a series of highly traditional illustrations for Israel Zangwill's *Ghetto Comedies* (a volume of short stories fictionalising the Jewish émigré experience in England and America and a sequel to his celebrated *Children of the Ghetto*), which adhere to the prevalent English Victorian stereotypical depictions of 'the Jew'. In 1909 Amshewitz captured the young Rosenberg in a formal, traditional, romantic portrait (fig. 10), showing the aspiring poet deep in thought with pen poised.[21] In his review of Amshewitz's work, Rosenberg later commented on this 'portrait of a young poet, gazing as if out of "dream dimmed" eyes, holding the pen in his hand, apparently waiting for inspiration [...]. It is well studied, except for the mannered and unpleasant way the forms of the shadows repeat themselves, which makes it appear as though style were aimed at rather than exact interpretation.'[22] Tellingly, Rosenberg's description also reinforces his credentials as a poet while entirely omitting any reference to himself as a painter.

Rosenberg also found an early literary mentor in the Whitechapel librarian Morley Dainow, who was 'much impressed both by his confidence and his sensitivity'. Dainow encouraged Rosenberg by criticising his poetry and soon discovered that Rosenberg was already 'perfectly convinced that his vocation in life was that of a Poet and Painter'.[23] According to Rosenberg's sister Minnie Dainow also took Rosenberg to the National Gallery 'and other art galleries, and suggested that he copy Old Masters.'[24]

When Rosenberg left school in 1904, his family could not afford for him to pursue a career in art and shortly afterwards he was grudgingly apprenticed to Carl Hentschel, a firm of Fleet Street engravers. 'It is horrible to think', he wrote in a letter to Miss Winifreda Seaton (a schoolmistress whom he met at Amshewitz's studio, and who encouraged him to read and write poetry), 'that all these hours, when my days are full of vigour and my hands and soul craving for self-expression, I am bound, chained to this fiendish mangling-machine, without hope and almost desire of deliverance.'[25] He remained passionate about art and poetry, reading and drawing obsessively, attending evening classes and scribbling or reciting verses during meal-times.

It was also at this time that Rosenberg met Frank Lewis Emanuel (1865–1948), who was appointed his 'guardian' by the Jewish Board of Guardians during the term of his apprenticeship. Emanuel noted how Rosenberg 'chafed against being in trade' even 'an *art* trade in which his ability would at any rate have *some* play [...]' But he pointed out to Rosenberg 'how difficult it was for an artist – even provided with certain means – to earn a living as a painter and urged him first to learn an art trade – to fall back upon – so that in case of need he would not be destitute. Meanwhile he was encouraged to push forward his art on all *available* occasions so as to reach a point at which he would be justified on abandoning trade and launching out.'[26]

Another Jewish 'establishment' painter, as well as a respected printmaker, topographer and art critic, Emanuel had trained at the Slade and the Académie Julian in Paris, and, like Amshewitz was also an exhibitor at the Royal Academy, as well as Chief Examiner with the Royal Drawing Society and for many years a special artist with the *Manchester Guardian*. As an art specialist and a member of the Maccabeans,[27] he was also a member of the advisory committee for the Whitechapel Art Gallery's 1906 exhibition *Jewish Art and Antiquities*.[28] At his studio Emanuel presided over a club of artists and art teachers known as 'the Limners', which he described as 'a body of artists and art teachers [...] trusting enough to listen to my criticism of their work.' He awarded them prizes 'of prints and such like – found little jobs for some of them now and then and had exhibitions to which the public came and purchased in my studio and elsewhere'. In short, Emanuel was an important patron for an aspiring artist. However,

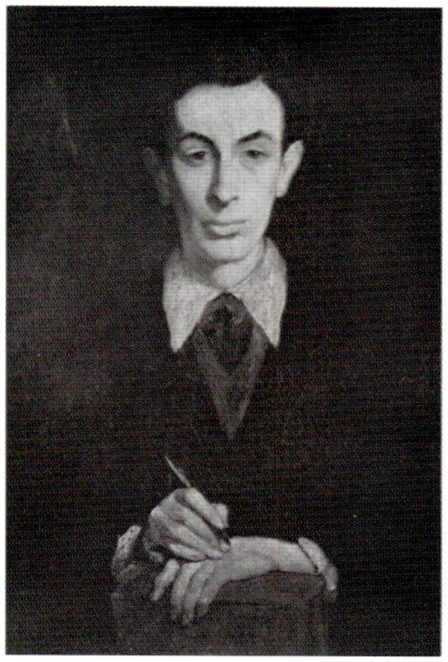

FIG. 10
JOHN AMSHEWITZ
Portrait of Isaac Rosenberg, 1909

FIG. 53
Morris Goldstein, c.1911–12

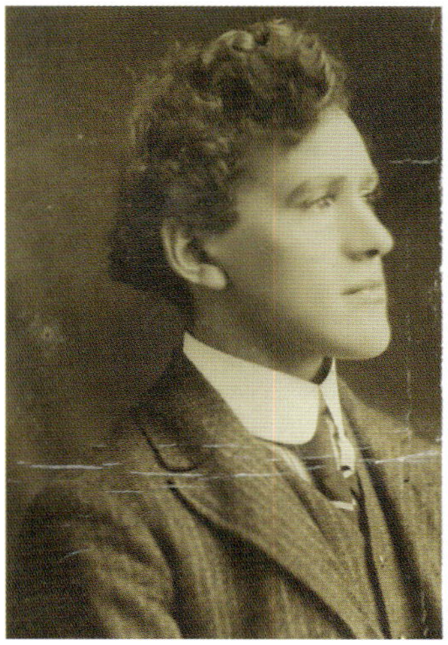

his patronage had political, as well as patrician, overtones. He felt that the Limners provided 'an opportunity to bring East and West end together and under the mutual interest of art to foster such social intercourse as would lessen class feeling', particularly for Rosenberg, 'whose circumstances had rendered him very bitter and despondent [...]. I got him and several other East End artists enrolled. I took care to give him and others like him [...] special encouragement and consideration.'[29] He even included Rosenberg as a contributor to *A Piece of Mosaic: being the book of the Palestine Exhibition and Bazaar* of 1912.[30]

After Emanuel's death, Rosenberg's earliest known *Self-Portrait* (1906, cat no. 2), a left profile executed in faint pencil on the reverse of his poem 'In arts' lone paths I wander deep', was found among his effects.[31] The portrait, as Joseph Cohen suggests, is 'a serious, slightly romanticized' image of the painter-poet, 'more reminiscent of a death-mask than a living adolescent',[32] in the tradition of Benjamin Robert Haydon's portrait sketches of the young Keats. A second profile of Rosenberg (*c.* 1910–12, fig. 2), known only in reproduction and also believed to be a self-portrait, with its high cheekbones and disordered curls, perpetuates this image of the melancholic romantic, as opposed to the tidy, formal pose of Amshewitz's portrait. Only, in 1912, under the influence of the Slade, did Rosenberg begin to shed this persona in his own self-portraits and evolve a leaner, more distinct contemporary image, which owed more to modernism than tradition. Among his contemporaries, however, Clara Birnberg (Clare Winsten), H C Hammond,[33] and to a lesser extent David Bomberg, who all made portrait studies of Rosenberg, the old, romantic image was the most enduring.

Emanuel's influence and the 'brilliant promise' he saw in the young student are apparent in works such as Rosenberg's exquisite sanguine *Head of a Barrister* (cat no. 5), one of his finest early portraits, executed in 1910. Emanuel described it as 'very beautiful', subsequently awarding Rosenberg a Limners' prize and purchasing the work himself.[34] But he was not pleased when Rosenberg later shrugged off his influence, commenting that 'Unfortunately Rosenberg had not the knack of showing to those who went out of their way to help him – that he appreciated their efforts.'[35]

More than a traditionalist, Emanuel loathed what he called 'mad modernistic styles'[36] and lost no opportunity in putting forward his decidedly anti-modernist views. In his obituary the *Jewish Chronicle*'s correspondent described Emanuel as 'vigorous in his condemnations of what he called the "modern-art swindle" and [he] founded the British League for the Rescue of Art, to combat the influence of Picasso and other modernists.'[37] When Jacob Kramer's controversial painting *The Jew* was published in the press in 1917, Emanuel wrote acerbically to the *Jewish World*, accusing the modernists of collaborating with the press to form a cartel against the traditionalists, fulminating against 'these tom-fools of the art and literary world [...] simply carrying their destructive, revolutionary and anarchistic lives and ideas into the peaceful realms of art and beauty.'[38] Emanuel later regretted what he called the 'nasty and unhealthy

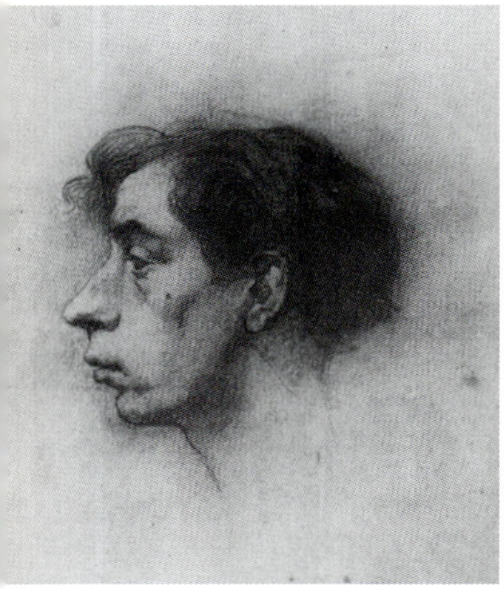

FIG. 2
ISAAC ROSENBERG
*Self-Portrait, c.*1910–12

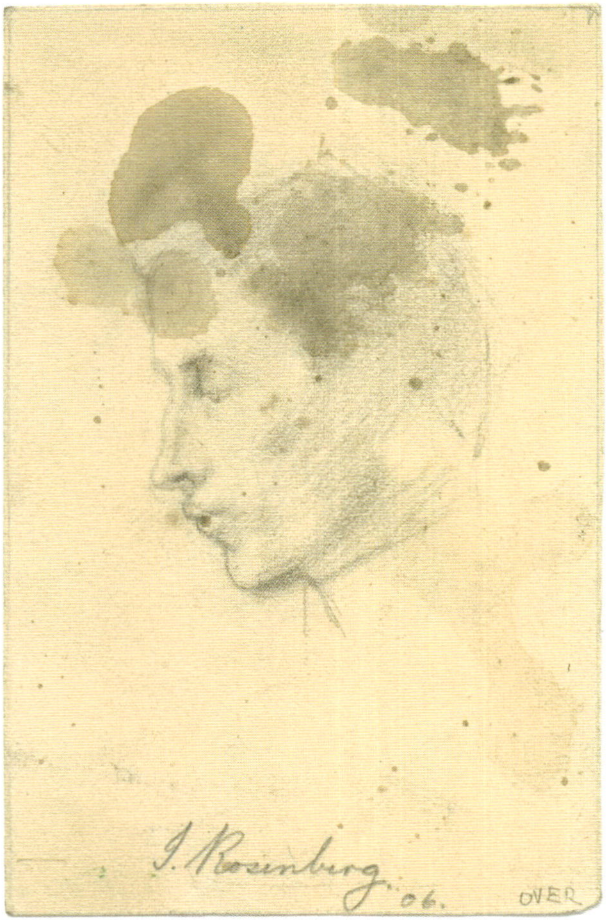

2
ISAAC ROSENBERG
Self-Portrait, 1906

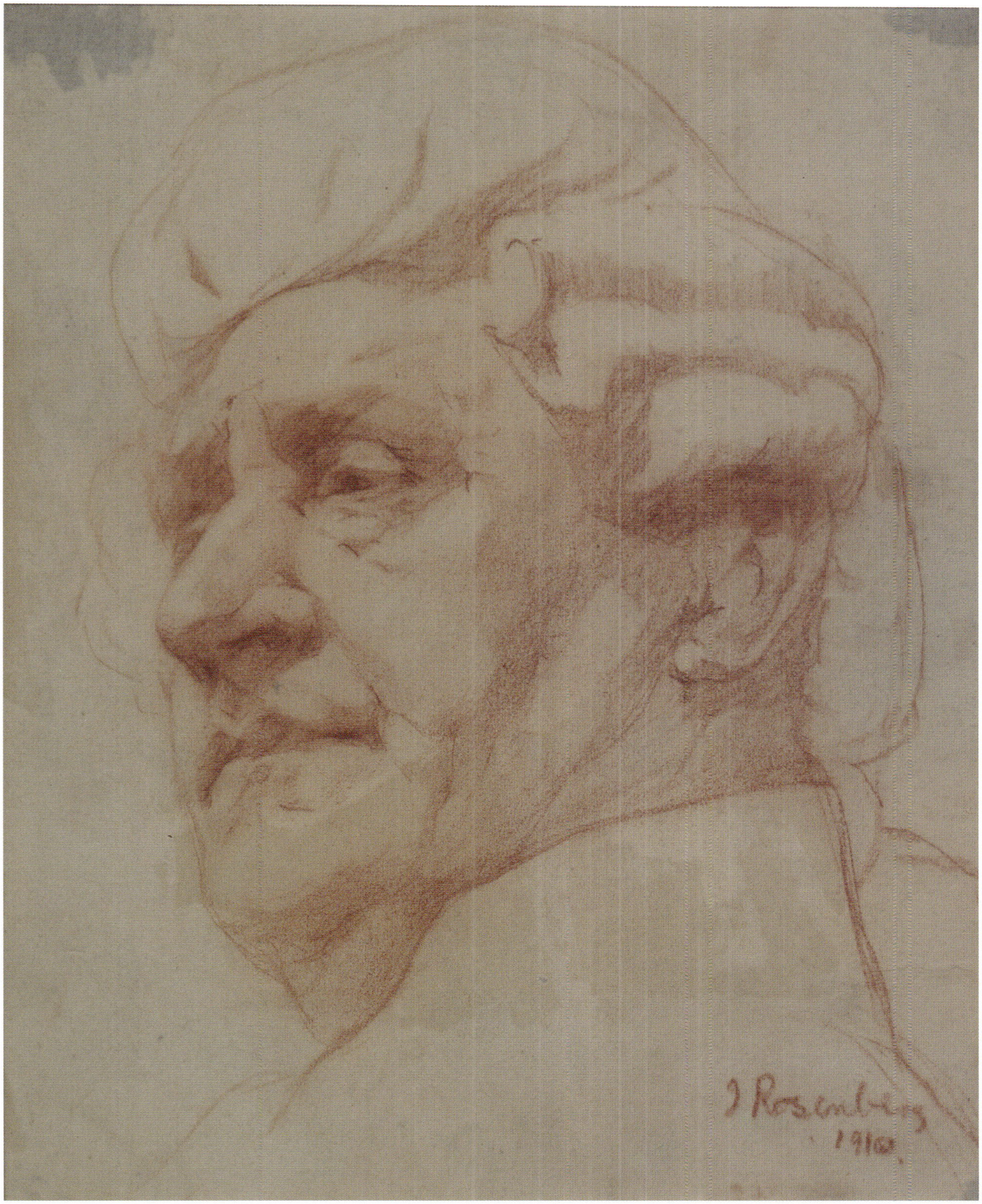

5
ISAAC ROSENBERG
Head of a Barrister, 1910

7
ISAAC ROSENBERG
Head of a Monk, *c.*1908–11

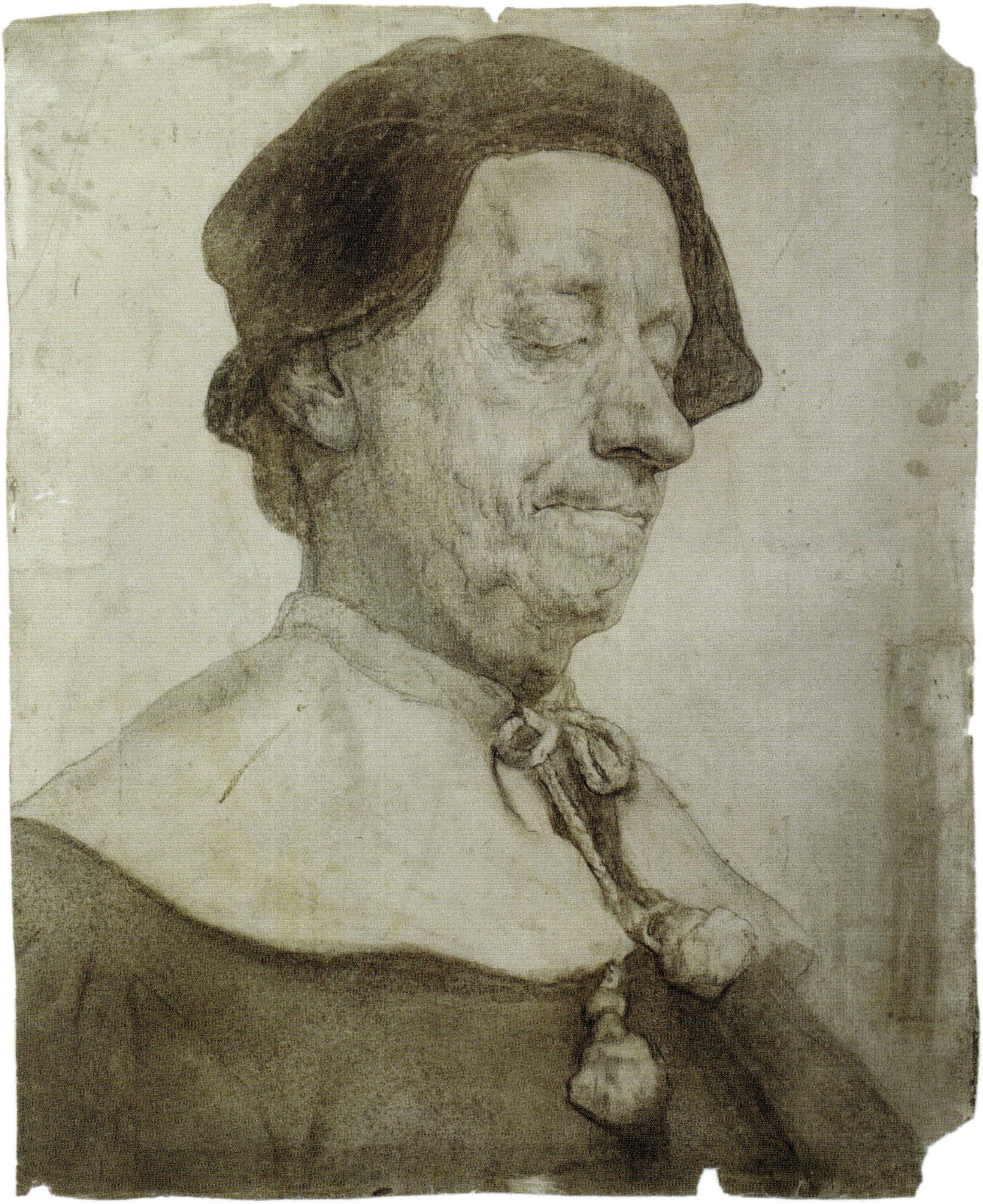

"atmosphere"' of the Slade and its 'traceable' effect on Rosenberg's art work, telling the poet Laurence Binyon that 'the art produced there was morbid, artificial and unclean', a bad influence on 'any young artist and doubly so for the already socialistic East End boys, who really required fresh air and sunshine let into their work and their lives to make their lives and achievements healthier and happier.'[39]

Following Emanuel's advice, Rosenberg had begun to attend evening classes at Bolt Court (1907–08), choosing (probably reluctantly) the industrial course over the fine arts taken up by his friend Morris Goldstein. Paul Nash, a fellow pupil on the Fine Arts course with Goldstein, who also became one of Rosenberg's contemporaries at the Slade, commented that 'the whole purpose of the school was avowedly practical. You were there to equip yourself for making a living.'[40] David Bomberg later confirmed this, recalling that at Bolt Court the 'standard was high in relation to the printing trade but not to painting.'[41]

From 1907–09, while continuing to attend Bolt Court,[42] Rosenberg, encouraged by Amshewitz, began to attend additional evening classes in fine art at Birkbeck College,[43] where he quickly distinguished himself. At the close of 1907, Rosenberg won first prize for drawing from the Antique and second prize for tonal drawing.[44] He also attended life-classes, almost certainly for the first time, winning the Mason prize for life drawing in 1908, the Birkbeck College Pocock prize (for a nude in oils) in 1909, and a Certificate of Honour for timed life drawing.[45] His remarkable facility for portraiture, demonstrated in the fine naturalistic drawing, *Head of a Monk* (*c.* 1908–11, cat no. 7, listed in his memorial exhibition as a 'Birkbeck Art School Study'),[46] was also recognised during this period. The work was awarded a national book prize and praised in the *Birkbeck College Student's Magazine*.[47]

In 1911 Rosenberg met the group known as the Whitechapel Boys, of which he was to become such a prominent member. All were aspiring writers and neighbours in the East End. Joseph Leftwich (1892–1984), then working as a furrier in a sweatshop, named the group which, besides himself, comprised John (also known as Jack or Jimmy) Rodker (1894–1955), an unlikely civil servant who later became a modernist poet, translator and publisher of among others T S Eliot, Ezra Pound and James Joyce; and Samuel or 'Simy' Weinstein (1893–1991), then a teacher in an East End Board school, who would become a published poet and biographer of George Bernard Shaw (as well as the future husband of 'Whitechapel Girl' Clara Birnberg). In the immediate pre-war years, this close-knit group and a number of their fellow Jewish contemporaries met frequently, often daily, at the Whitechapel Art Gallery, the library next door, Toynbee Hall in Commercial Street and the Young Socialist League in Stepney to discuss their ideas about art, literature and politics.

Rosenberg caught their attention one evening in January 1911 when, stopping abruptly under a lamppost, he pulled out some scraps of paper and began to read his poetry aloud. Impressed both by the dramatic gesture and the poetry itself, they nonetheless found Rosenberg himself unprepossessing. Leftwich described him as 'very short, sickly, plain-featured, awkward and shuffling in his walk, his voice was monotonous and he stammered a bit. He was also depressingly self-absorbed, and he awed us a little. He did not smile once all that first evening.'[48]

Despite his diffidence Rosenberg was not only absorbed into the writers' group but also provided the link that brought the Whitechapel writers and artists together. Crucially, he had already established friendships with a number of Whitechapel artists: Goldstein, his old friend from Stepney Green and Bolt Court, and David Bomberg (1890–1957)[49] – another reluctant apprentice – whom Rosenberg met through his family's 'paying guest' or lodger, Mitchell,[50] at the Whitechapel Art Gallery. There Rosenberg also met two further art students, Mark Gertler and Mark Weiner (afterwards Wayner), whose Aunt Barbara would often feed them when, hungry and broke but

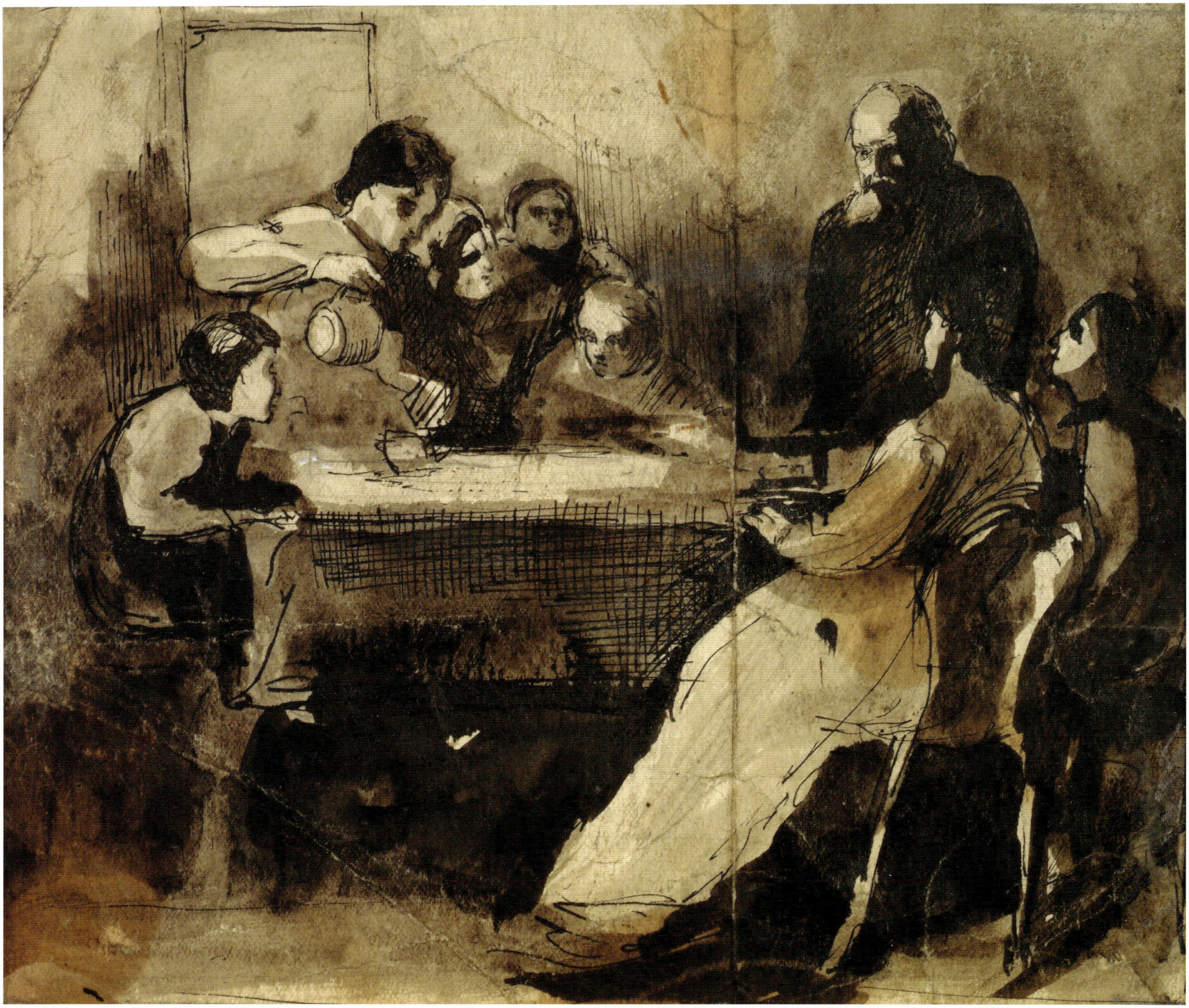

4
ISAAC ROSENBERG
Family Group at a Meal, *c.*1910

full of ideas, they met up to outline their plans for the future. As Ian Parsons (who later edited Rosenberg's *Collected Works*) has commented, 'it is difficult to over-estimate the stimulus, emotional and intellectual, which [Rosenberg] derived from his close friendships' with the Whitechapel Boys.[51]

Unable to afford either professional models or proper studios, the Whitechapel artists often worked at home, usually in the kitchen. Gertler, the first to obtain his own studio, at various times lent it to or shared it with Bomberg, Goldstein and possibly Kramer. Bomberg meanwhile lent his to Rosenberg, and all of them later met there to discuss painting. Rosenberg's studio, Leftwich later recalled, was 'a long narrow passage, which was the family living room. The dresser, crammed with crockery, occupied most of the space; the table, at a corner of which Rosenberg sat sketching, was rickety and littered with cups and plates.'[52] The artists were also dependent on their families as their earliest models: Barnett Rosenberg, Louis Gertler and Max Kramer, their wives and their children, frequently sat for their artist sons at home. In *Family Group at a Meal* (*c.*1910, cat no. 4) Rosenberg also provided a clear visual record of a way of life which was gradually being eroded. The picture has been folded a little off centre, perhaps to isolate the group around the table to the left, perhaps because Rosenberg did not value it, but most likely, simply because he was notoriously disorganised and untidy.[53]

In this period Rosenberg executed several early self-portraits 'with a mirror propped up on the rickety table', probably because, as his nephew Isaac Horvitch commented, 'it was simply that he had no other sitters.'[54] Stephen Winsten once called and found Rosenberg 'gazing intently at himself in a mirror' at work in the kitchen on one of these self-portraits. The kitchen, Winsten noted, was 'a small room with very poor light, but it was the only room that had a mirror and where he could leave his paints about, as the parlour was kept for visitors and his bedroom was shared by a lodger.'[55]

Possibly also because of the continuing lack of money to pay professional sitters, reciprocal portraits were common among the group: Bomberg of Rosenberg (fig. 13, see below); Bomberg of Kramer; Kramer of Bomberg; Birnberg of Rosenberg (cat nos. 44, 45 and fig. 26) and Leftwich (fig. 27); and Rosenberg of Birnberg (cat no. 29).[56] Poems by Rosenberg and Leftwich also make reference to their Whitechapel peers[57] and for a time the writers collaborated on a composite novel.

Although this period was marked by friendship and co-operation among the Whitechapel Boys, there were also disagreements that arose from competitiveness and divergent ambitions. Bomberg called it 'jungle warfare'.[58] Winsten and Rodker fell out over politics and the relationship between Bomberg and Rosenberg was often spiky. Apparently, both Bomberg and Goldstein thought Rosenberg 'a good poet but no painter' – so there may be a hint of irony

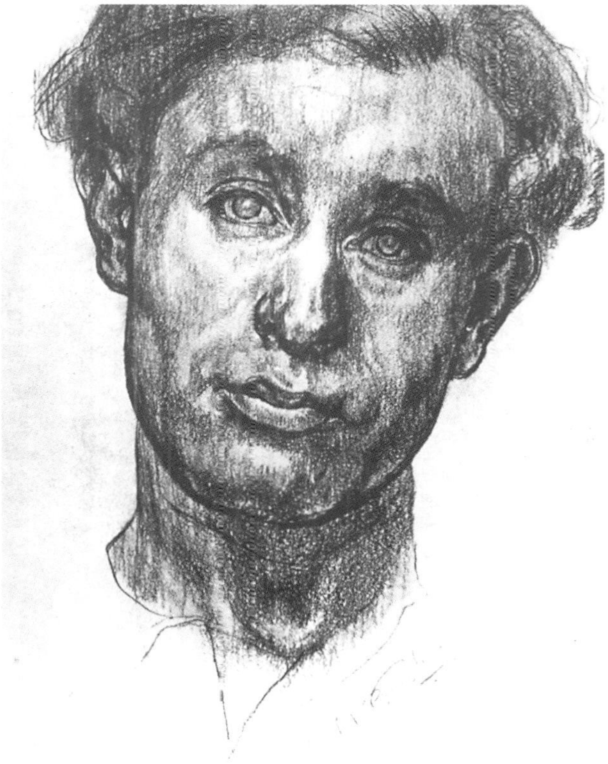

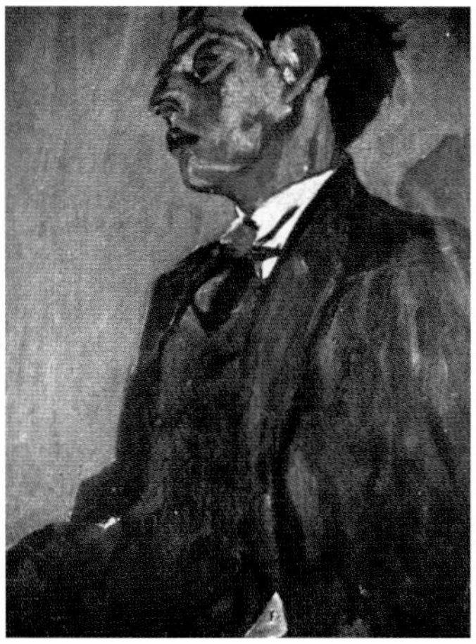

FIG. 13 *left*
DAVID BOMBERG
Head of a Poet (Isaac Rosenberg), 1913

FIG. 27 *above*
CLARE WINSTEN (CLARA BIRNBERG)
Portrait of Joseph Leftwich, *c.*1915

in the title of Bomberg's prizewinning study of Rosenberg entitled *Head of a Poet* (fig. 13), a highly accomplished, intelligent drawing, now sadly lost. Jean Moorcroft Wilson has argued that Rosenberg's membership of this group 'undoubtedly strengthened his resolve to become either a painter or a poet' and encouraged him to throw up his apprenticeship.[59] However, once he joined his contemporaries Gertler and Bomberg at the Slade, both their brilliance and competitiveness may have helped to push Rosenberg towards poetry.

Leftwich believed that Rosenberg's Jewish cultural background had an enormous significance on his development as both a poet and a painter.[60] Joseph Cohen, on the other hand, has observed how the 'distinctly Jewish element' in Rosenberg's work was 'reserved entirely for the poetry where his Jewish background fused with his English heritage to produce a peculiar tension from which sprang an eternal idiom.'[61] When reviewing the work of Amshewitz and Ospovat in 1912, Rosenberg opened his article by pointing out that 'without knowing the names of the artists, [...] one would not suspect for a moment the[ir] Jewish parentage'. Unlike the other Whitechapel painters, however, Rosenberg rarely explored his Jewish heritage or the contradictions of his upbringing in his own painting. Naturally, there are family portraits, including his only known portrait of a rabbi (his uncle Rabbi Peretz).[62] But Rosenberg produced neither concentrated interiors like Gertler's *Rabbi and Rabbitzen* (1913)[63] nor (though he wrote in the same review of 'the travail and sorrow of centuries' having given Jewish 'life a more poignant and intense interpretation') did he execute 'barbaric and symbolic' portraits of Jewish life like Gertler's *Portrait of the Artist's Mother* (1913).[64] There are no religious figure scenes like Gertler's *Talmudic Discussion* (1911)[65] or Kramer's *Day of Atonement* (1919).[66] Nor were there,

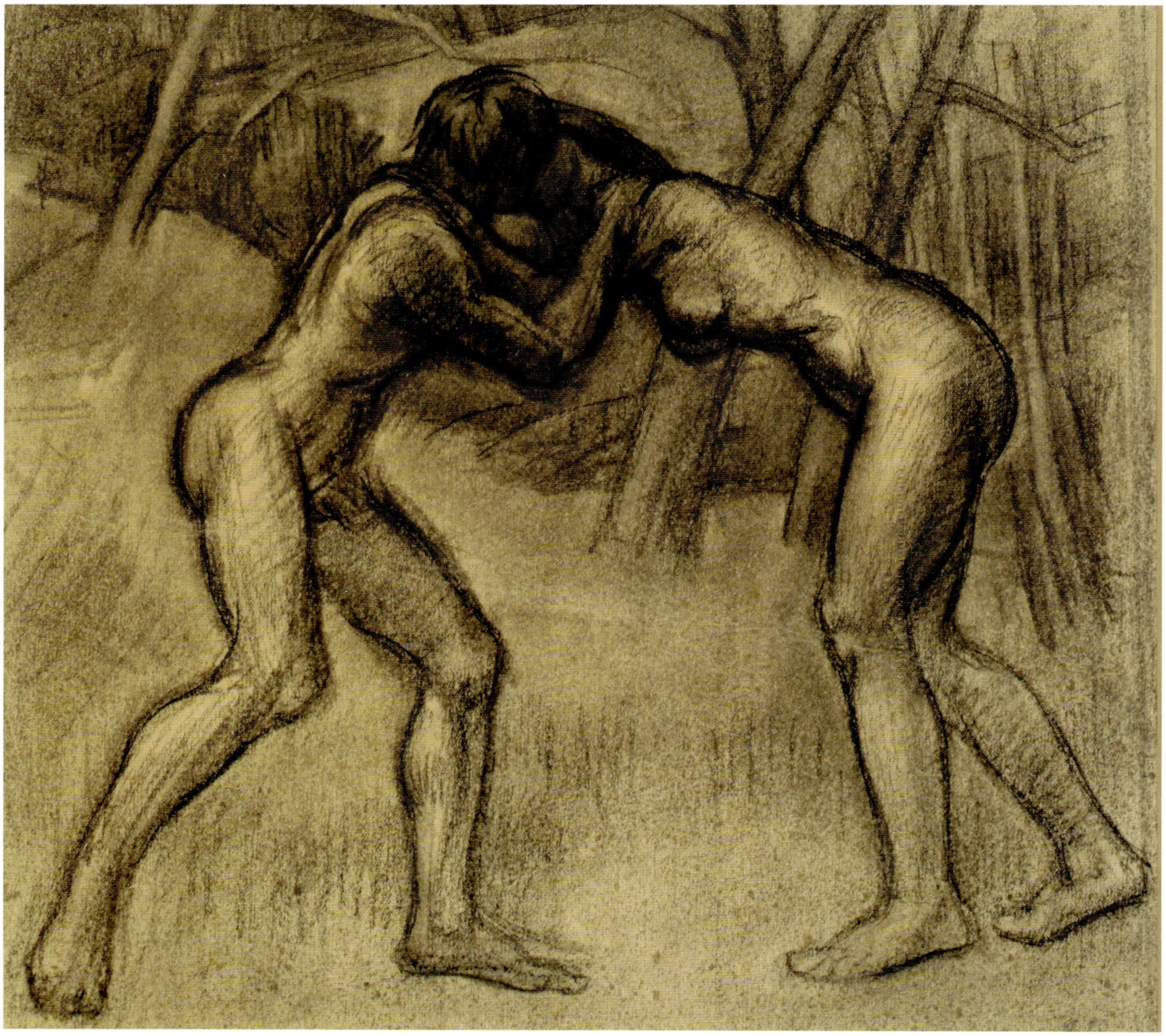

25
ISAAC ROSENBERG
The First Meeting of Adam and Eve,
1915

apparently, paintings of East End life like those which provided the starting point for Bomberg's pictures of wrestlers (*Ju-Jitsu*, *c.*1913), dockers (*In the Hold*, 1913–14) and bathers (*The Mud Bath*, 1914).[67]

There is, however, one notable exception: in 1912 in a Jewish literary and artistic miscellany supported by Emanuel called *A Piece of Mosaic* (cat no. 60), Rosenberg published an obscure drawing entitled *The Wharf* (fig. 7), now known only in reproduction, and not seen in the public domain for over 30 years.[68] The picture combines a local, urban landscape of the docks (including warehouses and a tug boat) in the background with a close-up of three East-End workers – probably dockers, recently much in the news on account of their strike over pay and conditions in the summer of 1911 – in the foreground. Posed as if for a photograph and pressed up close against the picture frame, the men have a forceful physical presence. The composition is dominated by the presence of the man on the right, who is clearly the leader of the group. Dressed in cloth cap and collarless shirt, with one eye closed and a cigarette clamped between his lips, he has the hardened face of a working man. His sleeves are rolled up to reveal huge, brawny arms, clearly accustomed to hard physical work but now idle. To his left a younger man leans toward him, his teeth gritted in a leer or a grimace; the head of a third man, less realised, is glimpsed behind them. A fourth, observed only from behind, sweeps the quay or dockside to their right. Instead of the calm, romanticised melancholy of Rosenberg's early landscapes, we have a dynamic scene of working-class life which he may well have observed firsthand at St Katherine's Dock. Rosenberg's attitude to his subjects is ambiguous; his accompanying verse 'Dim, watery lights, gleaming on gibbering faces, / Faces speechful, barren of soul and sordid' does not suggest any sympathy with the men he portrays.[69] Nevertheless, in subject-matter, execution and technique, this drawing is unique in his oeuvre. However, it relates closely to a topographical etching by Emanuel of the same subject in the Ben Uri collection.

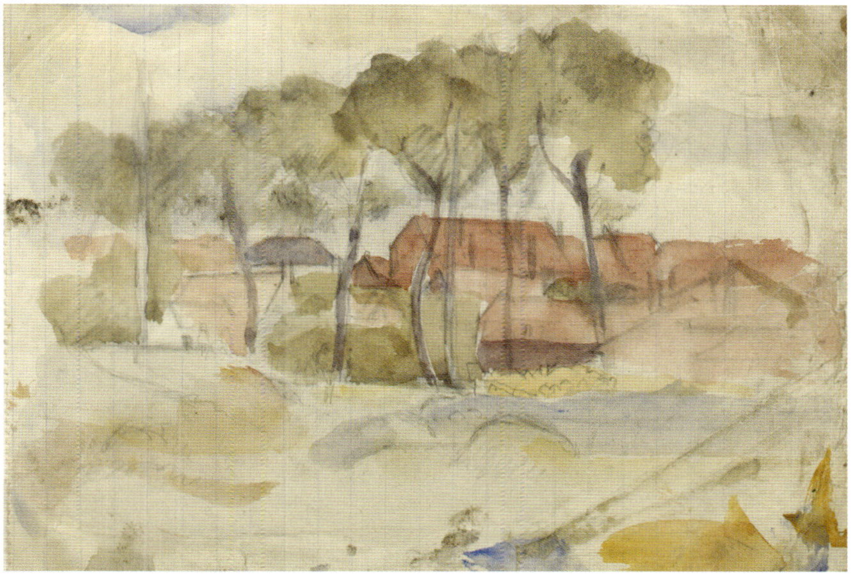

FIG. 1
ISAAC ROSENBERG
Untitled landscape [not dated]

Intriguingly, Bomberg implied in a letter to Leftwich that Rosenberg had early links to the more progressive Fitzroy Street and Camden Town Groups centred on Walter Sickert.[70] If true, Rosenberg appears to have benefited little from this connection; had it developed, compositions such as *The Wharf* may have taken quite a different turn. There is a suggestion – no more – in Bomberg's letter that Sickert may have dismissed Rosenberg in the same manner as Israel Zangwill would do when shown some of his early poetry.[71] Though an Impressionistic handling of paint is apparent in some of Rosenberg's early landscapes, *The Wharf* contains an element of the grotesque bordering on caricature far removed from the 'objective perceptual honesty'[72] of treatment and 'dispassionate accuracy'[73] of execution encouraged by Sickert and adopted by many of the Camden Town painters. Instead, Rosenberg's early landscapes are largely quiet, traditional and rural, employing a muted palette and showing the influence of painters in the National Gallery ranging from Whistler to Boudin and Puvis de Chavannes (the last an enduring influence). They give no hint of his urban, ghetto environment, which is instead glimpsed obliquely in his accomplished early portraits of family life.

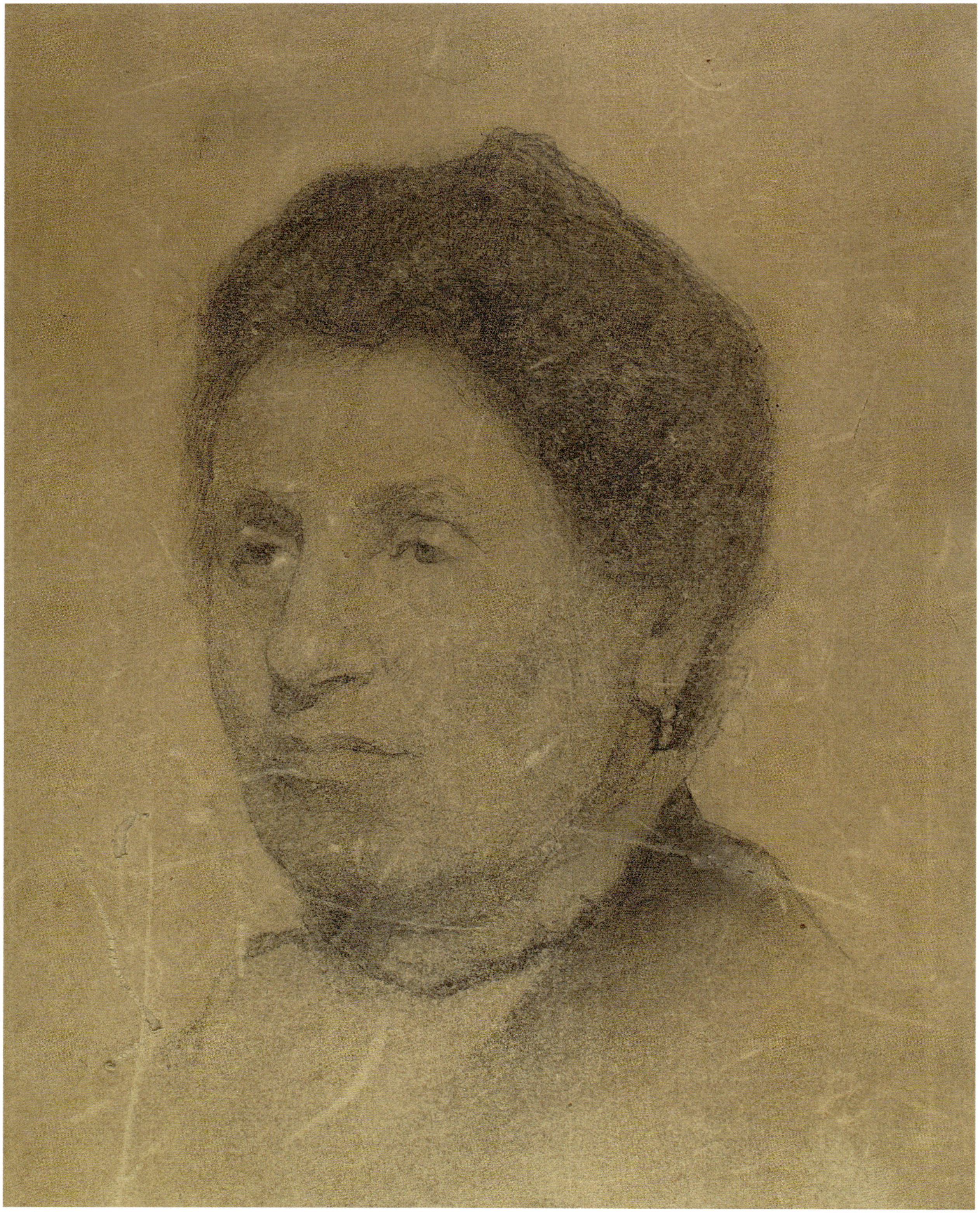

9 *left*
ISAAC ROSENBERG
The Artist's Mother, 1911

8 *right*
ISAAC ROSENBERG
The Artist's Father, 1911

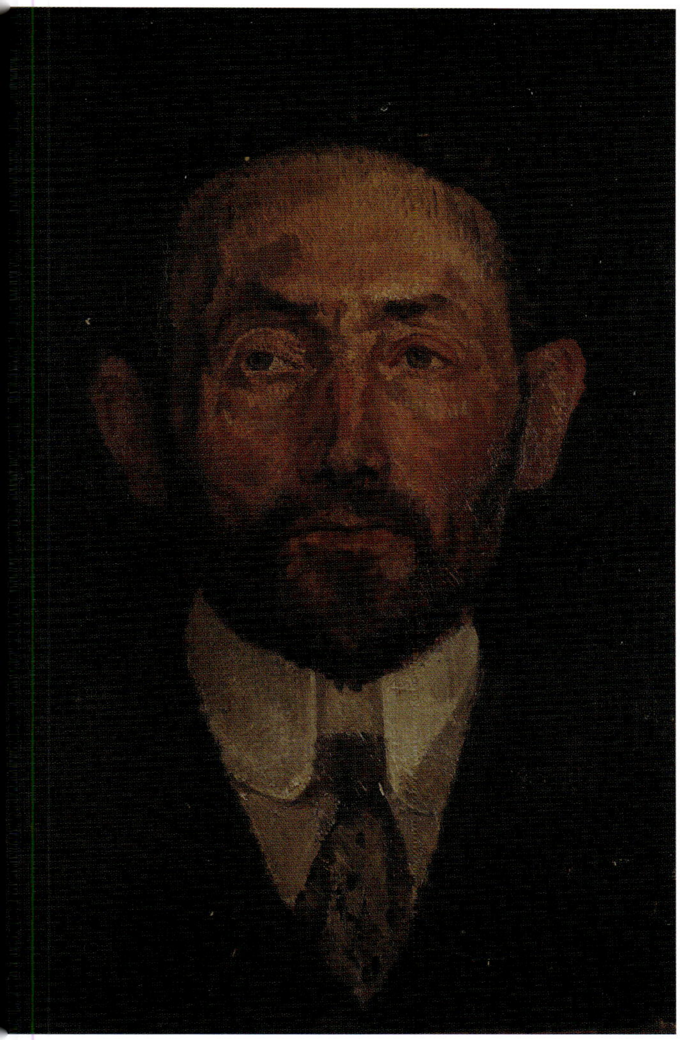

Rosenberg's sensitive early portrait *The Artist's Mother* (1911, cat no. 9), in black chalk and pencil, captures her resilience and a certain sternness, together with precise, almost photographic likeness. It is clearly the type of classic Edwardian portrait of which his mentors, Amshewitz and Emanuel, as well as his teachers at the Slade, would have approved. The handling has loosened marginally in his portrait in oil *The Artist's Father* (1911, cat no. 8), which, with its dark background (for which he was criticised) and finely-modelled features, hints both at his father's gentleness of character and his unhappiness. Taken together these two portraits form a natural pair such as the couple failed to achieve in life. Rosenberg's composition and treatment are reminiscent of Gertler's early portraits of his family, particularly *The Artist's Parents* (*c.* 1909–10) and *The Artist's Brother, Harry* (*c.* 1911),[74] completed while Gertler was at the Slade and possibly known to Rosenberg (whose work necessarily lacks the symbolic power of Gertler's double-portrait as well as something of its emotiveness). Gertler's approval was important to Rosenberg. Although in his 1914 essay 'Art',[75] it was Augustus John whom Rosenberg revered most (declaring that some of John's drawings 'could be hung side by side with da Vinci without suffering'), by 1915 Rosenberg placed Gertler 'easily next to John amongst our painters'.[76]

In March 1911, however, Rosenberg was still under the sway of Amshewitz. Leftwich recorded in his diary that Rosenberg was at work on a new self-portrait – in 'a violently green broad-brimmed Tyrolean' hat – originally intended for the Royal Academy (which Amshewitz had attended but which the other Whitechapel painters had already learned to despise). Leftwich noted that it was also to 'demonstrate to the Jewish Education Aid Society that he [Rosenberg] is in thorough earnest about taking up art as a life-work'.[77] Joseph Cohen believes that Rosenberg bought the hat as 'a grand gesture, full of significance' in order to 'symbolize his release from Hentschel's and to

FIG. 37
Rosenberg's parents and his sister, Minnie, 1889

FIG. 38
Isaac Rosenberg and his Siblings (with Rocking Horse), 1902

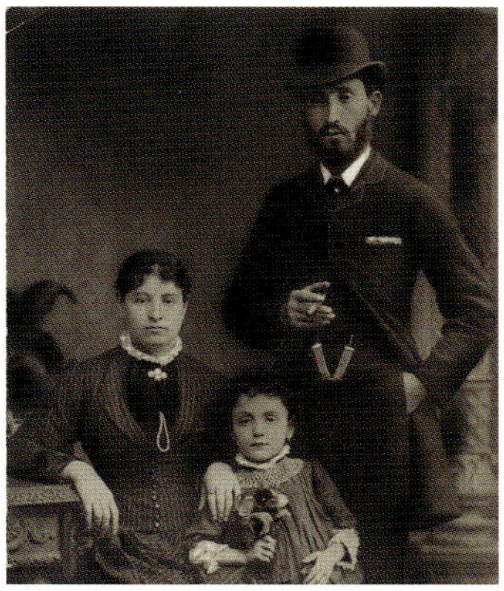

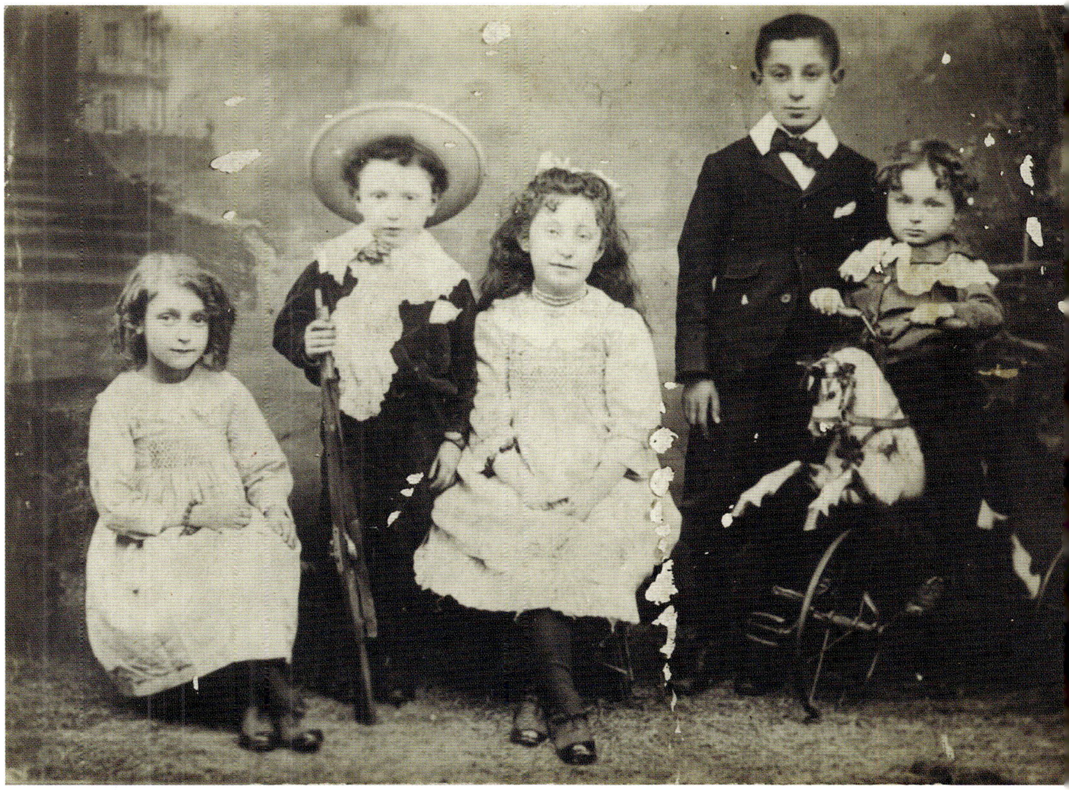

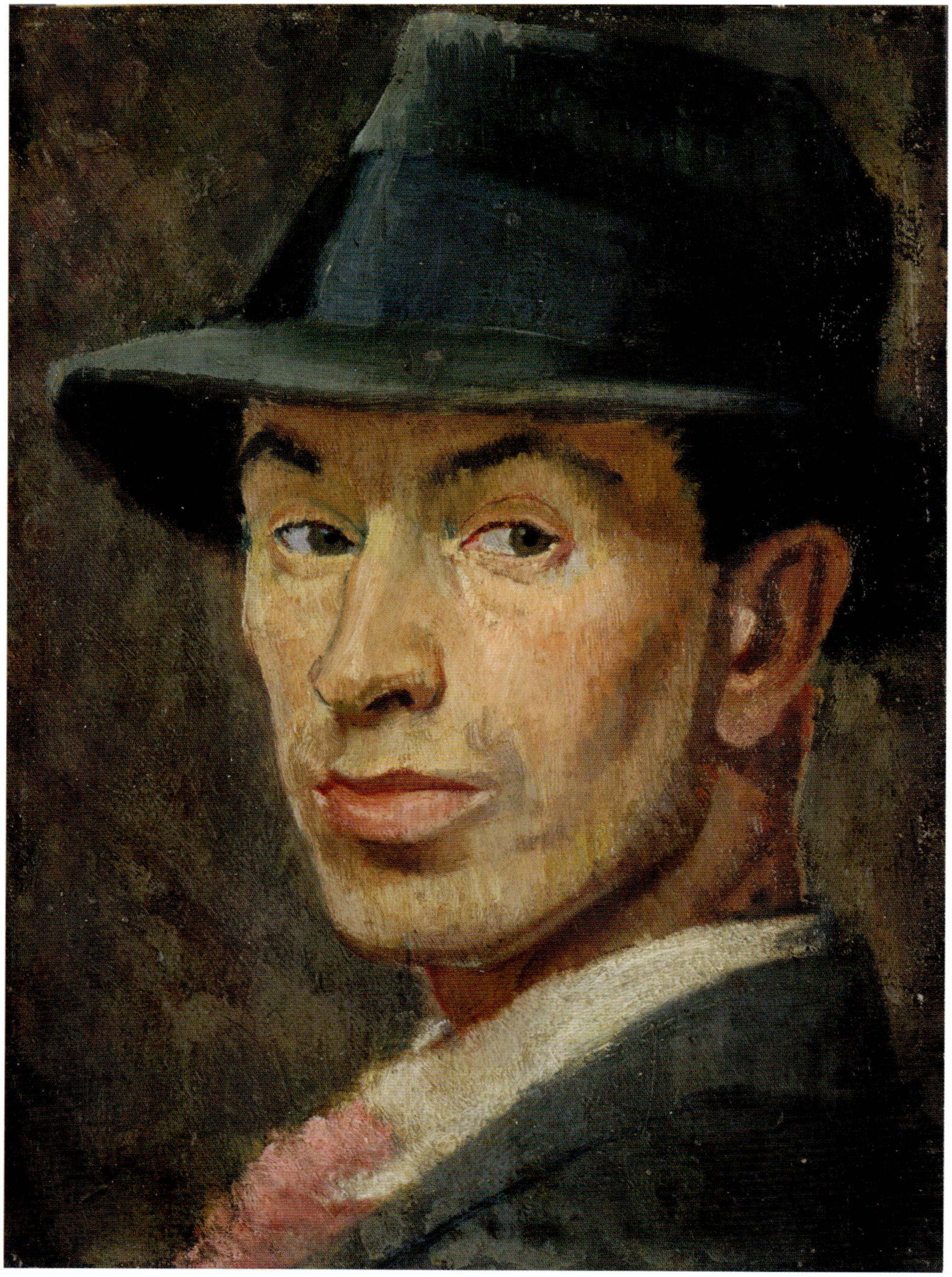

23
ISAAC ROSENBERG
Self-portrait with Trilby, 1914–15

celebrate having crossed the frontier into a brave new world'.[78] The hat was intended, as Lisa Tickner comments, to signal Rosenberg's 'emancipation from the ghetto and his entry into the world of art.'[79]

In early March the work in progress was inspected by Leftwich, Winsten and Rodker, who all considered it 'a very excellent likeness'. Leftwich went on to describe it in detail: 'the painting is bold and outstanding. The face is in shadow. The pose is very striking. It is a three-quarter length – quite a big canvas. He is standing up, wearing his overcoat with the collar turned up and his broad-brimmed Tyrolean hat on his head. Simy and Jimmy are [as] anxious as a Tic about it. We are quite sure that the Academy will accept it.'[80] This bravura attempt to take the Academy by storm failed, however, after Rosenberg went to borrow a frame from Amshewitz and the older painter suggested some improvements. Rosenberg, in trying to effect them, ended up spoiling the canvas. The extant finished oil (*c.* 1914, cat no. 22) is almost certainly a reworking of the same portrait and conforms to much of Leftwich's original description. Only the turned up collar has gone; the face remains slightly in shadow, but both composition and handling are free and bold and the pink tie is a flamboyant streak of colour. Rosenberg the modernist was struggling to emerge.

Rosenberg correctly sensed the dramatic potential of this portrait and reworked the image twice before perfecting it. *Self-Portrait with Trilby* (1914–15, cat no. 23), echoes the pose of the first portrait and retains the suit and pink tie but truncates the subject to head-and-shoulders and presents the figure facing left instead of right. This portrait has an engaging clarity and the composition is greatly simplified. However, it lacks both the depth and the punch of the final Tyrolean portrait (1915, cat no. 24) which reworks and refines the earlier portraits with a new confidence. Here Rosenberg finally achieves that sophisticated mixture of bravura pose and assured handling, underpinning the composition with the strong vertical brushstrokes employed in the portraits

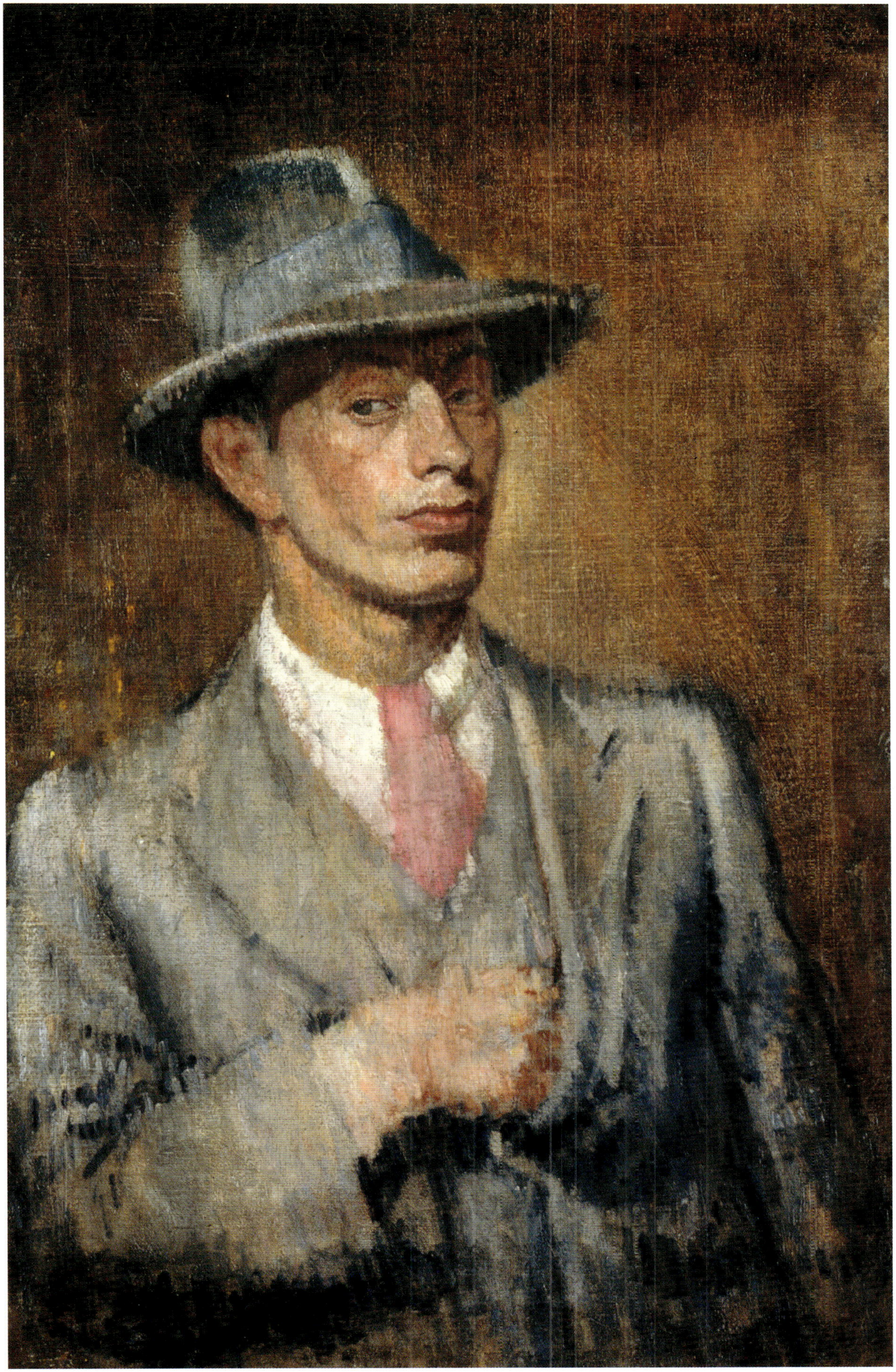

22
ISAAC ROSENBERG
Self-portrait with Trilby, c.1914

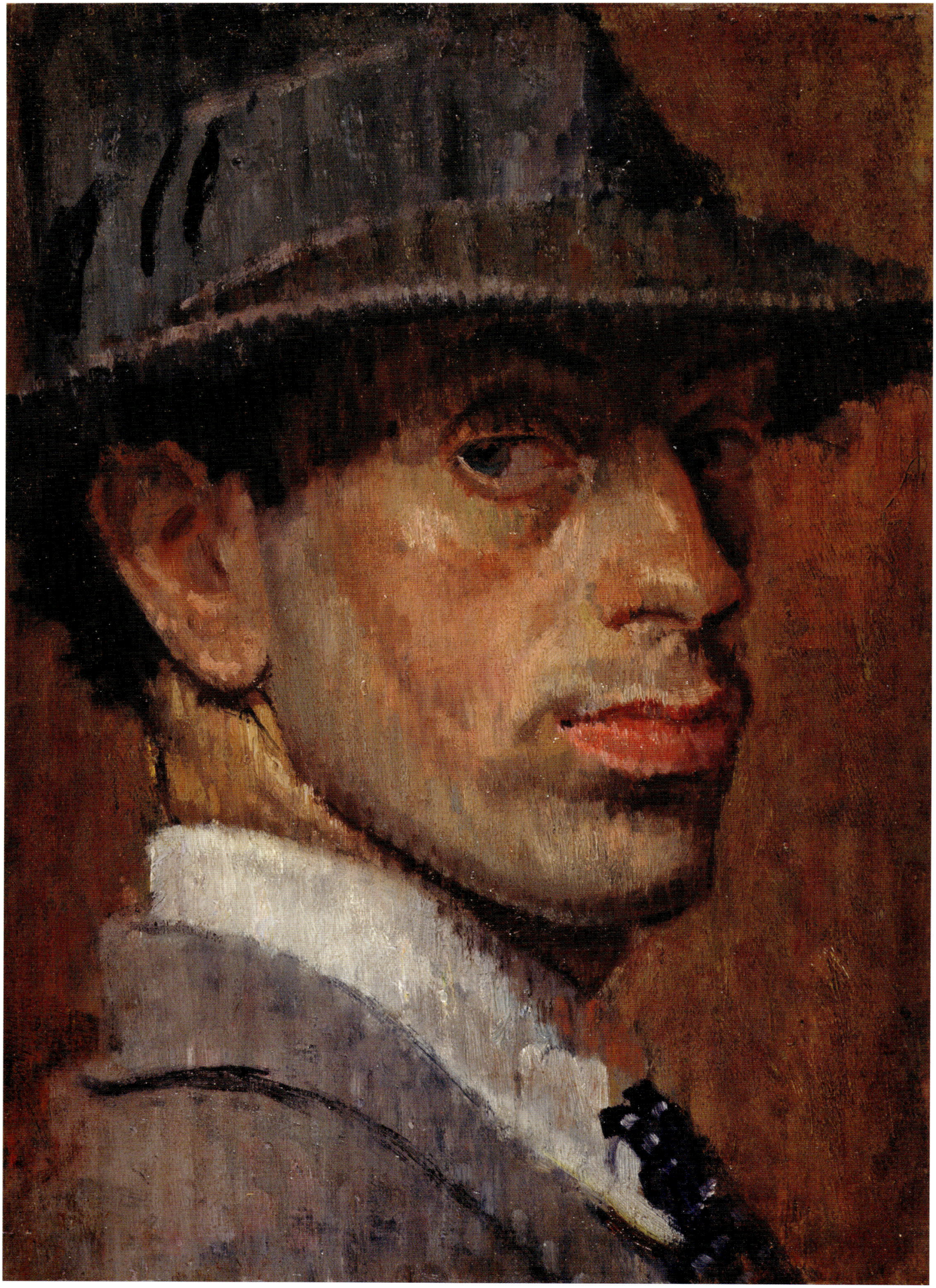

of *Sonia* (*c.*1915, cat no. 28) and *Clare Winsten* (Clara Birnberg, 1915, cat no. 29)[81] to create undoubtedly his most enduring image.

In an extract from her (unpublished) memoir, Rosenberg's friend Sonia Cohen explained the significance of Rosenberg's choice of clothing, which marked him out as one of the bohemians:

> Not only did artists and social revolutionaries separate themselves from philistines (bowler and silk hatted respectables) by wearing soft-brimmed sombreros, but their emancipated exclusiveness was further shown in the colour and form of their neckwear. A red tie was the sign of a social revolutionary; that is, a Social Democrat or Anarchist, and a black silk bow showed an artist – a poet or musician as well as a painter of pictures. The bows were tied under low cut 'rational' collars, being large and floppy like those worn by Paderewski and Puccini's artist in *La Bohème*, Fabians and such like intellectuals went bareheaded with long unoiled hair; and as far as I can remember these young men wore ties in Band of Hope blue.[82]

When Sonia first saw Rosenberg and Bomberg, making an entrance at the Whitechapel Reference library, she noted 'two young men [...], both of whom wore large brimmed black hats and neither had the bow or tie usual with this particular headgear.' Bomberg, 'the taller of the two wore an apple green or sometimes a yellow tie which invariably had a red stone pinned onto it' while Rosenberg, who she further described as 'he of the slow upturned smile, favoured pink ties' and, she noted, 'once had a whole neckcloth of pink'[83] (*Self-Portrait*, cat no. 6).

In March 1911, hoping to impress the Jewish Education Society, a charitable organisation that he thought might help him, Rosenberg was at work on a copy of Velázquez's *Philip IV* in the National Gallery, when he had the first of two extraordinary encounters. On 9 March George V arrived at the gallery on an official visit and most of the art students abandoned their work to go and watch him open some new rooms. Rosenberg, however, worked on, and the King, passing through, stopped for some moments to watch him at work. Just over a week later, again at work in front of *Philip IV*, Rosenberg found himself observed again, this time by a fellow painter, a middle-aged lady, with whom he soon became involved in a vigorous debate over the best masters to copy. To his surprise, his fellow debater turned out to be Lily Delissa Joseph (sister of Solomon J Solomon, RA), who explained to him her technique for landscape and interiors (based on a palette limited to white, cobalt and rose or orange madder), insisted on lending him her own colours, urged him to use them as soon as possible, and to call on her at her London home.[84]

Rosenberg executed his first painting using Delissa Joseph's methods only two days later in a landscape entitled *Highgate* and duly called on her. By May he found himself employed as tutor to her son, and was introduced to both her sister, Mrs Henrietta Löwy, and their mutual friend Mrs Herbert Cohen, whose strength of character is apparent in the portrait of her painted by Alfred Wolmark 45 years later (cat no. 46). Although Rosenberg spent a depressed and unproductive summer, culminating in a boat trip to St Helena, on his return he found that his life was about to change. The three ladies had decided to club together to cover his fees and send Rosenberg to the Slade School of Art. He would begin there in October 1911.

24
ISAAC ROSENBERG
Self-Portrait, 1915

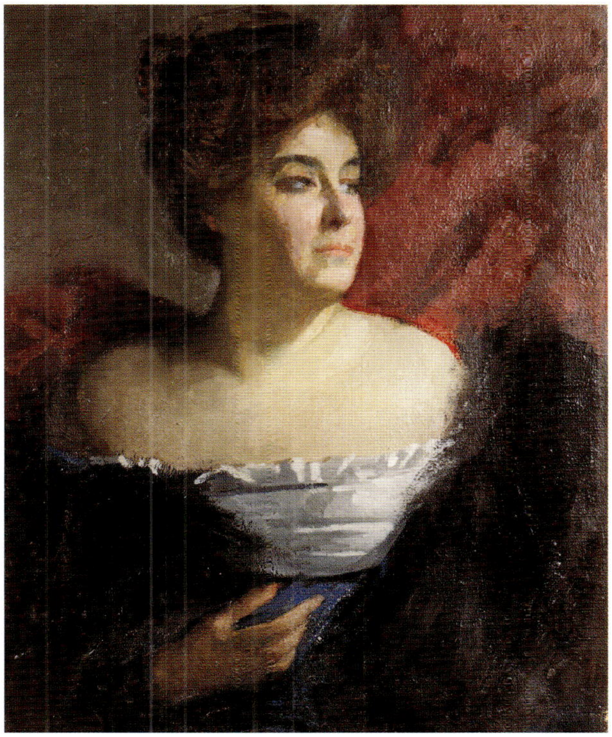

46
ALFRED WOLMARK
Portrait of Mrs Herbert Cohen, 1956

2

ISAAC ROSENBERG THE PAINTER
PART II: 'SHAKEN AND SHIVERED'

'Art is now, as it were, a volcano. Eruptions are continual, and immense cities of culture at its foot are shaken and shivered.'
Isaac Rosenberg, ART Part II, 1914[1]

'"The Slade, what is the Slade?" Nine-tenths of our readers will cry. Is it a building or a threshing machine? It is merely an art-school.'
Isaac Rosenberg, 'The Slade and its relations to the Universe'[2]

26
ISAAC ROSENBERG
Study of Nude Woman (Seated with Knee Raised), 1915

When Rosenberg arrived at the Slade in the autumn of 1911 it was, as he himself acknowledged, far more than 'merely an art-school': it was 'the finest school for drawing in England',[3] as well as the most progressive. Under a highly successful triumvirate of teaching staff – Fred Brown, Henry Tonks and Philip Wilson Steer – it nurtured some of the greatest talent of the day including Stanley Spencer, Paul Nash, William Roberts, C R W Nevinson, Edward Wadsworth, Dora Carrington and Ben Nicholson, alongside Rosenberg's fellow Whitechapel Boys, notably David Bomberg and Mark Gertler. Together these students formed what Tonks later described as the Slade's second 'crisis of brilliance'.[4] It was among such company that Rosenberg had to make his mark.

By 1911 there was a significant presence of Whitechapel Boys at the Slade. Gertler, who by then was only attending part-time, had become the first working-class Jewish student of his generation when he joined in 1908. His success encouraged others: Mark Weiner (afterwards Wayner), who stayed only briefly (half of the third term of 1909–10); Clara Birnberg, who joined in 1910; and Bomberg, who arrived several months before Rosenberg describing himself as 'Isaac's unofficial Guardian at the Slade'.[5] Three further Whitechapel Boys followed them: Bernard Meninsky, born in the Ukraine but brought up in Liverpool (1912–13); Rosenberg's friend from Bolt Court, Morris Goldstein (autumn 1912–13);[6] and Jacob Kramer, born, like Meninsky in the Ukraine and raised in Leeds (1913–14). All were set apart from the other students by their extreme poverty, walking in together daily to Gower Street to save money on the tube fare.[7]

In his last term Rosenberg would form a brief, unlikely friendship with Kramer who, at more than six feet tall, towered over Rosenberg's diminutive form. Formidably bulky and known for his boxing prowess, Kramer once rescued Rosenberg from an anti-Semitic bully when Rosenberg, upholding his father's pacifist principles, refused to fight back. Kramer admired Rosenberg's poetry, preserving some samples (now lost), and Rosenberg dedicated a verse to *J Kramer*,[8] probably out of gratitude as he had done with Amshewitz.

Excused the usual probationary period in the Antique room (a rare honour), Rosenberg immediately found himself in the men's life class ('I do nothing but draw – draw' he wrote to a friend).[9] Bomberg later described this experience as 'three years' work of sitting on a low donkey stool from ten to four drawing worm's eye views of the nude'.[10] Rosenberg was a conscientious student, even

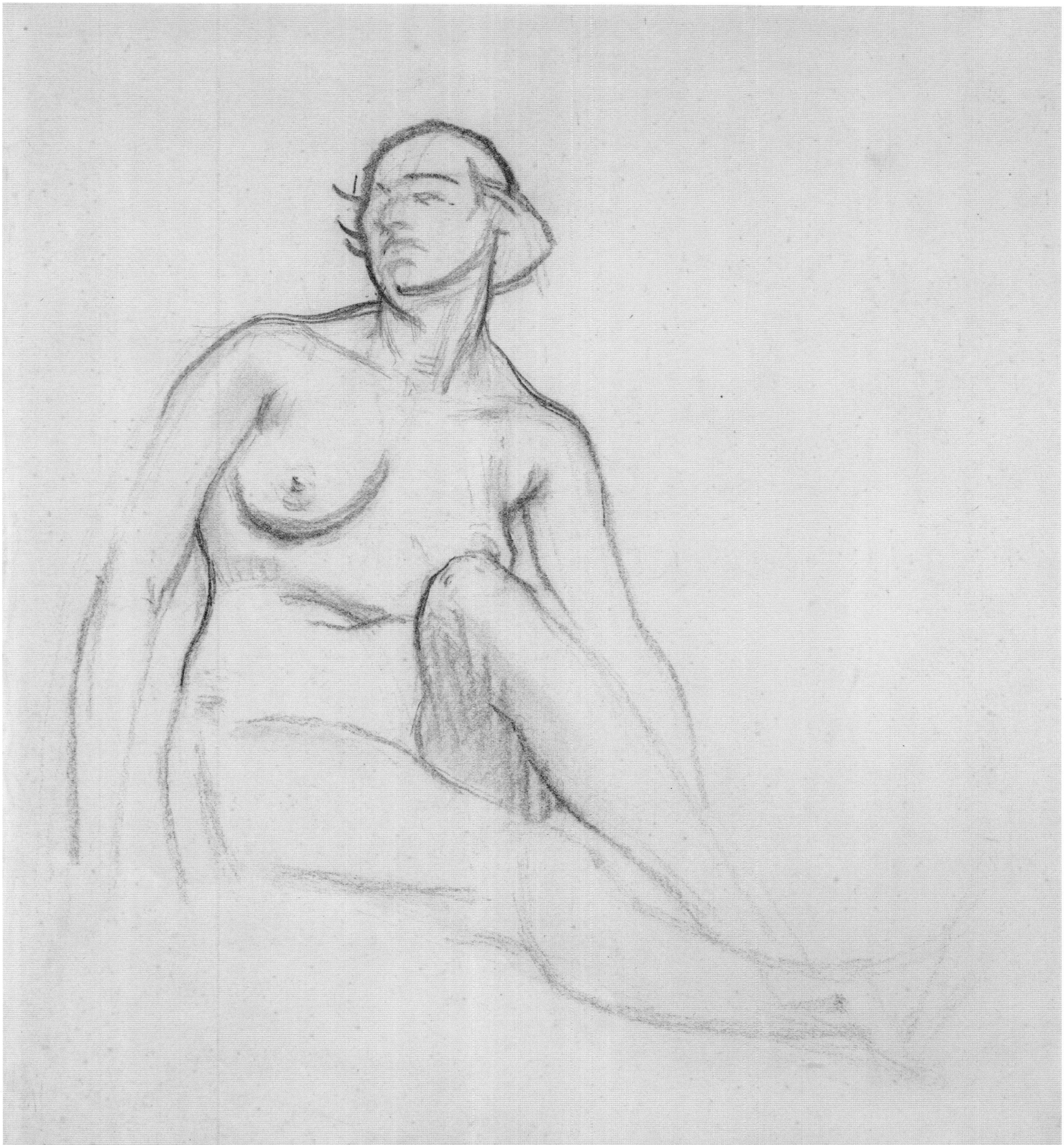

27
ISAAC ROSENBERG
Study of Nude Woman (Seen from Behind Walking), 1915

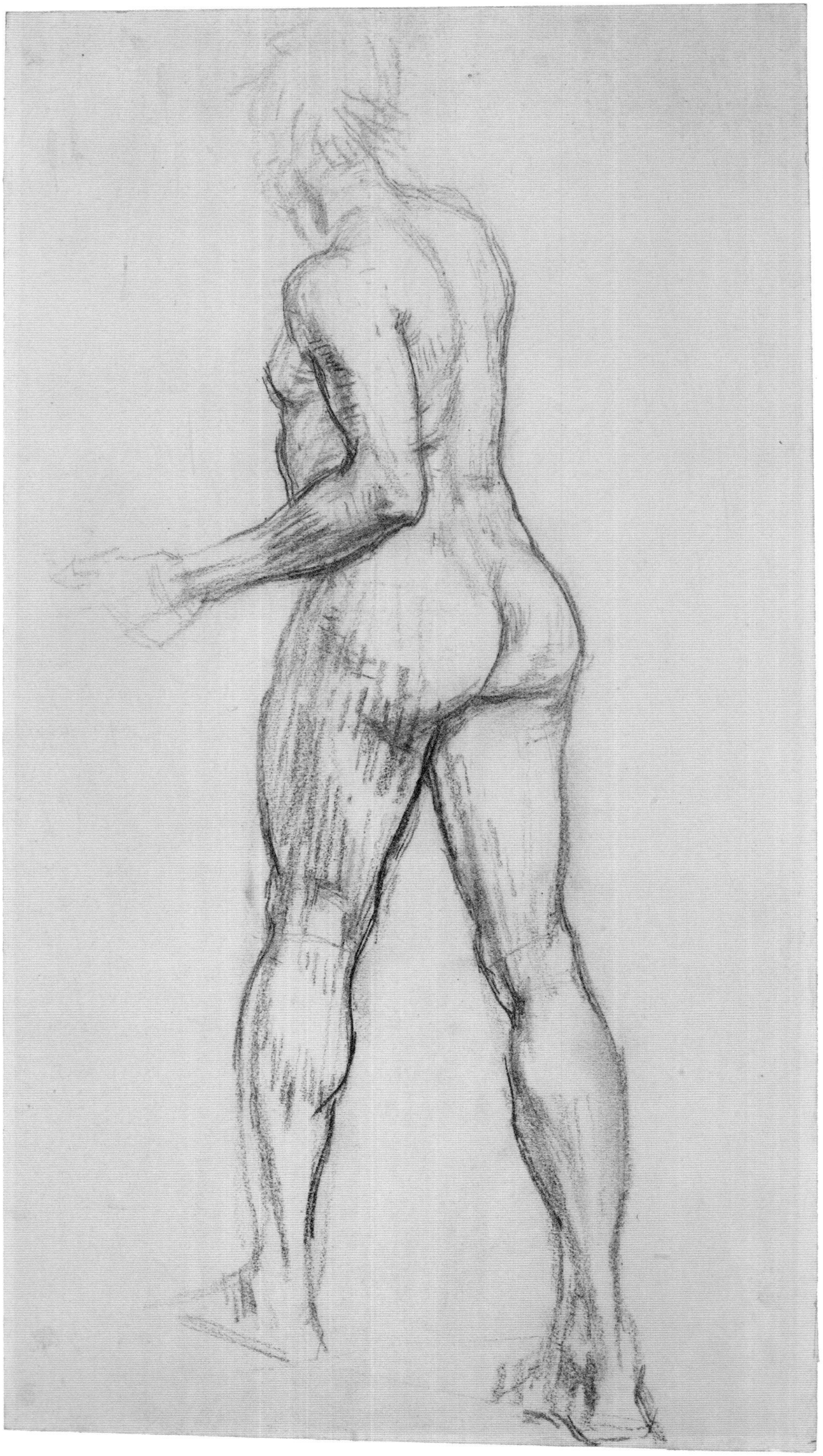

attending on Saturdays. His surviving nude studies in typical life-room poses (cat nos. 26 and 27)[11], are likely to date from this time. 'If he was not drawing, he was painting,' Joseph Cohen observed, 'copying the masters at the National Gallery when he didn't have a class. At weekends he did landscapes. And when he was not drawing or painting he was writing.'[12] Rosenberg described Tonks, the indomitable drawing master, as 'a most remarkable man. He talks wonderfully. So voluble and ready – crammed with ideas – most illuminating and suggestive – and witty.'[13] Under his tutelage Rosenberg learned to rid his drawings of superfluous detail, acquiring a clear, decisive line apparent in his *Self-Portrait* (1912, cat no. 15). Writing became temporarily displaced and in a letter to Laurence Binyon, Rosenberg admitted 'I find writing interferes with drawing a good deal, and is far more exhausting.'[14]

A report from C KoeChila, Professor Brown's assistant, confirms that Rosenberg was 'enthusiastic in his work [...], which certainly showed promise. He was skilful with the brush, and he gained a second Prize for Painting from the Head Model in the competitions, Session 1911–12.'[15] Almost all Rosenberg's surviving portraits have been executed in this head and shoulders format, and though the winning work has not been recorded, his sensitive and painterly *Self-Portrait* (1911, cat no. 6) is a superb example of his skill. In Steer's painting classes Rosenberg began to lighten his palette (see *The Fountain* (1911, cat no. 10) and *Trees* (1912, cat no. 12).

Rosenberg arrived at the Slade amid the excitement generated by Roger Fry's two Post-Impressionist exhibitions at the Grafton Galleries in 1910 and 1912, which caused such a revolution among painters of his generation. Gertler famously described

10
ISAAC ROSENBERG
The Fountain, 1911

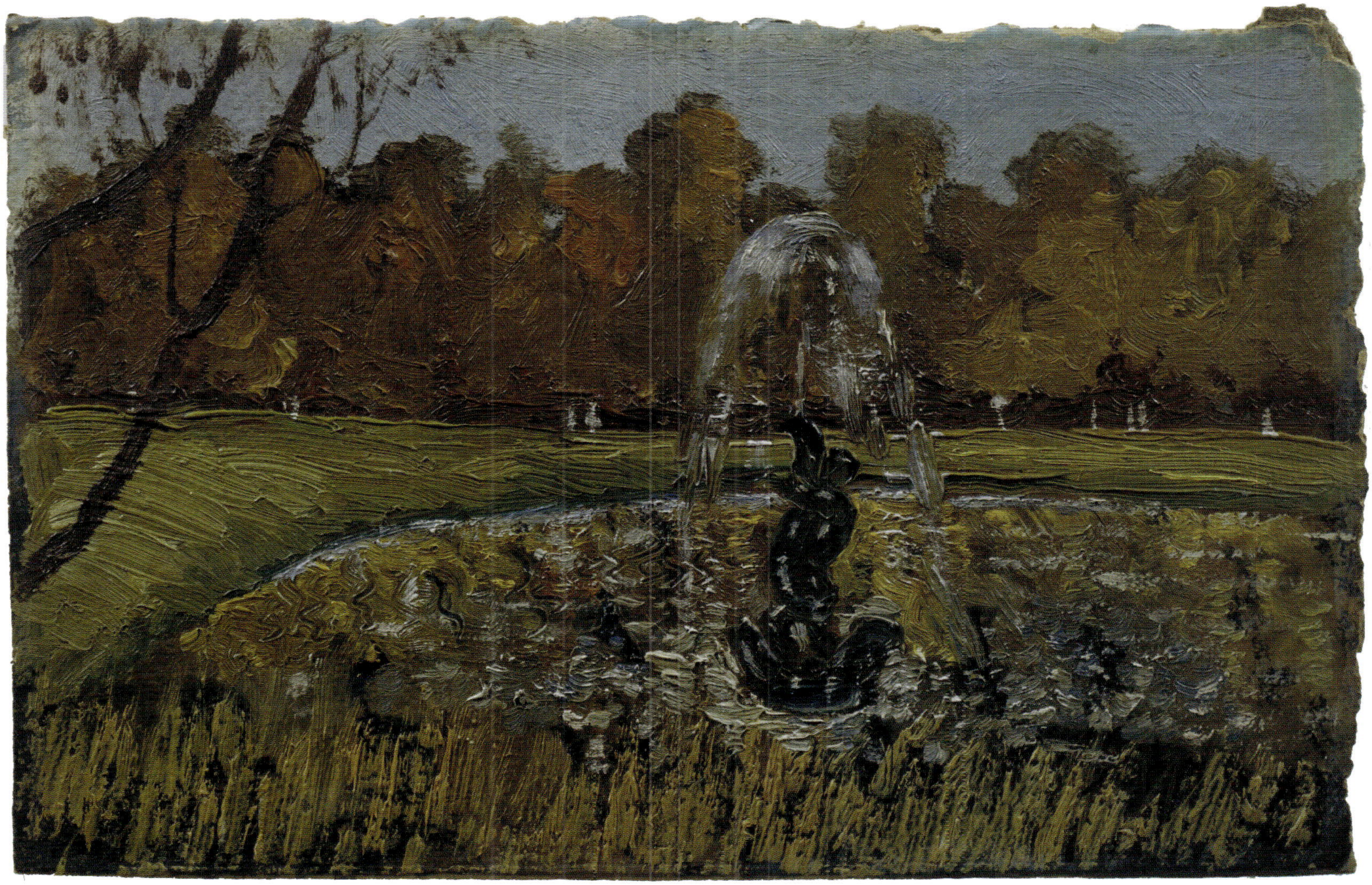

it as 'equivalent to the impact of the scientists of this age upon a simple student of Sir Isaac Newton.'[16] The emerging generation of painters, Rosenberg among them, all drew on the key techniques of Post-Impressionism, shedding some (but not all) of their Slade training in favour of simplification of definition, boldness of colour, exaggeration of individual components, flattening of forms and reduction of pictorial space. Yet Rosenberg was not naturally drawn to experimentation as a painter; his biographer Jean Moorcroft Wilson argues that he saved his innovation for his poetry.[17] Rosenberg's remarks on 'modern aims' and 'the fermented state of culture now in Europe' reflect his own struggle with 'the multiplexity, and elaborately interwoven texture of Modern life; the whole monstrous fabric of modernity' he observed, 'is rapidly increasing in complexity, and art, which is a sort of summing up, and intensification of the spirit of the age, increases its aims accordingly'.[18]

Rosenberg was attracted by the Post-Impressionism of Cézanne: 'To feel continuity in variety, both in colour and form, to feel freshness and intimacy – life and genuine communion of man's spirit with the universal spirit, was the aim of these men.'[19] But he recoiled from Futurism, even while reworking its vocabulary for his own purposes, writing in the alliterative prose of the aspirant poet of 'the Futurist, the last spark struck from this seething modernism, this mechanical age of speed and convulsive machinery [...]. Theirs is an ideal of strength and scorn. [...] Theirs is the terrible beauty of destruction and the furious energy in destroying. [...] To express these new ideals, they have invented forms abstract and mechanical, remote from and unassociated with natural objects, and by the rhythmic arrangement of these forms, to convey sensation.' Yet he deliberately undercut his own image of pulsating power with a more humble, prosaic – even comic – one, declaring: 'The only sensation I have ever got from a Futurist picture is that of a house falling'.[20]

Rosenberg's own experiments with modernism began almost immediately after he joined the Slade, in the multi-figure compositions, mostly on biblical themes, typical of Slade students in this period. *Sing Unto the Lord* (1911, fig. 3) is inspired by a biblical quotation from Exodus 15. 1–11, which Rosenberg wrote out and attached to the bottom of his

12
ISAAC ROSENBERG
Trees, 1912

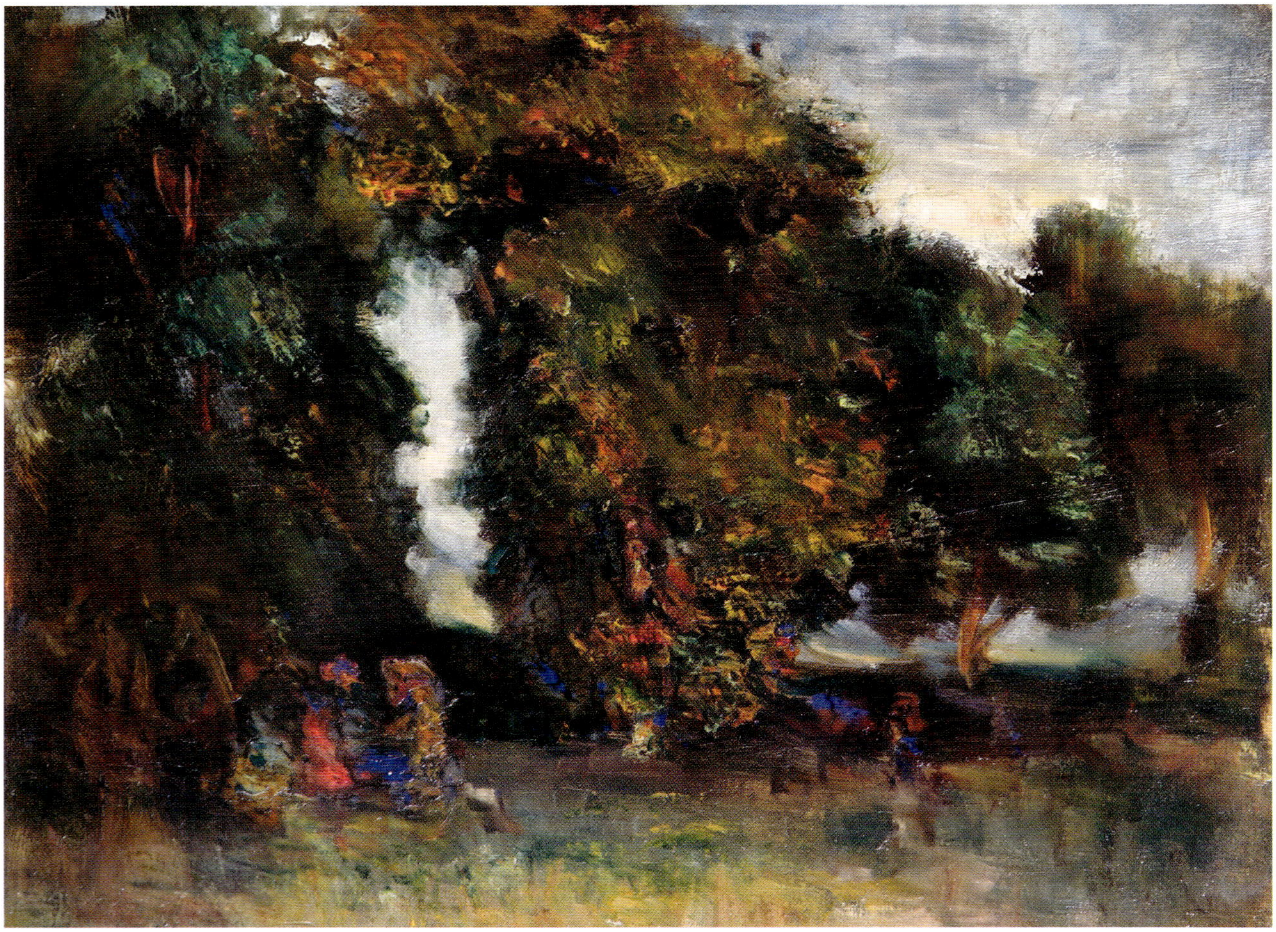

painting.[21] It shows three nude figures, one standing or wading on the left and gesturing towards two swimmers in the centre ground; their stark, dramatic poses are probably borrowed from life studies at the Slade, but are also reminiscent of Blake. It is possible that Rosenberg was influenced by Blake, though he later made it clear that he admired Blake's vision more than his draughtsmanship.[22] A more contemporary model may have been Duncan Grant's *Bathing*,[23] completed in the same year (though Grant's bathers are more stylised and his technique more advanced). Grant's depiction of the male body was influenced by Michelangelo, particularly his *Battle of Cascina*;[24] Rosenberg's swimmers are less idealised and muscular.

In 1912, probably under the influence of Bomberg, Rosenberg executed two of his boldest, embryo-modernist compositions: *Sacred Love* (1912, fig. 4) and *Joy* (1912).[25] *Sacred Love* was subsequently bought by Edward Marsh and hung in his spare bedroom, where 'it glowed with a strange, dream-like intensity, reminiscent of Blake – a lovely vision which for the next quarter of a century confronted on their waking all the guests in this little room.'[26] Although not a direct quotation from Blake, the subject of sacred love is suitably Blakean. Rosenberg depicts a modernist arcadia where young lovers meet against a backdrop of tree trunks delineated by thrusting diagonals, and a landscape broken up into flat areas of pastel colour. Further figures, whose actions are ambiguous rather than finally resolved, can be glimpsed behind them. The scene is partly suggestive of Gauguin's Tahitian canvases of local women[27] but is considerably softer in style and handling.

Another more direct model may have been Puvis de Chavannes's painting *Summer*,[28] with which *Sacred Love* shares its sylvan landscape, particularly the thrusting tree trunks, the draped female figures and the riverside setting. The kneeling pose of Rosenberg's central lover also echoes that of the naked boy hugging a lamb in *Summer* (although without the French artist's Christian overtones). Puvis de Chavannes was admired by Augustus John (one of the dominant influences at the Slade), whose large-scale imaginative compositions, such as *Lyric Fantasy*, reflect his influence.[29] Work by Puvis de Chavannes had also been shown at the Friday Club in 1910,[30] and influenced a number of Slade compositions.[31]

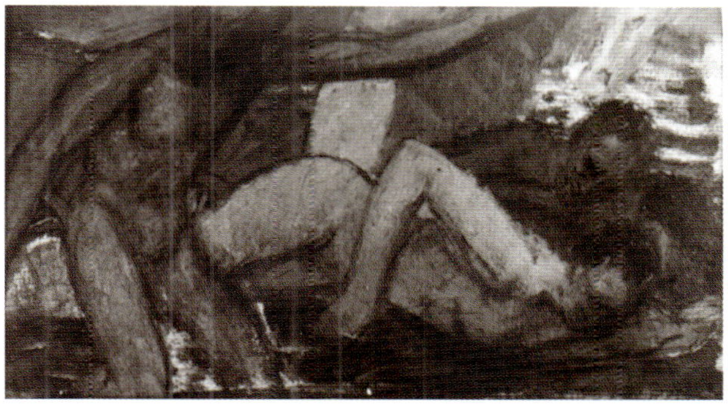

FIG. 3
ISAAC ROSENBERG
'Sing unto the Lord'
(aka *'The Song at Sea'*), 1911

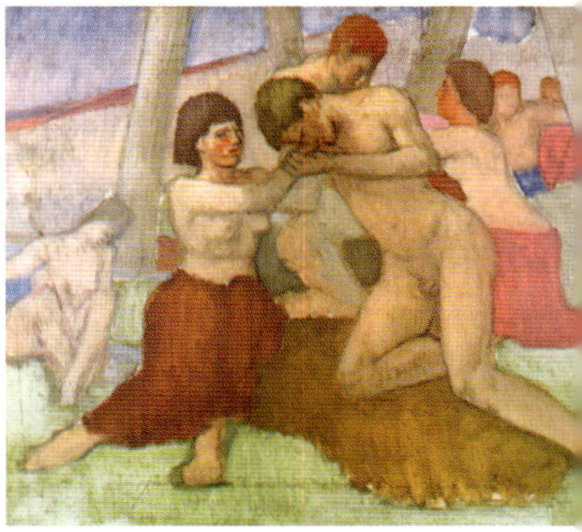

FIG. 4
ISAAC ROSENBERG
Sacred Love, 1912

Joy, Rosenberg's entry for the Slade summer competition of 1912, was executed during the holidays and submitted when classes resumed in the autumn.[32] By reason of its size alone (approx. 6ft × 4ft), this was one of Rosenberg's most ambitious canvases. Bomberg, whose studio Rosenberg occasionally borrowed – and where all the Whitechapel artists met to discuss painting in this period – was working simultaneously on his own composition, *Island of Joy* (7ft wide). Birnberg's *Dawn* (fig. 24, approx 5ft wide) was probably also executed for the same competition. Rosenberg began *Joy* in July[33] and worked on it 'frantically'.[34] He asked Ruth Löwy (daughter of one of his patrons Mrs Henrietta Löwy and a Slade contemporary), who modelled for one of the recumbent figures (*Ruth Löwy as the Sleeping Beauty*, fig. 6), to 'live in the garden of Joy' so that when she sat for him 'you will know what sort of expression to wear when I put you in my "garden of Joy"'.[35] But Ruth's sleeping face has more in common with Rossetti's portraits of Elizabeth Siddal and bears little relation to those of the six figures in Rosenberg's most starkly modernist composition *Hark, Hark, the Lark* (1912, cat no. 16),[36] which Joseph Cohen believes was the first composition study for *Joy* and 'intended to represent a group of nude figures of both sexes responding to the song of the bird winging overhead.' The study, as

16
ISAAC ROSENBERG
Hark, Hark, the Lark, 1912

Cohen points out, 'is practically devoid of Joy';[37] instead the figures with their upturned faces and outstretched arms appear to be imploring, beseeching, rather than rejoicing. In the pared-down modelling and expressiveness of his figures Rosenberg comes closest here to the work of Bomberg and William Roberts, suggesting a lively interchange of ideas.

By August 1912, Rosenberg had 'the working fever' and had 'started my picture again, having taken a violent dislike to my design – it is absolutely another thing now', though significantly, he described 'the literary idea' as 'the same. My colour conception is a wonderful scheme of rose silver and gold – just now it is all pink yellow and blue – but I have great hopes with it.' To realise this colour scheme he borrowed a pearl, which was 'just that iride[sce]nce – that shimmering quality' he sought 'to make the whole scheme of my picture.' He used a Miss Grimshaw, whom he found 'a good sitter – though her figure was much too scraggy for my purpose' and wanted a 'more titanic model' for the upper part.[38] Now, he told Ruth Löwy, it was 'a gorgeous scheme of rose pearl and gold – a dream picture', but 'everything', he continued ominously, 'now depends on the models (if I can afford any) and the types I get for them.'[39]

Rosenberg's excitement is palpable in his letters and led their readers to expect a magnificent composition, but his patron, Mrs Herbert Cohen, was hugely disappointed when she called to look at the result, which remained unfinished. She felt misled over the progress of the picture and their relationship – already in difficulties (all the Whitechapel boys came to resent the influence of their wealthy Anglo-Jewish patrons) – deteriorated. That autumn when Rosenberg failed to send in her cheque for the Slade's fees (he held it back since it was 5 shillings short),[40] she suspected him of being at best disingenuous, if not downright dishonest, and reduced his living allowance. At the Slade however, though he did not take the prize,[41] Rosenberg's entry was 'well praised – the Pro – said it showed a hopeful future – had great charm etc but I wanted more study.'[42]

Cohen describes the final painting (now lost) as using a dozen figures in 'a fantasy of ecstatic representations'.[43] This was exactly the sort of composition to which Mrs Cohen (and Emanuel) objected. Both used the word 'unhealthy'[44] to describe this style of painting, while Laurence Binyon later wrote that Rosenberg's work became 'tinged with the temper and the prevalent ideas of his own generation of students.' He summed up what he felt to be both the strengths and weaknesses of Rosenberg's art: 'He was full of ideas, was a capable draughtsman, and could conceive of an interesting design. Yet, [...] it did not seem to be for him the inevitable means of expression.' Binyon recalled seeing at Rosenberg's studio 'a large, ambitious composition – an oil painting [almost certainly *Joy*] – which I fancy was never completed'. It was, he recalled, 'saturated with symbolism and required a good deal of explanation.'[45]

Binyon's response suggests that Rosenberg was still blending other influences, particularly literary ones, with the new modernist ideas espoused by Bomberg, Roberts, and to a lesser extent, Birnberg. Binyon admired 'the mysteriousness' of Rosenberg's composition and thought that:

> the ideas which inspired the painting had suggested figures and groups and visionary glimpses of landscape which had passages of real beauty, though the whole work had grown impossibly complex with its convolutions of symbolic meaning. It reminded me of his poetry; and I think that represented his natural bent in art.

Binyon also remarked, tellingly, that had Rosenberg been born 'half a century earlier, he would have been an ardent disciple of Rossetti. But he could not escape from the mental atmosphere of his own generation, in which so "literary" a conception of painting was bound to wither in discouragement.'[46]

During this period Rosenberg wrote to Binyon of his admiration for Rossetti. It was no coincidence that two of the figures he revered most, Rossetti and Blake, were also both poets and painters:

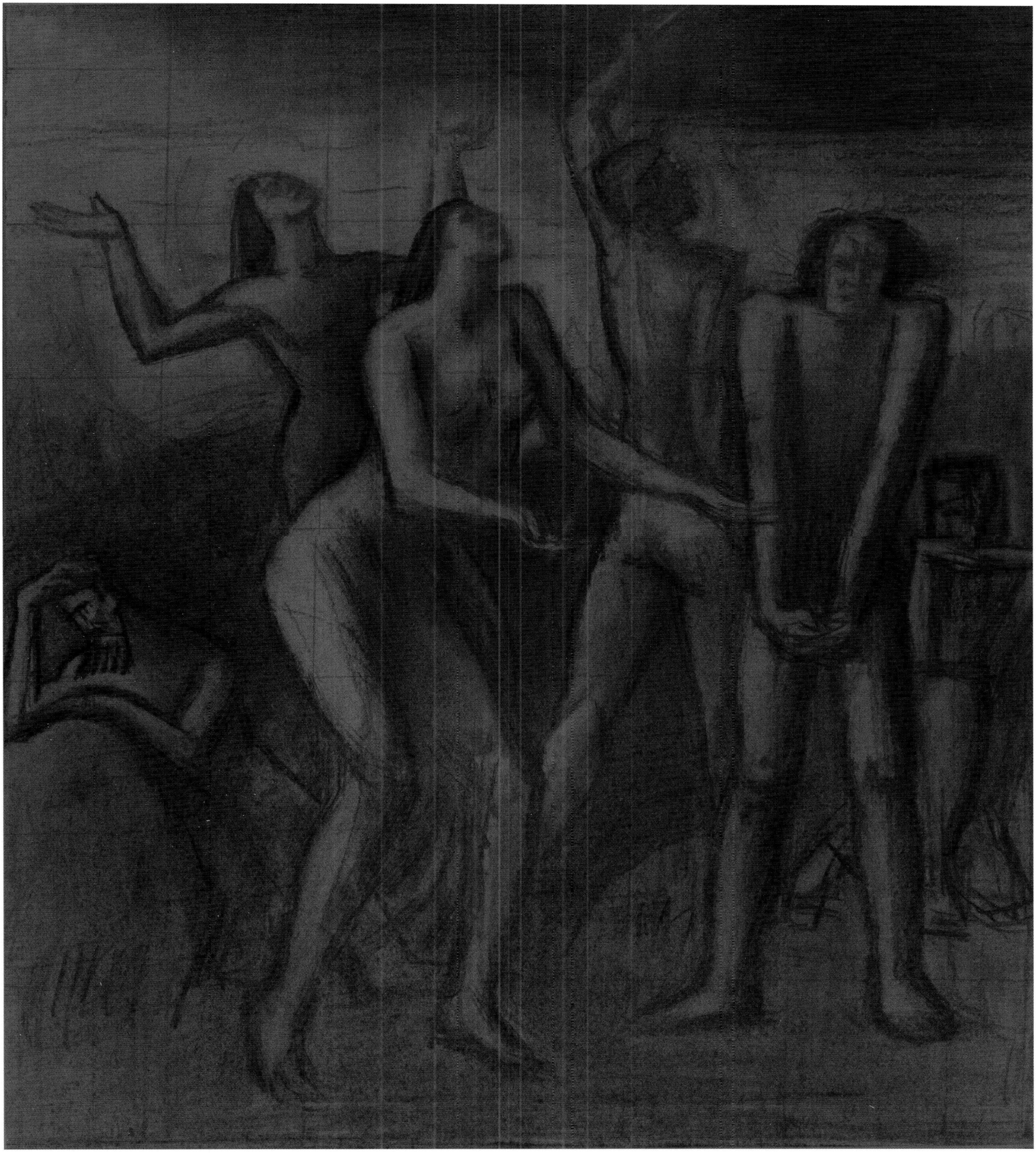

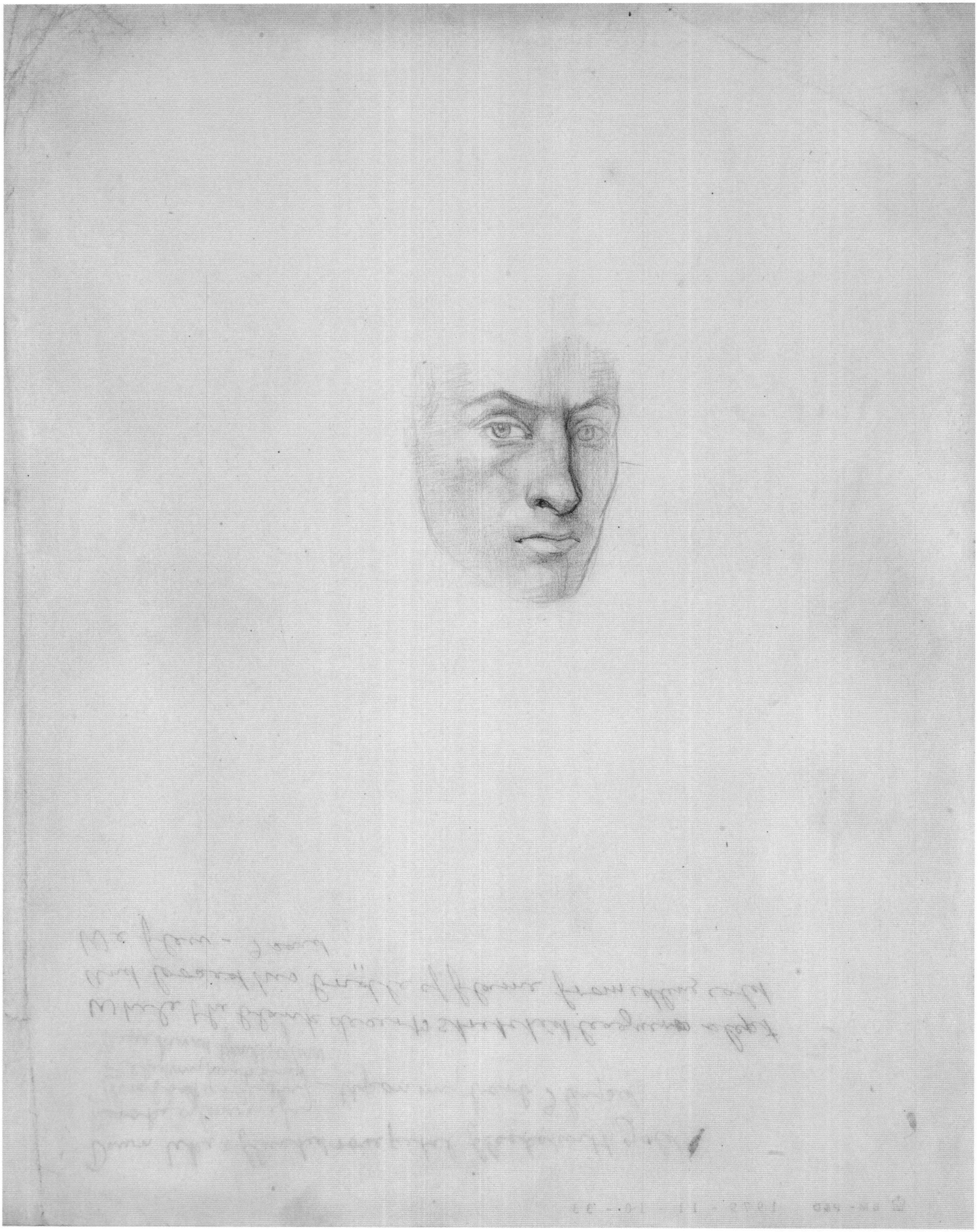

Amongst modern artists Rossetti appeals very much to me & also his poems. I think his *Beata Beatrix*[47] has as much of the divine insight as any Lippi [sic] Lippi – more I should say, because in it Rossetti has deified a human passion and not as the Italians did humanized deity. I do not know much of early Italian art, but I consider that form of art – <u>Art</u> [sic].

For emotional fervour and lyrical ecstacy [sic], expression through passionate colour and definite design, – because instead of confining themselves to rules of architectural line, they took the infinitude of nature to build their designs from; because instead of appearing an affectation of beauty – a moment frozen into canvas – they have the grace & quality – the spontaneity of unselfconscious and childlike nature – infinity of suggestion – that is as much part & voice of the artists soul [sic] as the song to the bird.'[48]

Rosenberg also told Binyon that he had 'not yet done anything in painting or drawing which I would care to show [...]. Of course I would like to do imaginative work but I have hardly attempted anything – practising portraiture mostly as I feel that is the most paying – & one must live.'[49] However disparaging this comment about portraiture sounds, Rosenberg must have recognized his own gift in this medium. Writing to the poet Gordon Bottomley from France in August 1916, Rosenberg requested that when he returned to England 'I will be allowed to make a drawing of you; as a rule the poets are unlucky in their painters; but I am eager to draw the poets I like'.[50] He apparently made the same request to Lascelles Abercrombie: 'a poet to paint a poet', as he put it in a letter to Marsh.[51]

Head of a Male Figure (*c.* 1911, cat no. 11) – probably a self-portrait – with its scribbled verse fragments on the reverse,[52] indicates that drawing and writing both remained vital, often interwoven strands of Rosenberg's creative output. The Slade, however, was dedicated to moulding fine artists, not poets, and this dichotomy may have been behind Rosenberg's poor relationship with Professor Brown. Rosenberg was never to be an ultra-modernist, an iconoclast like Bomberg, but he had enough confidence and self-possession not to allow himself to be suffocated by the Slade. Bomberg later recalled: 'Prof Brown never showed any appreciation for Isaac's drawing – somewhat more for his Painting[.] Professor Brown once stopped me in the corridor, Rosenberg will have to leave[.] No one, not Augustus John, William Orpen or Sir William Rothenstein would ever presume to argue with Professor Brown – but Rosenberg did – that was an outstanding incident, like Blasphemy in the Synagogue, a very courageous thing to do, in my opinion'.[53]

Rosenberg's problems with Brown (who, although its ultimate authority, usually emerges as self-effacing from most accounts of the Slade) began in 1910 when he applied to the Jewish Educational Aid Society (JEAS) for a loan to finance his studies at the Slade. Originally known as the Maccabeans, the JEAS was a unique Jewish charitable organisation, established in 1896 to help talented young Jewish children escape the ghetto by progressing to secondary education. When it later widened its scope 'in the direction of helping all promising students needing assistance', it opened its doors to the majority of the Whitechapel Boys, including Gertler, Bomberg, Rosenberg, Kramer, Meninsky, Wayner and Goldstein, many of whom, like Rosenberg, had been forced to endure commercial apprenticeships before JEAS funds helped them to the Slade. However in 1910, when Rosenberg first applied for financial help, despite the backing of two of its most prominent members, Solomon J Solomon, RA, and the critic Marion H Spielmann,[54] he was turned down after Brown proved 'reluctant' to admit him.[55]

As David Boyd Haycock has commented, Rosenberg objected to what he called 'the paradox of the Slade': the push 'to attain to a completeness of vision' which resulted in 'a total sinking of all conscious personality, a complete absorption and forgetfulness in nature.'[56] Boyd Haycock believes that it was because of this that Rosenberg 'eventually quit the Slade and devoted his creative attention to poetry and drama instead.'[57] The situation was further complicated by Rosenberg's overriding need to earn a living, which later pushed him towards the army, just as the war pushed him away from painting and towards poetry. Joseph Cohen has suggested that

11
ISAAC ROSENBERG
Head of a Male Figure, *c.*1911

Rosenberg's Slade training prepared him for this and that perhaps its 'greatest benefit was to make him a better poet. Its unrelenting, incessant emphasis upon the logic of the sharp, clear line, economical and spare, was a lesson he needed to have drummed home. Though he had a hard time learning it, that lesson was as important in composing verse as in drawing.'[58]

Rosenberg's reputation as a painter may also have been undermined early on by the tendency to class him (retrospectively this was expressed more strongly) as poet first and painter second. The JEAS, when turning Rosenberg down for a loan in 1910 had noted in the minute book that he 'also had a good talent for writing poetry'.[59] Even his early mentor Frank Emanuel would finally come down on the side of Rosenberg the poet, rather than Rosenberg the painter, calling him 'a great poet' and believing that 'therein lay his greater strength.'[60] Binyon's famous assertion that Rosenberg was more a poet than painter (which after all originated with Rosenberg himself) is also repeated on his Slade record, and after Rosenberg's death Tonks remembered him 'primarily as the young poet who died in the 1914–18 war rather than as an art student.'[61] Clearly, at the Slade, Rosenberg already had a reputation as a poet – fostered perhaps by Bomberg – but probably unchallenged, perhaps even encouraged, by Rosenberg himself. Ultimately, Rosenberg's greatest problem as a painter was that his yearning for self-expression was more readily fulfilled in poetry.

In the autumn of 1912, after Mrs Cohen reduced his living allowance, Rosenberg turned again, like the majority of the Whitechapel Boys, to the JEAS for assistance. This time his application was successful. JEAS support extended beyond art school fees to cover dental care and a week in Paris for Gertler,[62] a trip to Rome for Meninsky, and a set of false teeth and a new suit of clothes for Kramer.[63] After Rosenberg began to experience eye-trouble, the JEAS paid for him to see a consultant.[64]

In contrast to Bomberg and Gertler, who exhibited regularly and attracted press attention from the first, Rosenberg failed to establish a reputation as an exhibitor while at the Slade. Stephen Winsten suggested that Rosenberg 'learnt to boast of his rejections at the [Royal] Academy'[65] – an institution popularly rejected and despised by 'advanced' Slade students. As an entrant for the 1913 Prix de Rome

FIG. 40
The Slade Picnic, 1912

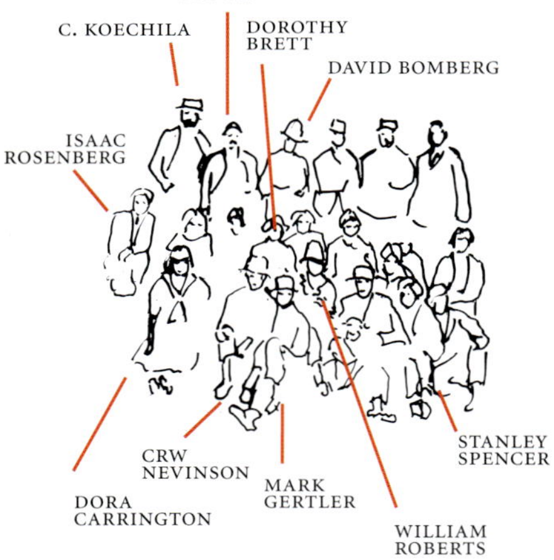

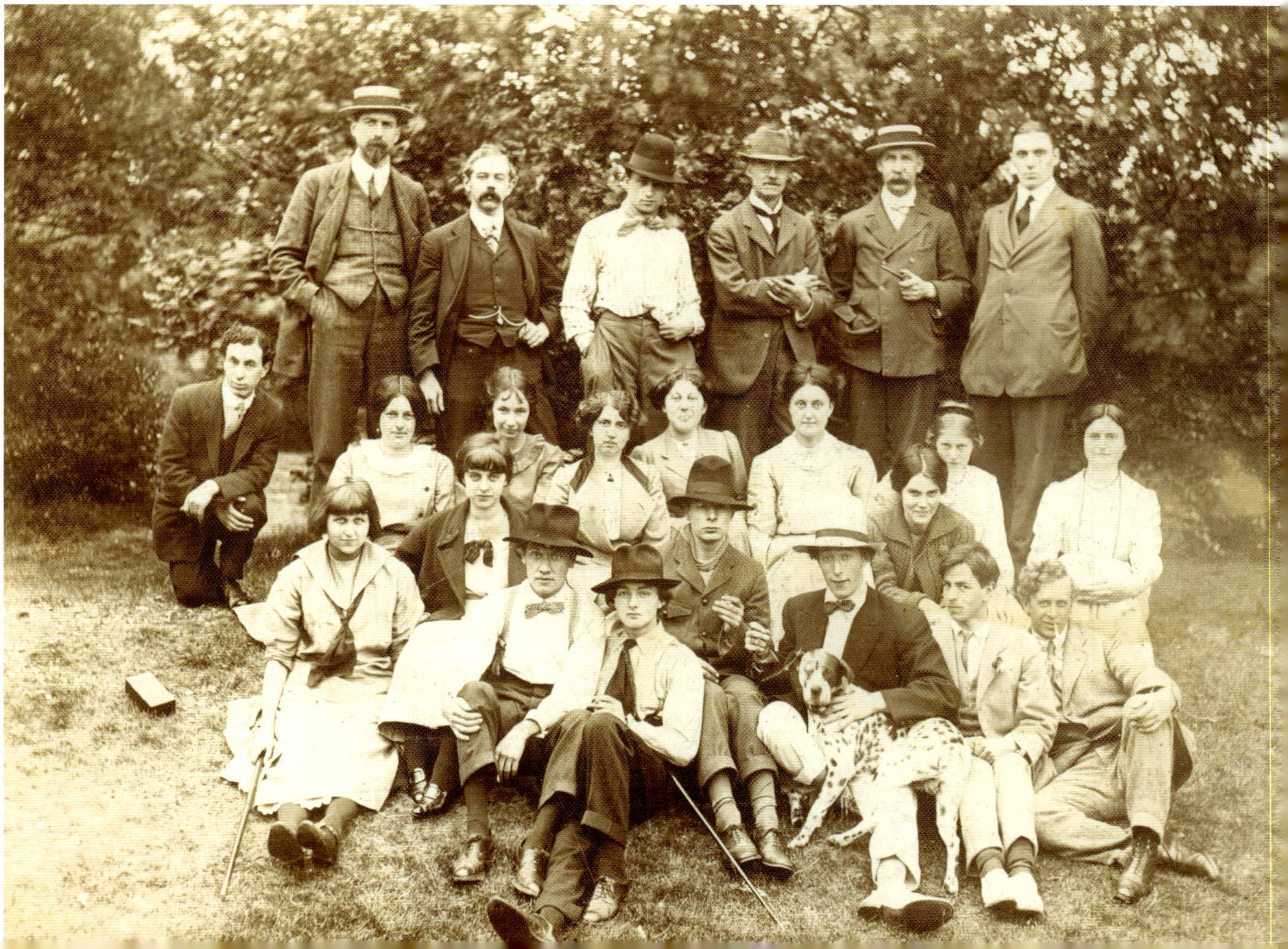

(he heard in spring that he had failed), Rosenberg did exhibit a number of works at the Imperial Institute Galleries in South Kensington, but no record of his exhibits has survived. Rosenberg was not a member of the Friday Club at which both Bomberg and Gertler showcased their early avant-garde work, nor did he exhibit with the Allied Artists' Association or join the London Group – though membership of the latter was notoriously difficult and even Gertler was not elected until his third attempt in February 1915.

Unlike Bomberg, however, and in spite of his strained relationship with Brown, Rosenberg received a satisfactory report from the Slade in May 1913 which suggested that he would benefit from a further year's tuition. In the event he stayed only two terms in his final year, leaving in March 1914 after the recurrence of lung trouble which a holiday to Bournemouth funded by the JEAS, and a trip to Isle of Wight with Bomberg the previous summer, had failed to cure.

Rosenberg's difficult relationship with Professor Brown perhaps accounts for his low profile at the New English Art Club (NEAC). Established a quarter of a century earlier to challenge the dominance of the Royal Academy and its adherence to Victorian classicism, the NEAC, which was run along French lines by elected juries, had done much to promote 'progressive English painting' in its first 20 years. The Slade painting master, Philip Wilson Steer, was a founder member; Fred Brown had drawn up the constitution and Tonks was an active jurist. Undoubtedly, the influence of the triumvirate encouraged talented Slade pupils to exhibit at the twice yearly shows. Most of the Whitechapel Boys, including Bomberg, Gertler, Kramer, Wolmark, Wayner, Schloss and Goldstein – as well as Rosenberg – exhibited at least one work there. Rosenberg was admitted to this company in his second year at the Slade when, advised by Brown,[66] he exhibited and sold (for £4) a *Sanguine drawing* at the winter show in 1912.[67] The sale allowed him to pay back a £2 loan from Mrs Cohen to cover the cost of printing his first volume of poems *Night and Day* in the spring of 1912.[68] However, after this he showed nothing further at the NEAC until well after he had left the Slade.

In 1913 Bomberg, recently fledged from the Slade but already with a reputation as a modernist, was asked (together with Epstein) to form a specifically 'Jewish Section' at the forthcoming Whitechapel Art exhibition, *Twentieth Century Art: A Review of Modern Movements*. It was, as the *Jewish Chronicle* noted a week after the show opened, 'the first real attempt to organise a collection of works by Jewish artists'.[69] Bomberg teased the press with his inflammatory pre-show publicity, and when the exhibition opened in May 1914, critics recognised that both the show as a whole and those modernists (like Bomberg) 'said to have abandoned representation entirely' were issuing a challenge to the hegemony of the Royal Academy: 'The Piccadilly artists would say, no doubt, that Whitechapel is the proper place for it and Billingsgate the proper language,' wrote one critic, concluding nonetheless that 'Art, like life, is at any rate more exciting in Whitechapel than Piccadilly. Something is happening there and nothing at all at Burlington House'.[70]

Now free of the Slade, this was Rosenberg's largest showing of work during his lifetime, and yet he played a very minor part in the exhibition as a whole. He exhibited five works in all, three of them portraits of which two were probably in oils: (no. 260) *My Father*,[71] (no. 295) *Portrait* and (no. 268) *Head of a Girl* (possibly cat no. 21), probably a drawing.[72] Rosenberg's other two works were literary subjects: (no. 273) *Murder of Lorenzo* (Keats)[73] and (no. 279) *The Judgement of Paris* – probably another drawing[74] – showing that Rosenberg, like Meninsky, as Lisa Tickner has commented, was still 'under the sway of broadly Pre-Raphaelite themes.'[75] Rosenberg's journey towards modernism, however tentative at this stage, was certainly not reflected by Bomberg's curatorial selection of his work. The *Jewish Chronicle* found the painting of Rosenberg's father muddy in colouring and weak in characterisation'[76] – though his sister Annie later claimed that it was 'highly commented

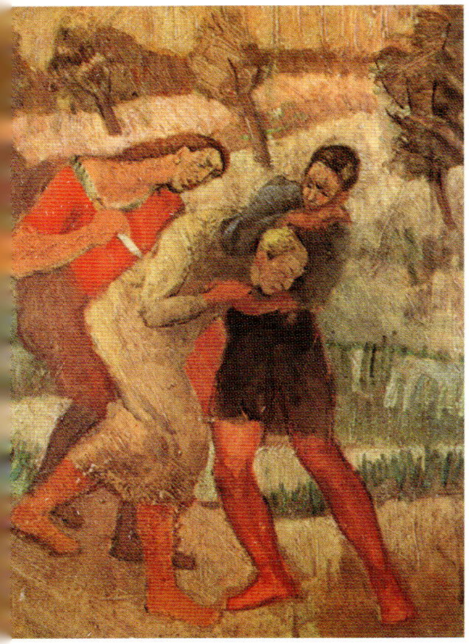

FIG. 5
ISAAC ROSENBERG
The Murder of Lorenzo, 1912

on'.[77] Otherwise, Rosenberg seems to have received scant press attention.[78] In contrast to Bomberg and Gertler, he remained as little-known and little-recognised after the exhibition as before it.

Despite this, during 1912–14 Rosenberg had embarked on his most prolific period as an artist, creating an extraordinary series of highly accomplished self-portraits, which, taken together, chart his increasing engagement with early British modernism and demonstrate his transition from his earlier, more naturalistic style. In all the later portraits Rosenberg wears the same green suit (probably the 'family' suit (fig. 42), which he shared with his brothers) but with a variety of neckwear. The least successful of these, *Self-Portrait in a Pink Tie* (1914, cat no. 18) has a sharpness and leanness reflected in the thin handling of paint and the flattening of the image against the board, but demonstrating a complete break with the early romantic self-portraits. In *Self-Portrait in a Red Tie* (1914, cat no. 17), the composition is as bold and radical as the flaming red of what Sonia Cohen would have recognised as Rosenberg's 'social revolutionary's' tie.[79] The artist more than fills the lower picture frame – his shoulders spilling out to either side giving him an appearance of strength which is reflected in the confidently tilted head, unsmiling yet assured, perfectly balanced against the gold frame of the picture behind him. It is likely that this extremely accomplished early modernist portrait is the one about which Rosenberg wrote to Marsh from South Africa in the autumn of 1914, calling it 'very gay and cocky' and commenting, 'I think [it] will go down well.'[80]

In poor health (his lungs continued to bother him causing him 'to cough very vehemently at times'[81]) and unable to find work, Rosenberg travelled to South Africa early in June, his fare paid by the JEAS. He went to stay with his sister Minnie who had married and moved to Cape Town the previous summer. Although frustrated to find that 'nobody seems to have money here, and not an ounce of interest in Art',[82] Rosenberg came to see this as an opportunity. After he was asked 'whether the futurists exhibited at the Royal Academy', he took a leaf out of Bomberg's book and decided to 'kick up a row' by giving 'a series of lectures on modern art [...] in great style', asking Marsh to supply the relevant reproductions. It is highly unlikely that Rosenberg would have attempted anything like this back in London, where he might have been inhibited by the energy and success of Bomberg and Gertler.[83] He did, however, re-publish the lectures in England in the *Jewish Standard* in 1915.[84] In South Africa he was commissioned by Sir Herbert Stanley to paint two babies (for a fee of £15) and he lectured at the studio of the South African painter Madge Cook (whose portrait he drew in gratitude). He was also invited to spend some time in 'a pretty suburb with a very pretty name, Rondesbosch', at the home of 'a Miss Molteno', a great admirer of his poetry, and, also Rosenberg told his parents, the 'sister of the speaker to House of Parliament here.'[85]

However, despite the impressiveness of the South African countryside, few paintings and no landscapes have survived from this trip, partly, Rosenberg claimed, because he lost a number of canvases over the side during embarkation on his return. Among the surviving works is the delicate, yet sensual, Augustus John-influenced profile drawing of the actress Marda

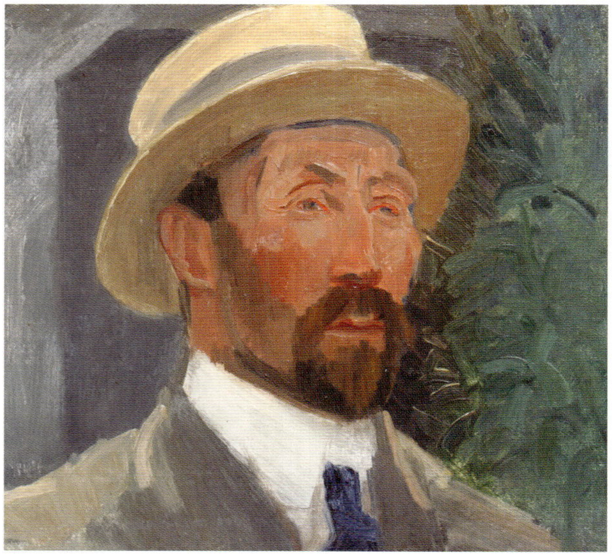

FIG. 8
ISAAC ROSENBERG
Portrait of the Artist's Father, *c.*1914

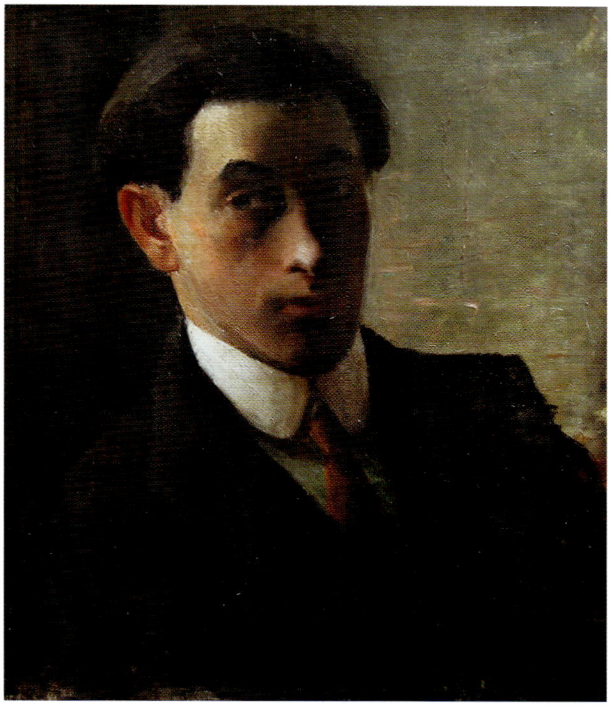

20
ISAAC ROSENBERG
Self-Portrait, 1914

Vanne (1914, cat no. 19),[86] with whom Rosenberg may have had a brief affair. He also painted two black sitters and at least two self-portraits in South Africa. After war was declared Rosenberg responded with a poem entitled 'On Receiving News of the War', but he remained in South Africa for the time being and the conflict had no immediate effect on his painting. 'By the time you get this things will only have just begun I'm afraid' he wrote presciently to Edward Marsh, 'Europe will have just stepped into its bath of blood. I will be waiting with beautiful drying towels of painted canvas, and precious ointments to smear and heal the soul; and lovely music and poems. But I really hope to have a nice lot of pictures and poems by the time all is settled again; and Europe is repenting of her savageries.'[87]

That autumn Rosenberg arranged for the publication of his lectures under the title 'Art'. The lectures, together with two of his poems, were published in December 1914–January 1915 in the magazine *South African Women in Council*, edited by the mother of his artist-friend, Madge Cook. However, as his sister Annie put it: 'the public, [with] the exception of a small minority, did not seem to be intellectual enough to grasp the beauty of his works'[88] and, disappointed, he left Cape Town in February to begin the long voyage home. He arrived back in London in March 1915.

Post-Slade and post-South Africa, out of work and with little prospect of finding any, Rosenberg completed some of the finest portraits of his short career during perhaps his bleakest moments. Notable among them is the splendid portrait of Sonia Cohen, (cat no. 28), a former sweatshop worker and aspiring actress with whom he was probably in love. It was painted in May 1915 during several sittings when Sonia, then pregnant,[89] was living with Rosenberg's Whitechapel friend, the poet, critic (and later publisher of the modernists) John Rodker.

Like the best of Rosenberg's portraits in this period, *Portrait of Sonia* is characterised by strong, broad vertical brushstrokes which give the sitter a certain dynamism that belies her static pose, and a vivid crimson background reminiscent of the work of the colourist Alfred Wolmark, a treatment which it shares with the portrait of Clare Winsten (Clara Birnberg) painted in the same year. Skilfully blending traditionalist and modernist techniques, *Portrait of Sonia* has been called 'probably his best surviving work'.[90] Rosenberg wrote to Marsh about it, telling him 'I've done a lovely picture I'd like you to see. It's a girl who sat for Da Vinci, and hasn't changed a hair, since, in a deep blue gown against a dull crimson ground.'[91]

Rosenberg's interest in madonnas had been established early on with his faithful copies of two paintings by Correggio in the National Gallery: *Copy of a Madonna and Child*[92] and *Venus Cupid and Mercury* (c.1910, cat no. 3)[93], probably executed while he was a student at Birkbeck.[94] Rosenberg's *Portrait of Sonia* clearly references Leonardo da Vinci's *The Virgin of the Rocks*,[95] in which the Virgin wears a cloak of a similar deep blue fastened at the neck with a black brooch. Sonia too wears a brooch, though her

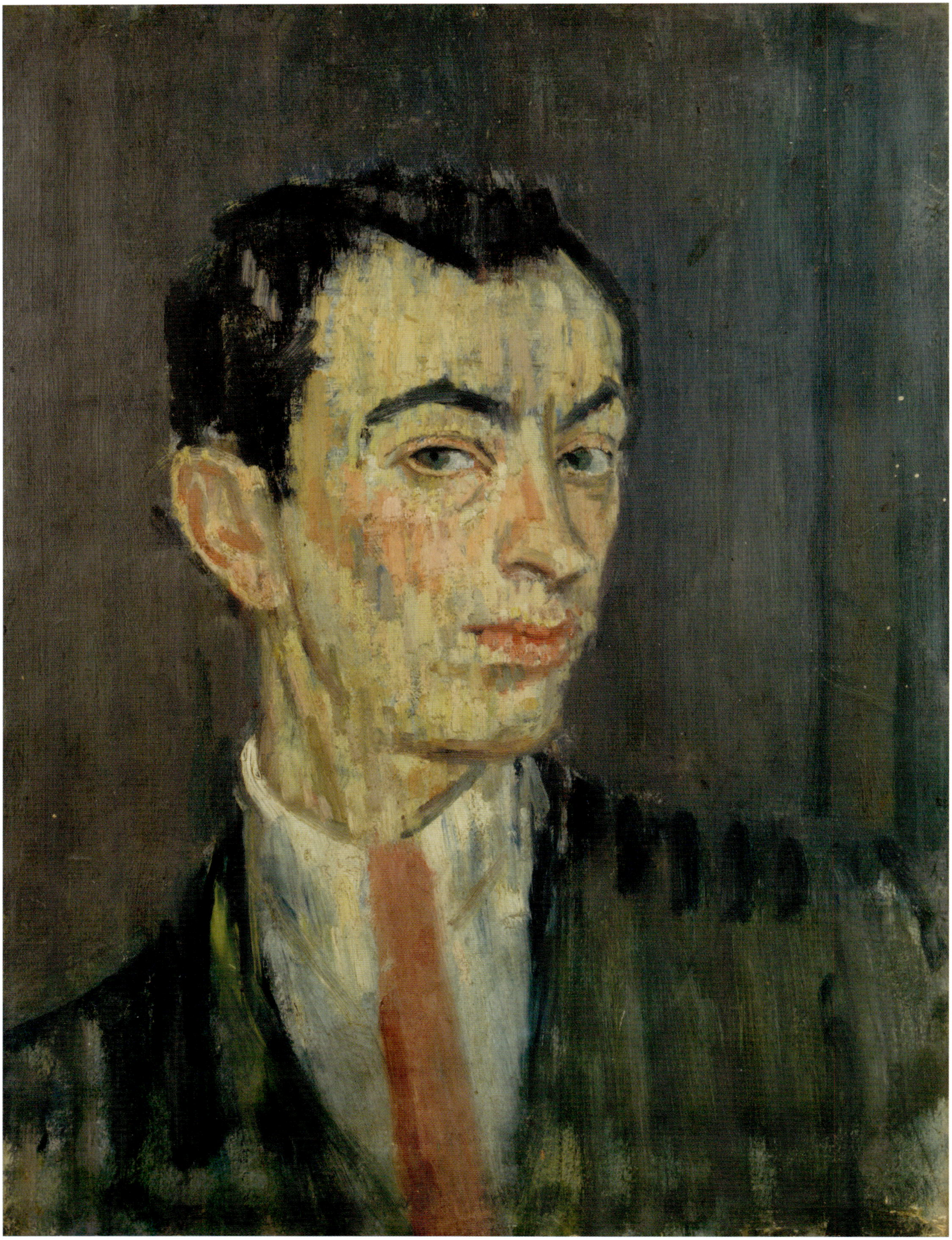

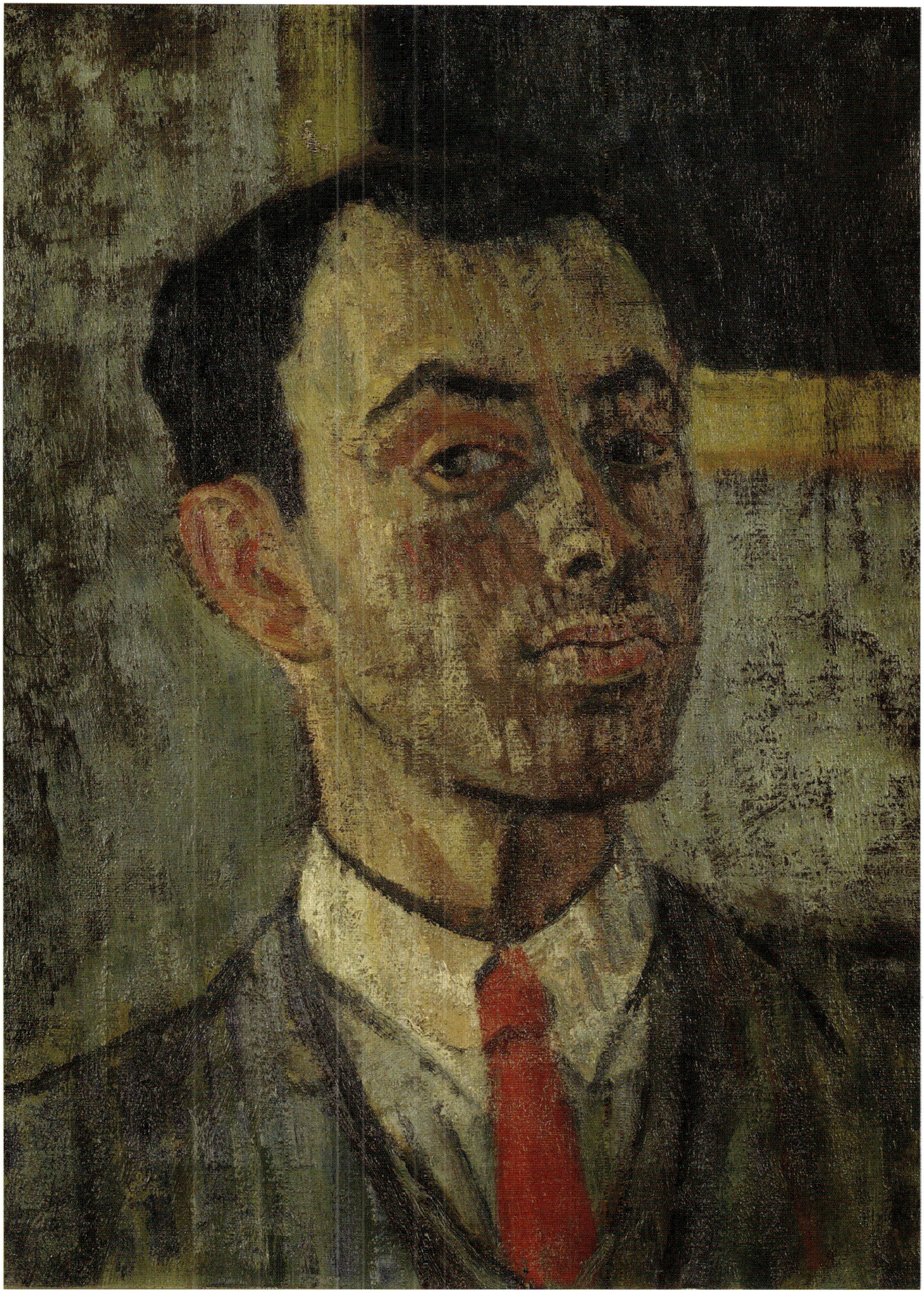

18 *left*
ISAAC ROSENBERG
Self-Portrait in a Pink Tie, 1914

17 *right*
ISAAC ROSENBERG
Self-Portrait in a Red Tie, 1914

expression is averted rather than downward-looking like Leonardo's Virgin. Rosenberg had successfully captured the Virgin's downward gaze a year earlier in a fine madonna-like portrait of his sister Minnie (fig. 9). Family reports tell us that Minnie was gazing down at her child, but Rosenberg omits the baby from the picture, leaving us instead with an expression of radiant serenity. In his lecture entitled 'ART', Rosenberg had described Leonardo da Vinci as having 'a mind of unhuman vastness, of the deepest poetry, and extraordinary logic and invention [...]. His drawings, particularly of women's heads, for perfect loveliness and pure realisation of form have never been surpassed.'[96]

The portrait of *Clare Winsten* (*née* Clara Birnberg, cat no. 29), who had been with Rosenberg at the Slade and married his friend the Whitechapel writer Stephen Winsten, was almost certainly completed in 1915, the same year as *Portrait of Sonia*. Although Rosenberg clearly described the latter as 'unfinished',[97] it is difficult to see how he could have improved it. By contrast, the portrait of Clare appears less finished: the paint has been applied more thinly, particularly in the background and lower half of the picture, so that the canvas shows through in several places; the vertical black brushstrokes are more numerous and there is an apparently unresolved section of green paint on the lower left.

The vertical brushstroke technique used in Rosenberg's portraits of Sonia and Clare apparently originated in *Head of a Woman: Grey and Red* (1912, cat no. 14),[98] which can be read as a transitional stage in the development of Rosenberg's handling. However, in this earlier work the vertical brushstrokes are applied principally to the face, which is less finely modelled than in the later portraits, while an area of shading to the left side anticipates Rosenberg's best-known *Self-Portrait* (1915, cat no. 24). The grey

FIG. 11
BASSANO
Marda Vanne, 1921

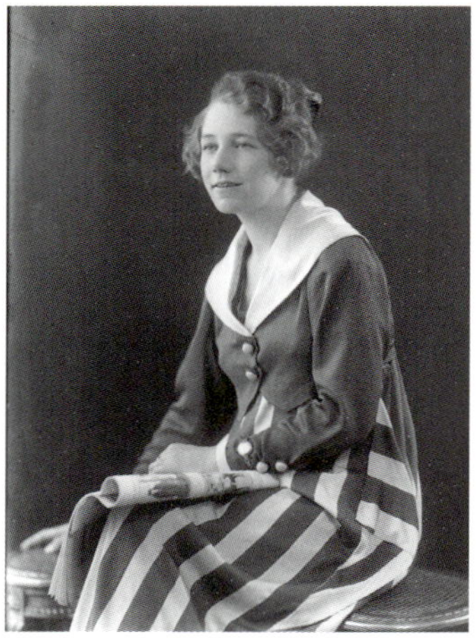

19
ISAAC ROSENBERG
Portrait of Marda Vanne, 1914

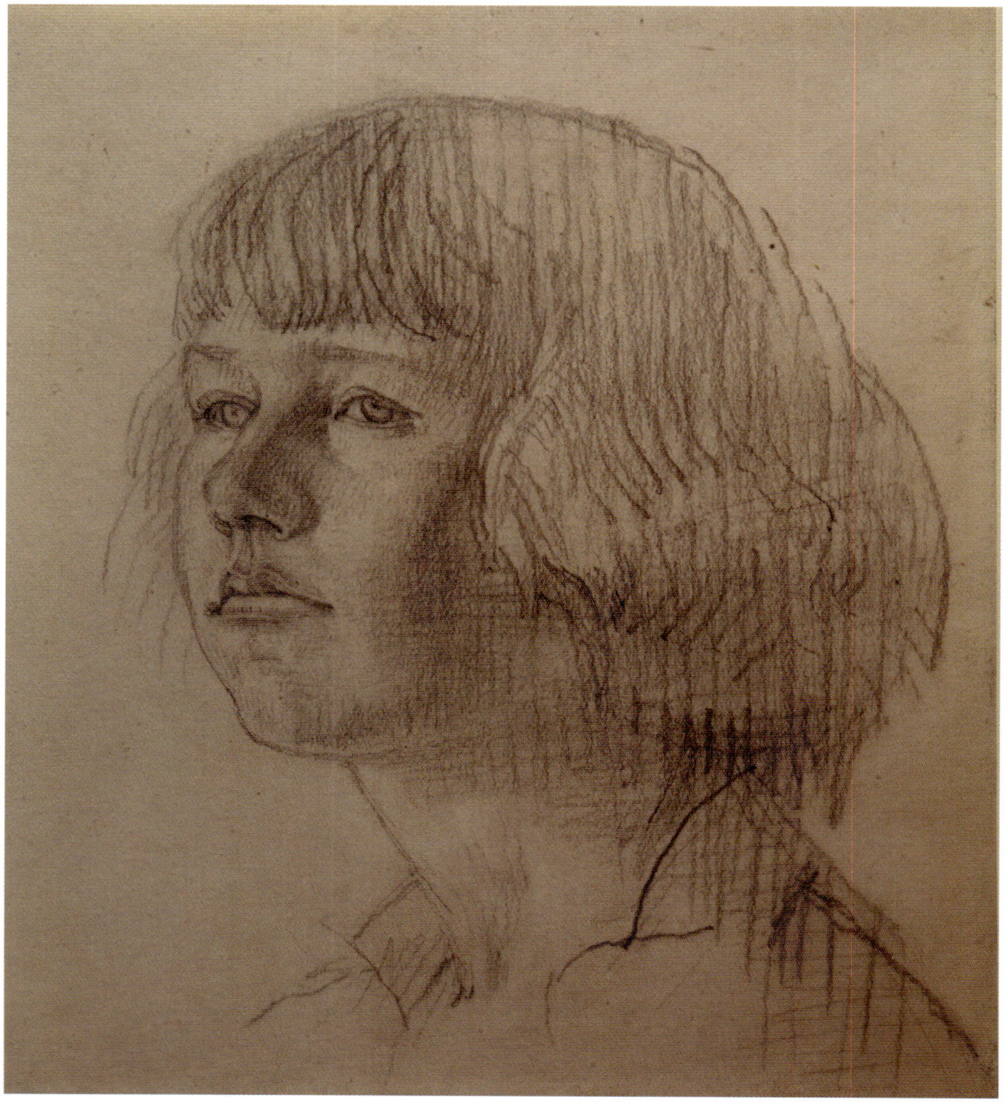

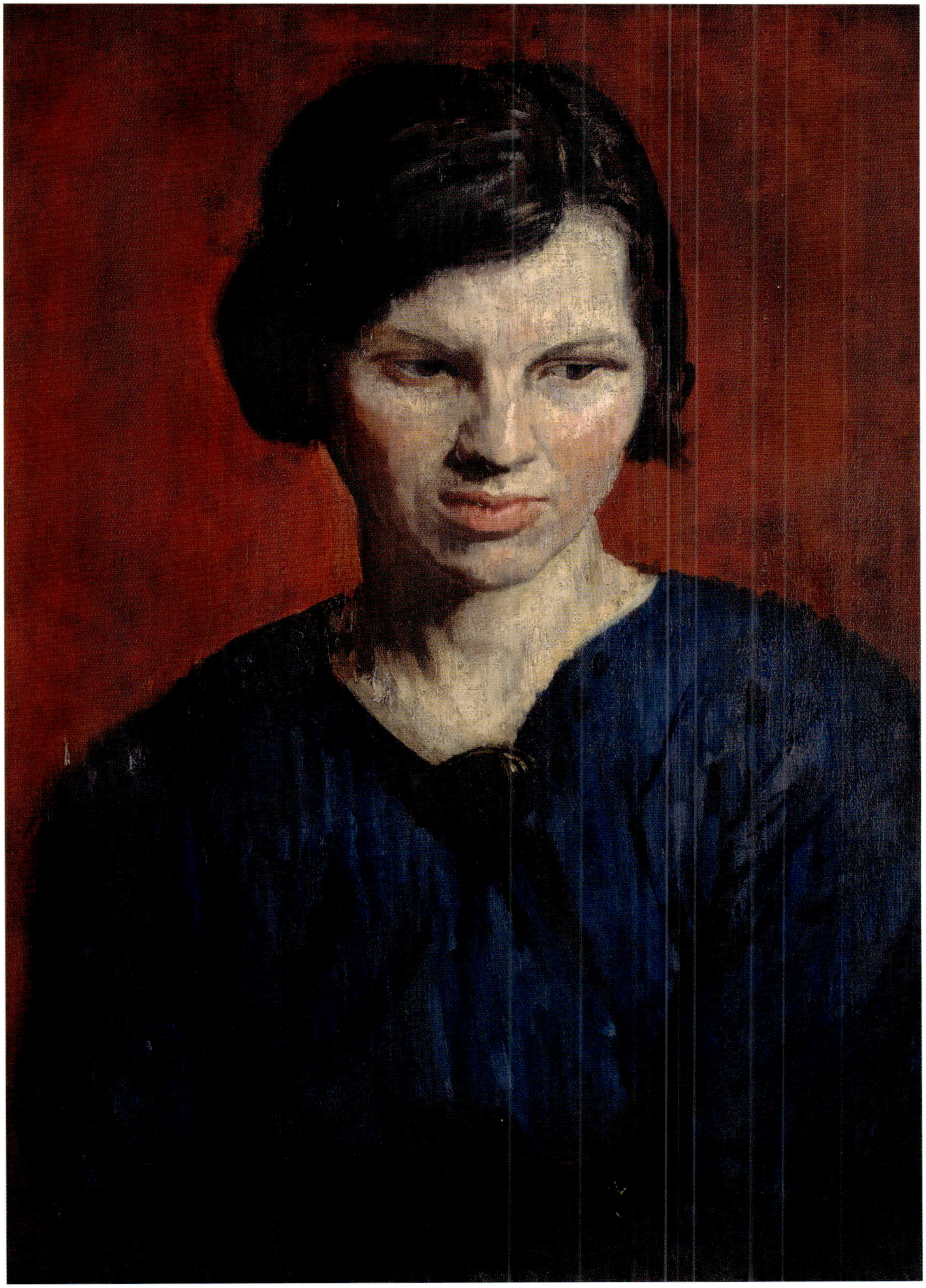

28
ISAAC ROSENBERG
Portrait of Sonia, c.1915

FIG. 45
Sonia Cohen, c.1913

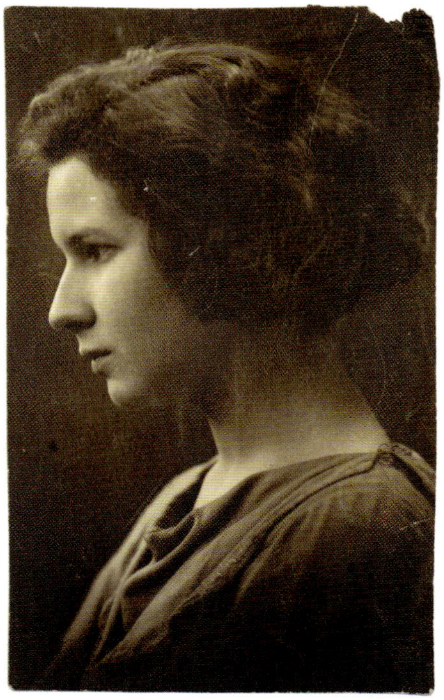

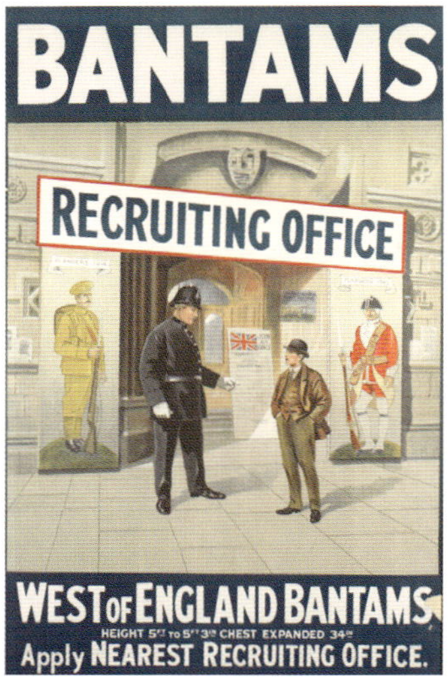

FIG. 34
Bantam Regiment poster, *c.*1914–16

background of *Head of a Woman* also marks an intermediate stage between the muddy Edwardian brown of *The Artist's Father* (cat no. 8) and the vibrant modern red of the portraits of Sonia and Clare which serves to liberate the sitters from their surroundings and gives them a contemporary edge. Rosenberg's satisfaction with *Head of a Woman: Grey and Red* is proved by his decision to submit this painting to the NEAC in the winter of 1915. It was accepted, but by then he had been forced, at least temporarily, to give up painting altogether. The NEAC catalogue cites his correspondence address as the military hospital in Bury St Edmunds. He was now a private with the Bantam Battalion of the 12th Suffolk Regiment.[99]

Rosenberg enlisted in October 1915, without telling either family or friends. He had considered volunteering throughout the summer and his letters show him see-sawing between 'the immorality of joining with no patriotic convictions',[100] and the 'strong temptation to join when you are making no money', as he put it in a letter to Ezra Pound.[101] Although he knew that his mother would be horrified by his decision, he believed that she would benefit financially. In taking this drastic step however, he effectively cut short his painting career.

FIG. 9
ISAAC ROSENBERG
Minnie Horvitch, the Artist's Sister, 1914

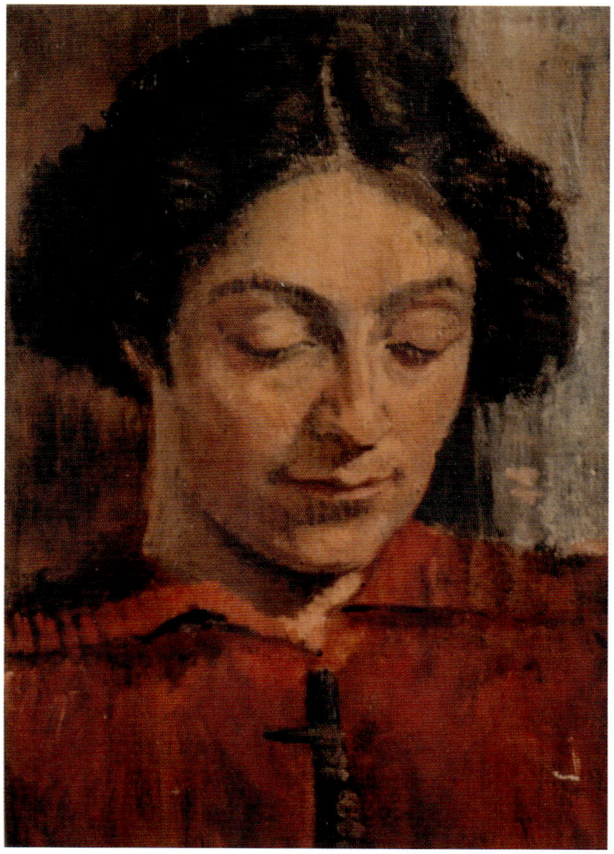

From winter 1915 until his death at the Front on April Fool's Day 1918, Rosenberg's art took on a new focus. Drawing now became his primary means of visual expression and rapid sketches appeared alongside poems on scraps of paper and the backs of letters recording, often with great poignancy, his life as a private in training and at the Front.

Since 'the idea of killing'[102] upset him, Rosenberg had sought a place in the Royal Army Medical Corps. Considered too short, he was sent instead to the Recruiting Depot at Bury St Edmunds, Suffolk, to join the Bantam Battalion of 12 Suffolk Regiment 40th Division (fig. 34). The regiment not only took men between 5' and 5' 3' – below regulation height – but also those, like Rosenberg, who, with his weak lungs, had failed the standard medical requirements. He could subsequently joke about this, writing to Edward Marsh in 1916 that the King, when inspecting them, 'must have waited for us to stand up a good while. At a distance we look like soldiers sitting down, you know, legs so short.'[103] Bomberg later commented that Rosenberg 'should never have been accepted for active service but the MO who pass[ed] him A1 turned his head away not to see the facts'.[104]

Kitchener's cost-cutting in the early years of the war made recruitment depots and training camps hopelessly overcrowded and ill-equipped, as a letter from Rosenberg to Sydney Schiff makes clear:

> I have to eat out of a basin together with some horribly smelling scavenger who sneezes into it etc. It is most revolting, at least up to now – I don't mind the hard sleeping the stiff marches etc but this is unbearable. Besides my being a Jew makes it bad amongst these wretches.[105]

Three years on little seemed to have changed when Jacob Kramer wrote to Herbert Read from his camp in Wales during the last months of the War

> I haven't begun my training yet, as yesterday I have been inoculated by the doctor [...]. I am wasting my time here – none of them here know that I paint or draw, as otherwise the captain would have put me on [...] easier work. [...] I am about fed up wasting my time day by day in the hut, listening to the continual vulgar talk which makes me sick and my mind dull.[106]

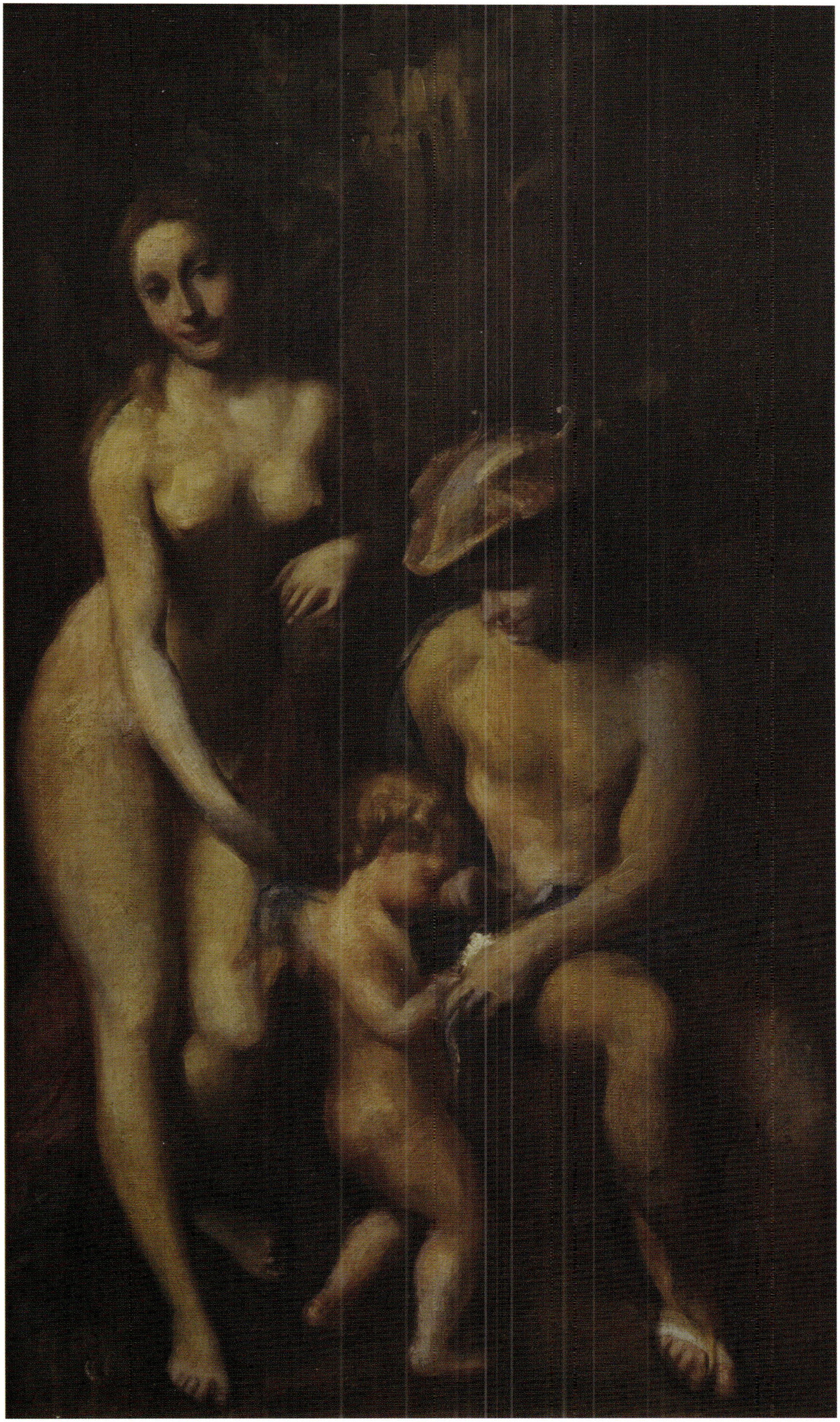

3
ISAAC ROSENBERG
Copy of Correggio's Venus, Cupid and Mercury, c.1910

14 *left*
ISAAC ROSENBERG
Head of a Woman 'Grey and Red', 1912

29 *opposite*
ISAAC ROSENBERG
Clare Winsten, 1915

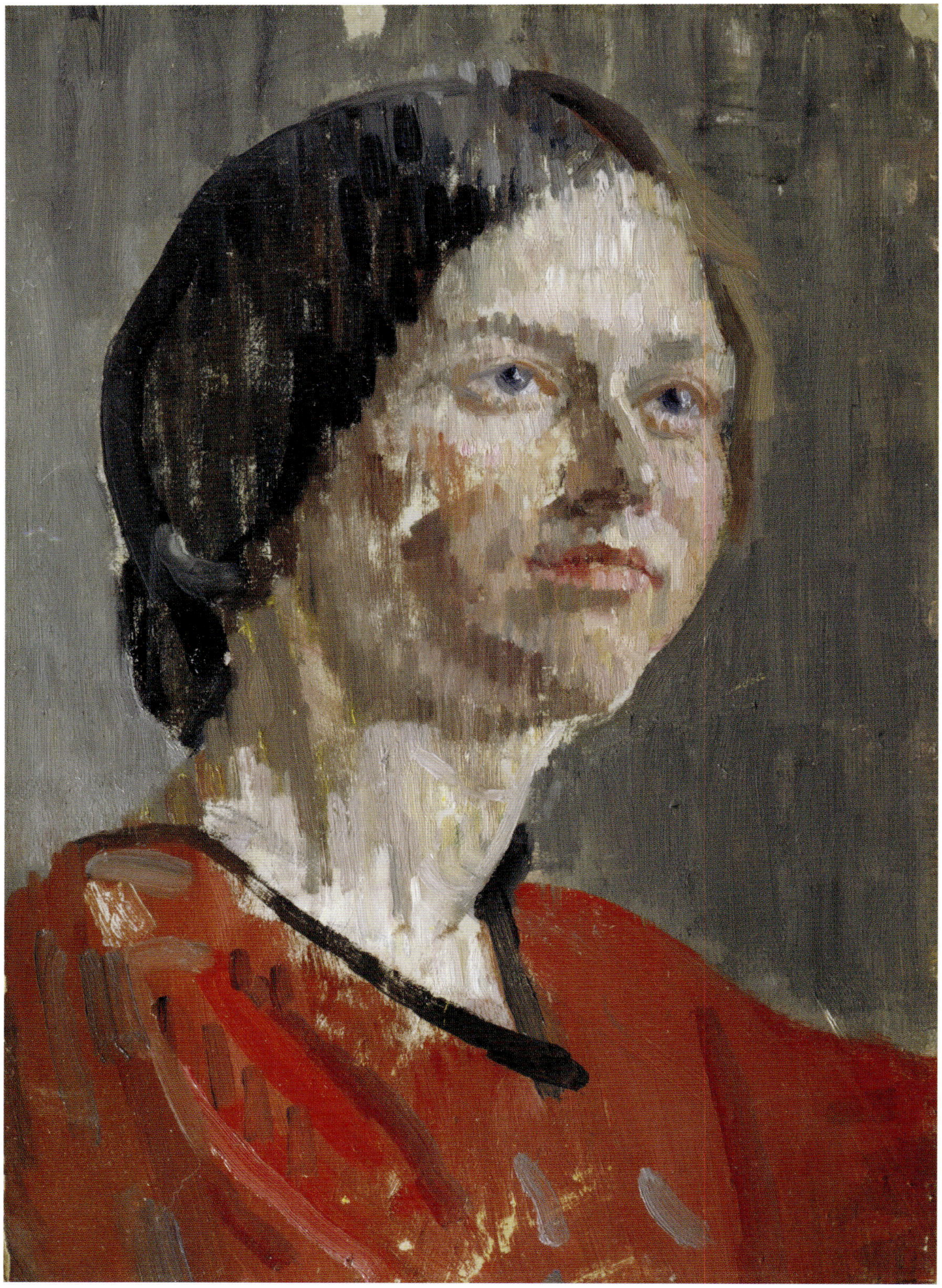

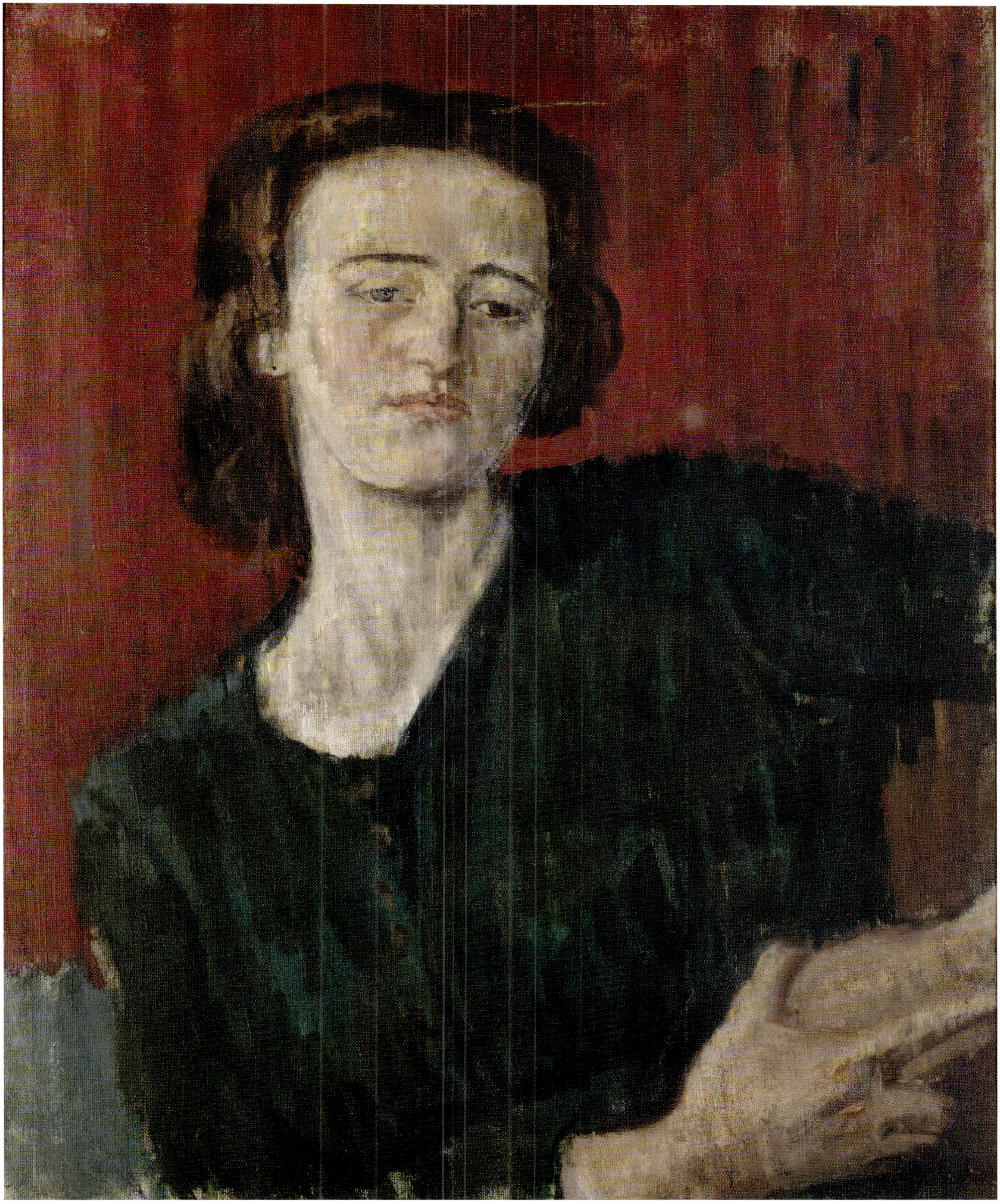

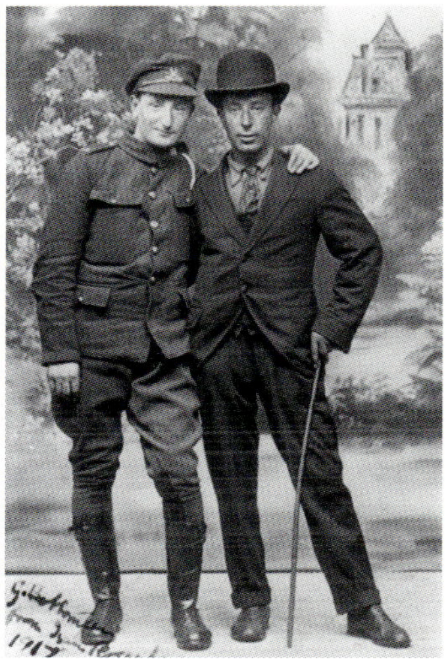

FIG. 43
Isaac Rosenberg in the 'Family Suit', 1917

Bomberg's military ink drawing, *The Billet* (1915, cat no. 31), executed prior to his joining up and exhibited unsold at the NEAC spring show in 1915, captures the crush, fatigue and boredom of new recruits whose poor accommodation often included a shared iron bed. Dark, angular, and modernist, the rigid vertical bars of the bedstead stand as much for the constraints and authority of military life as for the stifling of artistic endeavour.

Scarcely a month after joining up Rosenberg was in hospital, having slipped on the parade ground and cut both his hands 'rather badly'. Despite this mishap he sketched a few of his fellow soldiers in the hospital and, seeing 'heaps of subject matter all over',[107] told Schiff that if he could get 'a very small watercolour box with a decent sketch block, pencil, paper about 12 × 10, I might do something Sundays.'[108] From now on, however, any serious painting was impossible – even drawing was difficult – 'we get no private time', he explained to Schiff[109] – and only a handful of drawings (mostly in letters) have survived from his time in training and in the trenches.

Accustomed to hardship, Rosenberg soon accepted the harsh conditions of military life; he wrote to Marsh with wry stoicism, 'I find that the actual duties though they are difficult and require all one's sticking power are not in themselves unpleasant. It is the brutal militaristic bullying meanness of the way they're served out to us.'[110] In any event, Rosenberg must have acquitted his duties sufficiently well as he was offered a promotion to lance corporal, which he declined.

Rosenberg had not divorced himself from painting completely – his contributions to the NEAC in December 1915 bore his new address at the military hospital, though after receiving an acceptance addressed to 'Isaac Bomberg', he naturally feared they had been mis-catalogued.[111] He wrote to Miss Seaton that one of them was 'likely to be sold',[112] and continued to offer Marsh 'the pick of any drawing I do after this if I get clear.'[113] But with the writing of 'Marching – as seen from the left file', his first poem

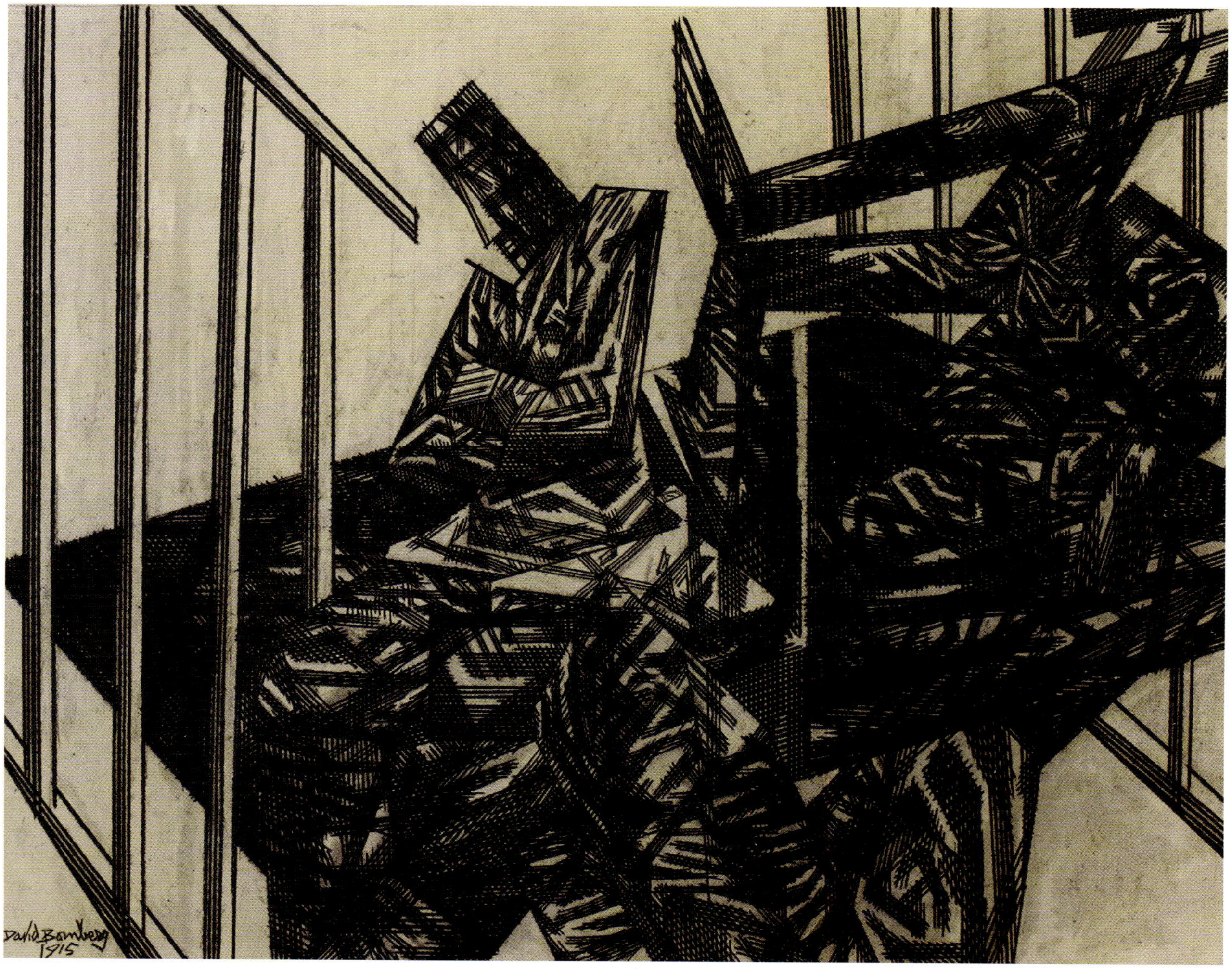

31
DAVID BOMBERG
The Billet, 1915

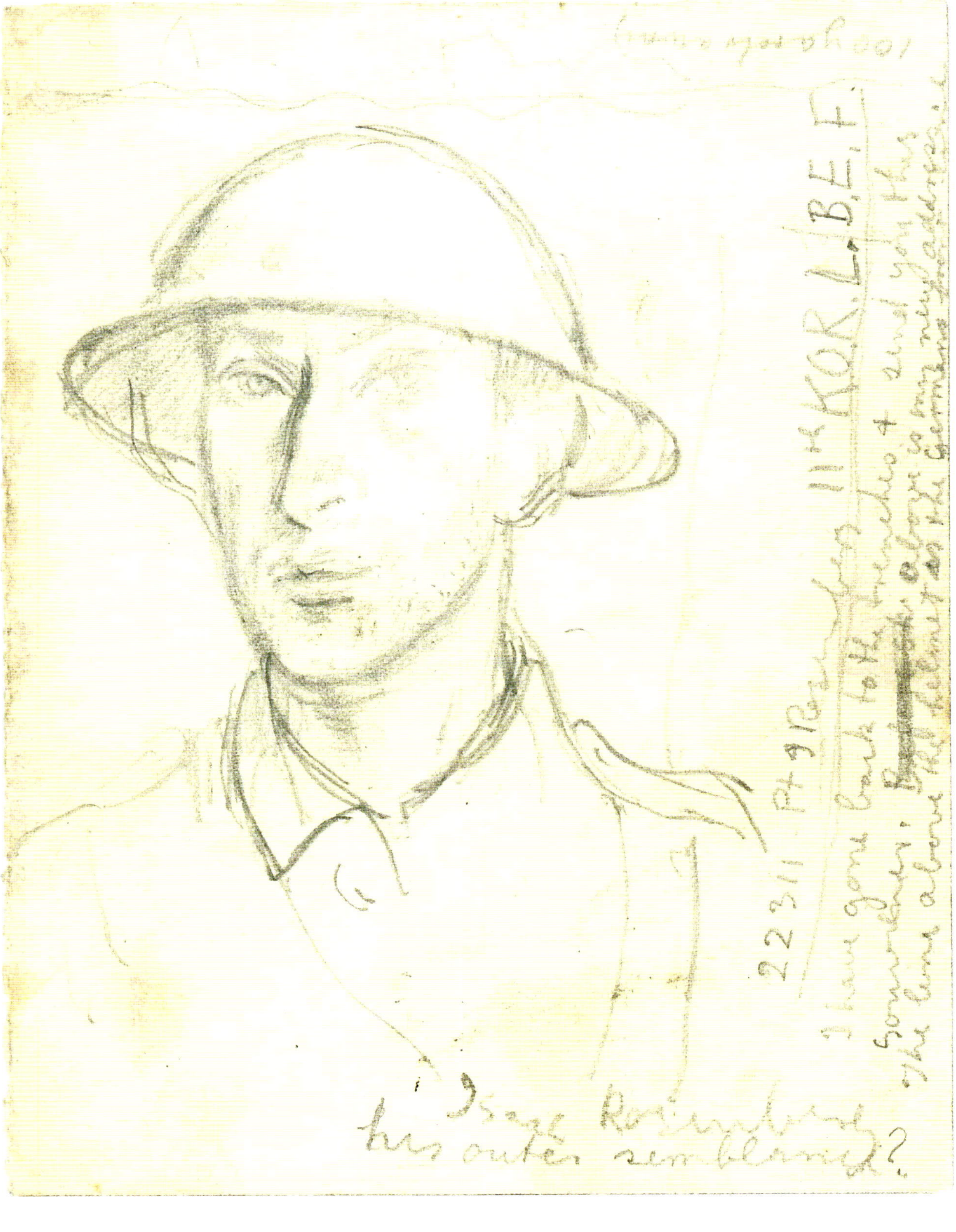

53
ISAAC ROSENBERG
Untitled Letter *Self-Portrait Sketch in Tin Helmet*, 1916 or after

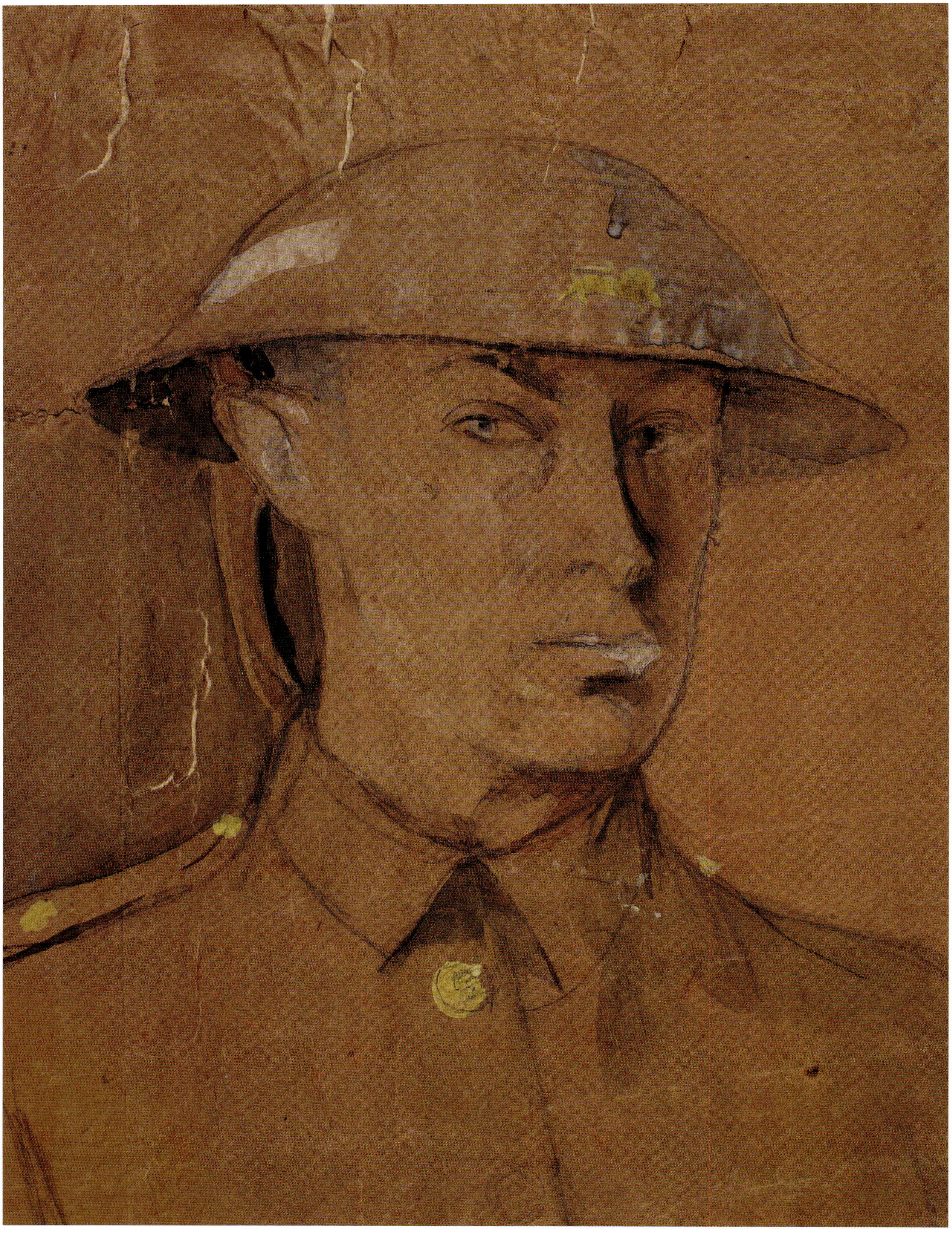

since joining up, his priorities began to shift. Although he was soon too tired to give 'poetry or painting a thought, he felt 'as if I were casting my coat, I mean, like a snake or a butterfly.'[114] From now on, during the short time remaining to him he channelled his creative energy into his poetry with such force that his vision as a poet gradually eclipsed that of the painter, although crucially (as Jean Moorcroft Wilson makes clear in her essay), his vision as a painter underpinned that of the poet.

In early January 1916 Rosenberg was transferred to the 12th South Lancashire Regiment at Blackdown Camp, Farnborough, Hampshire, and his position improved marginally: 'I am known as a poet and artist, as our second in command is a Jewish officer who knows of me from his people,'[115] he explained to Schiff but he had to acknowledge that his 'public' was effectively 'still in the womb'.[116] In March he was transferred again to the 11th Battalion King's Own Royal Lancasters (KORL) also at Blackdown Camp as Private Isaac Rosenberg, no. 22311. 'Nobody', he wrote to the poet Lascelles Abercrombie, 'but a private in the army knows what it is to be a slave.'[117] During six days embarkation leave in May he arranged for the printing of his play, *Moses*, by Reuben Cohen under the imprint of Paragon Press.

In June Rosenberg embarked with his unit for France. The cramped conditions on the voyage over resulted in his poem 'The Troop Ship'. Things did not improve when soon afterwards, in the build up to the Somme offensive,[118] Rosenberg's unit went into training for trench life. Hampered by appalling weather, the soldiers battled to stay dry and to snatch any brief moments of respite, sleeping standing up or squatting in holes dug out of the trench walls. In a letter to RC Trevelyan, Rosenberg included 'a very crude sketch of how I look here in this dugout' (*Self Portrait with Marmalade Jar*, 1916, cat no. 51). Rapidly sketched, it is a wryly humorous and concise self-portrait, with knees drawn up and hands folded beneath the chinstrap of his round helmet; a large rodent is seen scurrying away from a tin marked 'marmalade'.

While the conditions cramped the painter, however, they freed the poet as Rosenberg acknowledged: 'I believe I am a poet', he wrote firmly in the same letter. By late July 1916, despite the conditions, he was planning for the future: 'to teach drawing at a school a few days in the week, which leaves plenty of leisure to write, as I am convinced I am more deep and true as a poet than painter.'[119] He was in the trenches by August and briefly considered camouflage work.[120] The experience resulted in his poem 'Break of Day in the Trenches'.

Rosenberg's final self-portrait (indeed his final finished work as a painter) is the unsentimental, yet poignant, *Self-Portrait in a Steel Helmet* (1916, cat no.30), which appears to relate closely to a sketch made in a letter, entitled *Self-Portrait Sketch in Tin Helmet* (*c*.1916, cat no. 53). Executed in the trenches, in gouache and chalk on crumpled brown wrapping paper, possibly salvaged from a parcel sent from home, he joked of this portrait to his family that it was 'The New Fashion boiler hat – the trench hat.'[121]

30
ISAAC ROSENBERG
Self-Portrait in a Steel Helmet, 1916

Towards the end of 1916, despite the onset of winter – 'not the least of the horrors of war'[122] – Rosenberg found a new energy in his poetry. At Christmas in 'a patriotic gush[,] a jingo spasm', he sent Rodker (via Sonia) the poem 'Pozières',[123] with a remarkable ink sketch on the reverse (cat no. 49),[124] announcing 'A Merry Xmas from the 40th' – a rare example of his integrated verse and drawing. But the traditional season's greetings are strikingly at odds with both the text – which begins 'Glory! British Women! In your wombs you plotted This monstrous girth of glory' – and with the accompanying image of helmeted soldiers from both sides of the conflict. It is perhaps unsurprising that though Rosenberg submitted it as a design for the battalion's Christmas card, it was rejected.[125]

In January 1917, his health failed and Rosenberg was assigned to a Works Battalion behind the lines, but by late spring his condition had improved and

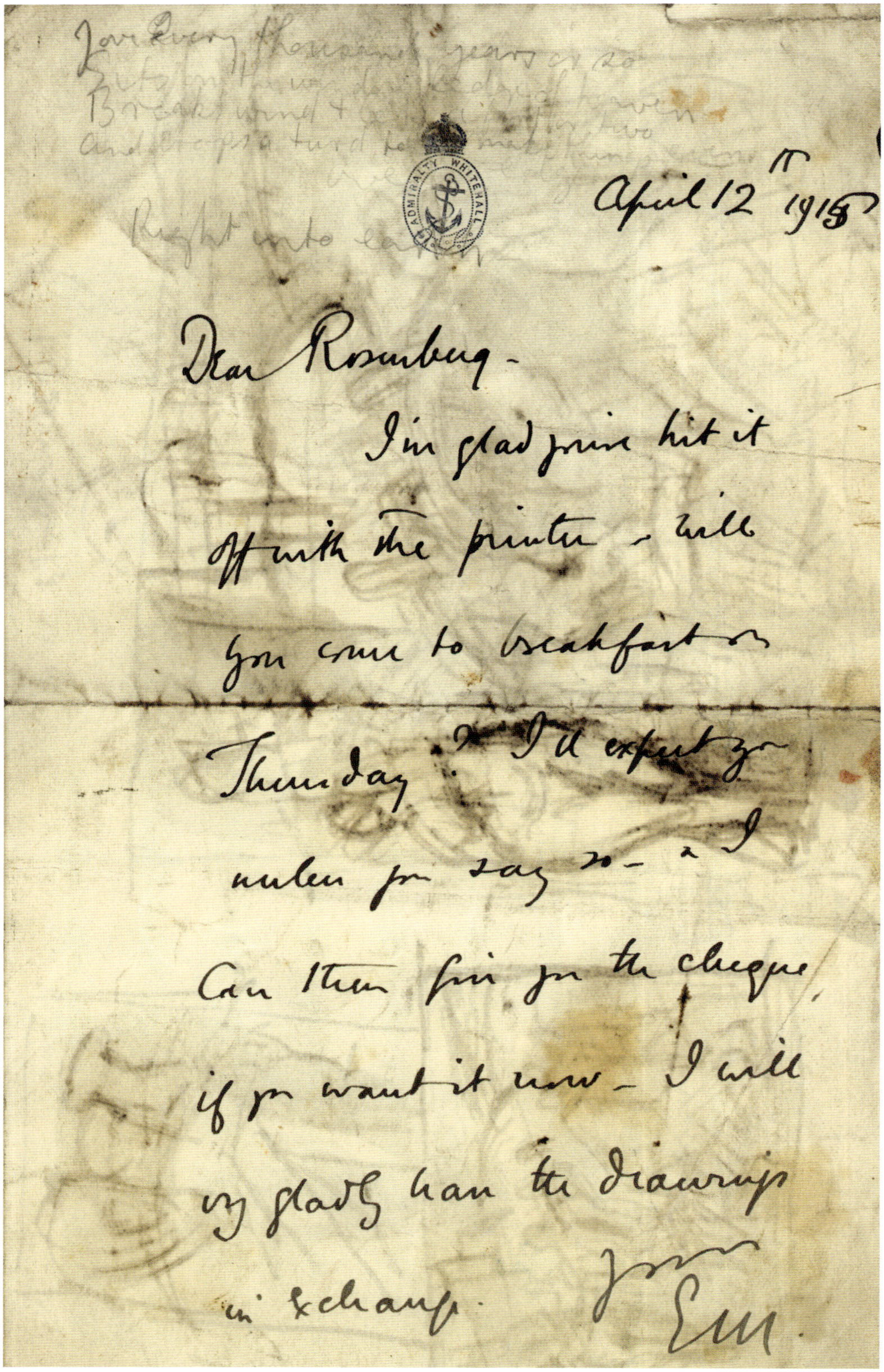

April 12th 1915

Dear Rosenberg –

I'm glad you've hit it off with the printer – will you come to breakfast on Thursday? I'll expect you unless you say no – & I can then give you the cheque if you want it now – I will very gladly have the drawings in exchange.

Yours

EM.

47
ISAAC ROSENBERG
Verso of *Three rough sketches: 39 Rosenau Road*, 1915

he was reassigned to 229 Field Company Royal Engineers, attached to 11th Battalion KORL. Although in the remaining 16 months of his life, Rosenberg wrote some of his finest poetry, he produced no more than a handful of drawings. 'An amusing little thing called "the louse hunt"', a sketch which he sent in a letter to Bottomley in February 1917, and which he hoped to work up later, has not survived.[126] But a final self-portrait sketch, also in a letter, gives the flavour of his military life: *Self-Portrait in Cap* (cat no. 52), inscribed 'I.R. July France. 1917', shows Rosenberg with unbuttoned shirt and cap pushed back to reveal in profile his familiar elongated features – the private for whom army life was now a business to be got through, but also, perhaps, the other-worldly poet, often criticised and sometimes punished for his careless appearance.

In September 1917 Rosenberg was granted ten days home leave and sought out his literary contacts Bottomley, Schiff and Trevelyan. He also met up with former Whitechapel Boy Jack Isaacs. Lost without the purposefulness of regimented army life however, he described himself as 'restless [. . .] and un-anchored'.[127] He visited Sonia and her daughter Joan, and worked again on her portrait. The war had already touched Sonia directly with the death of her younger brother Solomon in May, while on active service in France; he was only 23 years old.

When Rosenberg returned to France he was no longer attached to the Royal Engineers, but was sent to rejoin his regiment. Struck down with influenza in October he was admitted to hospital where he remained for two months until he was returned to the trenches in January 1918, which, he admitted to Marsh 'are terrible now. We spend most of our time pulling each other out of the mud.'[128] Although declared fit by the doctor, he knew that his strength was failing.

On 7 February Rosenberg was transferred to the 8th Platoon B Company, 1st Battalion of the KORL in the 4th Division (the 11th had been broken up owing to a shortage of men). During the latter part of March they moved back and forth to the Front at the Greenland Hill Sector near Arras, initially holding the line south of Gavrelle but then falling back to Fampoux after being overrun. On 28 March they returned to the Front and it was from there that he wrote his last letter to Marsh enclosing his final poem, 'Through these pale cold days', having only an inch of candle, he was forced to 'measure my letter by the light'.[129] He also mentioned tantalisingly that during 'our little interlude of rest from the line I managed to do a bit of sketching – somebody had colours – and they weren't so bad, I don't think I have forgotten my art after all.'[130] None of these works has survived but Rosenberg's letter shows that despite recognising himself as poet first and painter second, he never finally closed the chapter on his art.

After the Germans launched a full-scale attack, Rosenberg's unit lost 70 men. On the last day of March 1918, he was detailed for a wiring patrol and set off into the night, never to return. His remains were later found with those of his comrades but, unlike those of Solomon Cohen, they could not be individually identified. He was named simply as one of the eleven members of the battalion who had been killed.

Private Isaac Rosenberg no. 22311 is now buried in Bailleul Road East British Cemetery, north east of Arras in Northern France. Beneath the Star of David, the carved inscription on his headstone reads – 'Artist and Poet' – finally resolving in death the creative dilemma that had both inspired and perplexed Rosenberg throughout his creative life.[131]

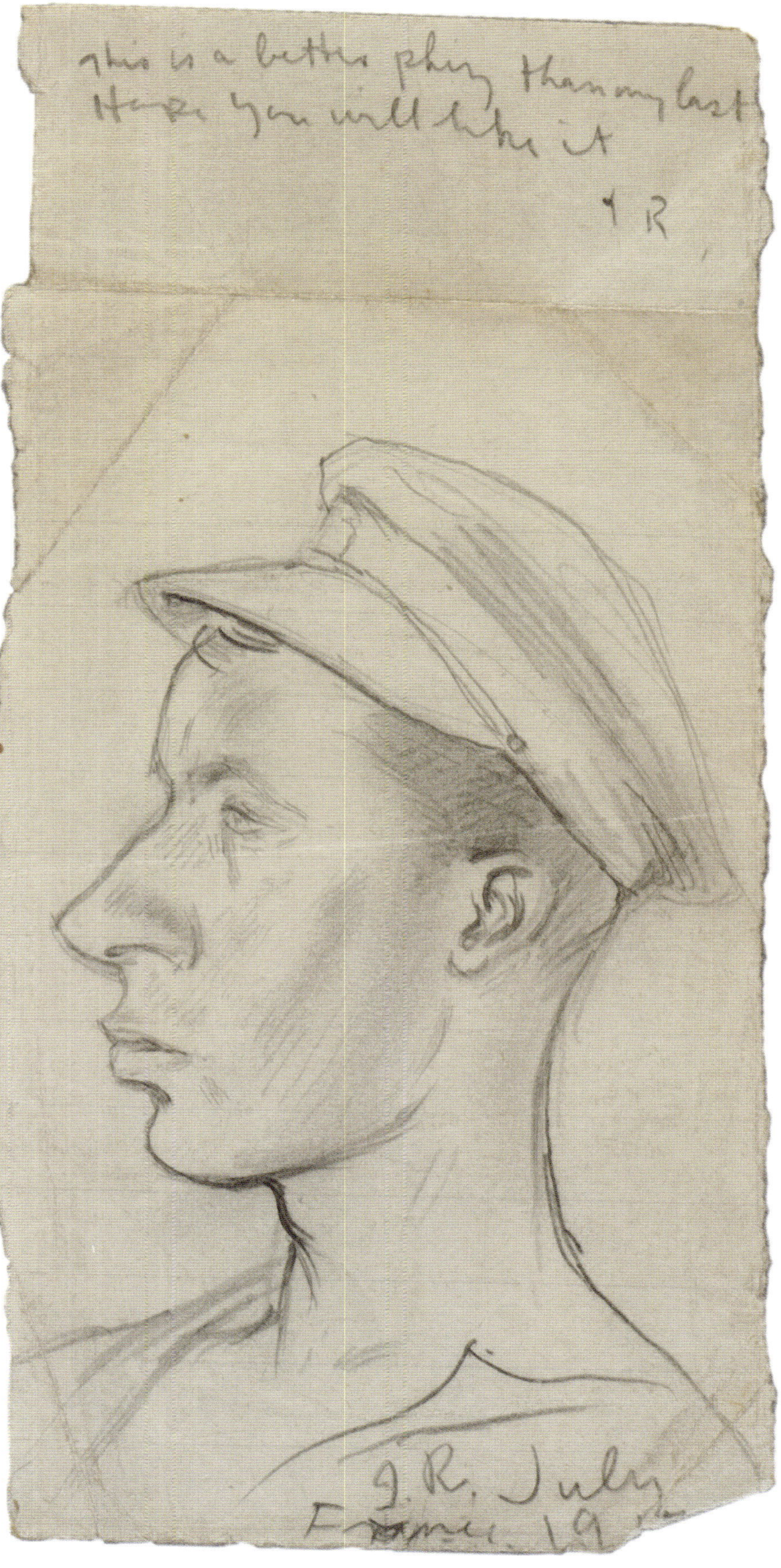

52
ISAAC ROSENBERG
Self-Portrait in Cap, 1917

3

ISAAC ROSENBERG: POET AND PAINTER

'By imagination in paint we do not encroach on the domain of the writer; we give what the writer cannot give, with all his advantages, the visible aspect of things, which the writer can only suggest.'[1]
ISAAC ROSENBERG, 'The Pre-Raphaelites and Imagination in Paint'

Siegfried Sassoon claimed 'genius' for Rosenberg, T S Eliot thought him the 'most remarkable' of the First World War poets and F R Leavis equated him with Wilfred Owen but found him 'even more interesting technically'.[2] A crucial part of that 'interest', I believe, and of Rosenberg's greatness and originality, sprang from the painter's vision he brought to bear on his poetry. This is particularly evident in his war poems, which are unique not least in the strength of their visual impact.

It was his artistic talent that manifested itself first and the area in which he received the greatest professional help. But it was not the arena in which his originality would emerge most clearly, possibly because of this rigorous training. Another reason for Rosenberg's superiority as a poet may lie in his character, background and the conditions that prevailed in pre-war England. In 1912 the art world still operated on a system of patronage, whereby poor, aspiring artists were dependent on wealthy art-lovers or philanthropists to support them and commission work from them. Painting, with a need for a studio, canvases, oil paints, and other expensive equipment was far more dependent on patronage than writing. Only the most outstanding talents such as Bomberg could afford to be independent and even he would suffer for it later on. Lacking Gertler's charm and social ease, Rosenberg's one hope of succeeding as an artist would require him to suppress his most basic instinct, the need for independence.

The main reason Rosenberg was less successful as a painter than a poet, however, lay more in the nature of his creativity than in his character. His reference (in a letter to a friend) to the 'literary idea'[3] behind one of his most ambitious paintings, *Joy*, his Slade summer competition entry of 1912, is highly significant, suggesting as it does that he needed the stimulus of words and narrative to get his imagination working fully. Before he even began to paint *Joy* he had expressed his conception for it in poetry, so that the painting itself became more of a translation, or illustration, of an original idea than a primary expression of his vision. It is perhaps fitting that, while the painting would be lost, the poem would survive. The first stanza of 'The Garden of Joy' which he sent to Ruth Löwy, one of the models for his painting (fig.6, *Ruth Löwy as the Sleeping Beauty*), with the words 'live in the garden of Joy so that when you get back you will know what sort of expression to wear when I put you in my "garden of Joy"',[4] shows how clearly he had first envisaged his concept verbally.[5] The device of the dreamer-narrator used in 'The Garden of Joy', familiar to Rosenberg from Keats and other Romantics, and the conjuring up of the Garden

FIG. 6
ISAAC ROSENBERG
Ruth Löwy as the Sleeping Beauty, 1912

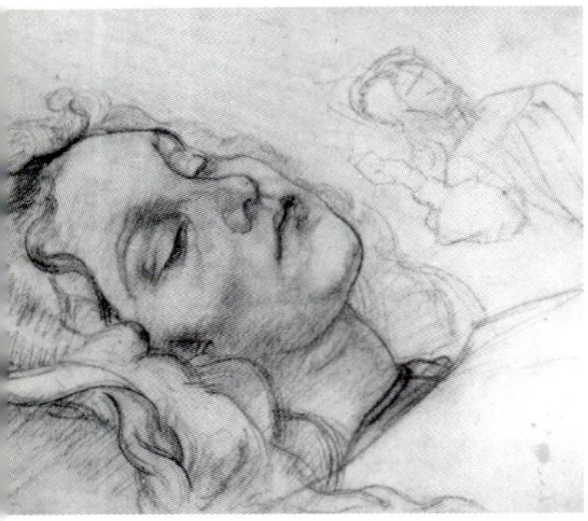

of Eden are essentially literary devices. The influence of that most literary of poets, Milton, whom Rosenberg had just been reading, is also evident, not just in the many echoes of *Paradise Lost*, but also in the Latinate, often archaic diction.

Laurence Binyon, a connoisseur of both art and poetry, since beside being an established poet he was Assistant Keeper in Prints and Drawings at the British Museum, felt that, though Rosenberg was a 'capable draughtsman' and 'could conceive an interesting design', art was not his 'inevitable means of expression'.[6] And of all the drawings and paintings Rosenberg showed him when they first met, it was *Joy* which confirmed Binyon's belief:

> [It was] a large ambitious composition—an oil-painting which I fancy was never completed. I cannot recall the nominal subject, but it was saturated with symbolism and required a good deal of explanation. I liked the mysteriousness of it, and the ideas which inspired the painting had suggested figures and groups and visionary landscapes which had passages of real beauty, though the whole work had grown impossibly complex with its convolutions of symbolic meaning. It reminded me of his poetry; and I think that represented his natural bent in art.[7]

Rosenberg himself recognised that there was a difference between imagination in art and imagination in literature. In a short prose piece on the Pre-Raphaelites he emphasised that 'by imagination in paint we do not encroach on the domain of the writer; we give what the writer cannot give, with all his advantages, the visible aspect of things, which the writer can only suggest'.[8] If Binyon was right, Rosenberg's imagination functioned most effectively as a poet, though enriched by his training as a painter.

Rosenberg's painter friends – Bomberg, Gertler and Kramer, among others – all suspected that his real genius lay with poetry. But he himself appears not to have realised this initially, vacillating for more than a decade between his two disciplines. It was only in late 1915, when desperation drove him to enlist in the army, that he was finally forced to choose. Conditions in his first unit, the Bantam Battalion of the 12th Suffolk Regiment and his two subsequent transfers to the 12th South Lancashire Regiment and 11th (later 1st) Battalion of the King's Own Royal Lancaster Regiment made it virtually impossible for him to carry on with his art. The only exceptions would be the two periods he spent in military hospitals, when kind friends sent painting materials and fellow-patients sat for him.

Apart from hospital, however, painting was largely out of the question and even poetry became very difficult. As a private he had less time and more physical labour than an officer. He also had fewer leaves, the period when the majority of officer-poets wrote the bulk of their war poems. His lack of privacy in army barracks made it almost impossible to concentrate and he warned one of his patrons, Sydney Schiff, early on 'not [to] expect any continuity or even coherence' from his writing.[9] Repeating a similar warning to another patron, Marsh, he described a further serious problem, which throws light on the nature of his war poetry once he begins to write it in earnest: 'There is always behind or through my object some pressing sense of foreign matter, immediate and not personal which hinders and disjoints what would otherwise have coherence and perhaps weight'.[10]

At the same time, it was precisely the 'pressing sense of foreign matter' and disjointedness which helps him to convey the reality of war so strongly in his verse. He had from the outset an acute awareness of the disruption and chaos looming, and not just for the ordinary soldier. The time was 'out of joint' for almost everyone and his ability to convey this sense of dislocation is one of his greatest gifts as a poet.

It was partly through chance that he had first turned to creative work in the army, when he found himself with time and materials to paint. But even he was already beginning to believe in himself 'more as a poet than a painter', convinced that he got 'more depth' into his writing[11] and at the first opportunity he returned to poetry. Donne's verse, one of only two books he had managed to bring with him, had not been enough to make him 'feel for poetry much' in his 'wretched surroundings'.[12] It was his own

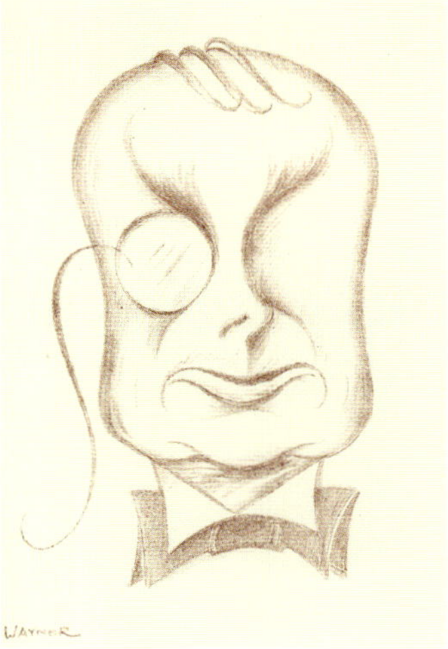

FIG. 21
MARK WAYNER
Sir Edward Marsh, 1943 or before

13
ISAAC ROSENBERG
Self-Portrait, 1912

'utmost distress of mind', he told the poet Lascelles Abercrombie, which sent him back to it, though the same mental state also made it difficult for him to write.[13]

His first real chance to write came during his four days' leave at Christmas. Shortly before it he tells Schiff that, having 'hardly given poetry or painting a thought' since he enlisted, he feels as if he were 'casting [his] coat [...] like a snake or a butterfly'.[14] It would still be a poet who emerged from the chrysalis, but one with wholly new experiences behind him. By the time leave expires he has written his first army poem, 'Marching':

Marching—As See from The Left File

My eyes catch ruddy necks
Sturdily pressed back,—
All a red brick moving glint.
Like flaming pendulums, hands
Swing across the khaki—
Mustard-coloured khaki—
To the automatic feet.

We husband the ancient glory
In these bared necks and hands
Not broke is the forge of Mars;
But a subtler brain beats iron
To shoe the hoofs of death,
(Who paws dynamic air now)
Blind fingers loose an iron cloud
To rain immortal darkness
On strong eyes.[15]

Rodker, whom Rosenberg met during his leave, believed 'Marching' to be a great work and sent it, on his behalf, to Harriet Monroe's *Poetry* magazine in Chicago. Rosenberg, who owned at least two copies of this prestigious magazine, mainly, I believe, because they contained poems by Pound, must have been greatly encouraged by this first response. Rodker's admiration was based partly on its 'ultra-modern' subject-matter,[16] underlining how instinctively Rosenberg gravitated towards modernist practice in verse as opposed to art. By Georgian poetry's rather conservative standard it would have seemed odd to find soldiers' strenuous daily activity 'poetic', which may explain Marsh's negative reaction when Rosenberg sent 'Marching' to him in late December 1915. (Another reason may, as Joseph Cohen has suggested, relate to the fact that in the letter which accompanied his poem, Rosenberg wrote to the highly patriotic Marsh 'I never joined the army for patriotic reasons. Nothing can justify war'.[17]) Yet it is evident that, however punishing Rosenberg had found marching initially and however routine it had become to him after a few months in the army, he also saw visual beauty in the sight of a solid wall of men – 'all a red brick moving glint'– swinging along in a uniform khaki formation with machine-like almost balletic co-ordination.

Bomberg, like Rosenberg, would eventually reject the Vorticists' worship of the machine, but he was still influenced by them at this time and it may have been one of Bomberg's paintings, works which anticipated sketches such as *War Scene*, that Rosenberg is partially envisaging here.[18] Even Gertler, when he came reluctantly to depict the war he loathed, would do so through a machine metaphor in *Merry-Go-Round* (fig. 16).[19] The emphasis on colour and shape in the first stanza of 'Marching' suggests strongly that Rosenberg's initial response had been that of a visual artist but that, lacking the time and materials to paint the scene, he had tried to capture it in words later.

It may have been this need to channel his dual creative energies into one medium, which gave him, he believed, 'more depth' as a poet from December 1915 onwards. The intensely concrete first stanza of 'Marching' leads on to a more abstract, metaphorical second, where the humble modern soldier is dignified with an 'ancient glory' by the poet, who uses the phrase to introduce the central paradox of the piece, the contrast between the living, vulnerable human beings with all their potential and the destructive, inhuman nature of the war in which they are involved, made worse in the twentieth century by its devastating machines. This last point is emphasised in another

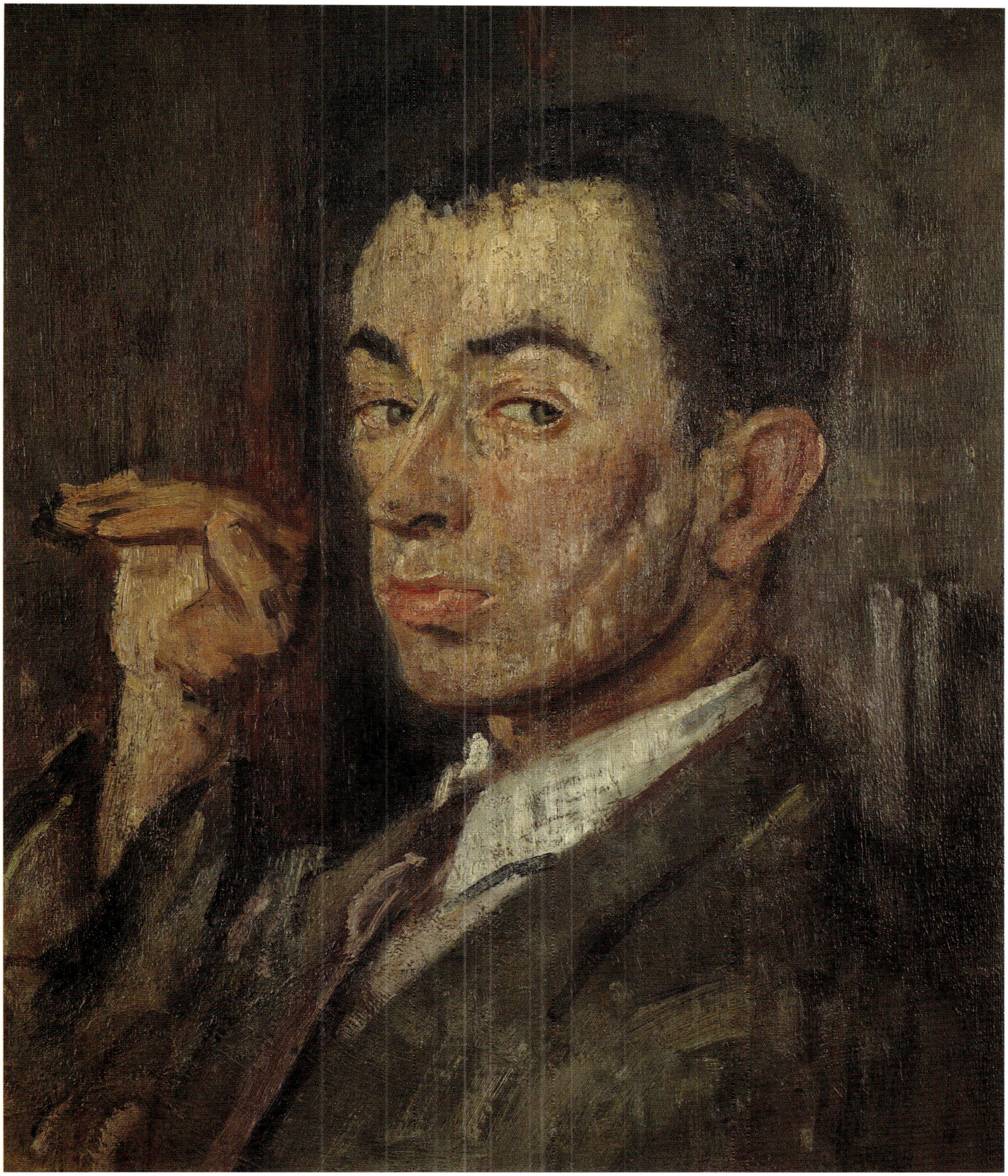

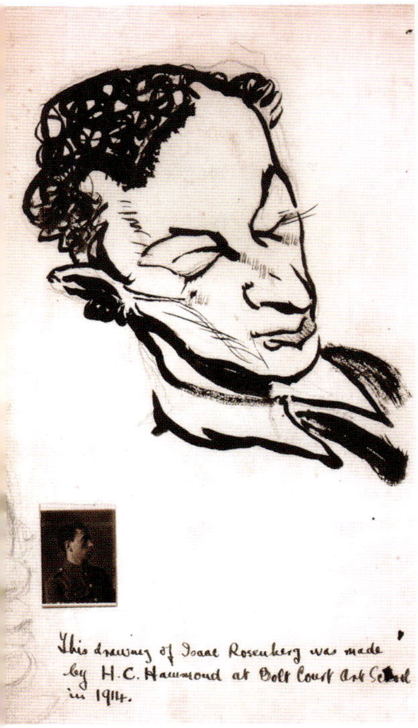

FIG. 17
H C HAMMOND
Portrait of Isaac Rosenberg
(not dated)

contrast set up between the ancient forge of Mars, where the Roman god of war 'beats iron/To shoe the hoofs of Death' and modern warfare, controlled by a 'subtler brain', a more impersonal ('blind') force, loosing 'an iron cloud' of destruction from the sky (aeroplanes have replaced horses). The soldiers, made 'immortal' by the 'rain' of ammunition, are also deprived of their sight as they plunge into the 'darkness' of death.

In struggling to paraphrase 'Marching' the full complexity of Rosenberg's concentrated language becomes evident. Through it he is able to convey not just the similarities and differences between ancient and modern warfare and its positive as well as negative aspects, but it also enables him to make his reader visualise the actual (the marching soldiers), the mythological (the forge of Mars) and the abstract (war and death) simultaneously. Though he feared that Marsh would find the few lines he added as 'vague' as the original poem, there is a great deal of concrete detail in it, even down to the wet winter weather he was himself experiencing, pinning this exploration of the nature of war firmly to earth.

In many respects 'Marching' differs from the kind of war poetry being written by almost all the other First World War poets. Rosenberg's treatment of war is also quite different: neither satiric like Sassoon, nor grieving like Owen, the closest writer to him is another painter-poet, David Jones, someone equally open to both the visual and experimental who also relies heavily on mythology in his work. But it is not only a matter of technique, nor is it just because (like Jones's) it is written from the viewpoint of a private rather than an officer that Rosenberg's poetry is so different. It is also being written by a Jew with centuries of persecution behind him, who often identifies with the persecuted rather than the persecutor, but who always looks at things from his own, fresh angle of vision.

It is his training as an artist, however, that most distinguishes Rosenberg and the link between his two disciplines reveals itself clearly throughout his poetry. 'The Troop Ship', for instance, a subject he sketched, apparently, before turning it into a poem, is intensely visual. A reference in one of his letters suggests that he drew himself crammed onto the deck of an overcrowded ship as it left for France, a visualisation which manifests itself clearly in the subsequent poem and one which anticipates his later emphasis on the unnatural, 'grotesque' nature of war:

The Troop Ship

Grotesque and queerly huddled
Contortionists to twist
The sleepy soul to a sleep
We lie all sorts of ways
But cannot sleep
The wet wind is so cold,
And the lurching men so careless,
That, should you drop to a doze,
Wind's fumble or men's feet
Is on your face.[20]

Written either during a crossing, or shortly after arrival at Le Havre, the poem might almost have been a description of a night in the trenches, towards which the whole of the 40th Division were proceeding in June 1916.

In the case of 'Louse Hunting' the link between an initial sketch of the subject and the subsequent poem is even clearer. Ironically, it was an apparently staunch supporter of the old traditions, the poet Gordon Bottomley, who encouraged Rosenberg to write on such an unconventional theme, as well as being indirectly responsible for his very untraditional handling of such a subject as louse-hunting. Rosenberg had first conceived the idea of a poem of this kind in July 1916, shortly after completing 'Break of Day in the Trenches', but on another common trench pest, fleas, rather than lice. Bottomley responded on 8 August:

I thought your Flea Hunt was a great subject [...] But what a subject for a painter too; an absolutely untouched chance for a painter of nudes. Goya or Daumier could have made the real thing of it.[21]

Though Rosenberg replies that he thinks Bottomley should write such a poem, since he is not planning to compose any more verse 'till we've settled down again', he responds enthusiastically to Bottomley's painter references, agreeing that 'it is a thing Goya would go mad on'.[22]

Too exhausted and demoralised to write such a poem during the harsh winter of 1916–17, Rosenberg evidently brooded on Bottomley's remarks. By 5 January 1917 he is thinking about 'The Louse Hunt', but by 8 February has still not produced the piece. Inspired, however by those two great artists of the grotesque, Goya and Daumier, he has executed a drawing on the subject. Shortly after that he appears to have made his first attempt at the poem 'The Immortals'.[23]

It was Bottomley's response to his drawing rather than this poem, however, which appears to have encouraged Rosenberg to produce his more original handling of the subject in 'Louse Hunting'. While admiring his 'Rear Elevation of a Flea-Hunt' sketch, Bottomley had felt it was 'a *static* Flea Hunt' [my italics]:

I should like to see what you would make of the active Flea-Hunt, which you first described [he wrote on 19 March 1917], with the men jumping over candles and singeing the fleas. That would yield quite a different kind of composition, all moving and flowing lines, like a Witches' Sabbath of long slim bodies as if Botticelli had gone mad and designed a naked ballet for the Russian dancers.[24]

Heartened by Bottomley's interest and further inspired by the vision of the hunt as a 'Witches Sabbath' or 'Botticelli gone mad', Rosenberg returned to the subject, producing an almost exact poetic equivalent of Bottomley's letter, together with his earlier references to Goya and Daumier. But, as Bottomley pointed out, it had been Rosenberg's idea originally, 'all summarized in your letter of last summer', which had read:

Last night we had a funny hunt for fleas. All stripped by candlelight some Scots dancing over the candle & burning the fleas, & the funniest, drollest and dirtiest scenes of conversation ever imagined. Burns 'Jolly Beggars' is nothing to it.[25]

The result is an intensely visual recreation of, in Bottomley's appreciative words, 'a night scene in which Rosenberg took part [...] a barn full of naked soldiers – Scottish and others – singing, swearing, and laughing, in mad antics as they pursued the chase.'[26]

Louse Hunting

Nudes—stark aglisten
Yelling in lurid glee. Grinning faces of fiends
And raging limbs
Whirl over the floor one fire,
For a shirt verminously busy
Yon soldier tore from his throat
With oaths
Godhead might shrink at, but not the lice.
And soon the shirt was aflare
Over the candle he'd lit while we lay.
Then we all sprung up and stript
To hunt the vermin brood.
Soon like a demons' pantomime
The place was raging.
See the silhouettes agape,
See the gibbering shadows
Mixed with the battled arms on the wall.
See gargantuan hooked fingers
Dug in supreme flesh
To smutch the supreme littleness.
See the merry limbs in hot Highland fling
Because some wizard vermin
Charmed from the quiet this revel
When our ears were half lulled
By the dark music
Blown from Sleep's trumpet.[27]

The visual origins of this poem are far more evident here than in 'The Immortals'. The naked bodies of the soldiers 'stark aglisten' in the flames, their 'grinning faces' and contorted limbs, their silhouettes and 'shadows/Mixed with the battled arms on the wall' and their 'gargantuan hooked fingers' digging in their own flesh for lice bring the scene to

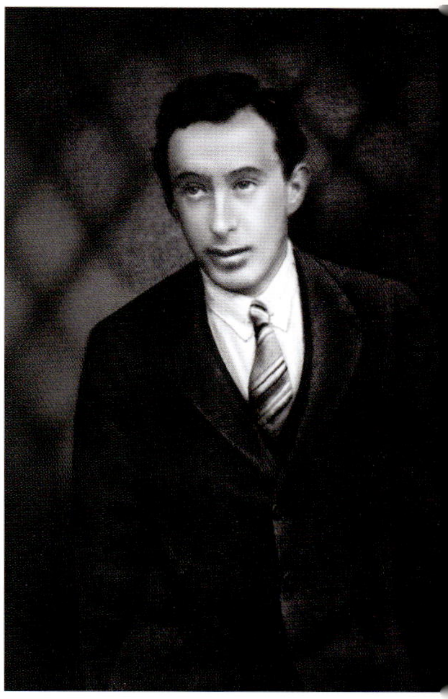

FIG. 39
Studio Portrait of Isaac Rosenberg, 1911

life in a manner worthy of Goya's blackest visions. The reader does not need to know, as the ex-Slade student Rosenberg probably did, that Daumier, dubbed the 'Michelangelo of caricaturists', was imprisoned for his lampoon of the French King Louis-Philippe as Rabelais' obese giant Gargantua, to appreciate the grotesque enlargement of the men's 'gargantuan hooked fingers'. Rosenberg's verse is at its best when, as here, his artistic vision is subsumed into his poetic one.

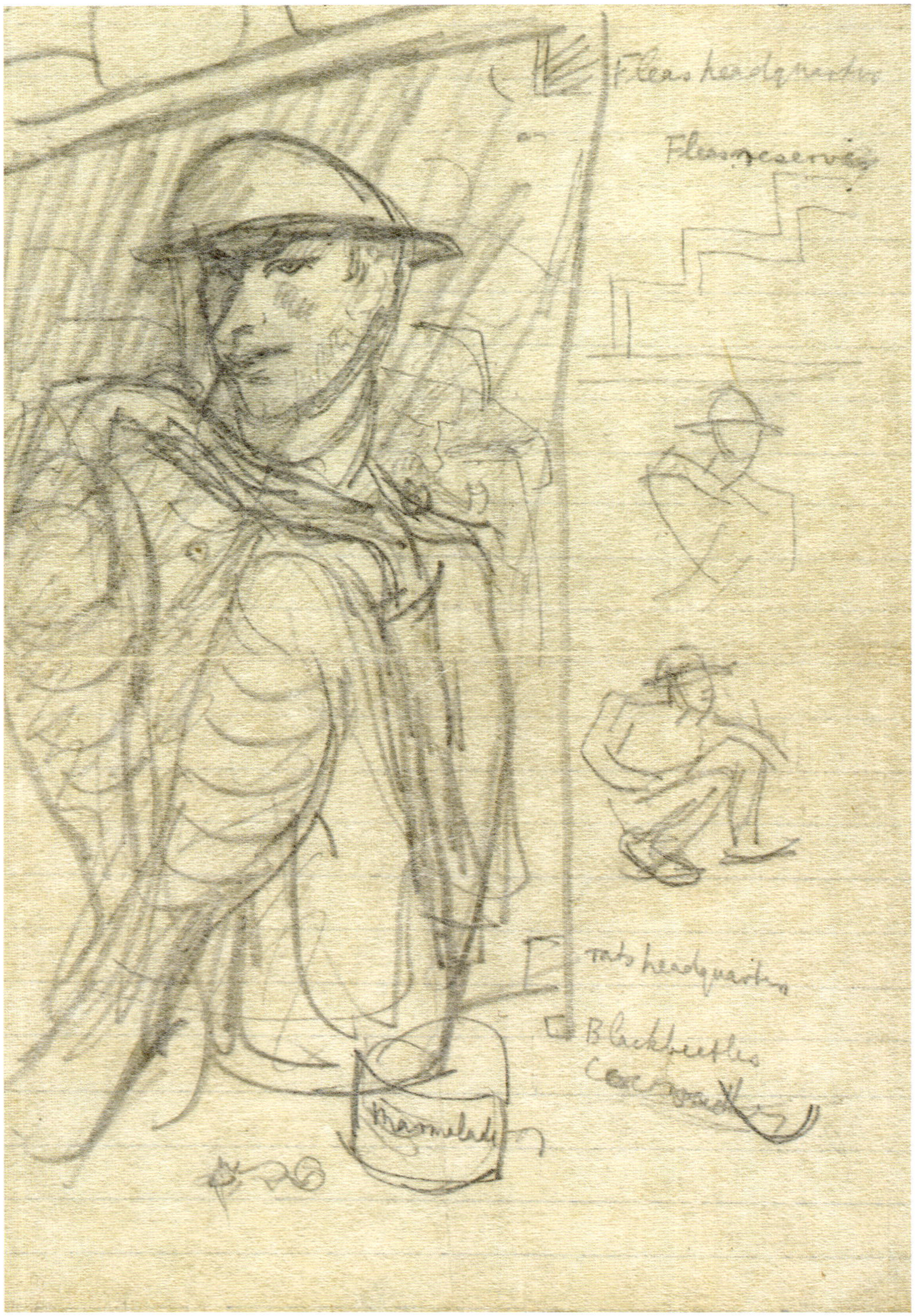

51
ISAAC ROSENBERG
Letter to R C Trevelyan
Self-Portrait with Marmalade Jar, *c.*1916

Even the friendly-looking rat of Rosenberg's sketch of himself (and his marmalade) in a dug-out (cat no. 51) may have left its mark on his poetry in the form of an uncharacteristically congenial rat in 'Break of Day in the Trenches'. His vivid recreation of the chalky-white trench, the blood-red poppy and the 'sleeping green' of no-man's-land certainly reveals the painter's eye.

More powerful still are the poems where an earlier, more fully realised work of art has evidently influenced a later poem. While 'Returning, We Hear the Larks', for instance, shows a debt to Shelley's 'To a Sky-lark', it owes even more, I believe, to his own charcoal drawing of the subject, *Hark, Hark, the Lark* (1912, cat no. 16), based on Meredith's 'The Lark Ascending':

> And every face to watch him raised
> Puts on the light of children praised [...]

Rosenberg's drawing depicts apprehension as well as joy in the faces of the six nude figures listening to the bird's song and this graphic rendering of the scene undoubtedly contributed to the central concept of 'Returning, We Hear the Larks'. (He had, for instance, already imagined their 'upturned list'ning faces' in his picture.) The nakedness of the men and women in the drawing suggests their vulnerability and while the soldiers in 'Returning, We Hear The Larks' are not literally naked (as they are in 'Louse Hunting'), they are metaphorically just as exposed to the potential danger in the sky. *Joy*, too, almost certainly inspired some of the other visual details of the poem. Since the picture itself is lost, this cannot now be proved, but the influence of the piece written in conjunction with it can, reading in part like a prose equivalent of the verse. 'Joy— joy— the birds sing, joy—' Rosenberg had written in its last sentence: '— the rivers, joy— the happy leaves, for the fear of Time haunts not, and the hands of fate are afar.'[28] The 'hands of fate' may be 'afar' in this earlier piece but, significantly, the writer is already conscious of them.

As Rosenberg develops as a war poet the link with his vision as an artist becomes less obvious but, if possible, even stronger. In his most wide-ranging poem on the subject, 'Dead Man's Dump', the transition from painter to poet is seamless. The narrator who takes us on this grotesque tour of the battlefield gives the reader an experience as visually as it is verbally intense, one which reflects his own feelings with the 229 Field Company, Royal Engineers, to which he had been seconded in the summer of 1917. His job with them involved carrying barbed wire and metal stakes up to the line in 'limber' carts, to repair any damage done to the tangled coils of barbed wire designed to protect the Allies from the enemy. One particularly unpleasant aspect of the job, he told Marsh, was 'running over dead bodies lying about'.[29] Though he clearly loathed the dangerous, macabre journey to no-man's-land, always undertaken at night, his poem on the subject ('Dead Man's Dump') shows how powerful an effect the desolate scene had on his imagination both as an artist and a poet:

> The plunging limbers over the shattered track
> Racketed with their rusty freight,
> Stuck out like many crowns of thorns,
> And the rusty stakes like sceptres old
> To stay the flood of brutish men
> Upon our brothers dear
>
> The wheels lurched over sprawled dead
> But pained them not, though their bones crunched,
> Their shut mouths made no moan,
> They lie there huddled, friend and foeman,
> Man born of man, and born of woman,
> And shells go crying over them
> From night till night and now.[30]

The painter has combined with the poet to give an arresting portrayal of this sinister night scene. The intense visualisation of the limber carts and their 'rusty freight' is complemented by the harsh sounds they make, the jagged, jerky rhythms reflecting their jolting progress over corpses and the underlying theme of sudden, brutal death. And the artist's vision of 'crowns of thorns' and 'sceptres old' is seized on by the poet to point, metaphorically, to latter-day Christs, the soldiers, which lends a dignity and nobility to their apparently meaningless deaths. Likewise, the picture conjured up of King Canute seated on the seashore, trying in vain to turn back the tide, allows the poet to suggest how ineffectual the barbed wire is likely to be in keeping back the enemy. The dead are shown lying 'sprawled' and 'huddled' side by side, regardless of which side they are on, silent in death, with only the shells to 'cry' for them. The following eleven stanzas are equally evocative both visually and aurally. It is a memorable opening and one typical of Rosenberg in its graphic detail and verbal music. The most dramatic moment in the poem, however, comes in the final two stanzas when Rosenberg projects himself into the mind and supine body of one of war's many victims at the very moment of his dying, then swiftly back in stark contrast to the drivers of the limber carts as they start on their return journey and bring the 'tour' – and the poem – to a close:

> Here is one not long dead;
> His dark hearing caught our far wheels,
> And the choked soul stretched weak hands
> To reach the living word the far wheels said,
> The blood-dazed intelligence beating for light,
> Crying through the suspense of the far torturing wheels
> Swift for the end to break,
> Or the wheels to break,
> Cried as the tide of the world broke over his sight.
>
> Will they come? Will they ever come?
> Even as the mixed hoofs of the mules,
> The quivering-bellied mules,
> And the rushing wheels all mixed
> With his tortured upturned sight,
> So we crashed round the bend,
> We heard his weak scream,
> We heard his very last sound,
> And our wheels grazed his dead face.[31]

The angle of vision, particularly in these last two stanzas is highly unusual – the dying soldier gazing up at the hooves and bellies of the approaching mules – and something Rosenberg, the painter-poet, can do exceptionally well. The 'normal' view of things has been, literally, distorted. Consciously or not, Rosenberg has, in a technique reminiscent of Post-Impressionism, rejected straightforward representation in favour of a selection of the most significant aspects of the scene. 'Dead Man's Dump' achieves in words what Stanley Spencer's Burghclere war murals achieve in paint.

So powerful was the effect of Rosenberg's painter's vision on his work as a poet that when Bottomley, a man well-versed in both arts, wanted a comparison for what he called the 'mysterious inscrutable texture' of Rosenberg's own favourite poem, 'Daughter's Of War', he felt obliged to include not just poets and musicians in his list but also at least three painters – Whistler, Titian and (the early) Dante Gabriel Rossetti.[32] And when, 20 years after first reading it, Bottomley still believed 'Daughters Of War' to be 'a finer war poem than anyone else achieved' in that conflict[33], he drew a comparison with one of England's greatest artist-poets, and one of Rosenberg's greatest 'ideals', Blake:

> [It is Rosenberg's] big achievement, his masterpiece, reaching up to a symbolism as great as Blake's from the still realistic level of 'Dead Man's Dump'.[34]

None of Rosenberg's few final poems achieves the visual intensity of 'Marching', 'Louse Hunting', 'Break Of Day in the Trenches', 'Returning, We Hear the Larks', 'Dead Man's Dump' or 'Daughters of War'. This may be partly because not long after completing the last of these Rosenberg found himself back in hospital in October 1917 and able, briefly, to paint again. Perhaps being able to channel his creative energy back into his first love, art, lessened his need to express his painter's vision through his poetry.

For the most part, however, and apart from one striking self-portrait of himself in gouache and chalk (cat no. 30) (in what Bottomley called his 'fine medieval helmet'[35]) and a few sketches of trench-life, when Rosenberg entered the army, he was obliged to leave his graphic work behind him. And this, as I have suggested, forced him to concentrate his creative energies into one channel deepening his vision as a poet and adding an ingredient to his work nowhere equalled in the other great voices of the First World War.

FIG. 41
Isaac Rosenberg in Uniform, 1917

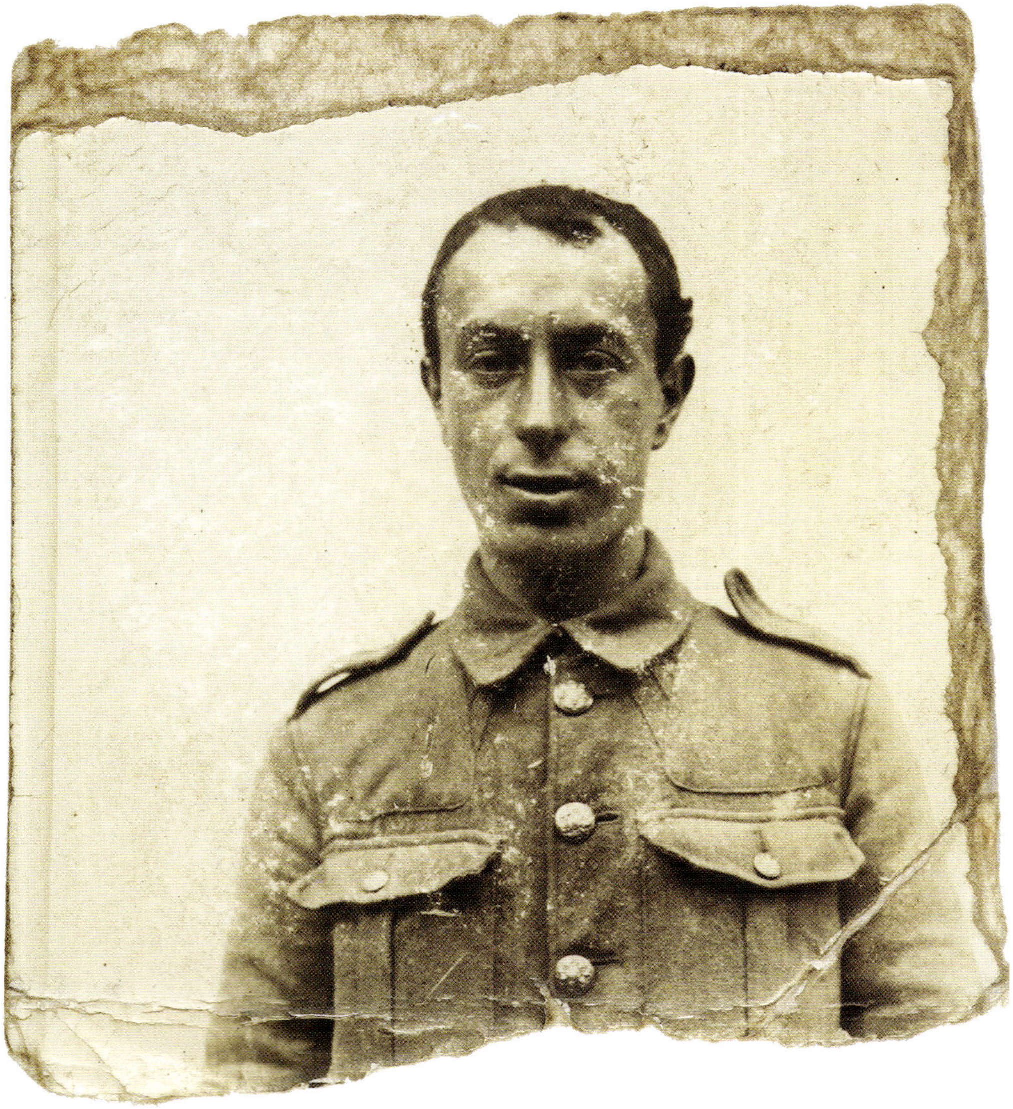

4

WHITECHAPEL AT WAR

THE WHITECHAPEL BOYS AND THE GREAT WAR

Winsten, Rosenberg, Rodker, I
How we are saddened and broken by
Struggles and teasing hopes and fears.
What awaits us in the coming years?
From '*Imminence*' (1912), JOSEPH LEFTWICH[1]

I never joined the army from patriotic reasons. Nothing can justify war. I suppose we must all fight to get the trouble over. Anyhow before the war I helped at home when I could and I did other things which helped to keep things going. I thought if I'd join there would be the separation allowance for my mother.
ISAAC ROSENBERG TO EDWARD MARSH, late December 1915[2]

For Whitechapel Boys Isaac Rosenberg and David Bomberg – both British-born Jews who enlisted towards the end of 1915 – volunteering prior to conscription was a matter of conviction. However, beyond Whitechapel, the mouthpieces of Anglo-Jewry began to apply pressure to the Jewish community-at-large as soon as the conflict began. Bold, graphic adverts in English and Yiddish in the *Jewish Chronicle* and *Jewish World* exhorted every Jew of appropriate age to do his duty towards Great Britain and join up. As early as October 1914, the *Jewish World* (fig. 34) declared: 'THE OLD SPIRIT OF THE MACABEES IS NOT DEAD. Every Able Bodied Unmarried Jew Between 19 and 45 should JOIN THE BRITISH ARMY. Join as Jews and be Proud of Your Race.'[3] These advertisements, as Mark Levene has written, endorsed the view that 'To belong in 1914 – that is, to belong to the nation – required what the French aptly called "l'impot du sang" a blood tax.'[4] To be fully integrated into Britain required Jews, at the very least, to be seen to be prepared to offer up their lives for their new homeland.

As the war progressed the situation became more difficult for Russian-born Jews who were perceived as foreigners, despite the alliance between Britain and Russia under which they were classified as 'friendly aliens' exempt from conscription. The first Military Service Act of January 1916 inaugurated conscription for single men between the ages of 18 and 41; the second Act compelled all men of serving age, unless exempt by military tribunal. The *Jewish Chronicle* diligently followed the work of these tribunals in a regular column entitled 'Russian Jews and Military Tribunals', casting a concerned but somewhat distanced eye over proceedings. Supposedly staffed with Yiddish and Russian interpreters, the tribunals were set up in London, Leeds, Manchester, Liverpool and Glasgow to consider applications from Russian Jews requesting exemption from conscription. Jacob Kramer, in a letter to Herbert Read towards the end of the war, wrote that he would 'probably appear before the Leeds Tribunary at the end of this month'[5]

The *Jewish Chronicle*'s 'special correspondent' broached this complex issue sympathetically in his column in October 1916, describing a spectrum of Russian Jews who 'ranged from the genuine refugee, bitterly and naturally opposed to military service, with its implied alternative of deportation, to the young Anglo-Russian who came here in his infancy, and who doesn't care a *beigel* for the war, its causes and its ultimate influence upon the Jewish destiny.'[6]

The non-naturalised East End Jews were not liable for service in the British army, nevertheless they were conspicuous on the streets of Whitechapel, as young

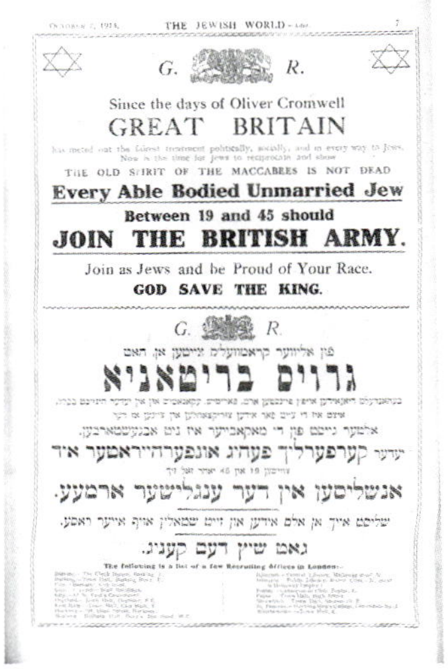
THE JEWISH WORLD

G. R.

Since the days of Oliver Cromwell
GREAT BRITAIN

THE OLD SPIRIT OF THE MACCABEES IS NOT DEAD
Every Able Bodied Unmarried Jew
Between 19 and 45 should
JOIN THE BRITISH ARMY.
Join as Jews and be Proud of Your Race.
GOD SAVE THE KING.

G. R.

גרויס בריטאניא

יעדער קערפערליך פעהיג אונפערהייראטער איד

אנשליסען אין דער ענגלישער ארמעע.

גאט שיץ דעם קעניג.

The following is a list of a few Recruiting Offices in London:—

FIG. 35
'Join the British Army' advertisement in *Jewish World*, October, 1914

men who were not away fighting. In autumn 1914, the writer Gilbert Cannan noted that Mark Gertler (who, like Rosenberg and Bomberg was British-born) was sometimes 'in despair, because his friends were looking askance at him because he was not in uniform.'[7] Gertler would soon leave Whitechapel but the problem was more acute for those who remained, particularly those of distinctive 'Jewish' appearance. Many were refugees from Russian oppression and there was a growing anxiety among the community at the possibility of having to return to serve under Britain's ally, the Tsar. As Deborah Maccoby has commented: 'the greatest dread of immigrant Jewish mothers from the Russian Empire was that their sons would be conscripted into the army; it brought back all their memories of the army in Russia, in which the Jewish soldiers had been so ill-treated that many of them had died before even reaching the Front, and those who did reach it were treated as cannon fodder.'[8]

This volatile situation led to increased political activity in the East End and in June 1916 the Foreign Jews' Protection Committee against Deportation to Russia and Compulsion (FJPC) – which numbered Israel Zangwill among its supporters – was established to protect the right of asylum and to protest against conscription and the threat of deportation. Despite the debate and protest, non-exempt Russian Jews continued to face the stark choice of either joining the British Army, or of being deported to Russia where they faced military service. Non-serving 'friendly' aliens were also compelled to register their movements with the police if they left their home town.

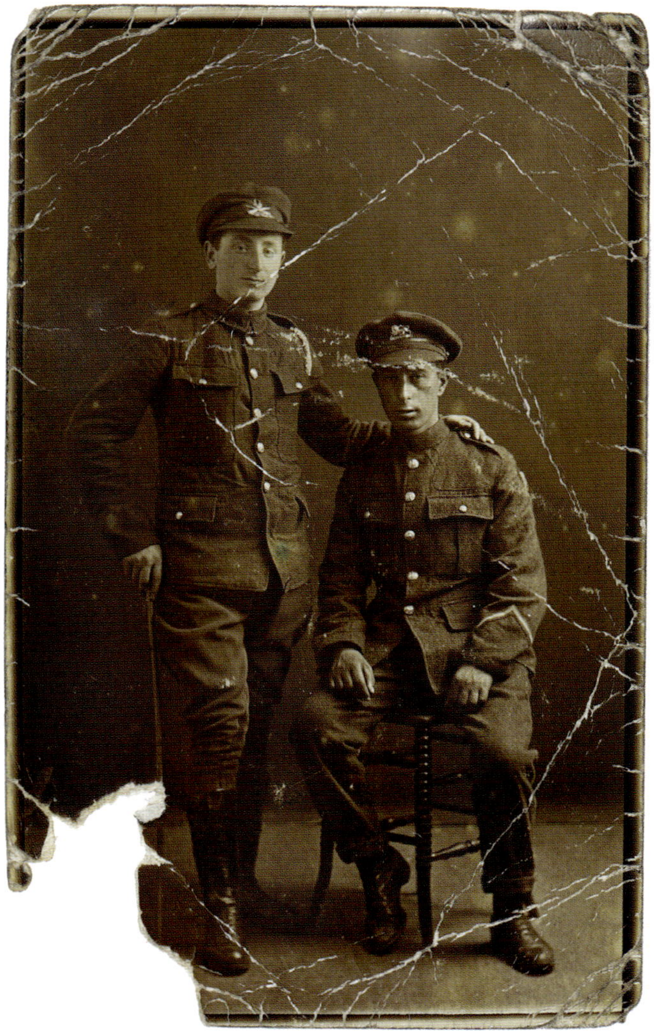

FIG. 42
Isaac Rosenberg and his Brother Elkon in Uniform, 1917

Furthermore, as Dr Jonathan Black, biographer of the war artists Edward Wadsworth and Eric Kennington, has suggested, Jews were often seen by the War Office as less than impressive fighting material. Reluctant to allow Jews to become officers in the combative branches of the services, the War Office tolerated them in the Labour Corps or Army Service Corps. Certainly, Talmudic scholars from the East End slums may have been poorer physical specimens than their well-nourished Anglo-Jewish 'West End' counterparts, but they were also emerging from a culture which placed no value on the pursuit of war. As the *Jewish Chronicle*'s 'special correspondent' commented: 'Are we going to press these gaunt, bearded brothers into khaki [...]? What can be the military value of these men? Observe them during the high festivals, on their way too and from the *Shool*, and ask yourself if they are the material whence fighting men are fashioned. The very idea is absurd.'[9]

Against this background, many of the Whitechapel Boys' parents, including Rosenberg's father Barnett, were pacifists. The threat – and in some cases appalling experience – of undergoing national service for the Tsar in their native countries motivated some of them to avoid the same fate for their children. As a young man in Galicia, Gertler's father Louis had shot himself in the foot to escape conscription, an extreme measure repeated by David Bomberg when serving in the army in 1917. Now, many of the older generation found that their children were being recruited for war by their adopted country. In the summer of 1914

Gertler witnessed many of his old Whitechapel neighbours ('no more Austrian in spirit than Hottentot!'[10]) being repatriated and his parents, who were themselves technically Austrian, were forced to become Poles to escape the label 'enemy alien'.

Moreover, for many of the younger British-born Jews, the 'old country' – in particular Russia – existed only as a terrifying mythological place in the stories told by the community elders. Louis Golding, the Jewish writer, described this notion in 'Forward from Babylon' ('The opening of a novel') published in the little magazine *Voices*:

> Russia – here was the first Babylon [. . .]. Philip's big eyes were round with horror of this immense inscrutable place. Everything they said was portentous, not wholly real. Many of their words attained a meaning only after laborious thinking.
>
> 'Kossacken – big as trees!'
>
> 'Big spikes in front of the Gubernator's house! Babies stuck! Rachel the parchment-maker's daughter caught up on a white horse. Never heard of again!'[11]

In an attempt to make Jewish conscription as attractive as possible, a formal Jewish fighting unit received government approval during summer 1917, a move which had been debated since the end of 1914 both inside and outside the community. *Jewish World* carried a dramatic full-page advertisement on its cover, as early as December 1914, declaring: 'BRITAIN has been all she could be to the Jews. Jews will be all they can be to Britain. Join the Special JEWISH UNIT',[12] and listed recruiting offices in Leadenhall Street, on the edge of Whitechapel (fig. 36). Those against the idea however, had protested at the formation of what they saw as a 'ghetto' regiment, an 'instrument of segregation'. Nevertheless, the increasing need for an appropriate environment for Jewish servicemen had been hinted at by Lord Derby in the *Jewish Chronicle* in November 1915, when he suggested that, 'in advance of conscription, Jewish recruits should join up in batches whereby they could be placed in battalions together which should have an inspiring effect upon young Jews and still further increase the number of Jewish recruits.'[13] A further attraction would be the provision of special facilities for religious observance and Yiddish speaking instructors.

The unit was formally designated as the 38th Battalion of the Royal Fusiliers and included British volunteers, as well as members of the former Zion Mule Corps and a large number of Russian Jews. It was composed of five battalions of different nationalities. In February 1918 the unit, in full dress kit, proudly paraded from Tower Hill to the Mansion House before returning to the East End via the Whitechapel Road. Headed by Colonel J H Patterson DSO, the 'Judeans' halted in front of the Pavilion Theatre to receive tributes. As the *Jewish Chronicle* observed: 'The march was unlike any other, more replete with significance [. . .]. It was a reply to the insistent taunt that has made existence a nightmare to the East End, that has sent menacing echoes into the heart of the West End [. . .]. It was Whitechapel's own come [sic] to be greeted – and cheered – and to be wept over – by its own.'[14]

The Royal Fusiliers would absorb more than one Whitechapel boy: Jacob Epstein[15] was conscripted as a Private in the 38th Battalion in 1917 and Bernard Meninsky served with the Fusiliers throughout. Jacob Kramer was also recommended to join the unit but chose to neglect this advice.[16] During his final month Rosenberg also wrote to Marsh that he had requested a transfer to the Jewish Battalion in Mesopotamia, drawn no doubt by the warm climate and the security of his own 'people', but such a request was unrealistic and ultimately unsuccessful.

Despite their shared European Jewish heritage, home backgrounds and artistic inclination, the Whitechapel Boys had no single experience of the war: they ranged from front-line soldier (Rosenberg and Bomberg), conscientious objector (Gertler, Rodker and Winsten) to those with tedious non-combatant roles (Meninsky and Kramer). Meninsky at least had the distinction of participating in the War Artist scheme.

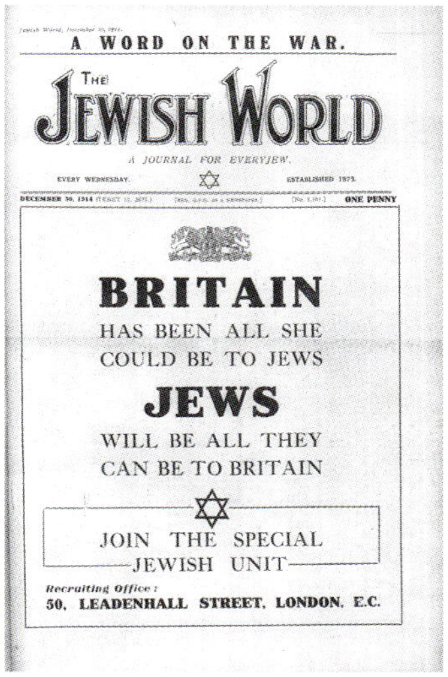
A WORD ON THE WAR.

THE JEWISH WORLD

A JOURNAL FOR EVERYJEW.

BRITAIN

HAS BEEN ALL SHE COULD BE TO JEWS

JEWS

WILL BE ALL THEY CAN BE TO BRITAIN

JOIN THE SPECIAL JEWISH UNIT

Recruiting Office:
50, LEADENHALL STREET, LONDON, E.C.

FIG. 36
'Join the Special Jewish Unit' advertisement in *Jewish World*, December, 1914

40
LONDON ART STUDIOS
*Isaac Rosenberg, c.*1915

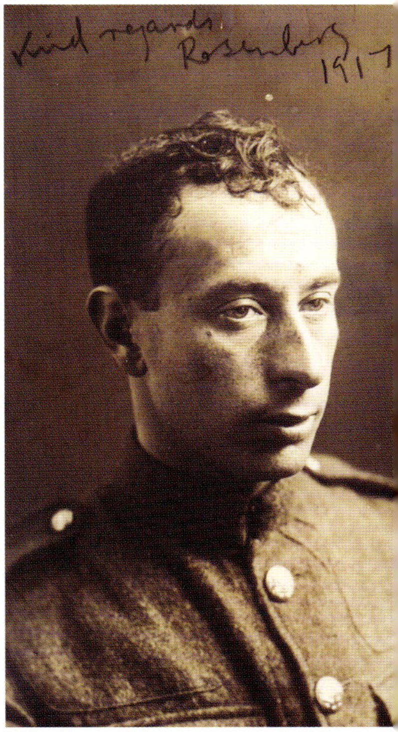

Bomberg, who enlisted, like Rosenberg, towards the end of 1915, joined the Royal Engineers and soon afterwards experienced the worst horror of trench warfare in France at first hand. Driven to desperation by the terrible conditions and by the death in action of one of his brothers, his drastic response was self-mutilation: he shot himself in the foot. Invalided out rather than severely punished (for what was considered an extremely serious offence), Bomberg was nevertheless soon returned to active service and posted as a runner for his unit. During this time, he began to write poetry and, in leave periods back in London, to work on a series of trench drawings. Richard Cork comments that it was perhaps the friendship with Rosenberg which stimulated this interest in verse and that Bomberg may 'even have made his first attempts at poetry in Rosenberg's company.'[17]

Bomberg's poems, such as 'Winter Night', 'Twenty Rounds' and 'Balloons', convey a full sense of horror and anguish:

> But the flight of the rising howitzer is ominous.
> War's rousing mastiffs, with lifted muzzles gaped!
> With throats torn. With passions pulsating painfully, —
> dulled thuds — dimly heard. Panting, — momentarily
> casting their ardent fever-breath — elongated pools of
> lighted blue — upon the heavy overhanging cloud.[18]

But his drawn images maintain a cooler emotional distance. Two drawings, probably dating from 1918, *Gunner Loading Shell* (cat no. 32) and *Soldier Patrolling Tunnel* (cat no. 33), as Cork indicates, clearly show a move away from the overtly fractured and more mechanical treatment of much of Bomberg's pre-war modernist work. A clear distinction is made between man and machine, although the dynamism of human limbs continued to fascinate Bomberg. He reintroduced this element of humanity markedly in the first version of *Sappers at Work*,[19] which he executed as a commission for the Canadian War Memorials' Fund. Bomberg was allowed to withdraw from active service to execute it and first produced a series of elaborate drawings. In the finished work, though he emphasized the 'flesh and blood

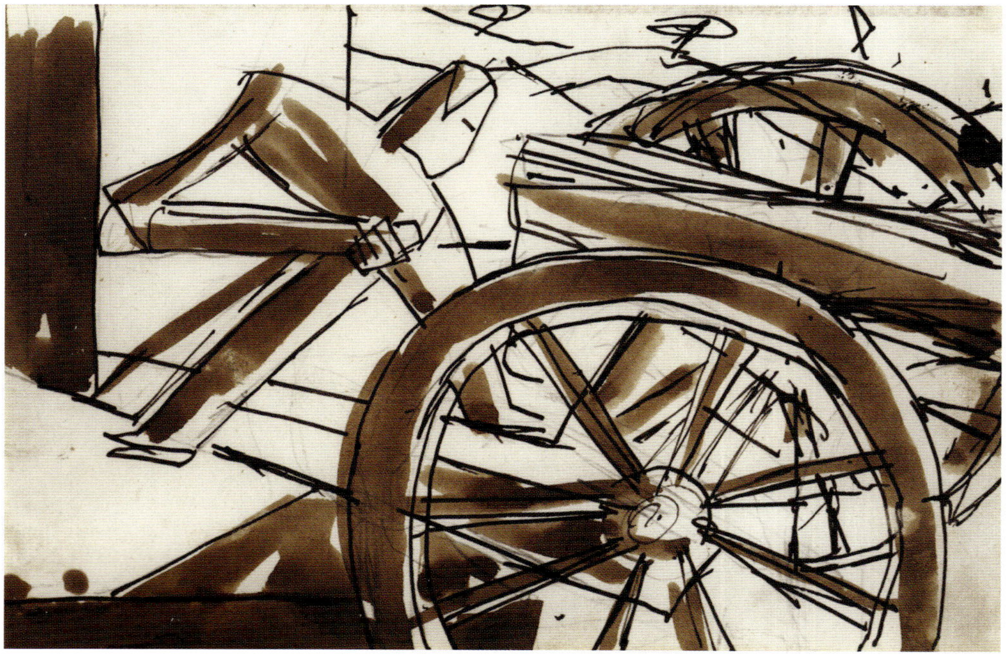

32
DAVID BOMBERG
Gunner Loading Shell, *c.*1918

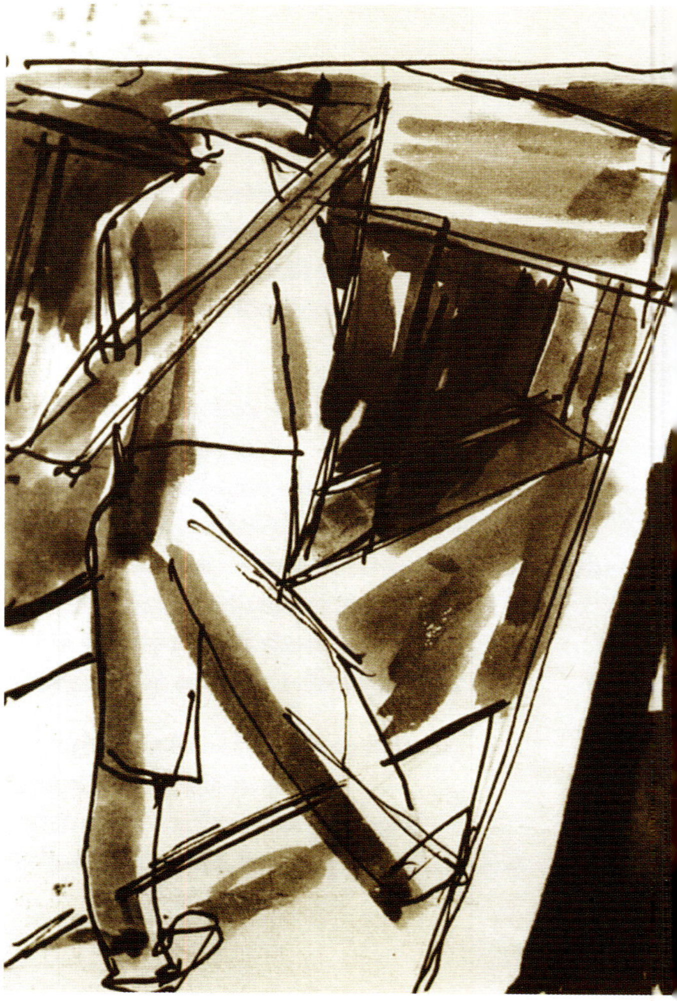

33
DAVID BOMBERG
Soldier Patrolling Tunnel, *c.*1918

vulnerability'[20] of his subjects, the painting was rejected by the art advisor P G Konody[21] who called it a 'futurist abortion'.[22] He painted a second more naturalistic version, which was accepted, but the experience left him deeply disillusioned. The armistice enabled Bomberg to return to painting, although in October 1919 he attempted to have some of his war poems published in *The Athenaeum*. The editor turned him down, but Joseph Leftwich claimed that they were first published (in Yiddish) in *Renesans* in 1920.[23]

Mark Gertler saw only one role for the artist in wartime: 'The best way we can help is to paint,' he wrote to Carrington.[24] Like the writers John Rodker and Stephen Winsten, he recoiled at the suggestion of fighting, calling it 'wretched sordid Butchery!!'[25] and as the war progressed his attitude hardened, particularly as he began to mix with members of the pacifist Bloomsbury set in London and with Lady Ottoline Morrell's wider circle of artists and writers at Garsington. There, pacifism was 'not only respectable but the orthodox religion'[26] and its supporters included the 'most notorious'[27] pacifists of the age: Lytton Strachey, D H Lawrence and Bertrand Russell who, on his return from lecturing in the United States at the outbreak of war, became the leading member of the 'No Conscription Fellowship' and spoke out publicly against the war. The Morrells' own pacifism was well known. As Liberal MP for Burnley, Philip Morrell had made a speech against Britain's involvement in the war in the House of Commons in August 1914, and was one of 30 Liberal MPs who insisted on including a clause of exemption for pacifists when the Military Service Act was passed in 1916. From then on Garsington swarmed with conscientious objectors sent to carry out work of 'national importance' on the farm.

In October 1915 Gertler broke with his (and Rosenberg's) patron Eddie Marsh, secretary to Winston Churchill in the Admiralty, over their differing attitudes to the war. 'Since the war,' he explained:

> You have gone in one direction and I in another. All the time I have been stifling my feelings. Firstly because of your kindness to me and secondly I did not want to hurt you. I am I believe what you call a 'Passivist'. I don't know exactly what that means, but I just hate this war and should really loathe to help in it.[28]

After the sinking of the Lusitania in May 1915[29], patriotic fever began to mount and by the autumn of that year, when Rosenberg and Bomberg joined up, 'atrocity rumours' were being used to blacken the enemy. Conservative critics like Sir Claude Phillips of the *Daily Telegraph* headed the campaign against radical art: 'Less than ever,' Phillips fulminated, 'do we feel inclined to look on with equanimity at these pranks in the domain of art, by which in piping times of peace it was possible to be mildly interested, or at any rate amused.'[30]

It was in this climate that Gertler exhibited his Blake-inspired *The Creation of Eve* (1914)[31] at the London Group's third show in November 1915, where it created public 'uproar!' and sent the critics 'quite mad with rage. God knows what they are wild about,' he wrote in genuine bewilderment,[32] and was astonished to find that 'some people in a rage [had] stuck a label on the belly of my poor little "Eve" with "Made in Germany" written on it!'.[33] The painting was dismissed by the *Daily Telegraph* as 'a deliberate piece of eccentricity'[34], declared 'unpleasantly sensationalist' by the *Observer*, condemned as 'merely a piece of impertinence, with a seasoning of blasphemy' by the *Pall Mall Gazette*, and finally damned as 'hunnishly indecent' by the *Morning Post*.[35] These criticisms, along with his German-sounding name, apparently linked Gertler's work to the 'sinister foreign subversion of British culture' suspected to be behind all experimental art in this period.

Following the introduction of the Military Service Act, Gertler presented himself 'trembling in every limb' at the local tribunal and recruiting office, only to be refused on account of his Austrian parentage.[36] 'What luck!' he told Dorothy Brett, 'now I am free to go on with my work. Perhaps some day "My Country" will thank God for my Austrian parentage which

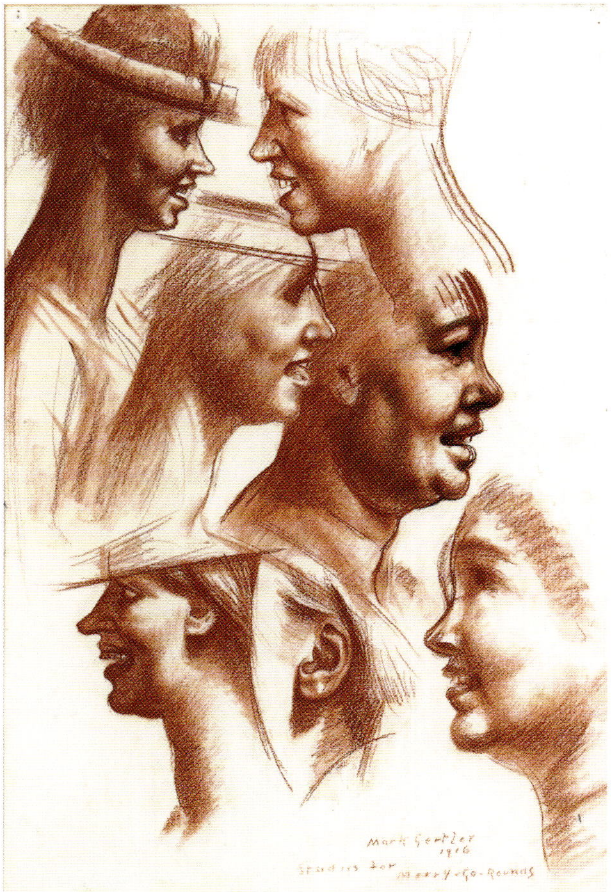

36
MARK GERTLER
Study for the Merry-go-round (aka *Studies of Heads*), 1916

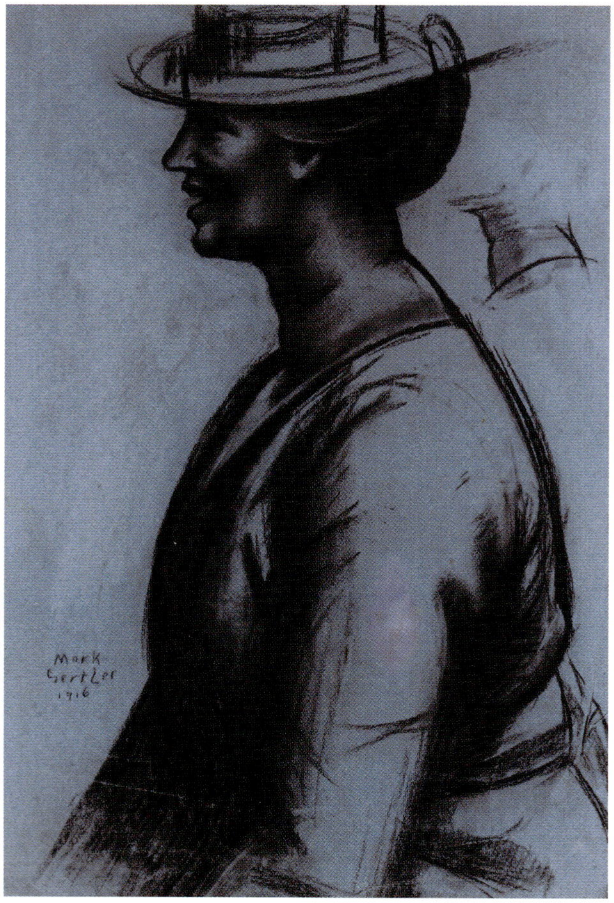

37
MARK GERTLER
Study for the Merry-go-round (aka *The Straw Hat*), 1916

enabled me to sit quiet and paint.'[37] The result was Gertler's savage anti-war masterpiece *Merry-Go-Round* (1916, fig. 16), his outstanding contribution to early British modernism, a nightmare vision of a carousel frozen in motion, the mouths of its riders (uniformed soldiers and their wives and sweethearts) opened in a long, unending scream. Strident oranges, yellows, reds and blues heighten the painting's dominant atmosphere of terror and violence, and it was immediately recognised by Gertler's circle as a satire on militarism.

Originally inspired by the Mayday fair on Hampstead Heath in 1915, but transformed into a metaphor for the futility and violence of war, the painting combines a pacifist vision of cultural disintegration with one of personal despair at Gertler's unhappy affair with Carrington (who would shortly leave him for the homosexual writer Lytton Strachey). Its strident colour scheme and mechanistic imagery also shows an awareness of Futurism and Vorticism, probably filtered through Bomberg and C R W Nevinson.

Gertler worked on studies for the painting throughout 1915–16. As 'war fear'[38] began to grip the nation, the image of the funfair became more sinister. During the many months it took to complete *Merry-Go-Round*, Gertler refused to show the canvas to anyone, including Vanessa Bell who called at his studio in March. As he added the finishing touches to the canvas, his pessimism increased: 'Lately', he wrote in May 1916, 'the whole horror of the War has come freshly upon me.'[39] He was worried by rumours that civilians were now being stopped on the London streets and asked to explain why they were not in uniform. Two carefully executed drawings of head and figure studies (cat nos. 36 and 37) reveal how Gertler's original conception darkened in the intervening months and in the finished canvas the figures of the riders have been pushed into caricature.

'Oh Lord, oh Lord, Have Mercy upon us! It is a devastating affair isn't it?' Lytton Strachey famously wrote after viewing the finished work in Gertler's studio. 'I felt that if I were to look at it for any length of time, I should be carried away suffering from shellshock. I admired it, of course, but as for *liking* it, one might as well think of liking a machine gun.'[40] After the reception of *The Creation of Eve*, Gertler's friend the lawyer (Jack) St John Hutchinson, who had already befriended and legally represented several conscientious objectors, worried that *Merry-Go-Round* would 'raise a tremendous outcry. The old, the wise, the professional critic will go mad with righteous indignation,' he predicted. 'And what strikes me is that these symptoms may drive them to write all sorts of rubbish about German art and German artists in their papers and may raise the question acutely and publicly as to your position.'[41] He advised Gertler that it might not be 'quite wise' to exhibit the picture at the Goupil Gallery and suggested a private showing instead. When Gertler did finally exhibit *Merry-Go-Round* at the London Group the following spring, despite attracting headlines such as 'THE MAN WHO HAS PAINTED A NOISE!',[42] the critics failed to detect its anti-militarism, and the question of Gertler's pacifism was not raised.

Gertler was finally called up in the last year of war and ordered to present himself at the headquarters of the Colours regiment on 4 March 1918. He told friends he had 'a conscientious objection to *fighting*,'[43] but Jack Hutchinson, together with Gertler's patron Monty Shearman, advised him to fill in an appeal form, objecting instead on the grounds of his Austrian parentage. At the local tribunal Gertler was told that his claim for exemption would be laid aside pending a medical examination and, to his great surprise, was rejected as 'medically unfit',[44] though it is not clear on exactly what grounds.[45] Like many of his Bloomsbury acquaintances, he was subsequently assigned to carry out work of 'national importance' on the Morrells' Garsington farm.

Gertler learned almost immediately of his probable commission as an Official War Artist,[46] which was confirmed in May by Alfred Yockney, secretary to the Official War Artists' scheme in Britain.[47] The scheme, which had been established in 1916, was run by a committee who advised the Ministry of Information on suitable appointments. William Rothenstein was among those commissioned in 1917, and later, in 1918, Richard (Dick) Carline at 22 would become the youngest of the commissioned war artists. It was these appointments from the younger ranks of British artists – among them C R W Nevinson, Paul Nash, William Roberts and Dick Carline's brother Sydney – that finally ignited Gertler's latent enthusiasm for the project. Once he learned that 'only young and modern painters have been chosen! Not a single RA!' he decided to accept 'on principle', because

> I look upon this as something very significant, I mean, that a more or less official committee, representing the Government should do this! And so strong is it, that they are actually withdrawing people like [Stanley] Spencer and 'Bobby' [William Roberts] from the Front! [...]. Yes, about Painting I am *Patriotic*![48]

In practice, this meant signing on with the committee for an initial six months, and painting at least one picture on a given subject. Gertler's was 'Air Raid Night in the Tube' – a subject for which he was well-qualified: during the relentless Zeppelin raids on London the previous autumn he had spent many nights in the basement 'listening to the almost continuous shriek and boombing [*sic*] of Guns.' The tube, he noted was 'crambed [*sic*] full of poor panic stricken people' taking shelter while London was 'almost continuously under fire.'[49] But when invited to the Ministry of Information to discuss the project, Gertler was dismayed by their restrictions (a preparatory sketch had first to be approved and even the size of the canvas – 'about 10 feet' – had already been stipulated). These restraints played on his fears about a lack of control to such a degree, that they quickly withered his initial enthusiasm,[50] and after a severe attack of depression he left the committee's original letter unanswered and his commission unfulfilled. Eventually it was cancelled, and *Merry-Go-Round* remains Gertler's only memorial to the First World War.[51]

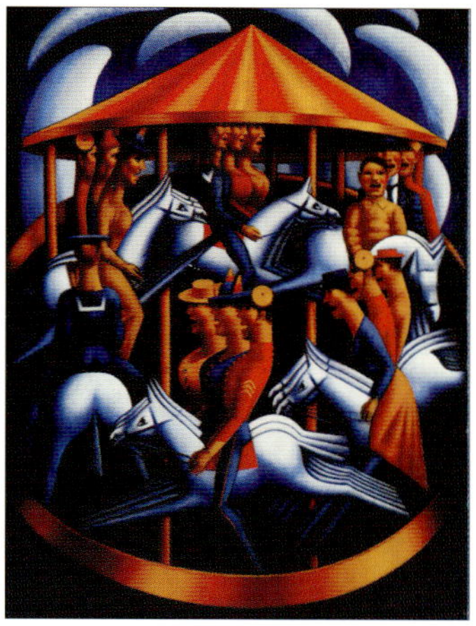

FIG. 16
MARK GERTLER
Merry-Go-Round, 1916

Ukrainian-born, but brought up in Liverpool prior to studying at the Slade through a JEAS grant, Bernard Meninsky was one of the first of the Whitechapel Boys to enlist. Although their eventual wartime experiences (and the final outcome) could not be more different, Meninsky, as his biographer John Russell Taylor suggests, probably joined up for similar reasons to Rosenberg – lack of work, no real prospects as a painter and a consciousness of standing out while others fought. A number of Meninsky's artist contemporaries, including the brothers Paul and John Nash and Charles Sargeant Jagger enlisted in the Artists' Rifles, but Meninsky, like many young men of Jewish descent, joined the Royal Fusiliers instead. Based in Plymouth, Meninsky passed an unremarkable and entirely dull war.

Naturalised as a British citizen during the last months of the War, Meninsky was finally invalided out in August 1918 due to neurasthenia, and offered a position as a Ministry of Information War Artist. Unlike Gertler, Meninsky clearly found no artistic conflict in creating such tightly controlled works whose images were no longer considered primarily as a contribution to propaganda but, rather, as a visual record. He accepted a contract of work under 'Scheme B', whereby the artist was 'put under exclusive contract for a period (six months minimum) and paid £300 a year for his pains (in addition to his military pay if he was still in service) as well as all his expenses.'[52] It may not have been as lucrative or as prestigious as the scheme for major commissions, but the resulting 'typical London scenes, during and after the arrival of a leave train from the front' (the brief given to Meninsky) including *On the Departure Platform, Victoria Station* (cat no. 42) and *Soldiers Arriving on Leave* (cat no. 41), are some of his most striking works. However, unlike his moving series of *Mother and Child* drawings from the same period, Meninsky's military scenes – probably because of his indirect experience of the conflict – seem curiously devoid of emotion. Sculptural and frieze-like, his soldiers appear to form a solid mass of limbs as they loiter on station platforms, while their faces are often turned away from the viewer, their expressions sketchy. One has the sense of a scene recorded but not *felt*.

Of the remaining Whitechapel Boys, all of the original writers were pacifists: John Rodker went on the run, sheltering with the poet R C Trevelyan, but was eventually captured and imprisoned in Dartmoor. Although Rosenberg could not have been present, intriguingly he drew a rough sketch of Rodker's arrest in south London on the back of a letter to Edward Marsh (cat no. 47). Stephen Winsten was probably imprisoned soon after his tribunal in 1916 and was taken first to Wormwood Scrubs then transferred to Wandsworth and still later to Bedford Prison for the remainder of the war. Both men underwent a number of privations and Rodker (certainly) and Winsten (probably) went on hunger strike. Both would later draw on their experiences in their writing: Rodker in

41
BERNARD MENINSKY
Sketch of Soldiers Arriving on Leave, 1918

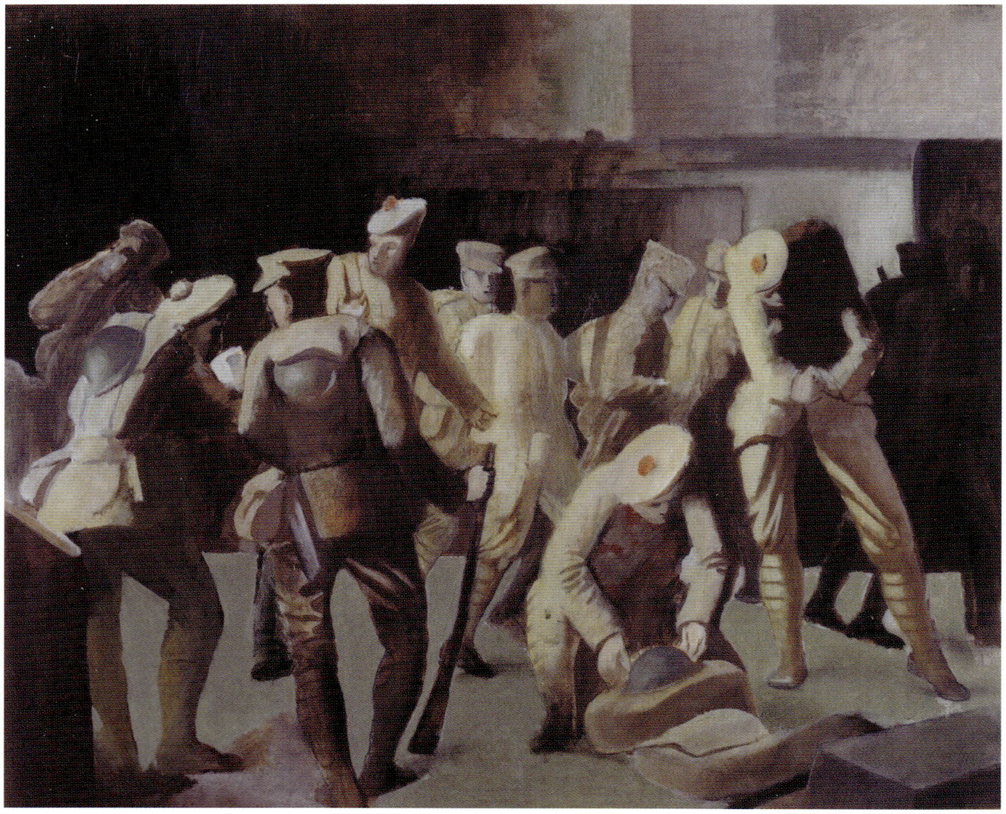

Memoirs of Other Fronts (1932)[53] and Winsten in his collection of poems, *Chains* (1920).[54]

Leftwich, who was not called up because of his Dutch birth, remained in Whitechapel, participating in a number of literary 'little magazines',[55] writing poetry and becoming a pivotal force in the setting up of two important home-grown Jewish cultural societies: the Ben Uri Art Society and the Jewish Association for Advancement in Arts and Sciences (JAAAS), both founded within weeks of each other in July 1915.

Although he was certainly in England at the time, Rosenberg was apparently not among those Whitechapel Boys present at the founding of the JAAAS. 'Open to Jewish Men and Women engaged in the Arts and Sciences', it was a forum for debate and mutual support. With the stated aim of 'focussing talent among Jews', it became known among its members as 'the Focussers'. At its inaugural meeting held at Toynbee Hall on 23 July 1915 to drum up grassroots support, nearly 100 members signed up, among them several from the ranks of the Whitechapel Boys, including Wolmark, Bomberg, Wayner, Leftwich, Rodker and Stephen Winsten, with Wayner and Rodker appointed to the provisional committee, Leftwich appointed Society Secretary and Wolmark elected Vice-President.[56] Subsequent meetings were held further west, with art classes hosted by Wolmark (who by August 1916 had become President) in his own home. Despite the enthusiasm of the Whitechapel Boys, the society seems to have foundered after 1917, when, tellingly, Wolmark began to use the unfilled pages of the membership book as his personal address book. By December 1917, when

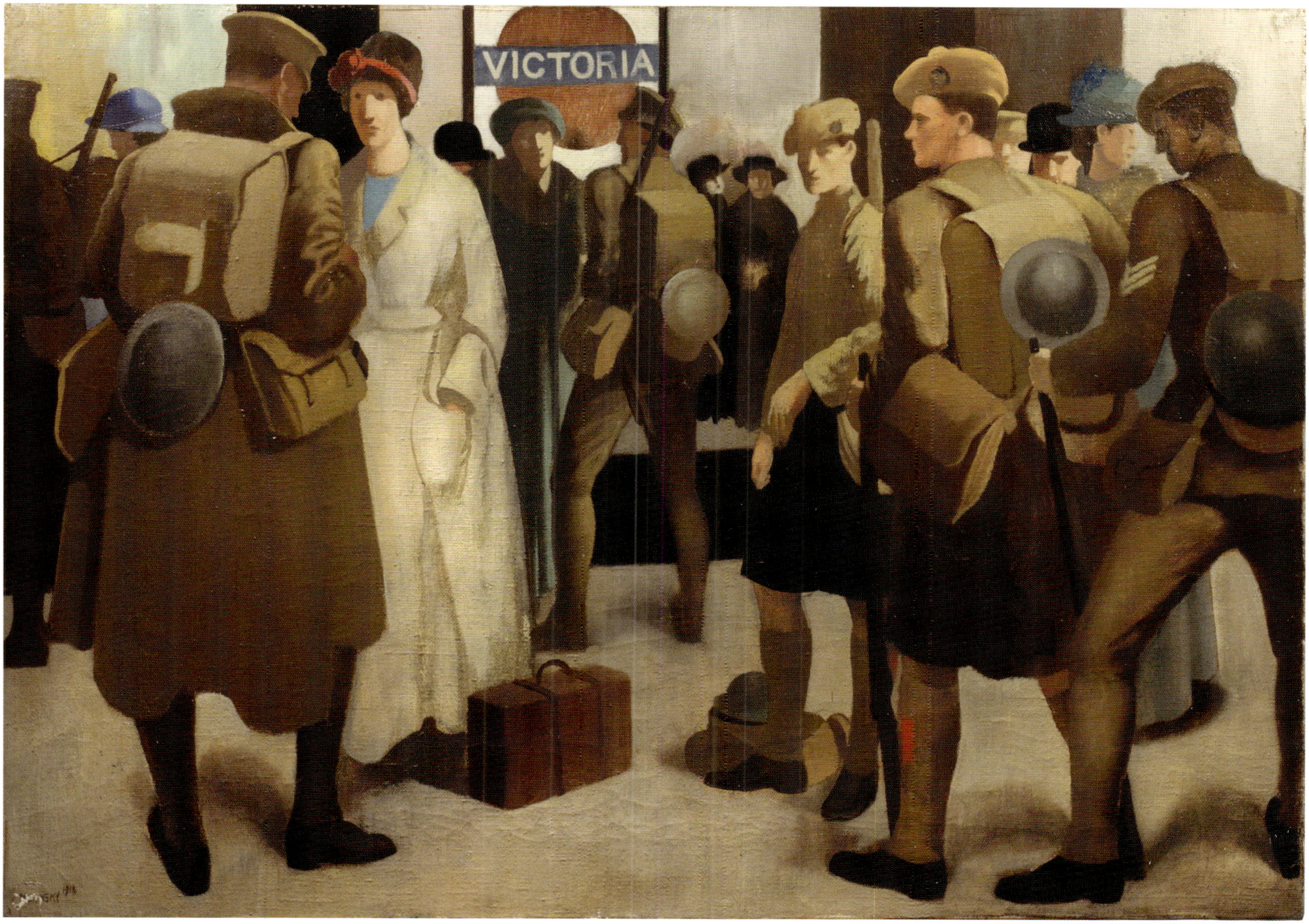

42
BERNARD MENINSKY
On the Departure Platform Victoria Station, 1918

Leftwich wrote to Rosenberg at the Front to try to enlist his support, the JAAAS was in trouble, overwhelmed by the 'exigencies' of war. Rosenberg showed a decided ambivalence towards joining the society, writing to Leftwich: 'Whats the idea of my joining your J affair, its no use to me out here, is it? Besides after the war, if things go well – I doubt whether I'd live in London. But you can put me down if you like.'[57]

From the older generation of Whitechapel Boys, Wolmark (37 at the outbreak of war) was officially 'passed as medically unfit for military service'[58] in 1915 owing to 'severe myopia'.[59] *Colour* magazine, to which he contributed prodigiously, featured a number of his striking colourist and poster-like paintings of uniformed officers (figs. 31 and 32).[60] One of them was a portrait of Norman Kohnstamm, the elder son of Wolmark's patrons, who was subsequently killed in action in France on 22 March 1918.[61] Despite not seeing active service, Wolmark had been concerned with war imagery since the first year of the war. In contrast to the single figure, formally posed, his painting *Soldiers Marching in Snow* (1915) depicts a soldier with shining helmet and rifle over whose shoulder marches a long file moving right, all in pale purple uniforms against a white ground and yellow sky, a scene perhaps inspired by a photograph but interpreted through Wolmark's unmistakeable colourist style.[62]

However his personal response to the war is best summed up by his large-scale canvas *The Medical Inspection* (fig. 33).[63] Wolmark made several attempts at this subject, and the large resulting canvas, finally completed in 1919,[64] with its strange palette of greens, purples and oranges, surely reflects not only his personal experience in undergoing a humiliating examination, but his considered reflection on the horrors of war: the smell of gas, bruised flesh, humanity stripped of any dignity.

Kramer, a Russian Jew and, since his father's death in May 1916, the sole breadwinner in his family, avoided joining up until the last months of the war. Despite his imposing physical presence, he was often in poor health and anxious that 'the ordinary routine of military work will affect me a great deal [...] having suffered from bad nerves for such a long time and at the same [time] being a grade III man on account of my eyesight'.[65]

Nevertheless, in early October 1918 Kramer was finally sent to distributing camp in Ripon to await his posting to a Russian Labour Camp in Wales. Deeply unhappy at his circumstances, Kramer wrote to Herbert Read again, anxiously asking for his help in arranging a more congenial placement. Remarkably, Read's written request to Kramer's commanding officer resulted in his becoming a regimental librarian with enough time to draw and paint a little (cat nos. 38 and 39):

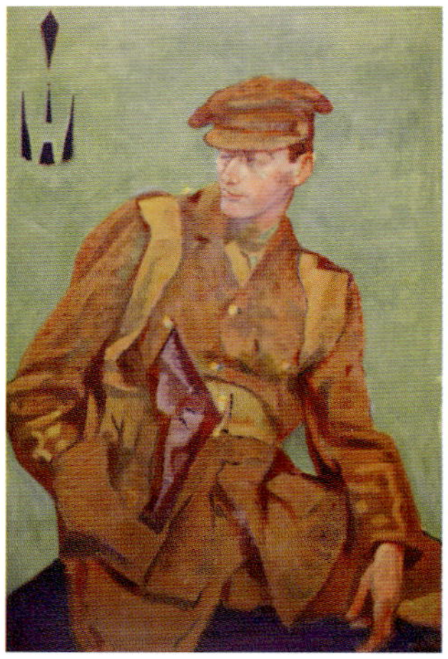

FIG. 31 *right*
ALFRED WOLMARK
Portrait of Norman Kohnstamm, *c.*1917

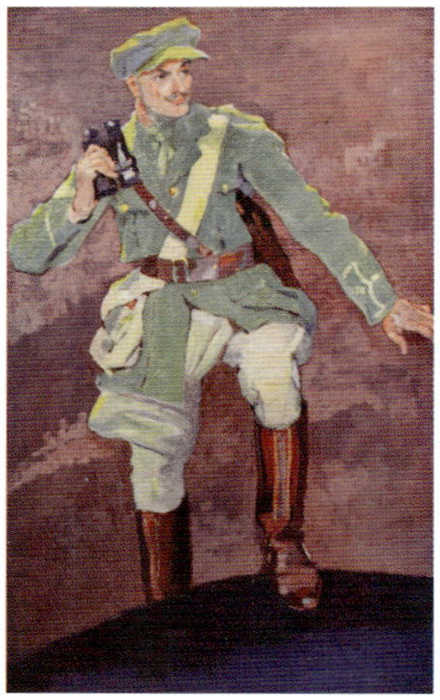

FIG. 32 *far right*
ALFRED WOLMARK
Soldier, *c.*1917

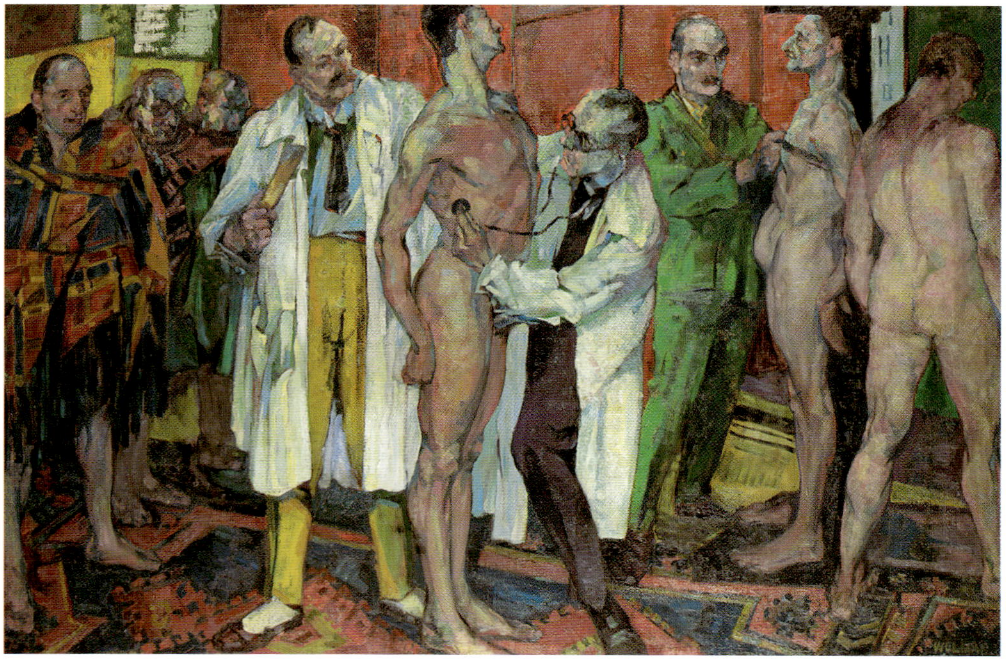

FIG. 33 *below*
ALFRED WOLMARK
The Medical Inspection, *c.*1919

> The Colonel is going to sit for me for a drawing and has been very much interested in my work – yesterday when I met him we had a discussion on the modern movement of art, and I am glad to say he liked my picture of 'the Jew' [...] if not for you I should have gone quite mad by the work I have done before – even now I feel the effects of the work I have done as when I hold a pencil my hands seem to tremble. However I am alright now and quite happy. I am beginning a series of compositions of military life – some day you must see them. They are done in ink and make quite interesting designs.[66]

Read replied with a salient piece of advice to Kramer the artist, applicable to each of the Whitechapel Boys: 'I expect you will gradually become indifferent to all the vulgarity and coarseness about you. And this good you will get out of it – You will come into contact with types of life which otherwise would have been unknown to you, and that is always valuable to an artist.'[67]

For the Whitechapel Boys, the war years and, for some, the direct experience of fighting provided a tremendous impetus to create work outside of the 'ghetto'. The war itself was, ironically, a fertile period – a critical event, as Read suggested – marked by the range of individual experiences and responses, where often one set of hardships was exchanged for another. All suffered financially and many of them physically, but only Rosenberg made the 'ultimate sacrifice'. Moreover, although he curtailed his painting career, in the little time he had, Rosenberg refocused his energies into poetry: 'determined that this war, with all its powers for devastation, shall not master my poeting; that is, if I am lucky enough to come through all right. I will not leave a corner of my consciousness covered up, but saturate myself with the strange and extraordinary new conditions of this life, and it will all refine itself into poetry later on.'[68]

The war undeniably cast a shadow over the life and work of the surviving Whitechapel Boys, and left an abiding sense of disillusionment, particularly among the artists. Bomberg, Gertler and Kramer each subsequently created a key work which expressed this sense of disenchantment and anticipated the

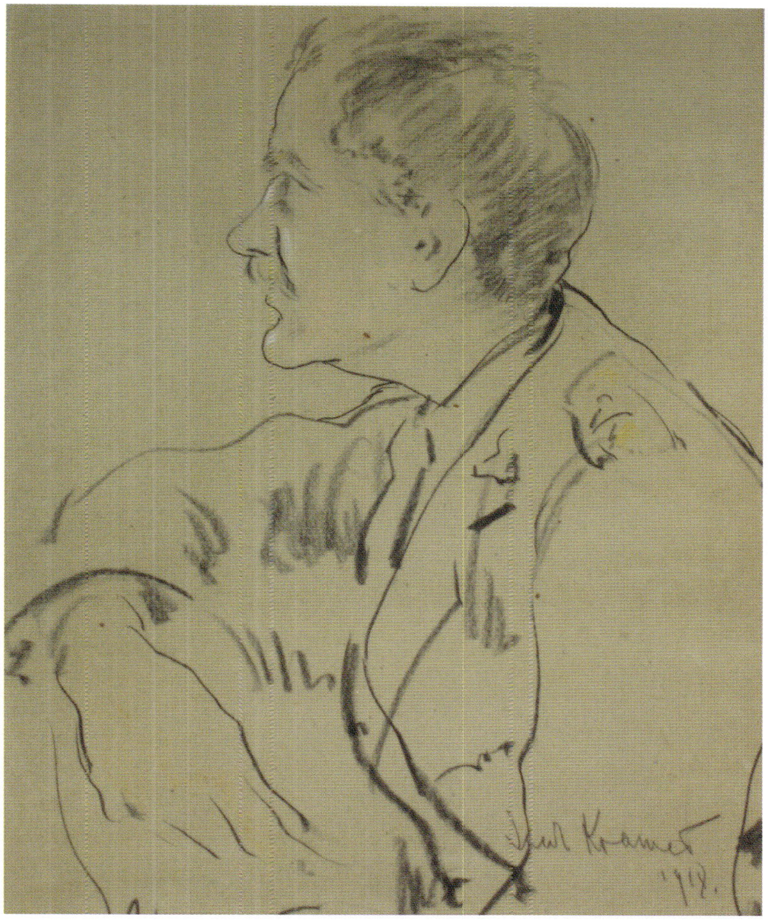

38
JACOB KRAMER
Military Portrait, 1918

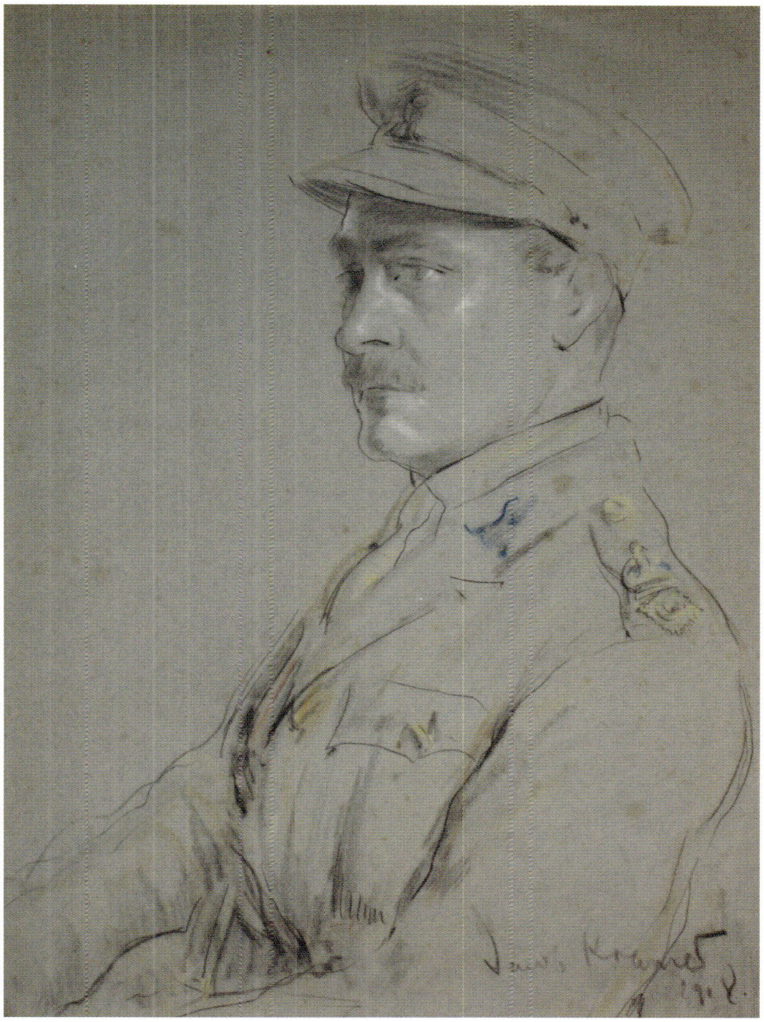

39
JACOB KRAMER
Military Portrait (with cap), 1918

49

ISAAC ROSENBERG

A Merry Xmas from the 40th: Design for a Christmas Card 1917

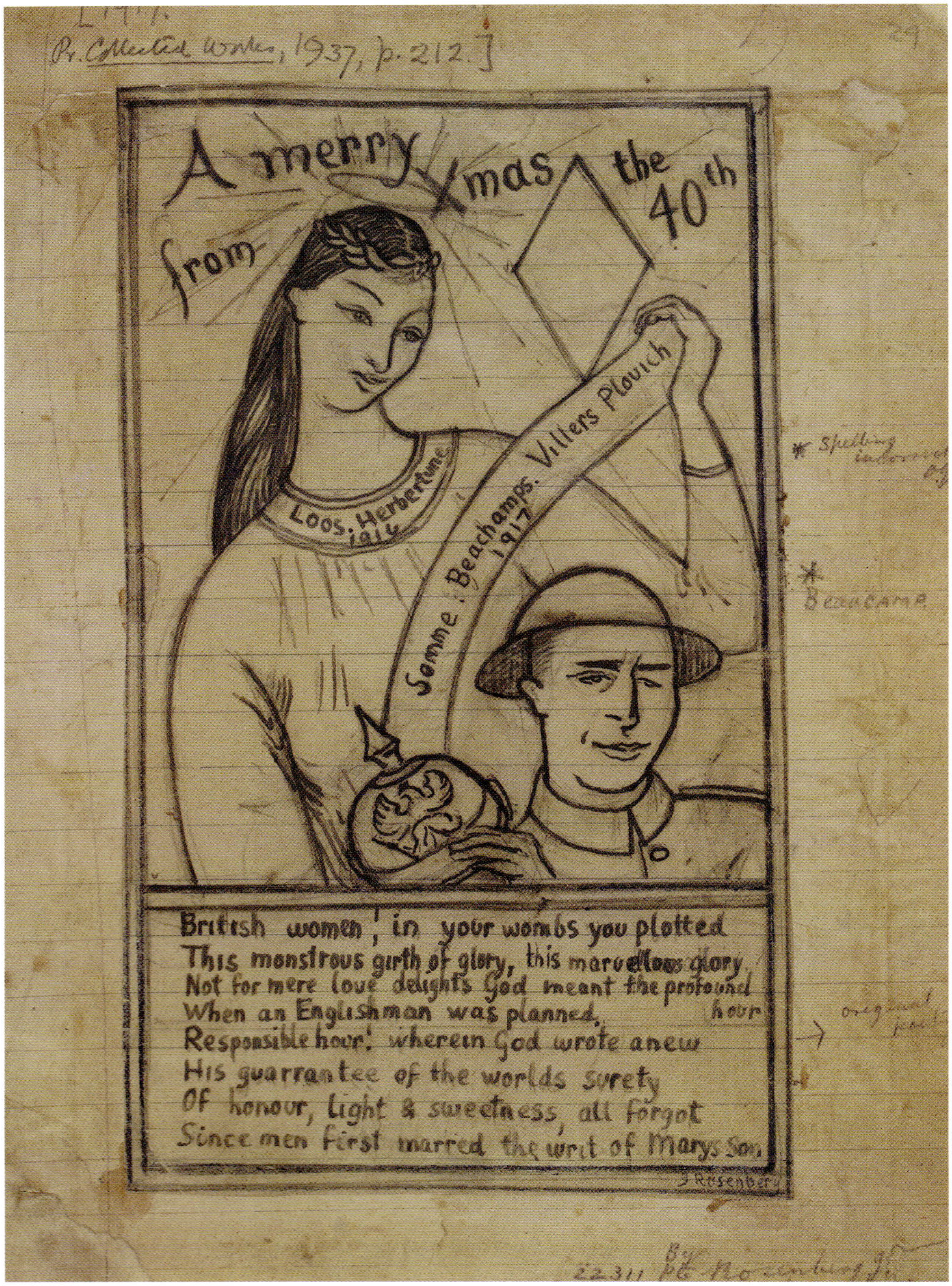

challenges of the new decade. Bomberg, who briefly returned to the East End, also returned to a familiar source of inspiration – the Jewish theatre – to reflect his increasing sense of isolation. *Ghetto Theatre* (1920),[69] a painting of dark, savage brilliance, depicts a joyless East-End Jewish theatre audience separated both from each other and the viewer by the imposing physical presence of the balcony rail. Their drab clothes, mask-like faces and closed body language not only express their sense of unfulfilled expectations but also prohibit any contact between them. The hunched figure of a man in the upper left foreground, leaning wearily on a stick, is symptomatic of Bomberg's dismal, post-war vision. Painted on the eve of his departure from the East End, it reveals that for him, the area was no longer a place of excitement and vitality.

Gertler, who had moved to Hampstead in 1915, in an attempt to deliberately throw off his roots, would never return to the East End. His troubled, introspective *Self-Portrait* (1920)[70] anticipates the diagnosis of tuberculosis, which, together with severe depression, frequently confined him to sanatoria throughout the next two decades.

Kramer created *The Day of Atonement*,[71] his seminal work in the canon of Anglo-Jewish art, within nine months of the armistice. His sense of alienation and his return to Leeds was perhaps intensified by his non-participation in the war. Nevertheless, the extended line of sightless, praying figures perhaps owes something to the sentiments conveyed in Rosenberg's powerful poem 'Marching':

> Like flaming pendulums, hands
> Swing across khaki –
> Mustard-coloured khaki –
> To the automatic feet.

Although the conflict served to scatter the group geographically, a spirit of co-operation and friendship remained between them. In the following decade, Bomberg, Gertler, Kramer, Brodzky and Meninsky (who was elected in 1919), all met as members of the London Group. Many also went on to participate in the 'little magazines' of the period and, almost all of them came together as part of the Ben Uri, the Jewish Art Society 'whose abiding influence permeate[s] far beyond their original aspirations almost 100 years later'.[72]

5

FIRST FRUITS
ISAAC ROSENBERG AND HIS CIRCLE IN PRINT

'Young writers desirous of making a footing in the world of literature will find this magazine the best means for communicating their first fruits in [sic] the world.'
REUBEN COHEN *The Jewish Standard*, 1 July 1915

Away from the grand gesture of the public venue and the rarefied atmosphere of the art gallery, 'little magazines',[1] as recent research has demonstrated, have become an increasingly valuable resource in documenting the development of modernism from the late nineteenth century through to the first decades of the twentieth century. Functioning somewhere between newspapers, critical art and literary journals, and the newly-coloured 'glossy' magazines (some like *Colour* were glossier than others), these publications, as the Modernist Magazine Project[2] suggests, provided 'an indispensable forum for modernist innovation and debate. They helped sustain small artistic communities, strengthened the resolve of small iconoclastic groups, keen to change the world, and gave many major modernists their first opportunities in print.'[3]

In a climate where anti-Semitism still lingered, these magazines, with their openness to material regardless of the identity of the contributor, became immensely fertile ground for the Whitechapel Boys, with the same roster of names appearing regularly across a range of publications: Bomberg, Gertler, Kramer, Leftwich, Meninsky, Rodker, Rosenberg and Winsten. As Leftwich recalled in a Ben Uri publication many years later, 'we all began to contribute to English literary magazines; Rosenberg, Rodker and I to *Colour*, Bomberg to *Blast*, Wyndham Lewis' Vorticist journal, Rodker to the *Egoist* [...] There was *Voices*, edited by Tom Moult where Louis Golding got his first work published.'[4] In the same article he described the various intersecting groups which made up the Whitechapel Boys: 'each was self-contained, but most of us knew each other, and sometimes we overlapped. Somehow we all linked together.'[5] This observation applies as much to the presence of the Whitechapel Boys in the 'little magazines' of the period as in their everyday lives.

The 'little magazines' were mostly small, independent ventures committed to new and experimental work across both literary and visual canons. Published monthly, quarterly or sporadically, some lasted for a single issue, others for more than a decade, morphing from one publication into another. They were often marked by fluidity in editorship and in contributors: the editor of one publication might contribute to a second and criticise a third. For example, *Art & Letters* (1917–20), initially founded by Herbert Read (1893–1968), Kramer's youthful mentor from Leeds) and Frank Rutter (1876–1937), Director of the Leeds City Art Gallery (1912–17) and founder of the Allied Artists' Association (AAA), was variously co-edited by Read, Rutter, Osbert Sitwell, Harold

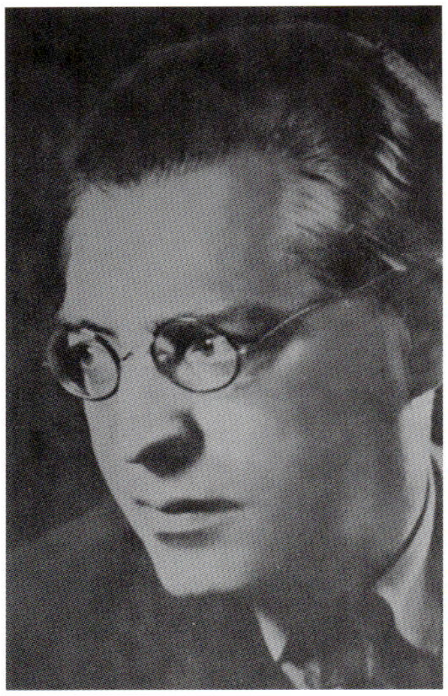

FIG. 52
Joseph Leftwich, 1937

Gilman and Charles Ginner, who were also all contributors. Rutter himself had previously edited *Art News*, the journal of the AAA (1909–15). Similarly, *New Paths: Verse, Prose, Pictures 1917–18* was co-edited by the publisher and writer C W Beaumont and M T H Sadler (the son of Kramer's earliest patron Michael Sadler, Vice–Chancellor of Leeds University and noted collector of modern art). Sadler *fils*, together with Scottish colourist J D Fergusson, had previously assisted editor John Middleton Murry at the birth of the avant-garde magazine *Rhythm* (1911–13), which showcased the work of many of the painters later associated with Vorticism.[6]

These magazines flourished not only because of this ready pool of energetic and visionary editors and contributors, but also through the increased use of images, both black-and-white and colour, bolstered by advances in photolithography techniques. A number of publications, such as *Colour* and its sister magazine *The Apple*, further encouraged artists to offer original artwork for sale, unusually taking no commission. Moreover, their formats were chosen to do justice to their art work. It was noted, for example, that 'the generous measurement' of *The Apple*'s pages, 'comparable in size to the long defunct *Form*', allowed for 'the reproduction of contemporary crayon and ink drawings with little or no reduction from the original', so that, it was claimed 'in this department *The Apple* takes at once the first place among contemporary art-journals, as *Colour* has held first place in regard to reproduction of paintings.'[7]

The rise of advertising also ensured a steady stream of revenue as well as a rich (if sometimes unintentionally humorous) juxtaposition of content. In Cohen and Rosenberg's collaboration, *Jewish Standard* in July 1915, Rosenberg's essays on 'Art'[8] are sandwiched between Cohen's articles on a variety of subjects, ranging from 'the condition of the Palestine Colonies' to 'the price of bread' and 'the needs of the incurable consumptive', the latter interspersed with adverts for humble, local East End goods and services such as 'Ben's Hairdressing' and 'Simco Flour'. Similarly, both *Renesans*, the Yiddish cultural journal which was supported by the Ben Uri Arts Society, and *Voices*, regularly carried adverts for Edward Good's 'Cameo Corner', a jewellery business belonging to one of the Ben Uri's founders, which claimed to offer 'all sorts of barbaric and beautiful things […] at prices within reach of all'.[9] Meanwhile, the modernist images of the artist contributors spilled over into the advertisements, with Elspeth Phelps Ltd of Albermarle Street using a simple, Modigliani-like outline of the 'modern woman', with bobbed hair and bare shoulders, to advertise 'Alluring clothes'.[10]

The war years, with the rationing of paper, showed no marked decrease in this flurry of publishing activity. Indeed, shortages could be made into a positive selling-point. In the pages of the June 1918 issue of *Art and Letters*[11] an advert for the forthcoming *New Paths* declared that its planned 7s 6d edition (as distinct from the numbered *Special Edition*) would be strictly limited (and, therefore, surely more desirable), 'owing to shortage of materials'. (The difference between *New Paths* and the *Jewish Standard's* likely readership was also marked out by the latter's lowly 1d price tag.)

In the first half of 1912 Rosenberg entered the public arena through the medium of print for the first time, and appeared in three publications almost

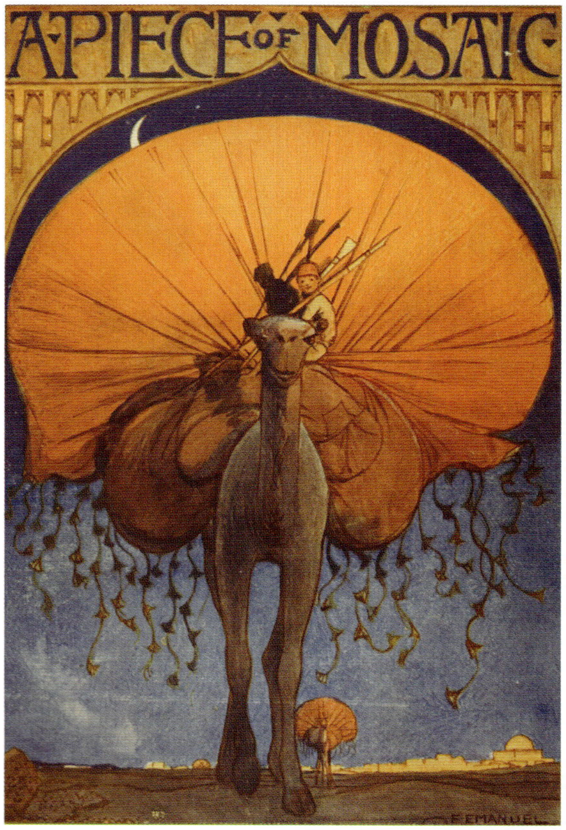

FIG. 15
FRANK EMANUEL
Cover design for A Piece of Mosaic, 1912

simultaneously. His inclusion in *A Piece of Mosaic: being the book of the Palestine Exhibition and Bazaar* (cat no. 60), edited by Cyril Picciotto and C M Kohan and published by T Fisher Unwin[12] in May 1912, probably came about through his friendship with Ruth Löwy (whose first cousin was married to Picciotto). She had suggested in March that Rosenberg send Picciotto samples of his writing. (Rosenberg had been 'very elated at Mr Picciotto liking my poems', though his prose, which Rosenberg himself dismissed as 'an early thing',[13] presumably, by its omission, Picciotto liked less.) However, Rosenberg's inclusion also probably owed something to his guardian Frank Emanuel,[14] who had advised the editors and 'throughout the preparation of this book most generously placed at our disposal the fruits of his taste and artistic experience.'[15]

Rosenberg's poem 'In the Workshop' (which Leftwich recalled hearing and admired), appeared beneath a reproduction of one of his drawings entitled *The Wharf* (fig. 7)[16] – the only occasion during his lifetime that Rosenberg's poetry and art would be published together.

Although *A Piece of Mosaic* functioned as a stand-alone text to accompany the Palestine exhibition and bazaar, which was held for two days in mid-May at the Portman Rooms in London, supported by the great and the good of Anglo-Jewry, the format of literary and artistic contributions was more closely related to that of a 'little magazine' than an exhibition guide. Indeed, Palestine was scarcely mentioned, despite the purpose of the event, as previewed in the *Jewish Chronicle*, 'to promote the industrial life of the Jews and Jewesses of Jerusalem [...] and the beauty and artistic value of the products of the ateliers of the Evalina de Rothschild School of Girls and the Bezalel School for Arts and Crafts.'[17] The paper also took the opportunity to promote *A Piece of Mosaic* as 'a wonderful half crown's worth [...] contain[ing] many notable literary and artistic contributors.'[18] Oddly, though Mark Gertler's name is advertised among the *Chronicle*'s list of contributors and Rosenberg's is omitted, this was reversed in the actual publication. It is not clear whether the paper made an error or whether the editors themselves made the substitution.

Both exhibition and publication were broadly Zionist in outlook, the latter in line with the internationalist views held by the publisher, T Fisher Unwin, although with its curious mixture of prose, poetry, scurrilous verses, fine art images and cartoons, it seemed to adhere little to the theme, besides including the poem 'Bezalel' by Professor Boris Schatz, the founder of the Bezalel School of Arts and Crafts in Jerusalem. Emanuel himself contributed the cover design (fig. 15), depicting an exotic Brangwyn-esque camel train in vivid colour which must have been far removed from the reality of the settlers' new life in the Middle East. Other contributors were drawn

FIG. 7
ISAAC ROSENBERG
The Wharf, 1912

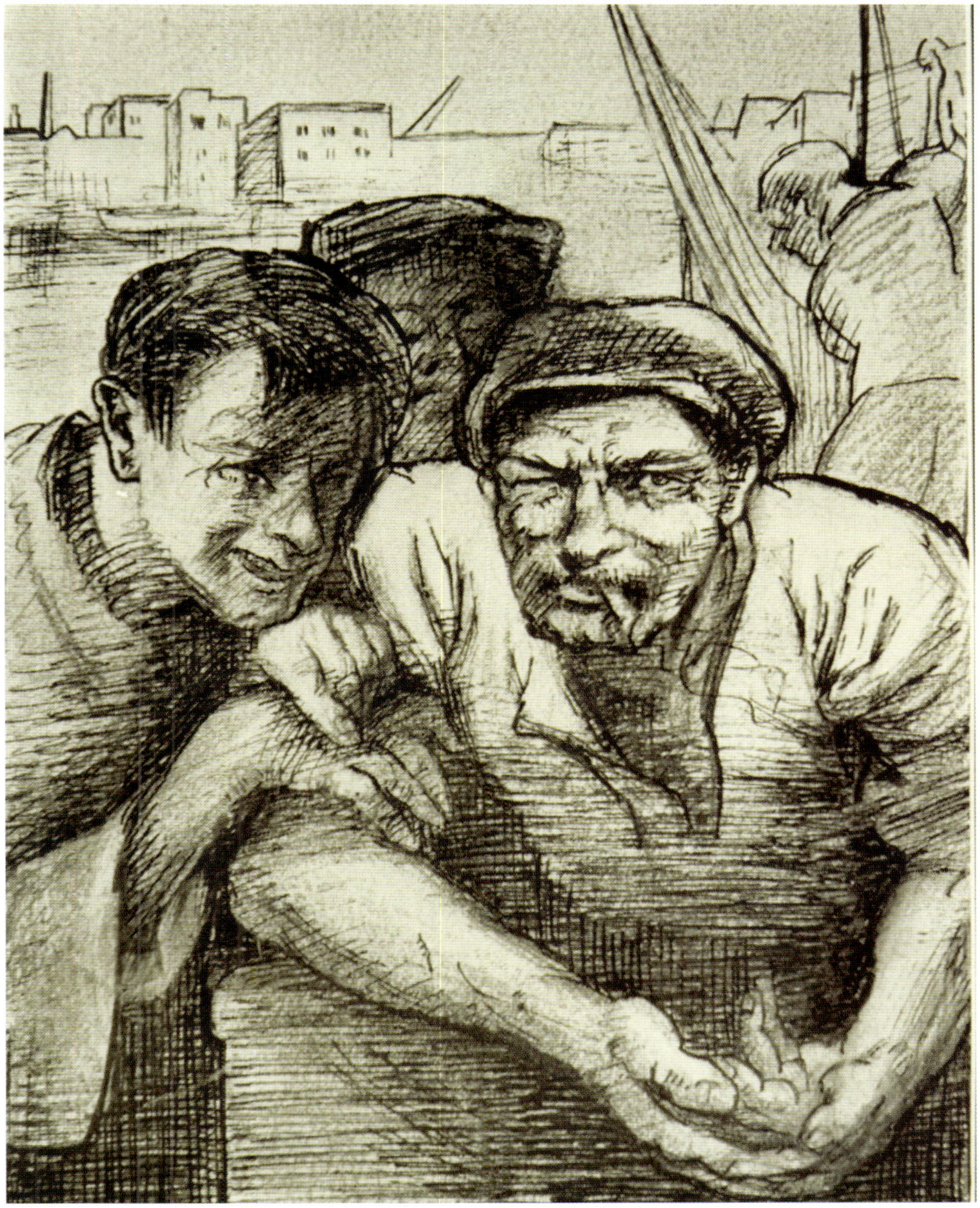

FIG. 54
Israel Narodiczky outside his Print Works, 1910

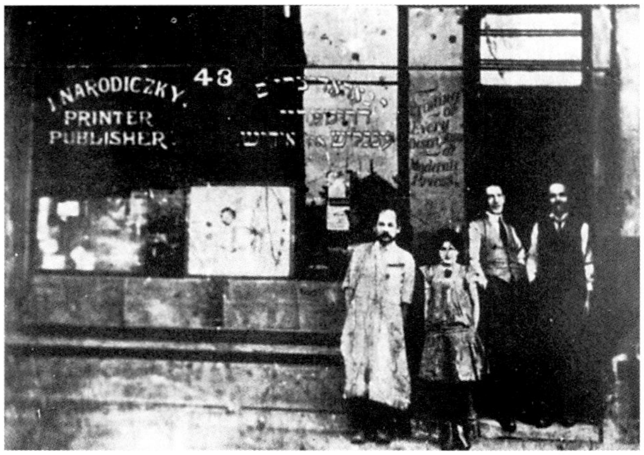

FIG. 51
'Inca' (Stephen Winsten), *c.*1921–22

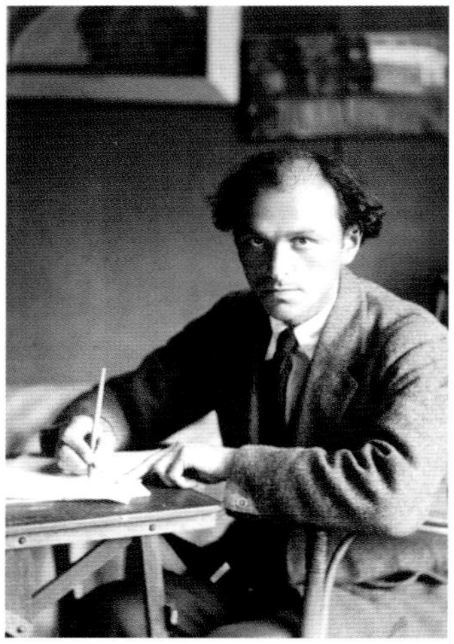

from established names across European and Anglo-Jewish contemporary cultural life, including Israel Zangwill, William and Albert Rothenstein, Arthur Schnitzler, J H Amshewitz, Lucien Pissarro, Solomon J Solomon and Herman Struck, august, if still mainly traditionalist, company for the newly-published Rosenberg, whose drawing was markedly different from the work of the other artist-contributors.

It was also in May 1912 that Rosenberg published his only exhibition review in the *Jewish Chronicle* ('Romance at the Baillie Galleries: The Works of J.H. Amshewitz and the Late H. Ospovat').[19] His main literary project for 1912, however, was the late-spring publication of his 24-page booklet of poems entitled *Night and Day* (cat no. 55), printed locally by Reuben Cohen at Israel Narodiczky's press in the Mile End Road (fig. 54) in an edition of 50. This was to be the first of a number of collaborations between Rosenberg and 'Cohen the printer', also known as 'Crazy' Cohen. A flamboyant character – 'tall and thin, with a flaming red beard' – Cohen had 'pretensions to a career in journalism. He had worked for a number of the small makeshift printshops [sic] in the East End and planned one day to set himself up as a printer, newspaper publisher, poet and tycoon, but he could never make enough money to feed his wife and child, let alone buy machinery for his own shop.'[20]

Israel Narodiczky (1874–1942), Ukrainian born and 'a lifelong Zionist and knowledgeable Hebraist',[21] had trained as a typesetter, publishing works in both Hebrew and Yiddish in his homeland, prior to arriving in Britain in 1896, on an unfinished journey to participate in the South African gold rush. He subsequently set up his unique Hebrew, Yiddish and English printing shop at 48 Mile End Road, providing some of the earliest examples of printed works in Yiddish in England. In 1900 he became the publisher of *Germinal*, the new periodical edited by Rudolph Rocker, the East End-based, German (non-Jewish) promoter of the Jewish workers' movement that so impressed many of the young Whitechapel writers, in particular Leftwich, Rodker and Winsten. Narodiczky's Mile End premises also became an unofficial salon for fellow Russian émigrés to discuss politics and literature. As Narodiczky's bibliographer, Marion Aptroot, comments, 'although he would have preferred to publish only Yiddish and Hebrew books, his main business was commercial printing which was financially more rewarding [...]. He was willing to print anything which he thought not to be racist, pornographic or illegal.'[22] Therefore, when in April 1915, Cohen privately printed Rosenberg's second volume of poems, *Youth* (cat no. 56), financed by the sale of three pictures to Edward Marsh, it emerged from the heterogeneous mix of Yiddish newspapers, theatre posters, political pamphlets and instructions for taking medicine, which all emanated haphazardly from Narodiczky's premises.[23]

Although Aptroot's bibliography omits it, Narodiczky also published in 1915 the three issues of the short-lived literary periodical *The Signature*, edited by D H Lawrence, Katherine Mansfield and John Middleton Murry. Narodiczky was also to become one of the founder-members of the Ben Uri Art Society, printing the *Ben Uri Album* in 1916, a remarkable collection of decorative designs by the Ben Uri's founder, the Russian-born artist Lazar Berson.[24]

On 1 July 1915 Rosenberg and Cohen published their collaboration *Jewish Standard*. Rosenberg modestly contributed the opening paragraphs of his lecture 'Art' which he had originally delivered in South

Africa and had previously published in the magazine *South African Women in Council*.[25] Despite Cohen at the helm, portentously declaring that 'Young writers desirous of making a footing in the world of literature will find this magazine the best means for communicating their first fruits in [sic] the world', the magazine lasted only a single issue. (Nevertheless, the notion of 'first fruit' must have found some resonance, since the following year, while on active service, Rosenberg wrote a poem of the same title.)

On 19 May 1916, during Rosenberg's six days' embarkation leave, Cohen also printed Rosenberg's final work, his play *Moses* (cat no. 48) on Narodiczky's press but under the name 'Paragon Printing Works'.

Founded in the summer of 1914 just prior to the outbreak of war, the glossy monthly magazine *Colour* was designed to showcase the relatively new (to England) process of full-colour printing. Although apparently edited anonymously, T Martin Wood prefaced each issue with fulsome comments about the range and quality of the illustrations to follow. *Colour* sat somewhat uneasily between the modernists and the establishment. Its strapline – 'The most fascinating magazine in the world' – certainly did not help and it was scorned by the avant-garde for its concentration on artwork from the traditionalists, such as Clausen, Strang and Brangwyn. Once war broke out, *Colour*'s broad scope led to a somewhat bizarre juxtaposition of images, so that it was not uncommon to find pleasant rural landscapes and fashionably-dressed ladies placed cheek-by-jowl with harsher modernist depictions of the conflict, by artists such as C R W Nevinson, Eric Kennington and the brothers Paul and John Nash.

Nevertheless, many of the Whitechapel Boys – Bomberg, Gertler, Kramer, Meninsky, Morris Goldstein and Horace Brodzky – published artwork here at least once, often (ironically) in striking monochrome.[26] Wolmark, by now a confirmed colourist (and medically unfit for military service), contributed prodigiously, including several covers as well as a number of formally-composed images of soldiers in uniform posed against striking backgrounds (figs. 31 and 32), which were closer to contemporary poster design than the darker images of his fellow modernists and highly suitable for reproduction. Others, like Wayner, whose 'decorative black and white work' had, according to the critic of the *Jewish Chronicle* received unqualified praise from some of our finest critics',[27] moved gradually from traditional realist depictions such as *The Jew* (September 1915), to sparer, more contemporary monochrome and graphic images, such as that of *Major L Rothschild* (fig. 20), of the Jewish Recruiting Committee, suggesting that he learned to tailor his work to the medium of print – and perhaps that the readership was becoming more appreciative, or at least more accepting, of modernist imagery.

Wayner may also have been influenced by Horace Brodzky (1885–1965), who specialised in printmaking, excelling in the reprographic-friendly mediums of the woodcut and linocut. Australian-born and of Ukrainian Jewish descent, Brodzky lived and worked in both New York and London, contributing to a number of little magazines in both cities. Coming from a journalistic background, he had begun to produce 'small portraits and caricatures for the Fleet Street papers'[28] early on in his London career. He also sold etchings through Dan Rider's bookshop in St Martin's Lane, meeting there the journalist Frank Harris, editor of *Hearth and Home*,[29] who published some of his early drawings. Harris later edited the weekly journal *Modern Society*, where Brodzky was briefly on the staff. Brodzky also met Katherine Mansfield and John Middleton Murry at Rider's, afterwards publishing drawings and woodcuts in *Rhythm*;[30] by 1912 he had even purchased his own etching press.[31] However, Brodzky was also a skilful colourist, placed by P G Konody, writing in *The Observer*, 'somewhere between Brangwyn and the post-impressionists. His design has real power,' Konody noted, adding 'his colour is truly dazzling in its fearless strength.'[32]

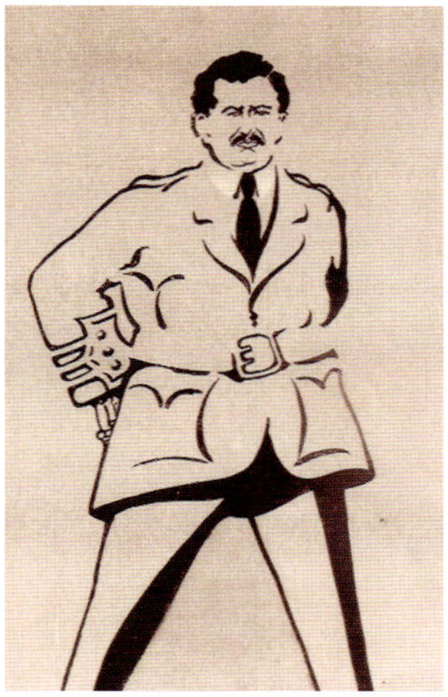

FIG. 20
MARK WAYNER
Major L Rothschild, c.1916

Neither a resident of the ghetto, nor a Slade student, Brodzky nevertheless developed close links with his Whitechapel artist peers[33], illustrated by a number of reciprocal portraits *c.*1913–15. Brodzky sketched Wolmark (*c.*1913)[34], Kramer (1915) and Epstein (1915),[35] and developed a close friendship with the French sculptor Henri Gaudier-Brzeska, who spent time sketching in the East End, transferring innumerable 'Jewish street hawkers [...] to paper, all without apparent effort.'[36] Brodzky and Gaudier-Brzeska's friendship resulted in further reciprocal works, including Brodzky's portrait oil of Gaudier-Brzeska (*c.*1913, cat no. 34) and Gaudier-Brzeska's etching of Brodkzy (1913, cat no. 35), inscribed 'all amico Del Sole Brodzky'. In 1913 Gaudier-Brzeska sculpted a mask of Brodzky,[37] as well as markedly modernist busts of Wolmark[38] and Frank Harris.[39]

Appropriately, Brodzky and Gaudier-Brzeska's friendship was initiated via the medium of print. Gaudier-Brzeska first contacted Brodzky after viewing his cover design – a starkly powerful woodcut entitled *The Ascetic* – for the December 1912 issue of *The Art Chronicle.*[40] The power and economy of Brodzky's black-and-white imagery, which so appealed to Gaudier-Brzeska, is further encapsulated in the monochrome linocut *A Woman Bathing*, ironically included in the launch issue of *Colour* in August 1914.[41]

Gaudier-Brzeska returned to France in September 1914 and enlisted in the army; he was killed in action in 1915. Brodzky returned to New York the same year (where he remained until 1923) and continued his printmaking career. Following the publication of *A Portfolio of Linocuts by Horace Brodzky* by Egmont Ares in 1920, he was praised by New York's *World Magazine* as 'a Graphic Artist of Independent Proclivities.'[42] According to his son John, Brodzky also at different times edited two New York magazines in which he promoted modern British

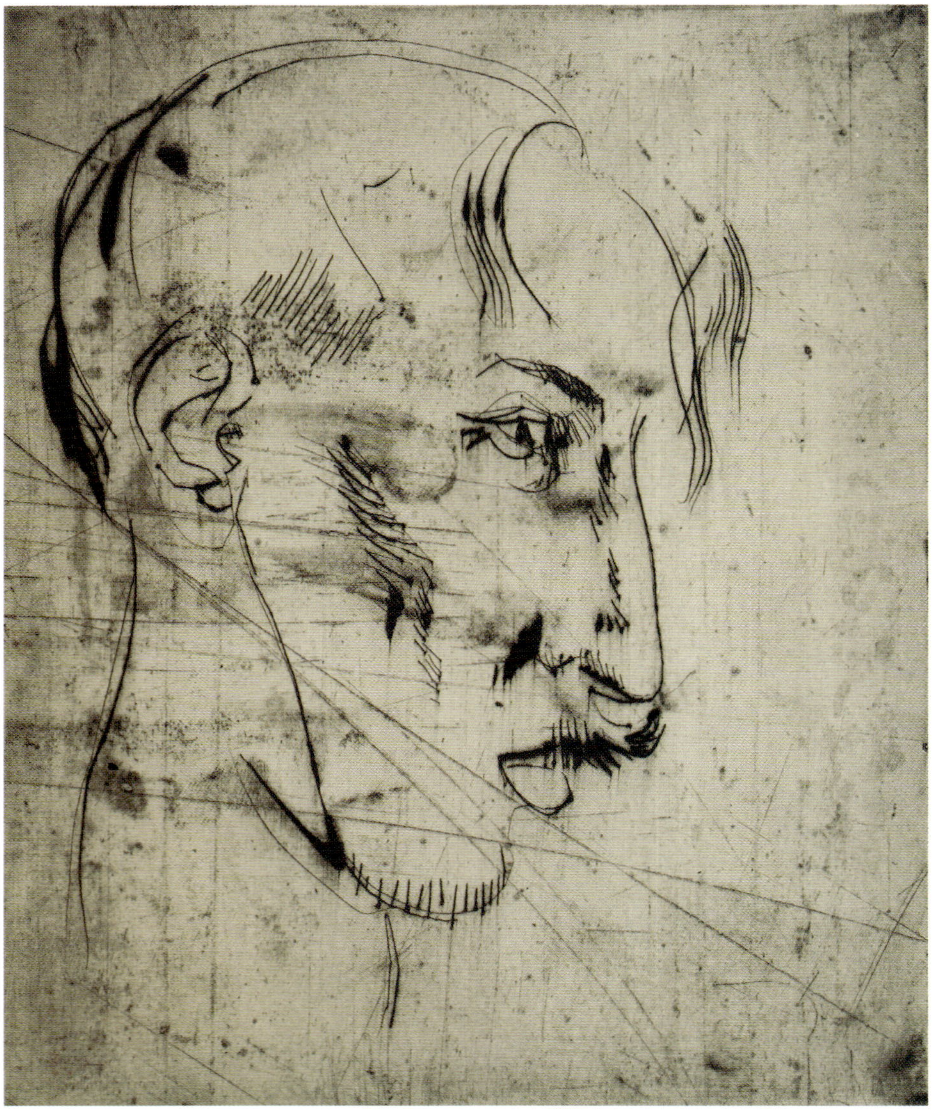

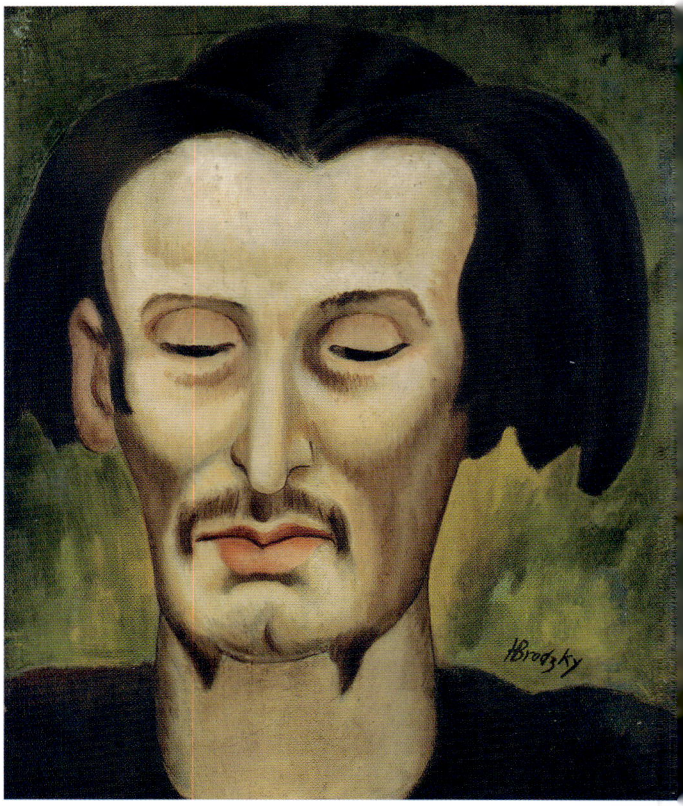

34 *above*
HORACE BRODZKY
Portrait of Henri Gaudier-Brzeska, *c.*1913

35 *left*
HENRI GAUDIER-BRZESKA
Portrait of Horace Brodzky, 1913

artists. The first, *Rainbow*, which ran for only three issues in 1920 and in which he 'promoted modern art and poetry', introduced New York to 'Isaac Rosenberg's poems, Epstein's sculpture and Gaudier-Brzeska work.'[43] In the second magazine, *Art Review*, Brodzky published the series of articles he wrote on Gaudier-Brzeska, which were later worked up into his biography of the artist. On his return to England, Brodzky briefly worked for *Colour*, under the editorship of Wilson Barratt.[44]

Leftwich was also a regular contributor to *Colour*. The April 1918 issue included the poem 'A Prayer', 'affectionately inscribed to my friend, Alfred A. Wolmark', while the October 1919 issue bizarrely mis-attributed Leftwich's memorial poem to Rosenberg, 'Killed in Action', to Rosenberg himself. And while it remains largely true, as Joseph Cohen has suggested, that 'few poets could have been more out of place' in the pages of such a 'chic, bourgeois, coffee-table publication'[45] than Rosenberg, he nevertheless found it a useful early mouthpiece for his poetry. 'Heart's First Word' and 'A Girl's Thoughts' were featured in consecutive summer issues in 1915 (though notably, unlike his contemporaries, Rosenberg never published art work in *Colour*).

Perhaps surprisingly, *Colour* also printed Yiddish material in translation including a folk story by Shalem Ash [sic] and a piece entitled '"The Rabbi and His Wife" from Yiddish of L Shapiro', both translated by Hannah Berman,[46] the latter sharing a page with *The Student* (possibly a self-portrait) by Morris Goldstein, published in 1917.[47] The regular critic 'TIS' (Herbert Furst, later art critic at *Apollo*) was also one of the earliest non-Jewish critics to acknowledge the formidable artistic contribution of the Whitechapel Boys (though he did not use this term and notably excluded Rosenberg and Gertler). Noting that these Jewish artists formed part of a unique group, he called them 'a remarkable phenomenon', commenting on 'the presence among the young Jews whose fathers have escaped from the suffering of the Russian pale, of so much artistic talent. Epstein, Wolmark, Kramer, Meninsky, Bomberg and Naviasky represent, I believe, the first English generation of Polish Jewry.'[48] Nevertheless, with its middle class credentials, *Colour* was ripe to be satirised by Wyndham Lewis in *Blast: Review of the Great English Vortex*.

Championed by Ezra Pound and with the irascible Lewis at its helm, this iconoclastic journal first sounded its rude trumpet in July 1914, proclaiming its official manifesto, which 'Blasted' England with typical aggression for (among other things) its 'climate [...] its sins and infections', but particularly its Victorian values, while 'blessing' it for its industrial strength and satirical tradition. In a pre-launch advertisement the Vorticists claimed to be 'the English Parallel Movement to Cubism and Expressionism', as well as the 'Death Blow to Impressionism and Futurism'. Indignantly repudiating the charge of Futurist influence (they were highly critical of the Italian movement and its blurred depiction of speed), the Vorticists, though associated with the dynamism of the new age, focused more sharply on form. Their visual language drew on Cubist techniques of fragmentation, combined with hard-edged, machine-inspired imagery, shot through with a palpable energy, but with a stillness at its core 'where all the energy is concentrated. And there, at the point of concentration,' Pound explained, 'is the Vorticist.'

Naturally, the voices of Lewis and Pound were dominant in *Blast*, but the first issue also carried original illustrations by Lewis himself, Wadsworth, Roberts, Epstein and Gaudier-Brzeska, and literary contributions from Rebecca West and Ford Madox Ford (under his pre-war name, Ford Madox Hueffer). Although planned as a quarterly, the second and (though not intended as such) final issue, the War Number, appeared belatedly in July 1915. In addition to Lewis's pro-Vorticist text and images, Ezra Pound and T S Eliot published prose and poetry, as well as 'the historic instructive aesthetics' of 'Vortex (written from the Trenches)' by Gaudier-Brzeska, composed just before his death in France. Lewis also reviewed the recent London Group exhibition, confining himself

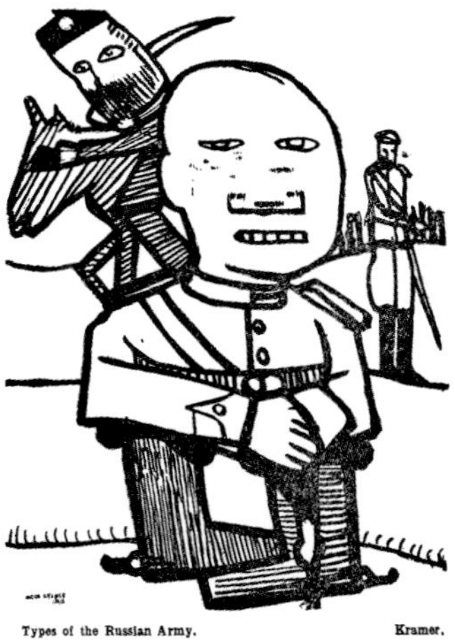

FIG. 18
JACOB KRAMER
Types of the Russian Army, 1915

to a 'consideration of the pictures in the Vorticist or Cubist section'.[49] He clearly considered that Kramer was sufficiently a 'Vorticist' to be included both in the article and as an individual contributor to *Blast* itself, with a curious satirical cartoon, *Types of the Russian Army* (fig. 18).[50] Perhaps here Kramer (still technically a Russian) was demonstrating in some small way his solidarity with his fellow artists who were experiencing the real theatre of war. Perhaps too, it also represented Lewis's idea of a 'good' satirical cartoon since in the same issue, in an article entitled 'Modern Caricature and Impressionism', he damned the 'ineffectiveness of the English variety'.[51] Although there is little evidence that Kramer's works were Vorticist in the same way as those of Bomberg or William Roberts, or even Lewis's own, Lewis also promised that Kramer's work would be included in the proposed third volume of *Blast*. Unfortunately this was never realised, as by then, as Lewis admitted, 'All of Europe was at war and a bigger blast than mine had rather taken the wind out of my sails.'[52]

The first edition of *Art and Letters*, an illustrated quarterly, was published in July 1917. It was co-founded by Frank Rutter and Herbert Read, with Osbert Sitwell and the Camden Town and London Group painters Harold Gilman and Charles Ginner as sometime editors. Sitwell (who also contributed to *Wheels*, edited by his sister Edith) eventually took on a third share. Born in the midst of the war, the publication originally had a very specific task in hand: 'Friends serving at the Front – some of whom contribute to this first issue – remind us that there are educated men in the Army who would gladly welcome an addition to the small number of publications which appeals to them. Engaged as their duty bids, on harrowing work of destruction, they exhort their elders at home never to lose sight of the supreme importance of creative art.'[53] As a serving officer Read was not permitted to take any public role in administering the project but was in effect joint-editor and contributed to the original costs. With his 'manifesto', he was clearly making a sly dig at what he felt to be the number of inferior publications already in circulation: 'Objections on the score of scarcity of paper and shortage of labour may surely be overruled when we remember the reams of paper wasted weekly and the hundreds of competitors daily misemployed on periodicals which give vulgar and illiterate expression to the most vile and debasing sentiment.'[54]

In the face of criticism from other more revolutionary quarters however, Read (writing his diary on active service during August 1917), defended the opening issue: 'It is not fair to judge *Art and Letters* by a first number appearing in war-time. It [...] is but a pale edition of what we do intend it finally to be. Against the *New Age* we intend to insist upon the primacy of beauty – even in economics. And hence a return to the socialism of Morris in preference to Karl Marx. Qualitative rather than quantitative ideas.'[55] He acknowledged its early limitations ('Of course, it isn't so "sumptuous" as it might be, or as it will be after the war') but also endorsed it as 'modern without being cranky. I think Ginner's article sums up the present position of modern art to perfection. [Charles][56] Marriott on dancing is good too.'[57]

Art and Letters survived until spring 1920 with a diverse selection of modernist contributors including Lewis, Eliot, Pound, John Nash, Orovida Pissarro and Gino Severini. For the winter 1918–19 issue, Lewis not only provided the cover design but also both prose and poetry with a war slant, alongside a melange of reproductions by Picasso, Edward Wadsworth and the late Gaudier-Brzeska, while Kramer contributed the drawing *Head of a Russian*. Rutter used the spring 1919 issue to advertise the opening of his own Adelphi Gallery,[58] at the same address as the magazine, with its intention of 'supply[ing] good work at democratic prices' and focusing on 'the best work of the younger generation'. It promised forthcoming exhibitions by Wadsworth (March–April) and Kramer (May). In the summer 1919 issue (cat no. 59) five of Rosenberg's poems were featured posthumously,[59] alongside his pencil study *Head of a Young Woman* (aka *Head of a*

Woman in Profile, 1914, cat no. 21) – only the second time his poetry and art had been published together – and an 'In Memorium'.[60]

Many of the Whitechapel Boys inevitably crossed-over with *New Paths* ('Verse-Prose-Pictures 1917–1918') co-edited by the publisher and writer C W Beaumont and M T H Sadler. Published in May 1918, one month after the death of Rosenberg, and with the war still ongoing, *New Paths* was 'Dedicated to the memory of Rupert Brooke, Gaudier-Brzeska, Gerard Chowne, Dixon Scott, A Noel Simmons, C H Sorley, Edward Thomas, Pelham Webb and to all those gallant gentlemen who, but for having died in the service of their country, would have been pioneers along the new paths of literature and art.'[61] It featured artwork by Gertler, Gaudier-Brzeska, Epstein, Kramer and Meninsky among others, arranged indiscriminately at the back of the volume rather than integrated into the text. Gaudier-Brzeska was represented by a pencil *Self-Portrait* and an early sculpture, *Weeping Figure*, and Gertler by a Cézanne-esque *Study for Bathers*. Kramer's *Day of Atonement* ('design for a woodcut') with its parade of mournful figures predated his highly significant painting of the same name. *New Paths* further promoted its serious and modern credentials by providing a comprehensive 'Bibliography of Some Recent Books of Verse'[62] and 'Bibliography of Noteworthy Young Novels'[63] alongside 'Pictures: Tendencies in Present-Day English Art'.[64] However, Rosenberg is notable by his omission as either painter or poet.

Voices: in poetry and prose was a new literary periodical much favoured by the Whitechapel Boys. Established and edited by Thomas Moult (1893–1974), a journalist and critic on subjects ranging from music, art and literature to sport, as well as being one of the Georgian poets, it first appeared in January 1919, nine months after Rosenberg's death. Founded 'immediately on the declaration of the Armistice in the belief that the barren years of the Arts since 1914 were about to be succeeded by rich aspiration among young artists towards the utmost freedom and strength of expression', *Voices* had distinctly pacifist leanings. An early issue included D H Lawrence's 'Rondeau of a Conscientious Objector'[65] and was dedicated to the pacifist writer Romain Rolland 'because of *Jean Christophe*'.[66] A selection of Stephen Winsten's poetry, written during his three-year imprisonment as a conscientious objector, appeared in the November 1919 issue,[67] prior to its publication in *Chains* (1920). However, in its second birthday issue (January 1921), Moult claimed that *Voices* was 'one of the few publications in which there has ever been printed any vital truth about the war as a human experience. For it is written, to a large extent, by men who fought in the war, and it is chiefly the poets among these men who are putting on record the only faithful account of the spiritual adventures of the combatant troops, anything of the sort having had to be suppressed, for temporary reasons, during the actual war, and being a drug in the market of the general press after it.'[68] The summer 1921 issue, which had a war theme, posthumously published Rosenberg's poem 'The One Lost', beginning

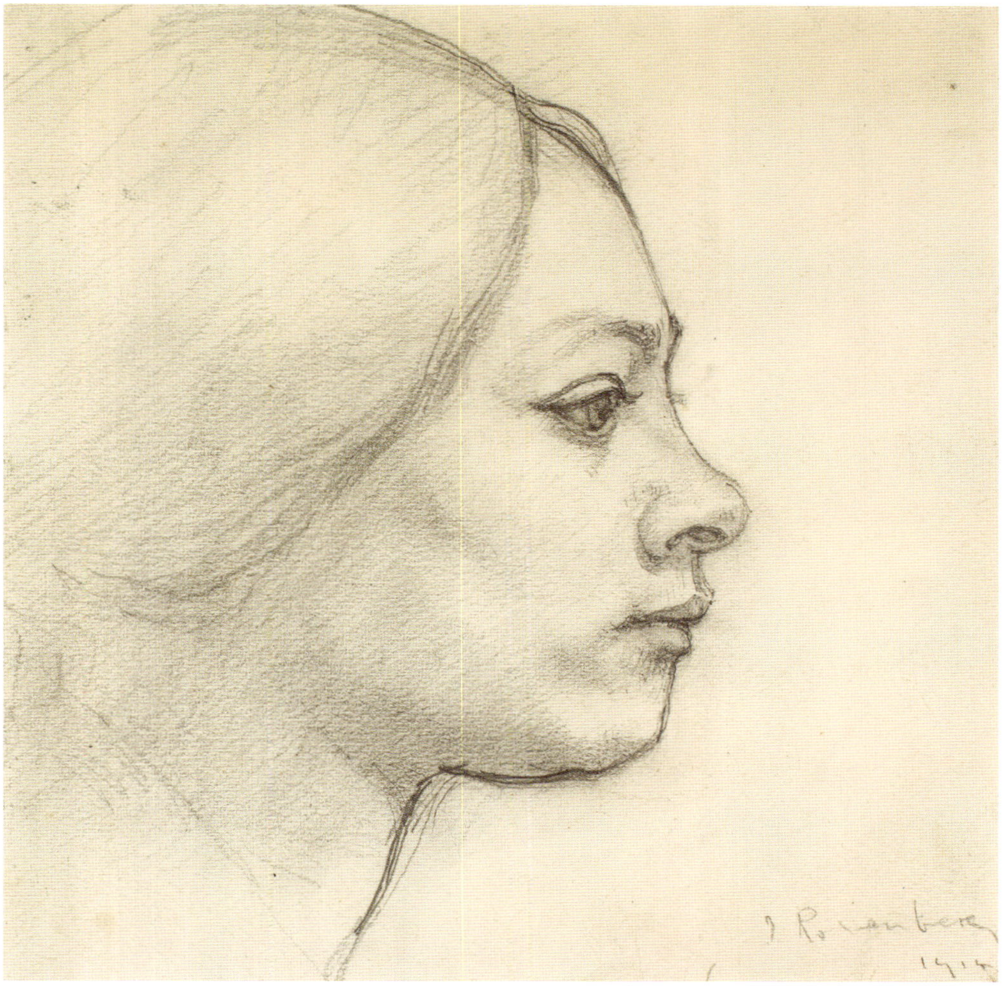

21
ISAAC ROSENBERG
Head of a Woman in Profile, 1914

'I mingle with your bones',[69] and a memorial tribute to Rosenberg by Samuel Roth (in which he commented wryly that 'this "Moses" of Rosenberg's, alas, is sometimes so little like a Jewish leader he talks almost like a contributor to the *Egoist*'[70]).

Voices provided a platform for newly-emerging writers, including A E Coppard, Louis Golding, F V Branford and Neville Cardus, as well as for the Whitechapel Boys. Indeed, its title was taken from a quote by Israel Zangwill, chronicler of the 'Ghetto': 'Voices, Voices we want – not echoes. Better the mistaken voice of honest individuality than the soulless bleat of the flock.'[71] After the publication of two further poems and a prose piece in the February 1920 issue,[72] 'S. Winsten', as he always signed himself, became a regular presence on the magazine. Throughout 1920, together with Moult and Louis Golding, he was one of the commentators in the regular column 'Notes on Present-Day Art'.[73]

Work by the Whitechapel artists, particularly those who were members of the London Group, such as Gertler, Bomberg and Kramer, as well as Clare Winsten, and associates such as Gaudier-Brzeska and Wyndham Lewis, was often reproduced or reviewed. Poems and prose by Israel Zangwill and Leftwich (as well as Stephen Winsten) were featured, as was an extract from the novel by Louis Golding *Forward from Babylon*, describing an immigrant Jewish family, now settled in England, looking back at times of persecution in Russia[74] (Kramer provided a woodcut to illustrate this which eventually appeared well over a year later in November 1920).[75]

In turn, Louis Golding regularly reviewed the Whitechapel Boys' contributions to the London Group and other exhibitions, often singling out Gertler and Bomberg for praise.[76] Both artists were generally positively reviewed by their contemporaries from the overlapping Whitechapel circles, such as S Winsten on David Bomberg, 'A Force in Modern Art',[77] and J[ack] Isaacs praising Gertler and Bomberg as the outstanding contributors to an exhibition at the Hampstead Gallery.[78]

But critical voices were also raised. O Raymond Drey (who had previously contributed art criticism to *Rhythm*),[79] wrote of Bomberg's *Russian Ballet book*, 'I am still at a loss to understand how so promising an artist could condescend (or was it a lapse?) to the trivialities of this little book.'[80] And in 1919, when reviewing Kramer's show at the *Adelphi*, Golding remarked, somewhat ambiguously, that he was struck by the emotional force of the 'terrifying rat-like stupidity' of Kramer's *Jews Praying*,[81] which he interpreted as 'a fierce comment upon the Jehovah who forbade images in paint or stone and in whose likeness those foreheads and curved spines were fashioned'.[82]

Operating in a mutually supportive and inclusive environment, the little magazines energetically advertised and promoted like publications and companion exhibitions – *Art & Letters* advertised *New Paths*, and *Voices* regularly devoted pages to fellow magazines under the heading 'Periodicals: A Survey of Contemporaries'. *The Apple* and latterly, in April 1920, *Renesans* (translated as 'Renaissance'), the new Yiddish art and literary monthly emanating from the East End, were complimented. The latter clearly captured the zeitgeist of which the Whitechapel Boys were so much a part:

> We welcome *The Renaissance* edited by Mr Leo Koenig [sic], which, we imagine is the only Jewish art-journal in existence. It has now reached its third number, and in the world-literature of Jewish artists it is quickly attaining to a leading place. Yiddish being the language of *The Renaissance*, and an international language also, there is no reason why this monthly journal should not circulate all over the globe.[83]

Despite this, *Renesans* enjoyed only a brief life, publishing six issues during 1920. Supported by the Ben Uri and edited by Leo Kenig, with Leftwich as Editorial Secretary, its features, all written or translated into Yiddish, included an article on Leo Bakst by Wolmark; Lucien Pissarro on his father Camille; poetry and prose by S Winsten (including a review of Bomberg's exhibition at the Adelphi Gallery) and Kramer's essay on art, 'Form and Shape',[84] which summed up his aesthetic philosophy.

Kramer and Bomberg also supplied cover mages. (Leftwich recalled many years later that Bomberg first published his war poetry in *Renesans*, but no evidence has been found to support this.[85]) Art by Simeon Solomon, Camille and Lucien Pissarro, Chagall, Modigliani, Kisling, Epstein, Bomberg, Kramer, Meninsky, Modigliani and Clara Klinghoffer was also reproduced, many of them for the first time in a Yiddish publication.

Moult also drew attention to *Renesans*' 'unique quality: there is no dependence in its pages on the well-established writers and artists; in letterpress and painting alike it is the younger men who are being encouraged.' In fact, this was hardly true of the painters, as the list above indicates. Solomon and Pissarro (father and son) could hardly be termed 'the younger men' and many of the Whitechapel Boys were by now established names. However, Moult did point to literature which might otherwise have been confined to a limited readership: 'Moysha Oyved's [sic] remarkable inspirational poetry, essays of a lofty spiritual tone by the editor [Kenig], and poetry by Mr. Joseph Leftwich [...] In its art and literary criticism *The Renaissance* discusses the work of the younger Jewish writers who are expressing themselves in English, and translations – exceedingly good – are made of work by English writers who express sentiments sympathetic to the Jewish temperament.'[86] Notably, Moult blamed 'a great journalistic failure in America' for intensifying 'the struggle which the promoters of *the Renaissance* are experiencing', concluding with a finality which perhaps suggested its imminent demise that it was 'a brave, a good work, however great and overwhelming ultimately that struggle may be.'[87]

Notably absent from all these publications, however, is John Rodker. In the years leading up to the war he had made his name as the 'poet of the ghetto' in some of the best-known modernist mouthpieces of the age including A R Orage's *The New Age: A Weekly Review of Politics, Literature and Art*,[88] which listed among its contributors Beatrice Hastings, T E Hulme, Katherine Mansfield, Ezra Pound and Herbert Read (commentators also reviewed modernist artists, such as Gertler, whose 'extraordinarily attractive' work was noticed by Anthony Ludovici in January 1913).[89] Rodker further contributed to *The Egoist*, Dora Marsden's successor to *The New Freewoman*, a bi-monthly which ran from 1914–19 and published major works by Eliot, Joyce and others, as well as to Lewis's *The Tyro*,[90] and Harriet Monroe's *Poetry: A Magazine of Verse* in Chicago.[91] (After Pound recommended some of Rosenberg's poetry to Monroe in summer 1915, Rodker sent in Rosenberg's 'Marching – As Seen From the Left File' in January 1916 and Rosenberg submitted his 'Break of Day in the Trenches' that September. Both poems were finally printed in the magazine in December 1916.)[92] Drawing on his Whitechapel cultural background and connections, Rodker also published essays ranging from 'The Theatre in Whitechapel' (*Poetry and Drama*)[93] to 'The New Movement in Art' (*The Dial Monthly*), where he also contributed an article on the Futurists and an explanatory caption to Bomberg's *Racehorses*.[94]

Both Rodker and Leftwich (the latter promoted, along with Miss Jean Guthrie-Smith, by Thomas Moult in *Voices* as 'the best of the poets')[95] contributed poetry to *The Apple [of Beauty and Discord]* (1920–21), the short-lived sister publication to *Colour*, published quarterly at a price of six shillings. Founded and edited by Herbert Furst (art critic for *Colour* and later *Apollo* and champion of the modern woodcut,[96] as well as a publisher), *The Apple*, 'like its arboreal namesake', the foreword suggested, was 'intended to be looked at, bought, enjoyed and digested by "high and low" without distinction [...] It is the hope of the editors that the juxtaposition of harshly opposite types of mind will prove to be a more healthy diet of thought than the peptonised preparations of the daily, weekly and monthly press.' Although a larger and less glossy format than its sibling, and intended 'to do for "Black and White" in Art what *Colour* Magazine is doing for Colour', *The Apple* published a similar contingent of artists and writers, in the main traditionalists but punctuated regularly by the contradictory or controversial offering of a modernist. Pound criticised the London museums ('The Curse'[97]), 'TIS' condemned Picasso and abstraction in 'Picassine Poisoning';[98] and work by Gaudier-Brzeska, Wadsworth and Lewis (*A Portrait of Ezra Pound*)[99] was reproduced. *The Apple* also sporadically featured work with a distinct Jewish/Yiddish appeal, including a number of short stories by Hannah Berman (who had also been published in *Colour*) and J L Peretz, the Yiddish author, also translated by Berman.[100]

Post-war, despite the efforts of *Renesans* and *The Apple*, the Whitechapel Boys gradually began to drift away both from the 'little magazines' and from each other. Bomberg withdrew from London life and Kramer returned to Leeds (although he provided Vorticist-inspired portraits for the *New Coterie* with its cover by William Roberts).[101] In 1923 when Gertler published two little-known essays on art, he did so outside the Whitechapel circle in *The Adelphi* – a newly-launched periodical under the editorship of John Middleton Murry and the Russian Jewish translator S S Koteliansky ('Kot'), Gertler's close-friend, who also worked with Leonard Woolf at the Hogarth Press. Rodker set up the Ovid Press in 1919, which lasted scarcely a year, but published within that period the first edition of Pound's *Hugh Selwyn Mauberley* (1920)[102] and portfolios of drawings by Lewis and Wadsworth.[103] At the same time, Rodker also replaced Pound as the London editor of the New York magazine *The Little Review*,[104] which declared candidly on its cover, 'A Magazine of the Arts: Making No Compromise with the Public Taste.'

FIG. 47
Whitechapel Scene with Ruderman's Store

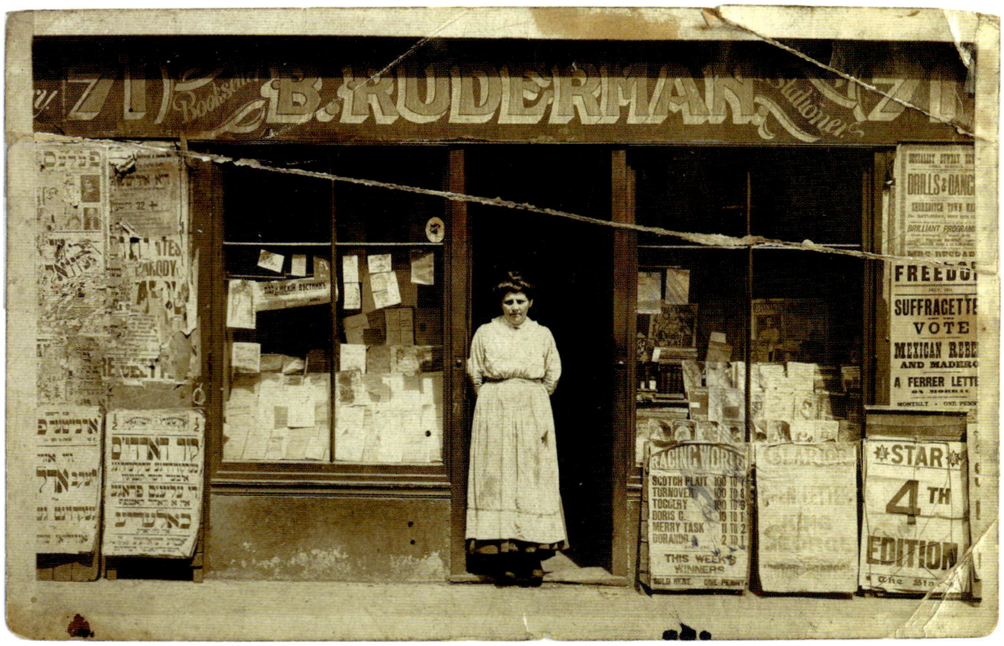

In a career dedicated to literature, most significantly as a publisher and translator, Rodker went on to publish the second edition of James Joyce's *Ulysses* and French translations of Joyce, as well as establishing a number of short-lived projects including the Casanova Society (1923–7, for limited editions), the J Rodker imprint (for Occult subjects), the Pushkin Press (1937–48), which published only a dozen titles, including Oliver Elton's English version of *Evgeny Onegin*; and finally, the Imago Publishing Company (1938–61), set up to publish Sigmund Freud after the psychoanalyst arrived in London in 1938 in flight from the Nazis, who destroyed the remaining stocks of his work. (Rodker worked with Freud's daughter Anna to publish a complete edition, which was eventually completed in 1952.) Leftwich continued to forge a career as a pioneer of Yiddish translation, publishing anthologies of Yiddish verse and literature, and survived to be a grand old man of letters and chief chronicler of the Whitechapel Boys.

In conclusion, the sheer energy and variety of the large number of 'little magazines' proliferating in the early modern British period provided an important voice for many of the Whitechapel Boys. Despite the ephemeral quality of many of these magazines, many of the writers established a sufficient literary presence to go forward with their future careers. For the artists these publications helped – both through exhibition reviews and perhaps more importantly, through the new medium of high-quality reproduction – to keep their names and work in the public arena. Rosenberg took little advantage of this new opportunity – only once appearing as combined poet and painter during his lifetime and never as a painter first and foremost. These early forays into print nevertheless provided him with an outlet for his poetry not readily available elsewhere. Despite only a small presence in the literary magazines of the period, Rosenberg undoubtedly went on to make one of the most important, original and lasting contributions to early twentieth-century literature.

6

FIGHTING ON DIFFERENT FRONTS
ISAAC ROSENBERG AND JOHN RODKER IN THE GREAT WAR

I feel I escaped, that I ought as much as the 9,000,000 be dead with them, that I have no right not to be dead and hate it that I did not live in and come through the perpetual no man's land of dun cloud and half-light, shot with shells, flares, explosions of all kinds, that made up part of my generation, the grey deadly world that is for most of us world without end, amen.

And Rosenberg my friend was blown to atoms and we are left with the cheap notepaper fading fast and the pencilled poems half rubbed out now [handwritten insertion, crossed out:] *poems of war not so much better than my own.*

Well! what do a few poems matter.[1]

JOHN RODKER *Memoirs of Other Fronts*

As far as John Rodker's own poetry of the Great War is concerned, one might be tempted to answer him 'not very much', a judgement that his crossing out in this typescript seems to anticipate. Isaac Rosenberg's poetry is in fact far better than Rodker's, and it is hard not to see this difference as a result of the isolation Rodker describes in the first paragraph. Whereas Rosenberg had volunteered for the army, Rodker was a conscientious objector. Rosenberg wrote coolly about a war he fought in, whereas Rodker penned hysterical verses about a conflict he was not part of, verses that come across as the output of a young man (perhaps one less mature than his years) using war as a pretext for shocking his audience. 'Hymn to Death 1914 And On', for example, with its soldiers resurrected only to re-enact their deaths, drew on the trope of the *danse macabre* that was itself hardly given new life. The poem's chief interest lies in the wildly eccentric typography of its first printing, with half the attraction being trying to work out how much of its look is wilful slipshodness and how much crude avant-garde gesture.

DANSE-MACABRE" Death
"Dried -guts "death

They clatter, girn, mow –
femur rattles skull
epiphyses shriek, grate –

Brain a shrunk pea
quintessential lusts -
rattles
rattles rattles
rattles.
O the 'bones ', the wonderful bones.
[God's the darkey][2]

This is nothing like Rosenberg's first effort after joining up, 'Marching—As Seen from the Left File':

Not broke is the forge of Mars;
But a subtler brain beats iron
To shoe the hoofs of death,
(Who paws dynamic air now).[3]

The care with which these lines are crafted – the classical reference subtly offset by the straightforwardly English, and monosyllabic, vocabulary, except for the weight placed on 'dynamic', and the way this word draws on its Greek meaning of 'force' – is worlds away from Rodker's slinging around of would-be scientific terms such as 'epiphyses'. Indeed, Rodker seems not to have

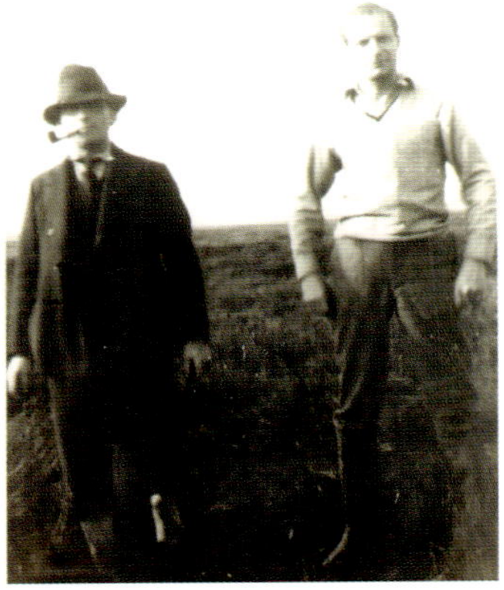

FIG. 46
John Rodker and David Bomberg, c.1938

understood the way Rosenberg's lines were supposed to fit together. While he was moving from army camp to camp, Rosenberg relied on Rodker's contact with *Poetry* magazine to get published. Discussing this poem with the editor, Harriet Monroe, Rodker decided the line 'Who paws dynamic air now' was a question rather than a relative clause.[4] This desire to turn part of a complex sentence into a simple separate question seems typical of Rodker's own writing style, paratactic and collagistic, never fully able to make the elements of his work cohere, evident even in the way the square brackets in 'Hymn to Death' are made to stand on their own. The incoherence of his poetry carries over into his most impressive piece of writing, *Memoirs of Other Fronts* (1932), published at the same time as many other books purporting to tell the 'truth about the war'. This, Rodker's only full-length novel, placed together fragments of his life without synthesis, like a rebus from which could be deciphered the workings of the society that had produced, and been produced by, the Great War. The ruthless self-scrutiny of this book led some reviewers (including L P Hartley, who was to write *The Go-Between* much later) to fear for its author's sanity;[5] but it has, perhaps, a parallel in the detached way that Rosenberg manages to present his own war experience.

And in this book more can be seen of what united Rodker and Rosenberg, even in the opposed roles of soldier and CO, beyond their friendship and their shared adolescence in Whitechapel. The facts that Rosenberg only joined up because he had no other source of income, and that he was waiting to be transferred to the Jewish Battalion when he died, are fairly well known. But Rodker too, who is known if for anything for his refusal to fight, describes himself as tempted to join a 'Foreign Legion' (presumably the abortive Jewish Legion of the early months of the war, as he had a British birth certificate).[6] As Rodker put it, the 'pacifist is fighting too, but on another front',[7] and their struggles were in part the result of the complicated pressures of war-time on British Jews that Mark Levene describes.

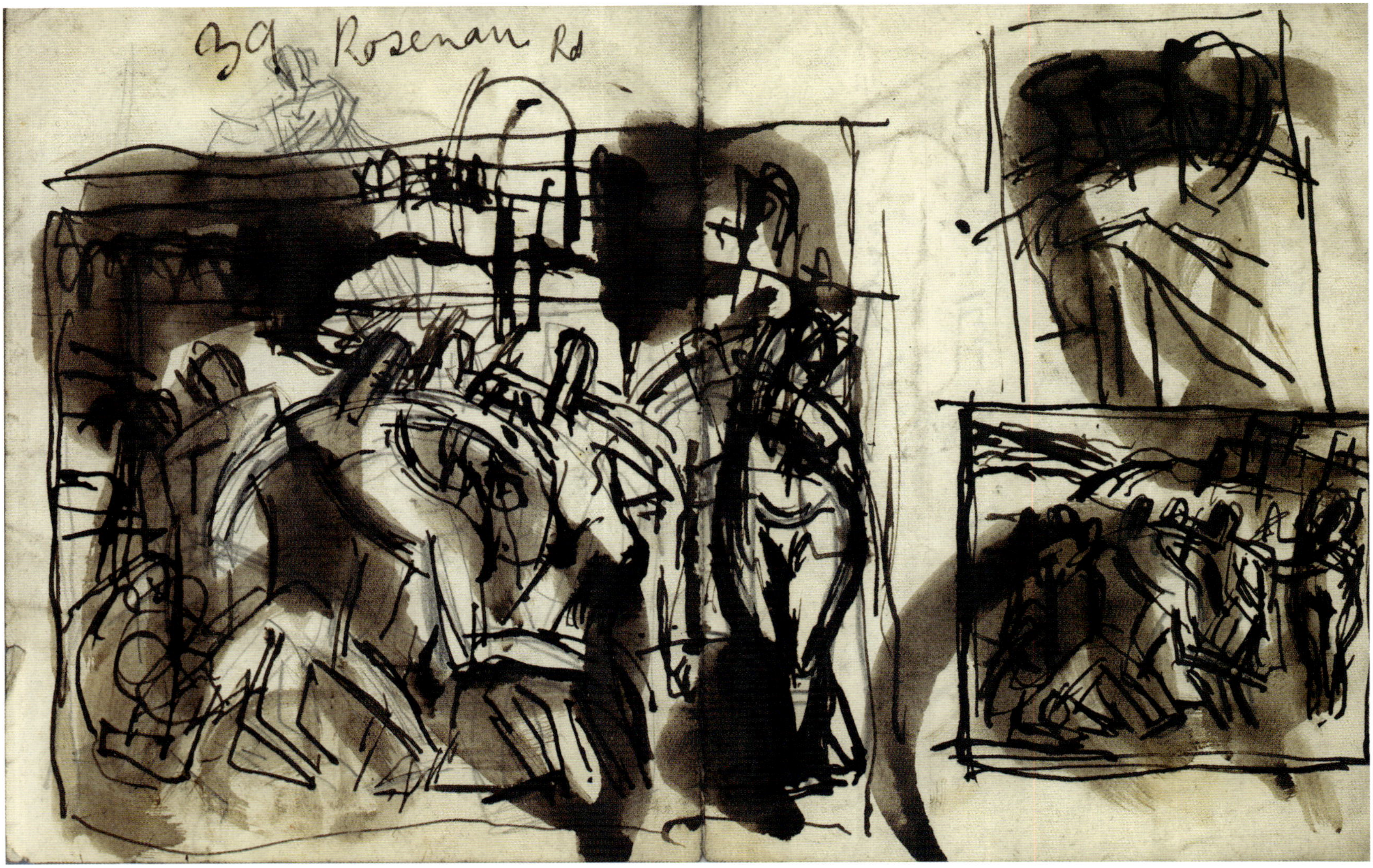

47
ISAAC ROSENBERG
Three rough sketches: 39 Rosenau Road, 1915

Personal identities, then as now, could be multi-layered, even in some sense schizophrenic, as different perspectives and ideas fought for control in the individual psyche. Throw in an entirely unexpected contingency such as war, and the result might be genuine confusion.[8]

One might say that Rodker was the more confused of the two, but the difficulties of identification with Englishness and English can be seen in both writers' work. Rosenberg's breaking from standard English in the line 'Not broke is the forge of Mars' (which cannot be put down to just poetic inversion) is matched by Rodker's use of not-quite-English English at crucial points in *Other Fronts*, where he also write that 'in Paris I feel English, in London a foreigner.'[9] It would be crudely reductive to see the ambivalent interest in vermin shown by both of them as an identification with anti-Semitic images of 'the Jew', but Rosenberg's intrigued, quizzical meditation on the rat in 'Break of Day in the Trenches', and Rodker's rather less subtle self-image as a poisoned rat in 'Hymn to Himself Atlas Twentieth Century' are both ways of thinking through a social situation in which they don't feel themselves fully to fit.

Any ambivalence of this use of rat-imagery was crushed completely in Wyndham Lewis's vicious caricature of Rodker in *The Apes of God* (1930) as Julius Ratner—'Joo Rat'—second-rate writer, publisher and pornographer. Rodker replied to Lewis in his extraordinary, uneven and unfinished *An Ape of Genius*, a collection of novelistic fragments illuminated by flashes of surreal brilliance that explode whatever structure it has rather than holding it together. Rodker characterised Lewis's anti-Semitism as a reaction to war and a continuation of war which countered the destruction of civilisation by destroying it even more, making his life, and his mind, a battlefield, haunted by the only creature that could survive there.

But after the cannonade, the crash and thunder the rumble and din, what comes? A sleek brown form scurries through undergrowth, and another, and another, with glistening eyes, sharp whiskers, pointed noses: appearing, disappearing. Rats! Rats! Furtive, yet cunning, yet daring, yet enterprising. Rats! The one thing that lived, that battened, that foraged that the bombardment could not prevail against.[10]

The rats here are clearly a reference to Julius Ratner, and have something of *The Waste Land* to them too; but Rodker is also, I think, drawing on 'Break of Day in the Trenches'.

> Droll rat, they would shoot you if they knew
> Your cosmopolitan sympathies.
> [...]
> It seems, odd thing, you grin as you pass
> Strong eyes, fine limbs, haughty athletes,
> Less chanced than you for life,
> Bonds to the whims of murder,
> Sprawled in the bowels of the earth,
> The torn fields of France.[11]

Neither the passage that I have just quoted by Rodker, nor the paragraphs in which he refers directly to Rosenberg that I began with, were ever published: the former because the novel was never finished

FIG. 19
WYNDHAM LEWIS
Portrait of John Rodker, 1923

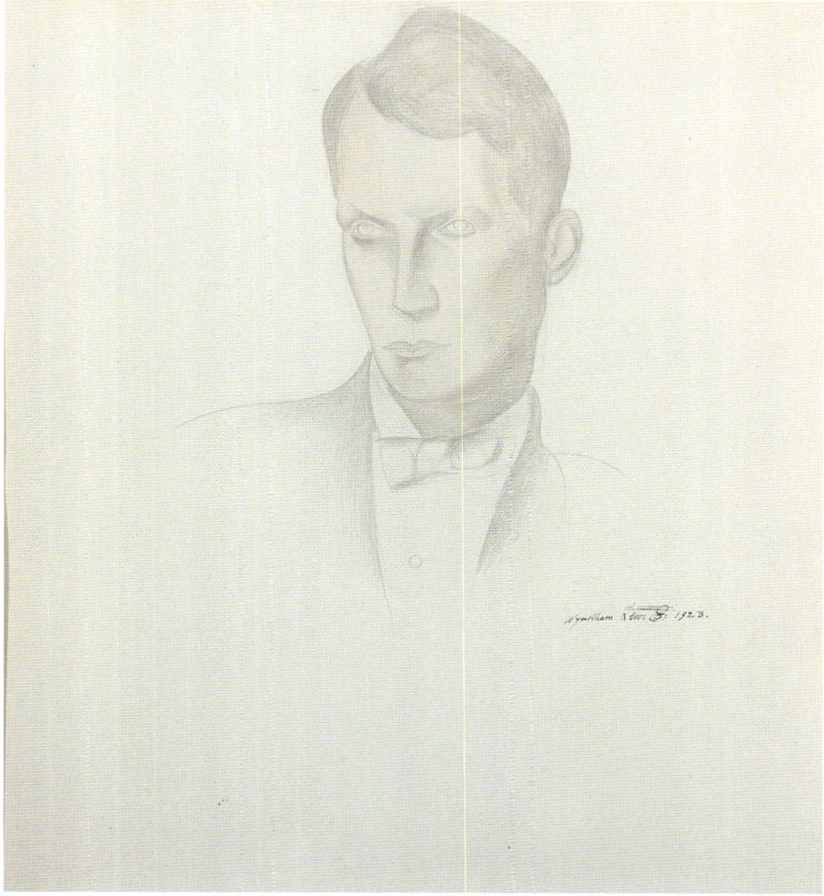

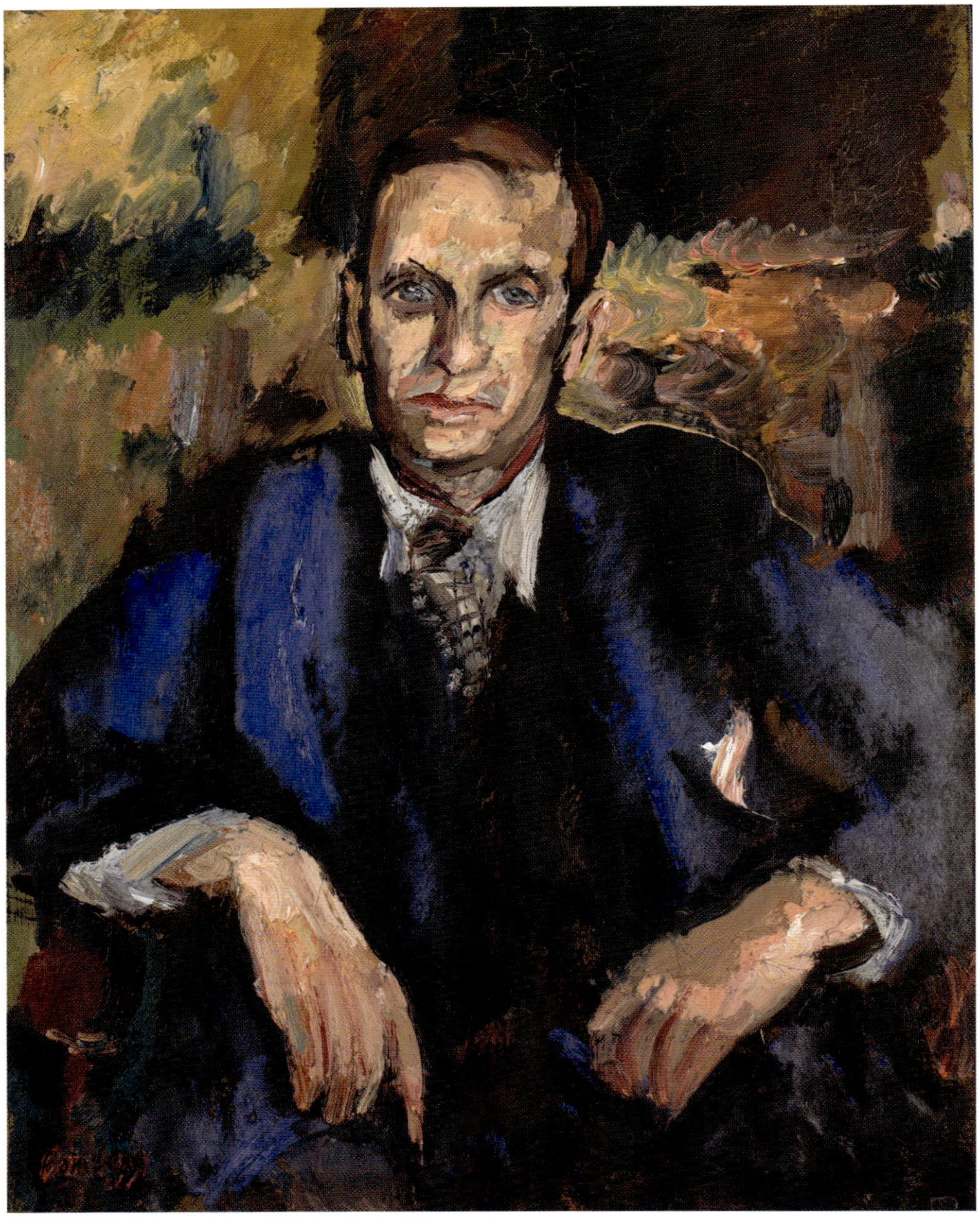

FIG. 14
DAVID BOMBERG
Portrait of John Rodker, c.1931

(indeed, it seems to me unfinishable), the latter because Rodker felt the need to strip all personal elements from *Other Fronts* in order to sharpen its social critique. But leaving out all evidence of his ties to his Jewish friends also, I think, indicates the strange position that he placed himself in with regard to his own Jewishness. Rodker's position, as someone close—too close, perhaps—to the Pound circle, meant that articulating his own Jewishness was a far harder, far more shameful thing to do. When he tried to do so, he was more circumscribed by stereotypes of Jews, including those used by Pound and Lewis, and only succeeded by stripping Jewishness of any particularity, making it into an undefined sense of foreignness. Nonetheless, his relationship with Rosenberg was a resource that he drew tentatively on at points to try to go beyond this position.

Where Rodker, it seems to me, failed in these efforts, Rosenberg clearly had more success. It may well be that his untimely death allows us to tell too easy a story of Jewish identification, with his *oeuvre* topped and tailed by verses on Jewish themes. Nevertheless, his writing – as an inspiration to Jon Silkin, for example – did remain 'usable' as well as 'ineffable', able to be made part of some kind of a lineage of Anglo-Jewish writing.[12] But the relationship between Rodker and Rosenberg, which I have shown here to be more important for Rodker than has been previously given credit, tells us a great deal about the struggles and complex identifications of Jewish writers and artists of the First World War.

7

WHITECHAPEL GIRL
CLARE WINSTEN (NÉE CLARA BIRNBERG, 1892–1984)

'Clare Winsten was a remarkable person [...] both a highly original artist and an active humanitarian during a period of far reaching artistic and social change [...] Although Winsten, like so many women of her generation did not have a formal career as an artist, her creativity and sensitivity permeated every aspect of her life.'[1]
'Clare Winsten (1894–1989): A Student at the Slade 1910–1912'

Among the 14 artists represented in the much-analysed 'Jewish Section', co-curated by David Bomberg and Jacob Epstein, at the Whitechapel Art Gallery's exhibition *Twentieth Century Art: A Review of Modern Movements* in 1914, is the name of a lone woman, Clara Birnberg, though she was also represented elsewhere in the exhibition. By 1913, as Lisa Tickner has observed, Birnberg was already 'quite the New Woman, a vegetarian and a member of the Women's Freedom League, studying at the Central School and at the Slade, working for Heal's and the Omega Workshops, with a studio in the City Road.'[2] In the same year, she executed the first (cat no. 44) of three portraits of Isaac Rosenberg and he returned the favour in 1915 with a splendid likeness in oil (cat no. 29).

But Winsten's credentials as a member of the Whitechapel group do not rest on this link alone. An émigré, like most of her Whitechapel contemporaries, she spent the latter half of her childhood in the East End, entered the Slade School of Art on a scholarship and studied there alongside many of the Whitechapel Boys. Her inclusion in Bomberg's 'Jewish Section' probably owed much to their early friendship at the Slade, though their relationship was fraught and probably short-lived. Bomberg also painted Birnberg and, for a while, in large-scale Slade compositions, they worked along similar modernist lines. Later, she chose her husband, the writer Simy Weinstein (Stephen Winsten), from among the Whitechapel Boys. In common with other members of the Whitechapel group, Clara was poor, talented, ambitious and vocal, and, like many of the Whitechapel writers, she was also overtly political. Not only a committed vegetarian and a member of the suffragette movement, she also became a pacifist during the First World War when her husband was imprisoned as a conscientious objector, an experience she later wrote about in her (unpublished) autobiography which affected her later life and work.

To date, Winsten's work, which is under-represented in public collections,[3] has been little analysed. Previously, a small number of largely traditional portrait drawings in the British Museum Print Room and a further portrait (of Rosenberg) in the Strang Collection, UCL, have been the only works in the public domain. However, a number of early experimental works, tentatively dated (largely on stylistic grounds) 1910–13, have recently emerged, which show that, like her Slade contemporaries, particularly Bomberg and William Roberts, she was familiar with and absorbed the influence of contemporaneous European avant-garde movements including Cubism, Futurism and the nascent

Vorticism early in her career, and explored these influences in her work. .

Born on 10 August 1892,[4] Clara was the second daughter of the three children of Michael A Birnberg[5] and his wife Fanny (née Feige Zellermayer), who were originally from Tarnopol in Galicia (now the Ukraine).[6] Fleeing pogroms, the Birnbergs emigrated to England around 1902,[7] travelling via Romania, where they spent well over a decade and where all three children – Gizella (known as Gerty, b.1884)),[8] Clara (b.1892) and Jonas (b. 1894 in Galatz)[9] – were probably born. They travelled on through Germany,[10] and eventually settled in the East End of London, in the heart of the Jewish community. Michael Birnberg, a former teacher,[11] was among those described by the Whitechapel writer Joseph Leftwich as 'one of the new anglo-Jewish "intellectuals" of Whitechapel'.[12] (He also put the fathers of fellow Whitechapel boys Samuel Winsten – Clara's future husband – and Isaac Rosenberg in the same category.) Like Rosenberg's father Barnett however, Michael's options narrowed after emigration and once the family had settled at 12 St Mark Street, the Minories,[13] he struggled to run a small business in Leman Street, Aldgate.[14] Sensitive to her origins, Birnberg referred to herself as a 'downstart', [15] a humourous nod to her later friend and neighbour George Bernard Shaw.

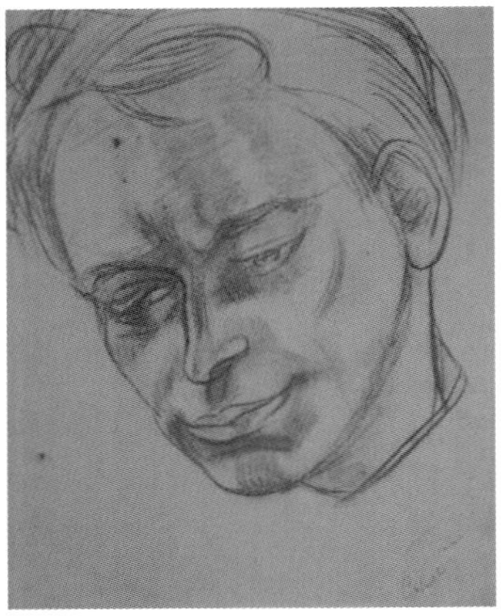

FIG. 29
CLARE WINSTEN
(CLARA BIRNBERG)
Portrait of Jonas (the Artist's Brother), c.1920

Initially educated at the Rutland Street Council School, Clara went on the Central Foundation Girls School (Tower Hamlets) from 1905–10, where it was noted that she spoke Romanian (at home they also spoke Yiddish, the communal language of the Jewish East End),[16] was 'artistic, disorderly, [...] talked a lot and didn't work as hard as her teachers would wish'. Her teachers believed that she needed to be 'more purposeful and thorough' and particularly noted her 'artistic temperament'. These remarks were repeated annually and summarised on her 'career card'[17] when she left in the summer of 1910, after winning a scholarship to the Royal Female School of Art.

Founded in 1842 in Queen Square, The Royal Female School of Art moved to Southampton Row in 1908 when it became part of the Central School of Art and Design (now Central St Martins), but kept its own separate staff and curriculum until it was fully incorporated in 1913. Originally known as the Female School of Design, its function was 'primarily to provide a training for working-class women', though it also accepted 'those of higher social standing who had fallen on hard times, to enable them to earn a living'.[18] At the time of its merger with the Central School, the majority of classes continued to be held in the evenings to enable students to continue working in their professions during the day.

It is not known whether Birnberg was ever apprenticed to a profession, but this would have been a likely option for someone of her class and background. Many of the Whitechapel Boys – Rosenberg, Gertler and Bomberg among them – began as apprentices, attending classes in the evenings at Birkbeck, the Regent St Poly and the Central School respectively, before attending the Slade full-time with the aid of the Jewish Educational Aid Society.[19] Although it was possible to transfer to the Slade after winning a scholarship from the Central (William Roberts did so in 1910), it is likely that Birnberg simply transferred her £40 scholarship from the London County Council to the Slade,[20] where she was admitted 'on the strength of her promise'.[21] However, her transfer from an institution where art was practised as a trade to one where it was regarded as a vocation would, in itself, have signalled a change in her future aspirations.

Birnberg was 18 when she arrived at the Slade in October 1910,[22] at a time when her fellow students were 'seething'[23] under the influence of Post-Impressionism, following Roger Fry's two seminal shows in 1910 and 1912. But her frustration is clear from her later recollection that during this time of experimentation, she was taught to look back to the example of masters such as Ingres, as well as to the work of Alphonse Legros, a former professor whose drawings covered the Slade's walls.[24] The legendary drawing master Tonks famously reduced many new students to tears with his sarcasm, but his clash with Birnberg, whom he apparently classed as 'a gifted student',[25] sounds tame in comparison to the experience of most:

Tonks: 'Do you really see things like that?'
I could only say: 'Yes of course!'
Tonks: 'Alright, go on.'[26]

However, Birnberg later claimed she was made 'miserable' by his negative remarks and described him as 'a woman-hater'.[27]

In her first year (1910–11) Birnberg studied drawing under Tonks five days a week. In practice this would have been mostly from the Antique (shared with the men), though all students were admitted to the (separate) men's or women's life room at the end of the day to make rapid sketches from the model. Most students had to undergo a probationary period before being awarded a Certificate for Drawing, gaining Professor Brown's agreement to move into the life room fulltime,[28] so we cannot be sure that Birnberg did so (though the fact that she went on to other classes in her second year, suggests that she made progress). It is likely that Birnberg's portrait head of *Abdul Baha* (1911, fig. 22),[29] a sensitive and accomplished drawing in the Slade manner, was executed in these classes. From 1911–12 Birnberg studied six days a week, taking, in addition to drawing, anatomy (also under Tonks, a former surgeon with a 'raking' eye), perspective (under George Thompson) and art history (under Roger Fry). Although there is no record of her studying painting (under Philip Wilson Steer), her autobiography[30] suggests that she did so.[31]

Traditionally, women had flourished under the Slade method of teaching: Lady Dorothy Stanley under Sir Edward Poynter; Laura Anning Bell, Mary Sargant Florence and the illustrator Kate Greenaway under Legros; and in the 1890s, Ethel Walker, Gwen John and Edna Waugh under the celebrated triumvirate of Brown, Tonks and Steer. Women had also, from the start, won a high proportion of the

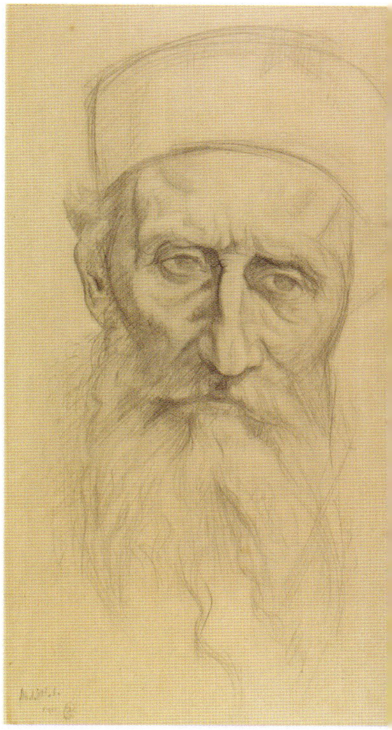

FIG. 22 *above*
CLARE WINSTEN (CLARA BIRNBERG)
Portrait of Abdul Baha, 1911

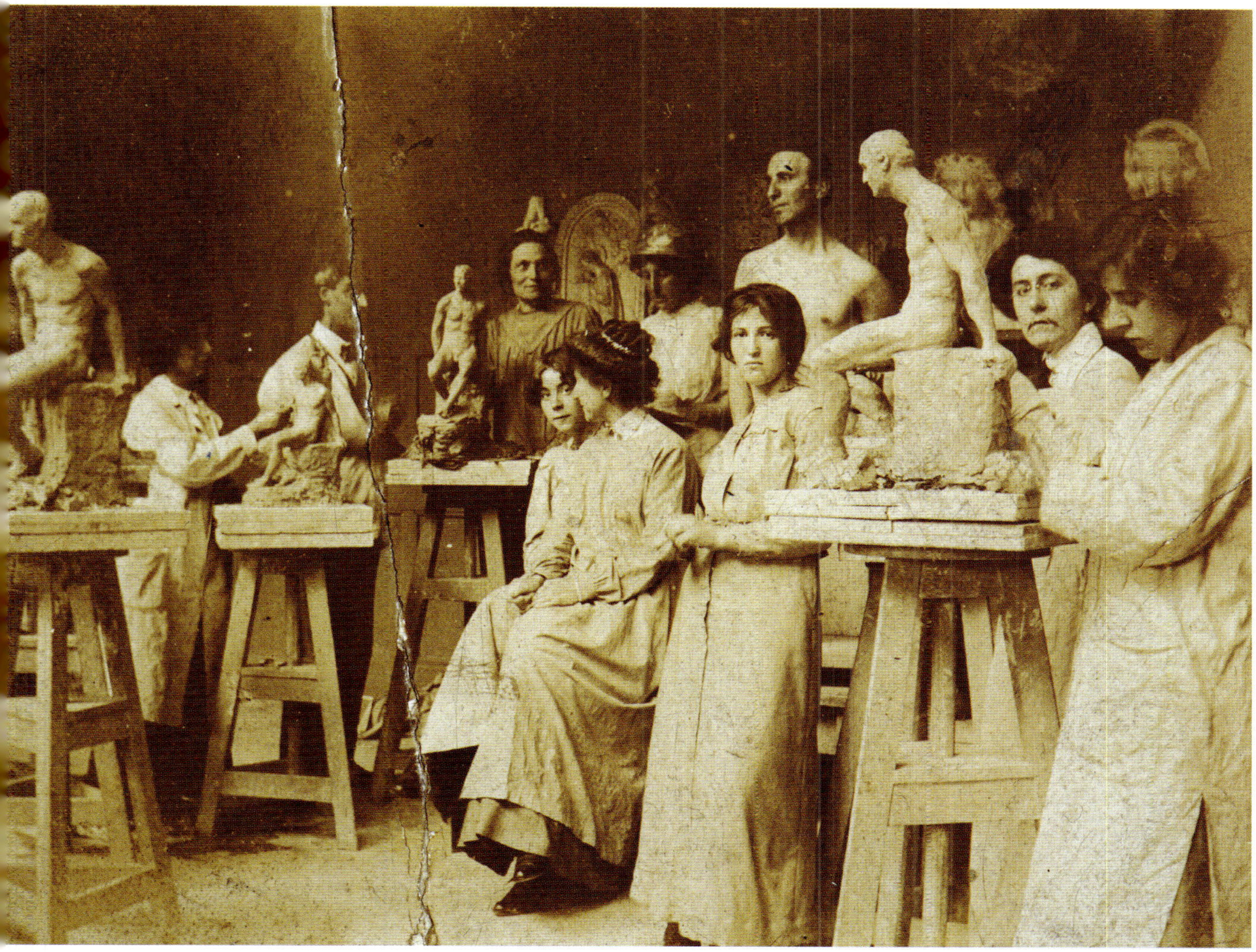

FIG. 48 *left*
Clara Birnberg [standing, 3rd from right] *in the Life-modelling Room (?at the Slade), c.*1910–12

Slade's scholarships and prizes and Birnberg's fellow women students included Dora Carrington (1893–1932), who carried off four prizes for Figure Painting and Composition. However, women were also subject to stricter controls: no woman, the rules stated, was to be admitted as a student of the college 'except upon the recommendation of the Lady Superintendent Miss Morison, and upon producing a satisfactory reference or introduction'. Naturally, this stipulation, which continued until after the First World War, did not apply to the men.

Women also outnumbered the men by almost four to one. Their intake included both aspiring artists and a number of middle- and upper-class students whose parents regarded the Slade as socially superior to the local branch schools but no more than a stage on their daughters' path to marriage, an attitude which clashed with Tonks's absolute dedication to high art. Although the Hon. Dorothy Brett (the daughter of Lord Esher) claimed that Professor Brown told her that they did not welcome her type (i.e. debutantes), records show that these students were an important part of the school. Not only did the ordinary fee payers keep the school running, they also provided pedestrian vehicles on the backs of which the outstanding pupils could climb – and shine.

Some of the male students, however, shared Tonks's impatience. Stanley Spencer is said to have told Birnberg that women artists were to him 'a contradiction in terms'.[32] C R W Nevinson – whose mother, Margaret, was one of the founders of the Women's Freedom League, which Birnberg herself would join – advised Carrington that as a female artist she would have 'quite simply a bloody struggle in front of you'. He was referring to that 'vile dead wall of prejudice & hatred against a woman or still worse that superficial summing out [sic] of your work as 'too clever' that so-called people of taste are addicted to [...] especially [to] women [as] you lose your youth.'[33]

However, Birnberg also felt isolated from the other female students, whom she believed to be 'chiefly [...] women from Kensington and Chelsea boasting of weekly trips to Paris and their dress designers.'[34] Their backgrounds could not have been more different from her own. These women were exemplified by the 'notable trio' of Lady Violet Charteris, Lady Diana Manners (both daughters of the Duke of Rutland) and Iris Tree:

> all spectacularly beautiful and dressed in the height of fashion. They were at the school for only a short time, but long enough to cause a sensation, and their work in the Antique received what [other female students] felt to be excessive attention from the staff, including even Tonks. The crowning touch was the group of handsome young men, in top hats and frock-coats, who took up position every morning in the entrance hall, waiting to take the beauties out to lunch.[35]

When another trio of female students, Carrington, Brett and Barbara Hiles, 'confessed their feeling of pique to their friend Gerald Shove, who was then sharing a house in Gower Street with Maynard Keynes, he presented himself at the Slade one day, attired for the occasion in top hat and frock-coat, and escorted them down the road to No. 3 for a luncheon of scrambled eggs, cooked by Hiles.'[36] Since, as Lisa Tickner has observed, 'around 1912 all the working-class students were male *and Jewish*, since only with philanthropic support could working-class students afford the fees',[37] it is clear that as the only working-class *female* Jewish student of her generation, Birnberg was particularly isolated.

Birnberg also seems to have kept an exceptionally low profile at the Slade: she does not appear in any of the known accounts by her many famous contemporaries (including the Whitechapel Boys); she is not listed as having won any prizes; and she does not appear in the famous Slade photograph of 1912. Nor did she establish a platform like many of the Whitechapel Boys at any of the contemporary exhibiting societies: the AAA (Allied Artists' Association), Friday Club or NEAC (New English Art Club) – the latter seen as a natural stepping stone for Slade pupils and where the majority of the Whitechapel Boys all exhibited at least one work.[38] Nor did she exhibit with more specialist societies such as the Society of Women Artists, founded in 1855,[39] or The Women's International Arts Club, possibly because she preferred to be judged alongside her male contemporaries as simply an artist and not specifically a *female* artist. Although some women (such as Carrington) were famously reticent about exhibiting, the fact that Birnberg signed and dated her work in this period suggests, as Stephen Chaplin has observed, that 'a public face was intended'.[40] Nevertheless, the Slade's usual success nurturing 'outsiders'[41] seems to have failed Birnberg.

She overlapped at the Slade with three of the principal Whitechapel Boys: Gertler, then only part-time in order to concentrate on 'Jewish subjects', Bomberg (1911–13) and Rosenberg (1911–14), the last two almost inseparable. Bomberg soon noticed Birnberg's good looks and during a period of intense admiration for Michelangelo, he cast her in the role of a Michelangelesque Sibyl. She recalled how 'he used to waylay me at the station and follow me everywhere,' and though she initially rebuffed his advances ('because I didn't like his manner – he was too forward') she eventually agreed after he cornered her in the library and asked her to pose for him, perhaps flattered when he told her 'I want to do a great painting of you in the style of Michelangelo.'[42] The sittings took place at Bomberg's home in Whitechapel, with Birnberg 'wearing Greek clothes, which fitted the Michelangelo idea.'[43] The painting, however, has not survived.

Bomberg's admiration for Michelangelo was at it most intense around 1911, however, the superficial

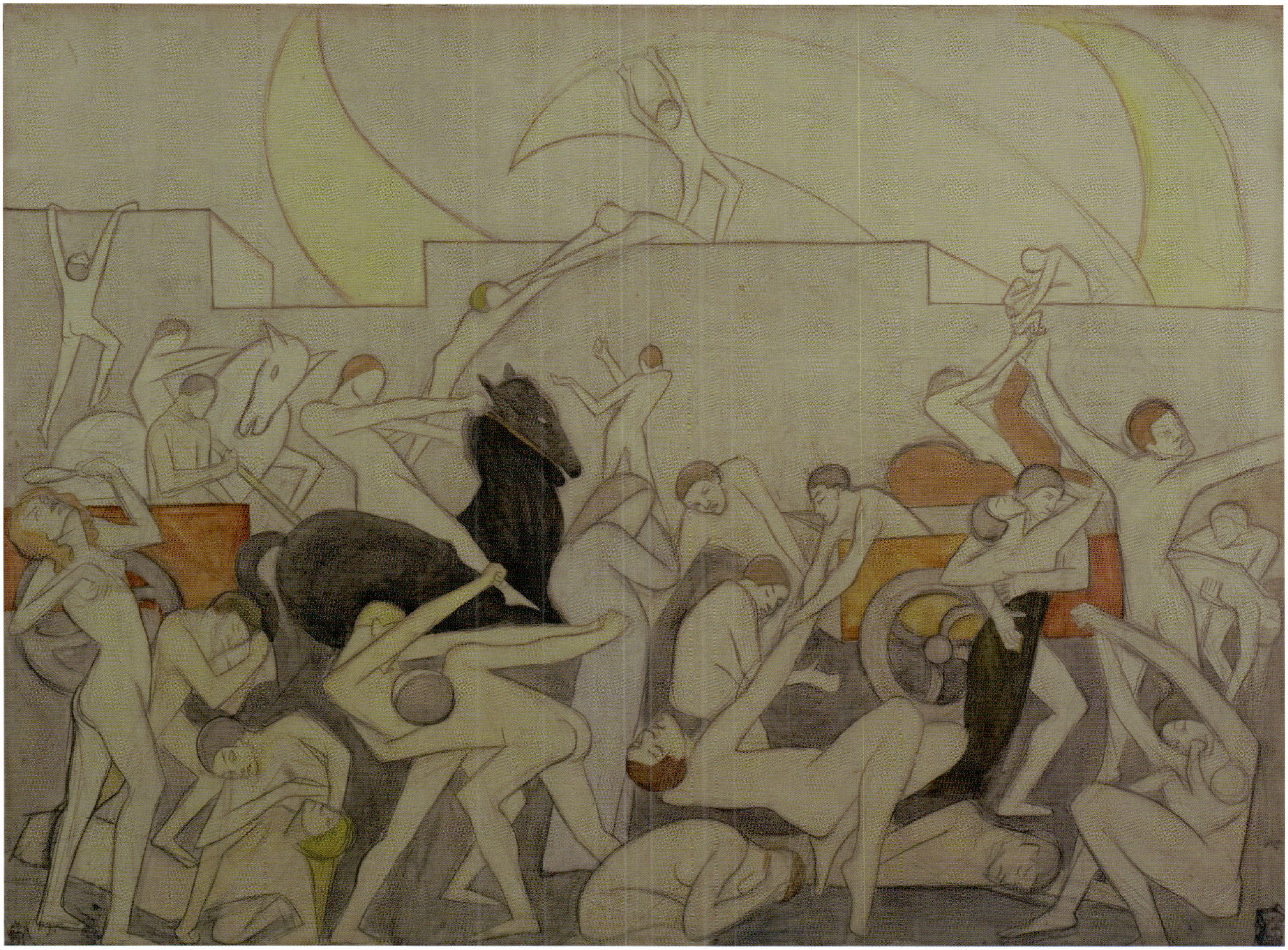

43
CLARE WINSTEN (CLARA BIRNBERG)
Attack, 1910

similarities between a number of their early works suggests that his relationship with Birnberg took place slightly later between 1911–13, when, under the influence of Post-Impressionism, she began to work along similar lines. Among these works is the large, unfinished watercolour, *Attack* (cat no. 43), possibly a study intended for transfer to canvas, and inscribed verso (probably in her daughter Theodora's hand) 'CLARE (WINSTEN) BIRN, 17 years old, 1910'. We cannot be certain about the dating therefore, but similarly ambitious, large-scale, multi-figure compositions on biblical themes were entered for the Slade summer competitions in 1911 and 1912. Birnberg's composition in *Attack*, has echoes of Uccello's *The Battle of San Romano*, which she would have known from the National Gallery. Her watercolour draws on a similar landscape format dominated by the image of the plunging horse in the centre ground. However, Birnberg's figures are not cast in heroic mood, nor do they share the same decorative quality. She also omits the thrusting lances, famously reinterpreted by Kandinsky in 1911, although her treatment of the horses apparently owes something to Franz Marc.[44] Instead, under the influence of Post-Impressionism – particularly Gauguin's flat, bold colouring – Birnberg's expressive figures display a variety of poses ranging from struggle to lament, pared down to their essentials. Behind them, the carts and wall are reduced to mere blocks, while in the background huge, curved, scimitar-like blades slice across the landscape.

Many of the same influences can be seen in one of Birnberg's most fascinating works from this period, to date her earliest known oil, entitled *Dawn* (aka *Morning*, *c*.1910–12, fig. 24), in which a dozen, naked figures on the left of the canvas – again simplified but expressive – stretch and unbend in the early morning sunlight, against a dramatic cliff-top setting overlooking the sea. This work also has strong affinities compositionally with Gauguin, particularly in the placing of the figures, and with Bomberg, in the dynamic vertical division of the canvas[45], as well as echoes of the mural painter Puvis de Chavannes. Conceptually, compositionally and technically, *Dawn* may be compared to the Slade summer competition entries by three other students in 1912: Bomberg's *Island of Joy* (*c*. 1912),[46] Rosenberg's *Hark, Hark, the Lark* (1912, cat no. 16), and William Roberts's *David Choosing the Three Days' Pestilence* (1912),[47] all of which feature figures in similar attitudes, though the context – waking, stretching or giving thanks – varies. Although not as large or accomplished as Bomberg's *Island of Joy* canvas, *Dawn* is still a substantial and impressive student work, which demonstrates Birnberg's potential.

FIG. 24 *right*
CLARE WINSTEN (CLARA BIRNBERG)
Dawn (aka *Morning*), *c*.1910–12

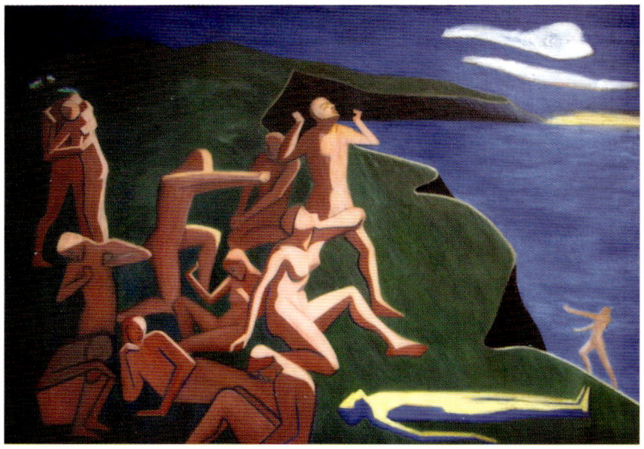

FIG. 12 *below*
DAVID BOMBERG
Vision of Ezekiel, 1912

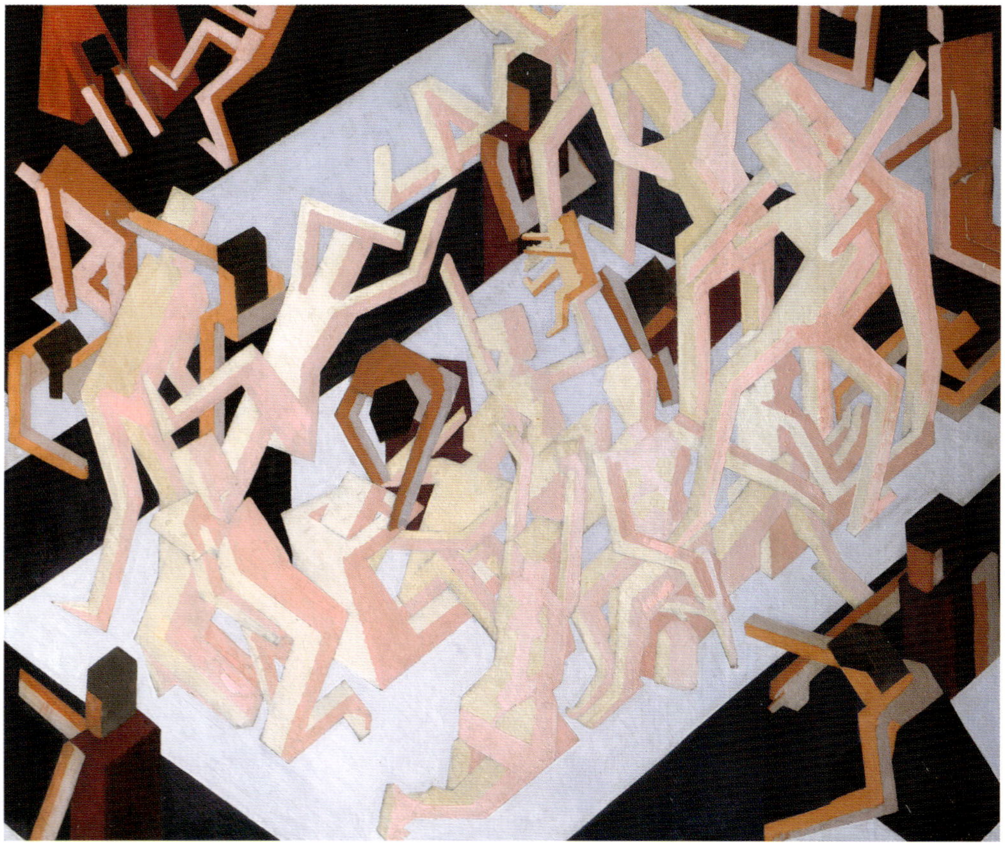

Two further untitled figurative studies, which clearly relate to the work of this period and move closer towards abstraction, also echo the work of Bomberg. The first (*Untitled*, c.1911),[48] employs a bold palette and shows the figures not only flattened but reduced to sharply-defined shapes: their heads and crossed limbs form triangles while in the centre there are a number of rudimentary hand-drawn black grids. The crudely-drawn figures are ambiguous: they may be awakening, as in *Dawn*, or struggling, as in *Attack*. However, the device of figures emerging from a grid was used several times in contemporaneous works by Bomberg including *Island of Joy* (c.1912),[49] *Study for Vision of Ezekiel* (c.1912)[50] and *Vision of Ezekiel* (1912, fig. 12).[51] In Birnberg's composition, a larger figure, presumably an adult, cradles a smaller one, presumably a child, anticipating Bomberg's studies for *In the Hold* (1913–14),[52]which show a child being passed over the heads of the passengers (or ship-builders) emerging from the grid-like hold.

In Birnberg's second untitled composition (*Untitled Figure Study*, c.1912, fig. 23), both technique and execution are more sophisticated and the composition is more finished than in her previous work. The figures appear to be actively struggling, locked in combat as their limbs thrash against a backdrop of black and green. In both studies, the figures push against the edges of the composition and spill over, still struggling. It is likely that the subject-matter is biblical[53] and it appears to relate closely to Bomberg's *Island of Joy*. Birnberg employs the same colouring for her figures, though they are not specifically grounded in the East End like Bomberg's dockers. The presence of a grid anticipates Bomberg's *Mud Bath* (1914).[54] While Bomberg moved closer to abstraction however, Birnberg's design remains essentially figurative. Her composition lacks the complexity of Bomberg's but is nonetheless taut and controlled. Like Bomberg, she shared with the nascent Vorticists a certain restlessness and dynamism in her active, colourful forms, but she appears to have stopped at this point, retreating from total

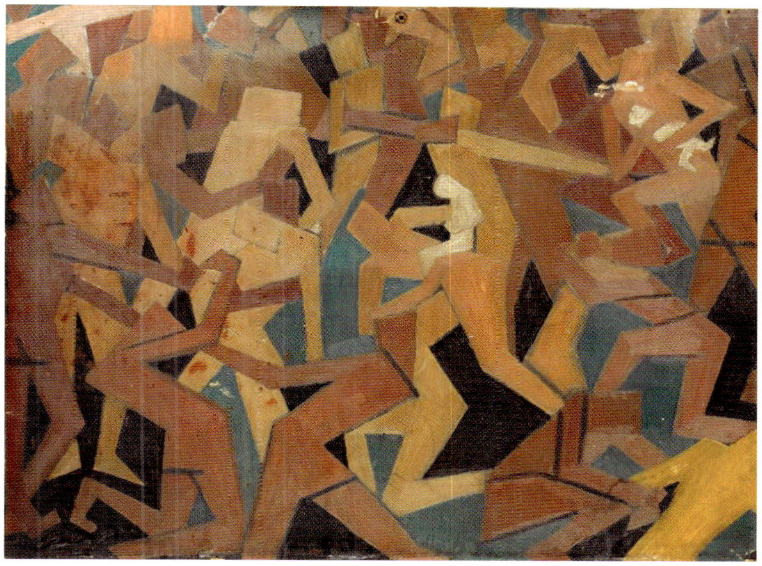

FIG. 23
CLARE WINSTEN (CLARA BIRNBERG)
Untitled Figure Study, c.1912

abstraction. It is impossible to know how closely she worked alongside Bomberg at this time, particularly since their relationship ended badly. Whatever really passed between them, Birnberg genuinely believed that 'her painting – freedom of mark and "inspiration" [had been] taken by Bomberg', and her bitterness against him rankled to the end of her life.[55]

Stephen Chaplin has noted the influence of the European modernists in Winsten's drawings: 'Those which appear to be early share a rhythmic simplification with the generation of Gaudier-Brzeska, and a heritage from Brancusi, Picasso of around 1908, and Matisse of the "Dance". Many of these were shown at the Strang in 1994 but were not photographed and most are no longer in the public domain.

Post-Slade, Birnberg's work appeared to return more directly to the figurative. *Female Head*, possibly a self-portrait (c.1910–20, fig. 25), with direct gaze and bobbed hair, shows strength of character as well as a bold, confident use of line, that of the 'New Woman'. Lisa Tickner observes how Birnberg embraced a number of personal freedoms in this period: she was 'a member of the Women's Freedom League,[56] studying at the Central School[57] and at the Slade, working for Heal's and the Omega Workshops,[58]

FIG. 25
CLARE WINSTEN (CLARA BIRNBERG)
Female Head (?Self-Portrait), c.1910–20

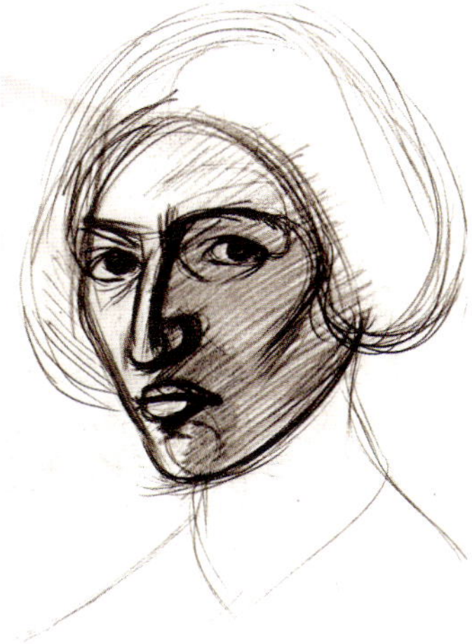

44
CLARE WINSTEN (CLARA BIRNBERG)
Portrait of Isaac Rosenberg, 1913

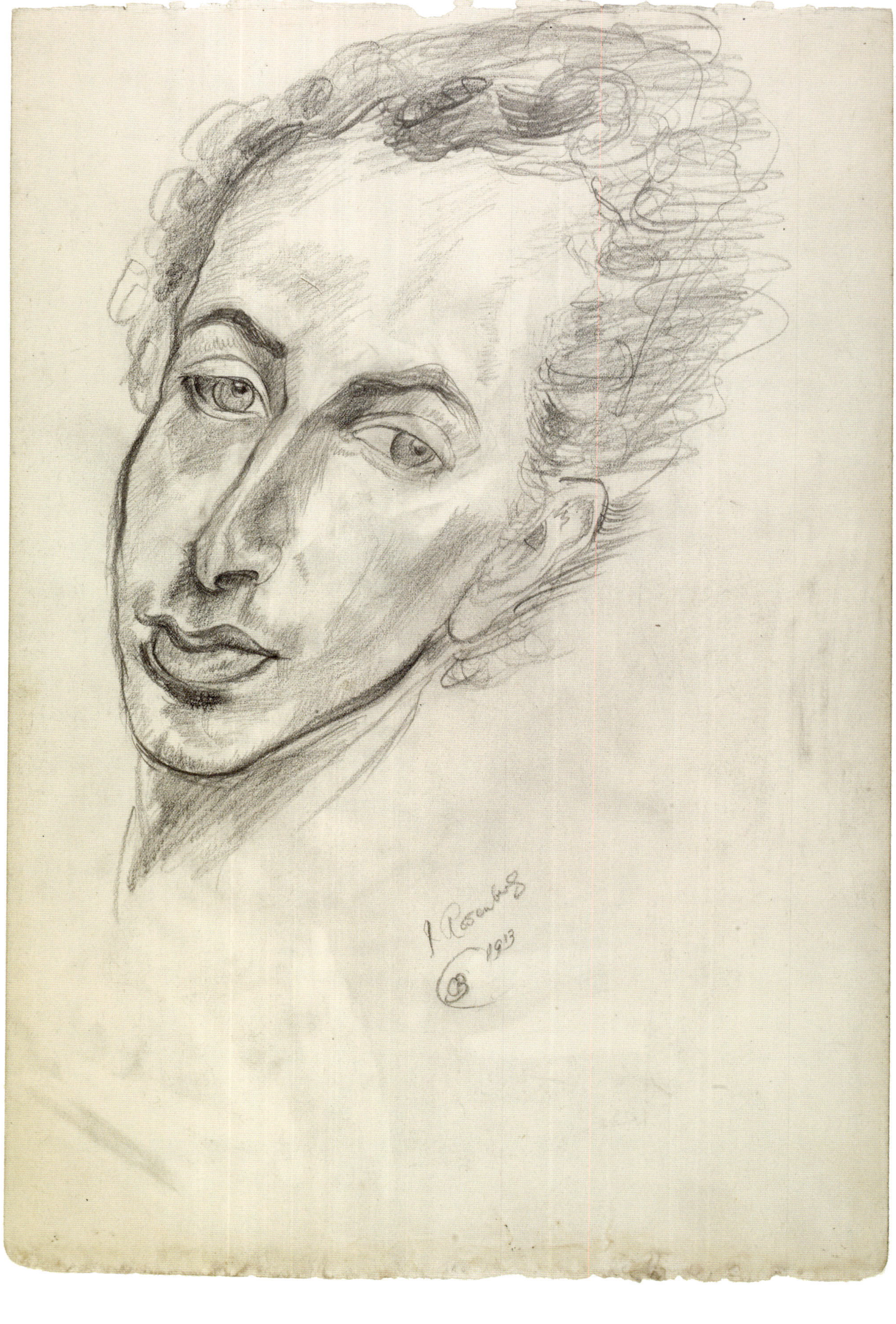

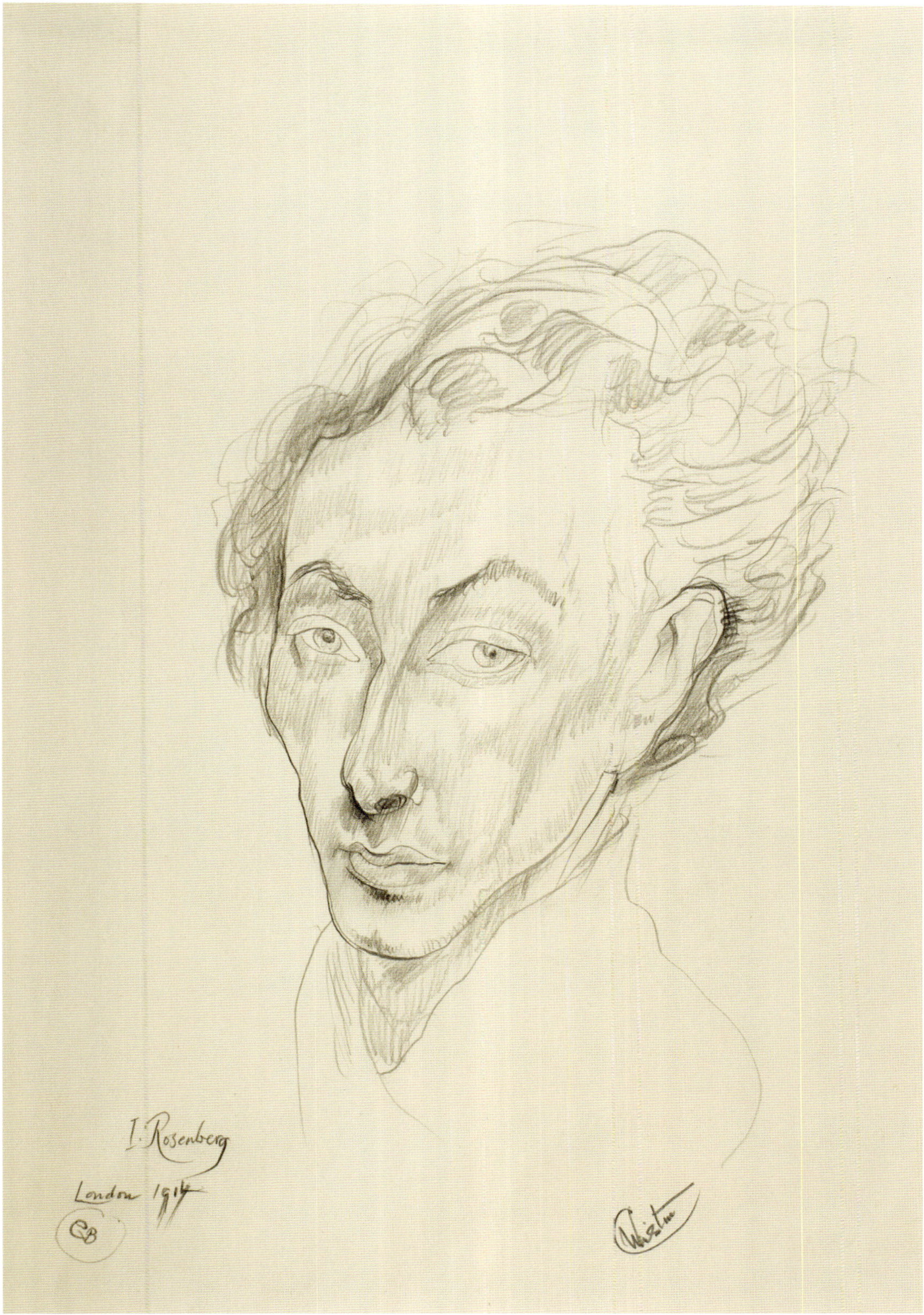

45

CLARE WINSTEN (CLARA BIRNBERG)

Portrait of Isaac Rosenberg, 1914

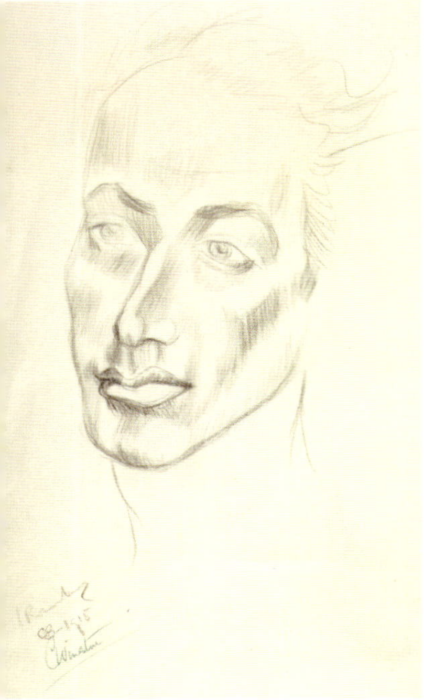

FIG. 26
CLARE WINSTEN (CLARA BIRNBERG)
Isaac Rosenberg, 1915

6 *opposite*
ISAAC ROSENBERG
Self-Portrait, 1911

with a studio in the City Road'.[59] Stephen Chaplin has noted how the act of cutting her hair short was 'a more personal witness to emancipation'.[60]

Birnberg clearly kept up her contact with Rosenberg after leaving the Slade and her earliest known portrait of him, a graphite study of his head, tilted to one side and inscribed 'I Rosenberg CB 1913' (cat no. 44), dates from this time. The face is sensitively drawn in the recognisable Italianate style favoured by Tonks, using soft shading on the neck and hair and a firmer, darker line around the jaw and cheekbone. The eyes, which stare straight out towards the viewer, are large and heavy-lidded, the eyebrows arched, the nose long and sensitive, the lips curled. Even without knowing the sitter it would be no surprise to learn that this is the portrait of an artist and poet.

Both the pose and the angle of the head appear to relate closely to Rosenberg's own *Self-Portrait* (cat no. 6) of three years earlier but Birnberg's portrait is softer, more romantic in mood. Although nothing is known of the sitting and Birnberg had already left the Slade by this time, it is interesting to note that David Bomberg's portrait of Rosenberg, *Head of a Poet* (fig. 13), which won the Tonks' prize for drawing at the Slade, was also executed in the same year. Bomberg is clearly the finer draughtsman: the slightly foreshortened view of his portrait – a favourite device at this stage of his work – shows greater skill and depth, as well as his indebtedness to Michelangelo. Yet Birnberg's is perhaps the greater likeness, and both portraits capture something of their subject's innate sensitivity.

Birnberg's second portrait of Rosenberg (cat no. 45), executed in pencil and inscribed 'I Rosenberg 1914', relates very closely to the first, but is deliberately wispier and more insubstantial: the high cheekbones are now hollow, the whole face is drawn and shadows appear beneath the eyes. Stephen Chaplin has commented on the 'emotional tension' of some of her early drawings, which range from the 'daemonic or formally reductive' to the 'sharply skeletal',[61] and it is tempting to see a foreshadowing of Rosenberg's early death in this etiolated, ghostly presence. A third, recently discovered drawing (fig. 26) of Rosenberg (signed 'CB – 1915', later signed again 'CWinsten'), concentrates on the lower face and is closest conceptually to the earlier drawing.

It is likely that Birnberg made her exhibiting debut at the Whitechapel Art Gallery's *Twentieth Century Art: A Review of Modern Movements*, in May–June 1914, where she only one of two contributors (the other was a male contemporary, Hubert Schloss) represented both within and without the much-debated 'Jewish Section',[62] co-curated by Bomberg and Epstein. The significance of this is difficult to assess: as Tickner has pointed out, 'the section was not as it were ethnically watertight. Neither "Britishness" nor "Jewishness" or any other component of identity and experience was considered in the catalogue or related to its social and aesthetic distinctions of movement and style.'[63] (Nevertheless, Birnberg's sensitivity to her origins and later anglicisation suggest how important identity was to her).

Despite the high number of exhibits overall (494), it was undoubtedly prestigious to have been included in such a wide-ranging review of modern British art, and to appear in such eminent company. Birnberg had one exhibit in the Lower Gallery, (no. 31) intriguingly entitled *Sketch for 'Fire' Composition*,[64] sandwiched between works by two other female contemporaries, the Vorticist Helen Saunders[65] and Amy Drucker,[66] whose work was placed next to one by Thérèse Lessore,[67] forming a small sub-section of work by women.

This section was followed by a display of objects from the Omega Workshops,[68] where Birnberg had worked in 1913, and it is possible that some of the objects she decorated were among them. Within the 'Jewish Section', she also had two works on display (nos. 300 and 303), both presumably works on paper and both entitled *Study of Head*. Tucked away in 'the passage' alongside drawings by Jacob Kramer, they were praised by a conservative press for showing

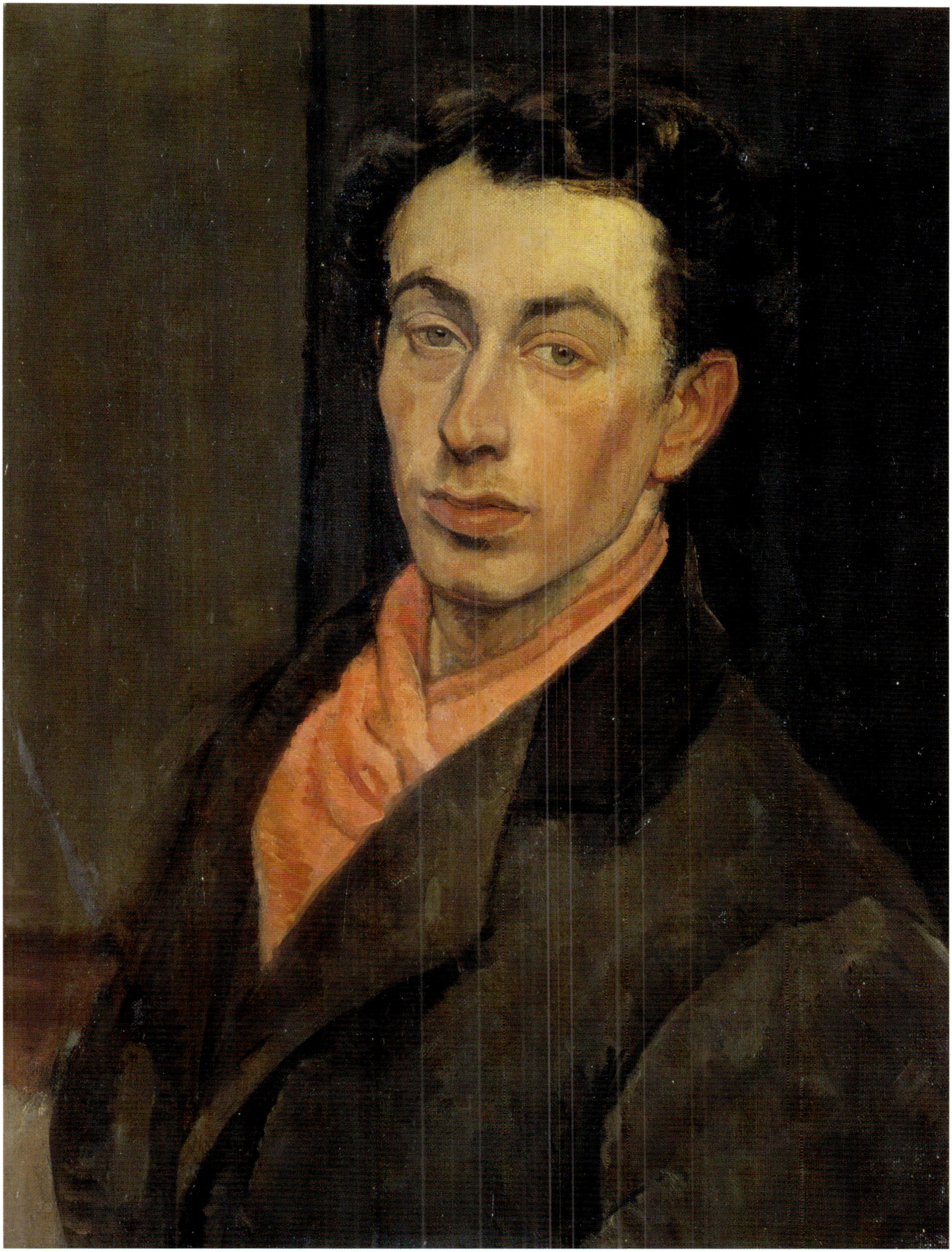

'fine delicacy and refinement of outlook.'[69] Tickner, who suggests that Birnberg's portraits of Rosenberg may have been among them, concludes that these drawings were 'probably quite conventional and would have diluted the bravura effect' of works elsewhere had they not been 'separated out as chiefly drawings and modest in scale'.[70] However, the title of Birnberg's *Sketch for 'Fire' Composition* hints at the inclusion of a more innovative, possibly even abstract composition. It is notable that either Birnberg as exhibitor, or perhaps more likely Bomberg as curator, took the decision not to exhibit her most innovative work in the 'Jewish Section' alongside his own.

Bomberg and Epstein were, in December 1913, both founder members of the London Group, a platform (certainly initially) for emerging British modernism, which held its first exhibition the following March, and which absorbed several Whitechapel Boys including Gertler, Jacob Kramer and Bernard Meninsky. Birnberg certainly aspired to membership of the London Group and put herself up for nomination but was rejected.[71] Both Epstein and Bomberg would also soon be associated with Wyndham Lewis's developing Vorticist movement.

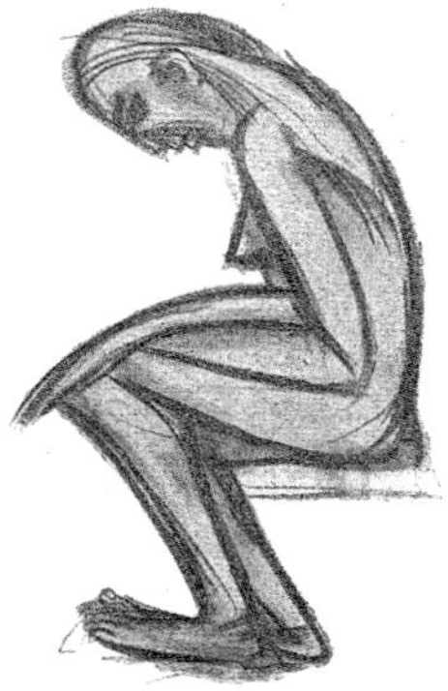

FIG. 30
CLARE WINSTEN (CLARA BIRNBERG)
*Seated Female Vorticist Figure, c.*1920

Birnberg's work never fully embraced the geometric abstraction favoured by the female Vorticists, Jessica Dismorr and Helen Saunders, though she would certainly have seen their work at the Whitechapel in 1914, and been aware of the publication of *Blast* in June 1914 and the Vorticist exhibition in June 1915. Two (undated) studies published in 1920 under the name 'C B Winsten',[72] show that her work was not untouched by this movement: a downward-looking, pensive female head and a Vorticist-influenced nude (*Seated Female Vorticist Figure, c.*1920, fig. 30), whose neatly-folded compact form is sharply defined by bold black contours, which emphasise both her curves and her jagged edges, and has close affinities to Jacob Kramer's *Vorticist Figure* (1920).[73] There is no indication that C B Winsten (as she signed her work post-war) was involved with the Vorticists, but she certainly knew Ezra Pound as her fine head study of him (fig 28.) in 1920 indicates. However, at this interesting juncture Birnberg's experiments with modernism appear to have largely stopped. It may simply have been that with the outbreak of the First World War her energies were redeployed into a number of other directions: the Women's Freedom League,[74] pacifism, her marriage to Stephen Winsten, the birth of their first child, Theodora (b. 1917), during his subsequent imprisonment, and afterwards, the birth of two further children: Ruth (b. 1920) and Christopher (b.1923).

C B Winsten maintained only an irregular presence in group exhibitions in London in the late twenties and early thirties in the Goupil Gallery salons.[75] And in 1937, a book entitled *Modern English Art*, by Christopher Blake – possibly a pseudonymn for her husband Stephen Winsten[76] – included three portraits by Winsten among works by Walter Sickert, Augustus John, Philip Wilson Steer, John Nash, Paul Nash, Laura Knight, C R W Nevinson, William Rothenstein, Duncan Grant, Edward Wadsworth, Edward Burra, Ben Nicholson and Alfred Wolmark.[77] However, the available evidence suggests[78] that thereafter Winsten's time was divided among her many activities and did not allow her to pursue a dedicated and sustained career as a painter.

It is not known exactly when Clara Birnberg met her husband. 'Simy' – variously known as Samuel or Simon[79] – Weinstein (1893–1991), later became Stephen Winsten. He and Clara had grown up only streets apart and it is possible that their fathers knew each other. Stephen's father, 'a bearded Jewish scholar-type' from Vilna (then part of Russia), was an expert on the Talmud and Jewish folklore. His children were also political and intellectual: Stephen's oldest brother, Rachmiel, stayed on in Russia and became a leader of the Bund (the Jewish Social Democratic Labour Party), founded in Vilna in 1897, going on to become a Soviet Commissar until he was 'purged' by Stalin.[80] One of his sisters, according to Leftwich, was ‘a pioneer Zionist, when Zionism in the East End and in Anglo-Jewry generally was a small movement. Her husband, Zalkind Stalbow, was active in the first Zionist group, the Bnai Zion, and active both in Tarbut and the Yiddish movement.’[81]

Little is known of Stephen Winsten’s early education. In 1908 he applied unsuccessfully to the JEAS for assistance. Leftwich implies in his 1911 diary that Winsten was public-school educated and proud of his learning.[82] Like most Whitechapel families, the Winstens were poor and shared their home with a lodger, ‘a talented Yiddish actor [called] Balsam’.[83] Together with Joseph Leftwich and John Rodker, Stephen Winsten was a member of the original Whitechapel Boys[84] and like them was intellectual, political, combative and collaborative. Under Rosenberg’s influence, they all wrote poetry and worked together on ‘a composite novel describing their common experiences, friendship and environment. Each would write one or two chapters a week, which they would then try to weld into a whole at the group meeting.’[85] By 1911 Winsten was a teacher in a Board School, with one of Rosenberg’s younger brothers among his pupils. At this time, he was particularly close to Leftwich, who often helped him plan the following day’s lessons in the evenings. Winsten enjoyed Rosenberg’s company: ‘I regarded him as an interesting bit of sculpture on which to gaze. I like the long, intellectual face, the pensive, twinkling eyes and the mystery he carried with him’,[86] but would soon fall out with Rodker, with whom he argued incessantly.

The Weinsteins (as they remained until after the war when they anglicised their names and took on new identities as S(tephen) and C(lare) B Winsten) probably married between 1914–16.[87] It was during this period that Clara sat to Rosenberg for her portrait in 1915, wearing a Florentine-style blue dress, which he merged with a modernist red background.[88] He captured a recognisable likeness in the wide forehead, even features and full mouth, but Clara’s expression is impassive and her mood impossible

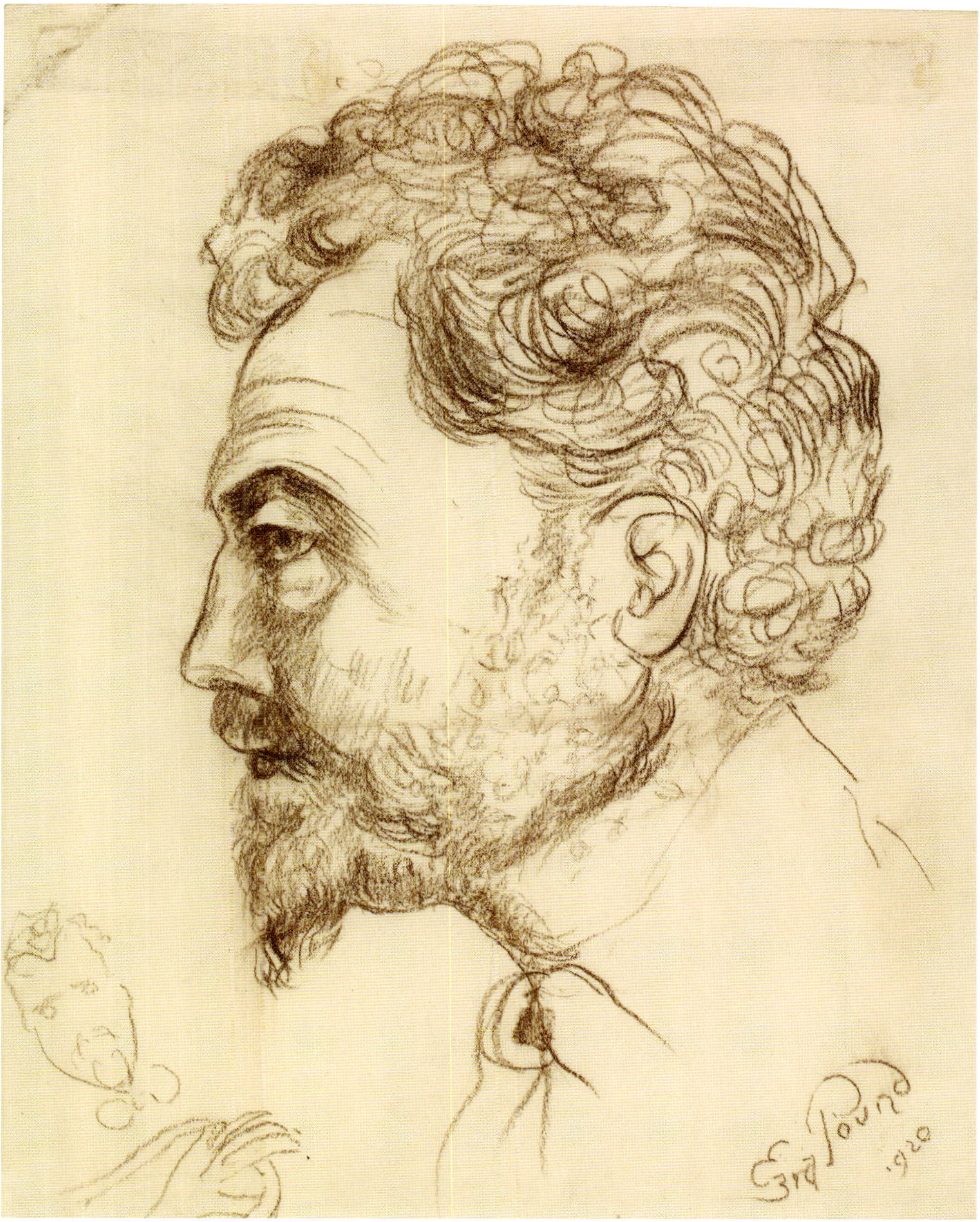

FIG. 28
CLARE WINSTEN (CLARA BIRNBERG)
*Portrait of Ezra Pound, c.*1920

to gage. In the same year, Rosenberg is listed (probably erroneously) as among those who joined Stephen Winsten and others at the foundation meeting of the Jewish Association of Arts and Sciences.[89] Through this group Winsten remained involved with the indigenous culture of the East End, becoming for a while Secretary of the Ben Uri Arts Society, which had also been established earlier in 1915.

The Winstens may have been among the thousands of anti-war protestors who gathered in Trafalgar Square on 2 August 1914. This opposition was behind the 1915 No-Conscription Fellowship headed by Bertrand Russell, which successfully campaigned to secure 'the conscience clause' in the 1916 Conscription Act: the right to claim exemption from military service. Over 16,000 men made that claim,[90] among them several of the Whitechapel Boys.[91] All had subsequently to attend a tribunal, comprising an interviewing panel with legal authority, to have the 'sincerity of their claims assessed'.[92] (Clara's brother Jonas was also a conscientious objector, though he was not imprisoned, and his future wife Naomi Bentwich was involved with Bertrand Russell and the No-Conscription Fellowship.)

Stephen Winsten was probably imprisoned soon after his tribunal in 1916 and was taken first to Wormwood Scrubs then transferred to Wandsworth Prison and still later to Bedford Prison. He spent the majority of his time at Wandsworth, where he may have contributed to the COs paper, known as *Old Lags Hansard,* which was once issued 'with an apology for late publication "owing to an official raid on our offices", the editor's cell.'[93] Harold Bing, a CO imprisoned in Winchester, and one of the instigators behind a prison magazine known as *The Winchester Whisperer*, recalled how it was 'written on thin brown sheets of toilet paper using the blunt end of a needle [...] [using] the ink supplied for monthly letters home. Just the one copy ("different people writing little essays or poems or humorous remarks, sometimes little cartoons or sketches") was passed secretly from one prisoner to another.'[94]

Stephen's imprisonment also inspired a collection of poems published under the title *Chains* (1920), which, as Jack Isaacs (who had been present at the inaugural meeting of the JAAS and reviewed the collection in *Voices* in 1920) pointed out, is most remarkable for its complete lack of bitterness. Nevertheless, glimpses of prison life can be gleaned from Winsten's poetry, though more from the titles than the substance. For instance, it is clear from the following that he underwent a number of privations: 'Prison Hunger' ('In sleep I dream, I eat and eat,/ Yet wake more hungry than before'); 'Bitter Cold (Wandsworth)' and 'Stillness of Wandsworth'. In 'The Workshop', where 'each sits on his hard stool and sews', Winsten suggest the monotony of prison life. 'The Wife: Husband on Hunger Strike' implies that, like fellow Whitechapel writer John Rodker, he also went on hunger strike for a time. 'To My Wife'

FIG. 49
Stephen ('Inca') and Clare Winsten in Clare's studio, c.1921–22

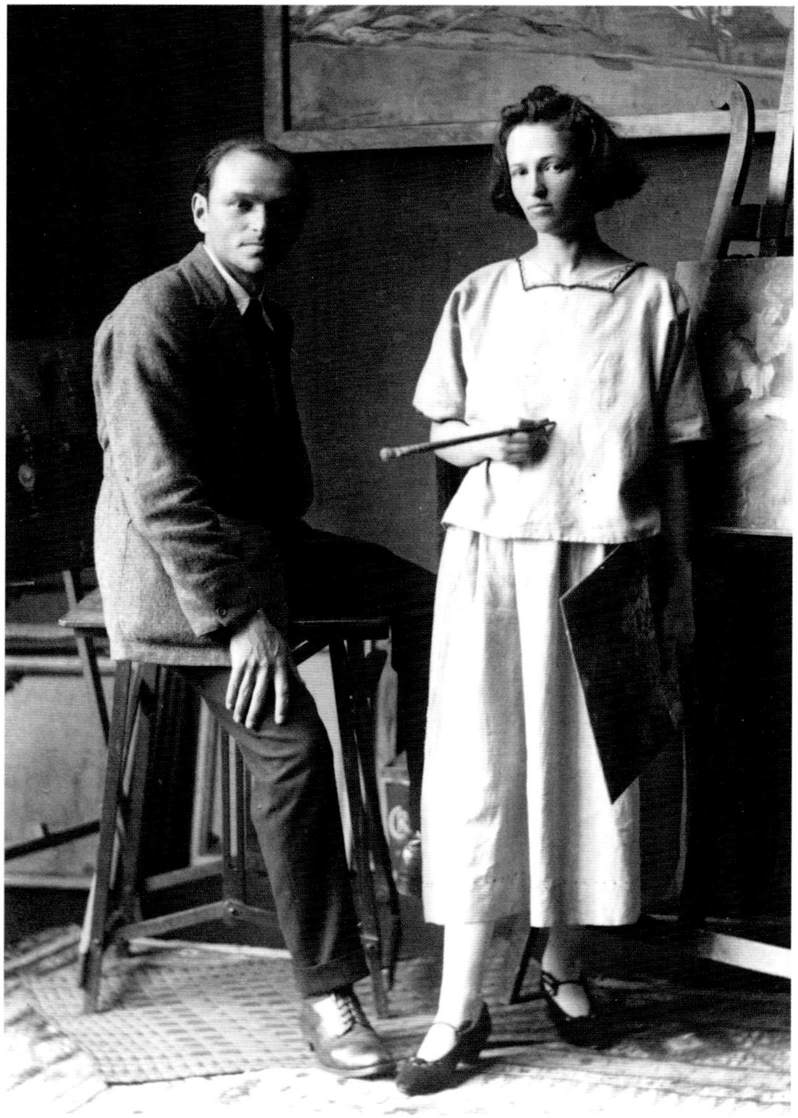

'Shall we forget/The long long years/When we were parted [...]' suggests the agony of separation and 'Becoming a Father in Prison' is followed by many fond references to his daughter Theo. In 'Recollection' the poet recalls passing 'the place my youth was spent,/My three best year, my golden year.'[95]

Pre-publication, ten of these poems were published in *Voices: in Poetry and Prose*, in November 1919,[96] together with two further poems and a prose piece in the February issue in 1920.[97] Thereafter, 'S. Winsten', as he always signed himself, became a regular presence in *Voices* throughout 1920, where he joined the editor, the journalist and writer Thomas Moult, as one of the commentators in the regular column 'Notes on Present-Day Art'.[98] Volume 3, March 1920, also included reproductions of two drawings by 'C. B. Winsten' (as she now signed her work), and in Vol 3, no 4, May 1920 in an article on 'The New Art Salon', Stephen Winsten included a specific, if modest, notice of his wife's work: 'The interesting experiment of C. B. Winsten in the small *Study of a Head* must be noticed. This is a brave attempt at colour speech; though the colour is strong and not toned down, the result certainly not extravagant; it is an earnest and striking method [...] of dealing with the living aspect of the face. It is also used to good effect in her landscapes.'[99]

Though the editorial work on *Voices* was unpaid, it at least provided Stephen with employment. It would have been difficult in any case, had he wanted to, to return to his pre-war employment of teaching since many advertisements for teachers stipulated 'No CO need apply'[100] (the Representation of the People act, passed on 6 February 1918, which granted the vote to women at 30, also disenfranchised conscientious objectors for five years). Stephen also subsequently became a commentator on art for *Renesans* (translated as 'Renaissance'), the Yiddish-language magazine set up and supported by the Ben Uri in 1920, and went on to edit the magazine *To-Morrow*.[101] (He also wrote at least two articles on Rosenberg and the early days of the Whitechapel Boys.[102])

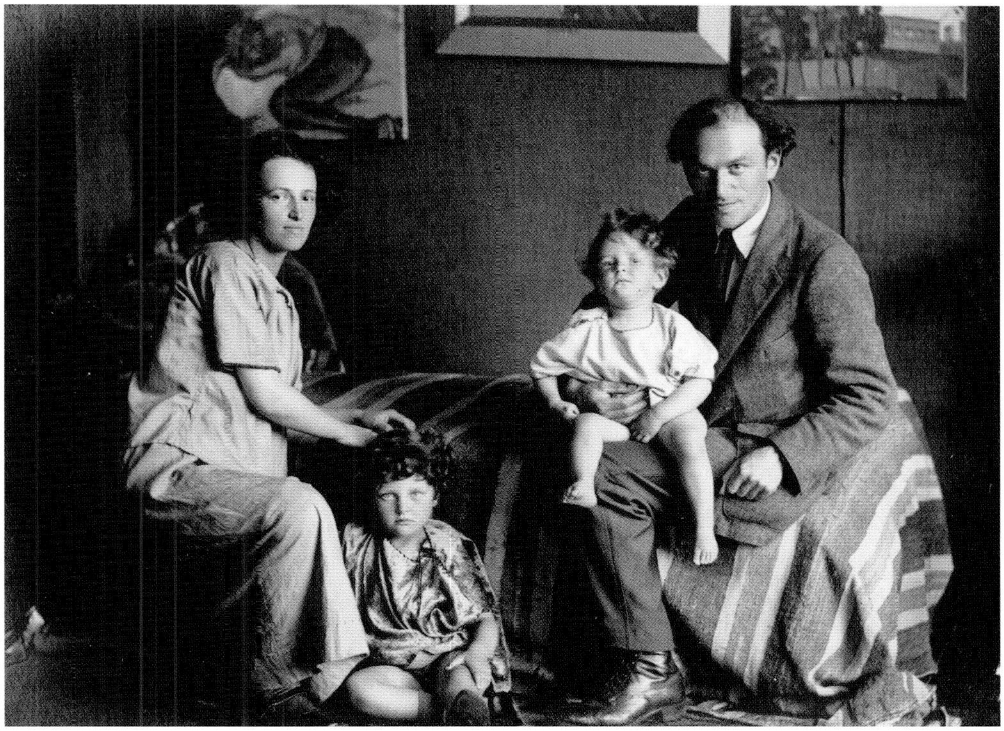

FIG. 50
Family group with Clare and Stephen ('Inca') Winsten and their daughters Theo and Ruth, c.1921–22

Later still, the Winstens apparently shook off their Jewish roots, embracing Quaker humanism (founded in 1939), though they remained lifelong pacifists, and Clare later modelled a bronze memorial sculpture to the pacifist and social work pioneer Jayne Addams *Mother and Child* (1968),[103] for Toynbee Hall in the East End, proving that she had not entirely severed her early Jewish links.

As humanists, pacifists and vegetarians, the Winstens were natural allies of the polemicist and playwright George Bernard Shaw when they became neighbours in the village of Ayot St Lawrence, Hertfordshire, in the late forties. Most of Stephen Winsten's works as a writer relate to this time. Over a decade (1946–56), he produced five books on Shaw, ranging from biography to reminiscences, which have led to accusations that he 'fashion[ed] a career out being Shaw's neighbour.' [104] However, Shaw certainly enjoyed the Winstens' company and, though he sat to many artists,[105] he also sat for at least three – probably more – portraits to Clare Winsten.[106] She also executed at least one bust of him, cast in an edition of three.[107] One of her drawings of him is in the British Museum (1946) and an oil (1945) is in a private collection.[108] Winsten painted a rather introspective portrait of the elderly playwright, white-haired and bearded and seated at his writing desk, his back reflected in the mirror behind. The writing pad in front of him contains the Shavian inscription, completed by Shaw himself in blue oil: 'I, Bernard Shaw, am sitting to Clare Winsten for her second/portrait of me in her studio in Ayot Saint Lawrence in this month of/May nineteen hundred and forty-five. They say the war ended the day/before yesterday; but…'.

Later Winsten sculpted a bronze figure of St Joan for Shaw's Corner, apparently at Shaw's request.[109] The art historian Gombrich, who knew the Winstens later in Oxford, described it as 'a statue that faithfully reflects the vision that Shaw had embodied in his play – a sturdy country girl, free of all sentimentality and […] artificial charm.'[110] In 1949 Clare 'collaborated' with Shaw on one of his last plays, *Buoyant Billions: a comedy of no manners in prose by Bernard Shaw and in pictures by Clare Winsten.*[111] Shaw also befriended the Winstens' children: paying for Christopher's education,[112] coaching Ruth at the Royal Academy of Arts,[113] and addressing a pamphlet, presumably to Theodora, entitled *My Dear Dorothea: a practical system of moral education for females, embodied in a letter to a young person of that sex* which was illustrated by Clare with a note by Stephen.[114]

In 1931, during his time in London,[115] Clare was given 'unrestricted access'[116] to Mahatma Gandhi[117] in order to execute his portrait.[118] According to Gombrich, Gandhi was so pleased with the final result 'that he took hold of her brush and signed his name in oil colour'.[119] Her other sitters included the film director Gabriel Pascal,[120] many writers, especially poets, including Robert Graves[121] and W H Auden,[122] and musicians, such as Benjamin Britten, Rostropovich and Shostakovich,[123] though she also executed landscapes. In her later years, her work moved towards abstraction; one of her imaginative late compositions, an untitled etching (1974), is at Newnham College, Cambridge. Late in life she wrote her (unpublished) autobiography. After her death in 1989, a retrospective of her Slade drawings was held at the Strang print room, UCL, in 1994.

Ultimately, the lack of work in the public domain and unevenness of Winsten's output suggests that after a number of early experimental works, war, motherhood and political concerns led to a dissipation of her early energies. As Stephen Chaplin has concluded, 'her interests were not restricted to art, but extended to how life could best be conducted. During a long and happy marriage, a partnership of concerns developed – pacifism, garden city living, vegetarianism, rethinking how children should be brought up […]. All this fed back into Clare's artistic projects, and she came to divide her time between family and friends, writing plays and novels, and periods of sustained painting.'[124]

Post-war, in common with her contemporaries, Winsten appears to have joined the *rappel à l'ordre* and her work became more naturalistic and less innovative. However, as the only woman to carve out a place among the Whitechapel Boys, for her early experiments with British modernism and for her Whitechapel connections, all of which paved the way for the emergence of future female artists such as Clara Klinghoffer (1900–70), Clare Winsten remains a fascinating figure: an early embryonic British modernist and a fully integrated member of the Whitechapel group.

CATALOGUE OF WORKS

WORKS BY ISAAC ROSENBERG

Dimensions are in centimetres, height before width

1
Caxton and Edward IV, 1901
Pen & ink and watercolour on paper
27 × 37
Inscribed 'I. Rosenberg Standard VII 18.12.01'
Mrs Gerda Horvitch

2
Self-Portrait, 1906
Pencil on soft card
11.8 × 7. 56
The Joseph Cohen Collection of World War I Literature/the Joseph M. Bruccoli Great War Collection, Thomas Cooper Library, University of South Carolina

3
Copy of Correggio's Venus, Cupid and Mercury, c.1910
Oil on canvas
71 × 42
Mrs Gerda Horvitch

4
Family Group at a Meal, c.1910
Ink & grey wash on paper,
13.6 × 16.2
Tullie House Museum & Art Gallery

5
Head of a Barrister, 1910
Red chalk on paper
17.8 × 14.7
The Joseph Cohen Collection of World War I Literature/the Joseph M Bruccoli Great War Collection, Thomas Cooper Library, University of South Carolina

6
Self-Portrait, 1911
Oil on canvas
49.5 × 38.7
Tate
Presented by David Burton 1972

7
Head of a Monk, c.1908–11
Pencil on board,
48.8 × 40
Imperial War Museum, London

8
The Artist's Father, 1911
Oil on cardboard,
41.2 × 30.5
Mrs Betty Silver

9
The Artist's Mother, 1911
Black chalk and pencil on paper mounted on board
25.4 × 20.6
Mrs Betty Silver

10
The Fountain, 1911
Oil on board
15.8 × 26
Imperial War Museum, London

11
Head of a Male Figure, c.1911
Graphite on paper
Verso inscribed with holograph poem 'Dawn like a flushed rose petal…'
25.3 × 20.3
British Museum

12
Trees, 1912
Oil on board
26.6 × 35.5
Imperial War Museum, London

13
Self-Portrait, 1912
Oil on board
45 × 40
Mrs Betty Silver

14
Head of a Woman 'Grey and Red', 1912
Oil on board
41.9 × 30.4
Imperial War Museum, London

15
Self-Portrait, 1912
Pencil on paper
36 × 28.5
The Joseph Cohen Collection of World War I Literature/the Joseph M Bruccoli Great War Collection, Thomas Cooper Library, University of South Carolina

16
Hark, Hark, the Lark, 1912
Charcoal and monochrome wash
38.5 × 33
The Joseph Cohen Collection of World War I Literature/the Joseph M Bruccoli Great War Collection, Thomas Cooper Library, University of South Carolina

17
Self-Portrait in a Red Tie, 1914
Oil on canvas
41.2 × 31
Mrs Betty Silver

18
Self Portrait in a Pink Tie, 1914
Oil on board
40 × 32.3
Imperial War Museum, London

19
Portrait of Marda Vanne, 1914
Pencil on board
40 × 32.3
Imperial War Museum, London

20
Self-Portrait, 1914
Oil on canvas
50.8 × 45.7
Doron D Swade

21
Head of a Woman in Profile, 1914
Pencil on paper
16 × 16.5
Private Collection

22
Self-portrait with Trilby (three-quarter length), c.1914
Oil on canvas
76.5 × 51
Private Collection, courtesy of Sotheby's

23
Self-portrait with Trilby (facing left), 1914–15
Oil on board
30 × 23
Mrs Gerda Horvitch

24
Self-Portrait, 1915
Oil on panel
29.5 × 22.2
National Portrait Gallery

25
The First Meeting of Adam and Eve, 1915
Charcoal on paper
24.5 × 27
Tullie House Museum & Art Gallery

26
Study of Nude Woman (Seated with Knee Raised), 1915
Charcoal on grey paper
35.8 × 32.6
British Museum

27
Study of Nude Woman (Seen from Behind Walking), 1915
Charcoal on grey paper
48.1 × 27.6
British Museum

28
Portrait of Sonia, c.1915
Oil on canvas
61 × 46
Joan Rodker

29
Clare Winsten, 1915
Oil on canvas
61 × 51
UCL Art Collections, University College London

30
Self-Portrait in a Steel Helmet, 1916
Black chalk and gouache on brown wrapping paper
24 × 19.5
Private Collection

WORKS BY OTHER ARTISTS

31
DAVID BOMBERG
The Billet, 1915
Black ink on paper
39.5 × 51
Victoria and Albert Museum, given by Mrs Lillian Bomberg

32
DAVID BOMBERG
Gunner Loading Shell, c.1918
Ink and wash on paper
12.7 × 19
Private Collection

33
DAVID BOMBERG
Soldier Patrolling Tunnel, c.1918
Ink and wash on paper
19 × 12.7
Private Collection

34
HORACE BRODZKY
Portrait of Henri Gaudier-Brzeska, c.1913
Oil on canvas
30.5 × 25.5
Private Collection

35
HENRI GAUDIER-BRZESKA
Portrait of Horace Brodzky, 1913
Drypoint on paper
Signed and numbered by printer: 'Brodzky imp. 2/2'
Signed, dated and annotated: 'all amico Del Sole Brodzky'
17.7 × 15
British Museum

36
MARK GERTLER
Study for the Merry-go-round (aka *Studies of Heads*)
Signed and dated (lr) 'Mark Gertler/1916 for Merry-go-rounds'
Red chalk on paper
56 × 38
Private Collection

37
MARK GERTLER
Study for the Merry-go-round (aka *The Straw Hat*)
Signed and dated (ml) 'Mark Gertler/1916'
Charcoal on blue paper
58.5 × 40.5
Private Collection

38
JACOB KRAMER
Military Portrait, 1918
Mixed media on paper
43.5 × 33
Jonathan Rosenthall

39
JACOB KRAMER
Military Portrait (with cap), 1918
Mixed media on paper
43.5 × 33.5
Jonathan Rosenthall

40
LONDON ART STUDIOS
Isaac Rosenberg, c.1915
Bromide print mounted on a postcard
12.8 × 7.8
National Portrait Gallery

41

BERNARD MENINSKY

Sketch of Soldiers Arriving on Leave, 1918

Oil on paper

42.5 × 58.3

Imperial War Museum, London

42

BERNARD MENINSKY

On the Departure Platform Victoria Station, 1918

Oil on canvas

50.8 × 76.5

Imperial War Museum, London

43

CLARE WINSTEN
[CLARA BIRNBERG]

Attack, 1910

Inscription verso 'CLARE WINSTEN) BIRN, 17 years old, 1910, "Attack"'

Watercolour on paper on card

56 × 76

Ben Uri Gallery, The London Jewish Museum of Art

44

CLARE WINSTEN
[CLARA BIRNBERG]

Portrait of Isaac Rosenberg

Inscribed 'I Rosenberg', dated 1913 and inscribed with monogram (CB)

Verso: Boats moored alongside quay

Graphite on paper

36 × 25.3

British Museum

45

CLARE WINSTEN
[CLARA BIRNBERG]

Portrait of Isaac Rosenberg, 1914

Pencil on paper

38.1 × 28

UCL Art Collections, University College London

46

ALFRED WOLMARK

Portrait of Mrs Herbert Cohen, 1956

Oil on canvas

74 × 62

Ben Uri Gallery, The London Jewish Museum of Art

MANUSCRIPTS

47

ISAAC ROSENBERG

Three rough sketches: 39 Rosenau Road

Pen and ink

12 April 1915

Verso: letter from Edward Marsh inviting Rosenberg to breakfast

The Joseph Cohen Collection of World War I Literature/the Joseph M Bruccoli Great War Collection, Thomas Cooper Library, University of South Carolina

48

ISAAC ROSENBERG

Title page, *Moses: A Verse Play*

(folio 2, Ms 48210)

12 × 14 × 23

1916

British Library

49

ISAAC ROSENBERG

A Merry Xmas from the 40th: Design for a Christmas Card

(folio 29, Ms 48210)

12 × 14 × 22

1917

British Library

50

ISAAC ROSENBERG

Letter to Sydney Schiff, *c.*July 1917

Facsimile

The Joseph Cohen Collection of World War I Literature/the Joseph M Bruccoli Great War Collection, Thomas Cooper Library, University of South Carolina

51

ISAAC ROSENBERG

Self-Portrait with Marmalade Jar

Verso: letter to R C Trevelyan, not dated [summer 1916]

Department of Documents, Imperial War Museum, London

52

ISAAC ROSENBERG

Self-Portrait in Cap

Verso: untitled Letter, 1917

Inscribed 'I. R. July France 1917'

Department of Documents, Imperial War Museum, London

53

ISAAC ROSENBERG

Self-Portrait Sketch in Tin Helmet

Verso: Untitled Letter, not dated [1916 or after]

Department of Documents, Imperial War Museum, London

EPHEMERA

54
Slade certificate, 1912
Awarded to Isaac Rosenberg
Bernard Wynick

55
ISAAC ROSENBERG
Night and Day, 1912
Oxford: Quarry Books, 1979
Facsimile edition of 25
Bernard Wynick

56
ISAAC ROSENBERG
Youth, 1915
Printed by I Narodiczky in
an edition of 100 copies
Inscribed to Mark Gertler
Luke Gertler

57
Letter from Israel Zangwill,
12 June, 1916
Bernard Wynick

58
LCC School Bolt Court
Medal, 1912
Awarded to Morris Goldstein
Raymond Francis

59
Art & Letters, Summer 1919
Bernard Wynick

60
A Piece of Mosaic being the book of the Palestine Exhibition and Bazaar, 1912
Edited by Cyril Picciotto
and C M Kohan
The Parkes Library,
University of Southampton

FIGURES REPRODUCED IN CATALOGUE ONLY

FIG. 1
ISAAC ROSENBERG
Untitled landscape
Original watercolour drawing
unsigned and undated
17 × 12.5
Berg Collection, New York Public Library

FIG. 2
ISAAC ROSENBERG
Self-Portrait (in profile facing left), *c.*1910–12
Pencil
19 × 14.6
Current whereabouts unknown,
formerly David Burton

FIG. 3
ISAAC ROSENBERG
'Sing unto the Lord'
(aka *'The Song at Sea'*), 1911
Oil on board
16.5 × 26
Mrs Ruth Garson

FIG. 4
ISAAC ROSENBERG
Sacred Love, 1912
Pencil and oil on board
47.5 × 61
Private Collection

FIG. 5
ISAAC ROSENBERG
The Murder of Lorenzo, 1912
Oil on board
30.4 × 24.8
Current whereabouts unknown

FIG. 6
ISAAC ROSENBERG
Ruth Löwy as the Sleeping Beauty, 1912
Red chalk
26.7 × 34.9
Current whereabouts unknown

FIG. 7
ISAAC ROSENBERG
The Wharf, 1912
Reproduced in *A Piece of Mosaic*
(unpaginated)
Edited by Cyril Piciotto and
C M Kohan
The Parkes Library, University of
Southampton

FIG. 8
ISAAC ROSENBERG
Portrait of the Artist's Father, *c.*1914
Oil on canvas
30.5 × 33
Private Collection, courtesy of
David Stern

FIG. 9
ISAAC ROSENBERG
Minnie Horvitch, the Artist's Sister, 1914
Oil on board
40.6 × 30.5
The Artist's Family
Current whereabouts unknown

FIG. 10
JOHN AMSHEWITZ
Portrait of Isaac Rosenberg, 1909
Reproduced in Amshewitz, S B
The Paintings of J H M Amshewitz RBA (London: B T Batsford Ltd, 1951), Plate 10
Current whereabouts unknown

FIG. 11

BASSANO

Marda Vanne

Whole-plate glass negative, 6 June 1921

National Portrait Gallery
Given by John Culme, 1996

FIG. 12

DAVID BOMBERG

Vision of Ezekiel, 1912

Oil on canvas

114.3 × 137.2

Tate
Purchased with assistance from the Morton Bequest through the Contemporary Art Society 1970

FIG. 13

DAVID BOMBERG

Head of a Poet (Isaac Rosenberg) 1913

72.6 × 27.9

Current whereabouts unknown

FIG. 14

DAVID BOMBERG

*Portrait of John Rodker c.*1931

Oil on canvas

71 × 58.5

Joan Rodker

FIG. 15

FRANK EMANUEL

Cover design for *A Piece of Mosaic*, 1912

Edited by Cyril Piciotto and C M Kohan

The Parkes Library,
University of Southampton

FIG. 16

MARK GERTLER

Merry-Go-Round, 1916

Oil on Canvas

189. 2 × 142.2

Tate

FIG. 17

H C HAMMOND

Portrait of Isaac Rosenberg

Current whereabouts unknown

FIG. 18

JACOB KRAMER

Types of the Russian Army, 1915

Reproduced in Wyndham Lewis, *Blast*, Vol 2, (London: John Lane, The Bodley Head, 1915), p. 31

Current whereabouts unknown

FIG. 19

WYNDHAM LEWIS

Portrait of John Rodker

1923

Private collection, courtesy Christie's

FIG. 20

MARK WAYNER

Major L Rothschild

Reproduced in *Colour*, Vol 4 (July 1916), p. 214

Current whereabouts unknown

FIG. 21

MARK WAYNER

Sir Edward Marsh, 1943 or before

Lithograph

35.6 × 24.2

National Portait Gallery
Archive Collection. Purchased, 2006–05

FIG. 22

CLARE WINSTEN
[CLARA BIRNBERG]

Portrait of Abdul Baha, 1911

Graphite on paper

42.1 × 25.4

British Museum

FIG. 23

CLARE WINSTEN
[CLARA BIRNBERG]

*Untitled Figure Study, c.*1912

Oil on board

49.5 × 68

Liss Fine Art

FIG. 24

CLARE WINSTEN
[CLARA BIRNBERG]

Dawn (aka *Morning*), *c.*1910–12

100 × 144

Turner Bennett

FIG. 25

CLARE WINSTEN
[CLARA BIRNBERG]

Female Head (?Self-Portrait) *c.*1910–20

Current whereabouts unknown

FIG. 26

CLARE WINSTEN
[CLARA BIRNBERG]

Portrait of Joseph Leftwich, *c.*1915

Reproduced in ed., Goldsmith, S J, *Joseph Leftwich at Eighty-Five: A Collective Evaluation* (London: The Federation of Jewish Relief Organisations, The Association of Jewish Writers and Journalists, The World Jewish Congress Yiddish Committee, 1978), p.5

Current whereabouts unknown

FIG. 27

CLARE WINSTEN
[CLARA BIRNBERG]

Portrait of Ezra Pound, 1920

[with separate head and hand studies at lower left]

Brown chalk on paper

21.1 × 25.1

British Museum

FIG. 28

CLARE WINSTEN
[CLARA BIRNBERG]

Portrait of Jonas (the Artist's Brother), *c.*1920

26.5 × 40.5

Pencil on paper

Benedict Birnberg

FIG. 29

CLARE WINSTEN
[CLARA BIRNBERG]

Seated Female Vorticist Figure, *c.*1920

Reproduced in *Voices*, Vol 3 (March 1920), opp. p. 78

Current whereabouts unknown

FIG. 30

ALFRED WOLMARK

Portrait of Norman Kohnstamm, *c.*1917

Signed with AW monogram (ul)
Reproduced in *Colour*, Vol 6 (March 1917), p. 61

Jerwood Foundation, London

FIG. 31

ALFRED WOLMARK

Soldier, *c.*1917

Reproduced in *Colour*, Vol 6 (May 1917), p. 117

Current whereabouts unknown

FIG. 32

ALFRED WOLMARK

The Medical Inspection *c.*1919

Oil on canvas

150 × 234

Private Collection, courtesy of Christie's

FIG. 33

Bantam Regiment poster, *c.*1914–16

Imperial War Museum, London

FIG. 34

'Join the British Army' advertisement

Jewish World (7 October 1914), p. 7

FIG. 35

'Join the Special Jewish Unit' advertisement

Jewish World, 30 December, 1914, p.1

PHOTOGRAPHS

FIG. 36
Barnett, Anna and Minnie Rosenberg, 1889
Bernard Wynick

FIG. 37
Isaac Rosenberg and his Siblings (with Rocking Horse), 1902
Bernard Wynick

FIG. 38
Studio Portrait of Isaac Rosenberg, 1911
Bernard Wynick

FIG. 39
The Slade Picnic, 1912
Bernard Wynick

FIG. 40
Isaac Rosenberg in Uniform, 1917
Bernard Wynick

FIG. 41
Isaac Rosenberg and his Brother Elkon in Uniform, 1917
Bernard Wynick

FIG. 42
Isaac Rosenberg in the 'Family Suit', 1917
Imperial War Museum,
Photographic Archive

FIG. 43
Cohen Family with Sonia and her brother Solomon, *c.*1905
Joan Rodker

FIG. 44
Sonia Cohen, *c.*1913
Joan Rodker

FIG. 45
John Rodker and David Bomberg, *c.*1928
Joan Rodker

FIG. 46
Whitechapel Scene with Ruderman's Store
Joan Rodker

FIG. 47
Clara Birnberg (Clare Winsten) in the Life-modelling Room (?at the Slade), *c.*1910–12
Slade Archive

FIG. 48
Stephen ('Inca') and Clare Winsten in Clare's studio, *c.*1921–22
Private Collection

FIG. 49
Family group with Clare and Stephen ('Inca') Winsten and their daughters Theo and Ruth, *c.*1921–22
Private Collection

FIG. 50
'Inca' (Stephen Winsten)
*c.*1921–22
Private Collection

FIG. 51
MARCEL STERNBERGER
Joseph Leftwich
Frontispiece from Joseph Leftwich
Along the Years: Poems 1911–1937
(London: Robert Anscombe and Company Ltd, 1937)
Printed by Mackays Limited, Cheltenham in an edition of 750 numbered copies

FIG. 52
Morris Goldstein, *c.*1911–12
Raymond Francis

FIG. 53
Israel Narodiczky outside his Print Works, 1910
Jewish Museum, London

FIG. 54
CLARE WINSTEN
Isaac Rosenberg, 1915
25 × 19
Private Collection

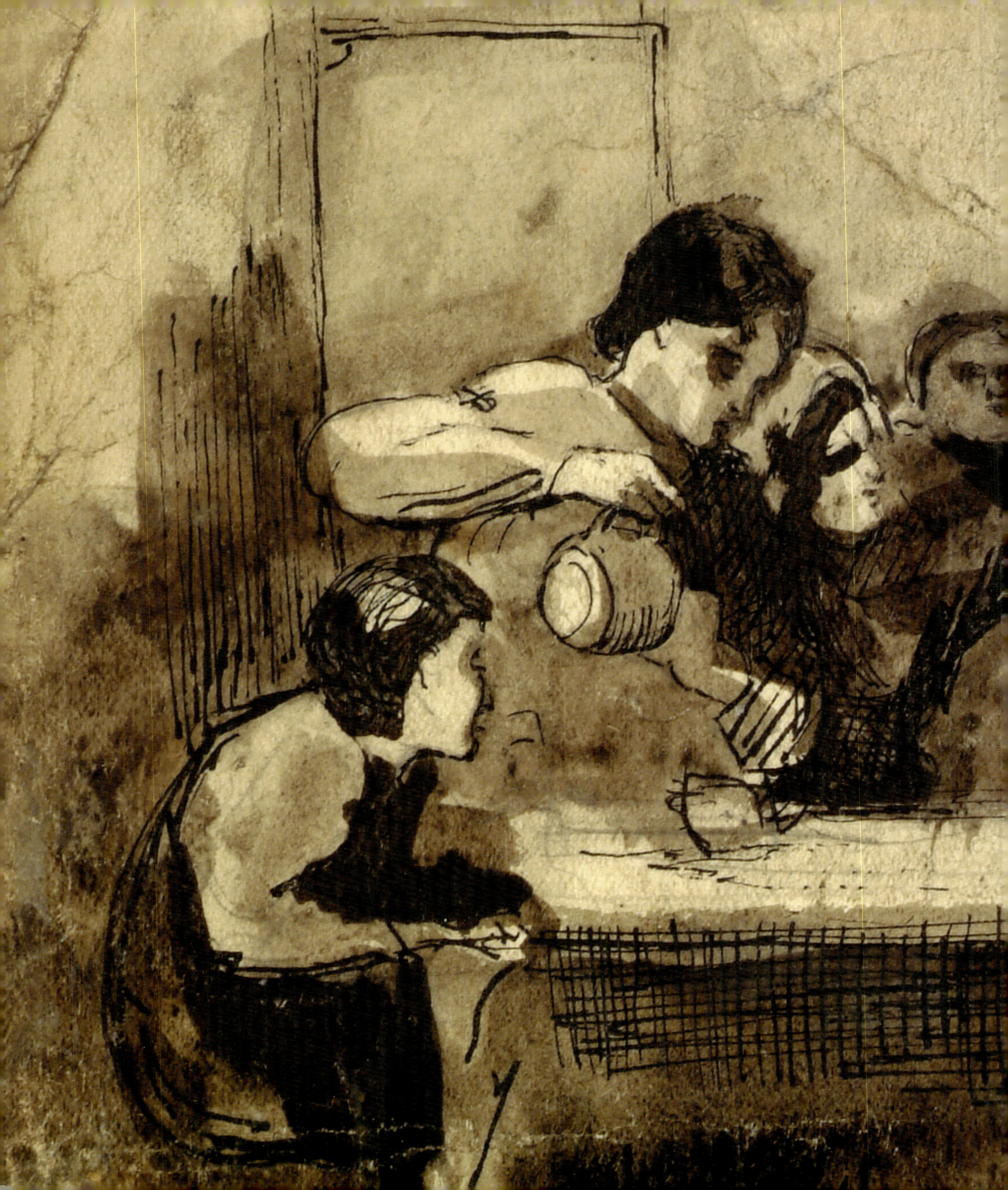

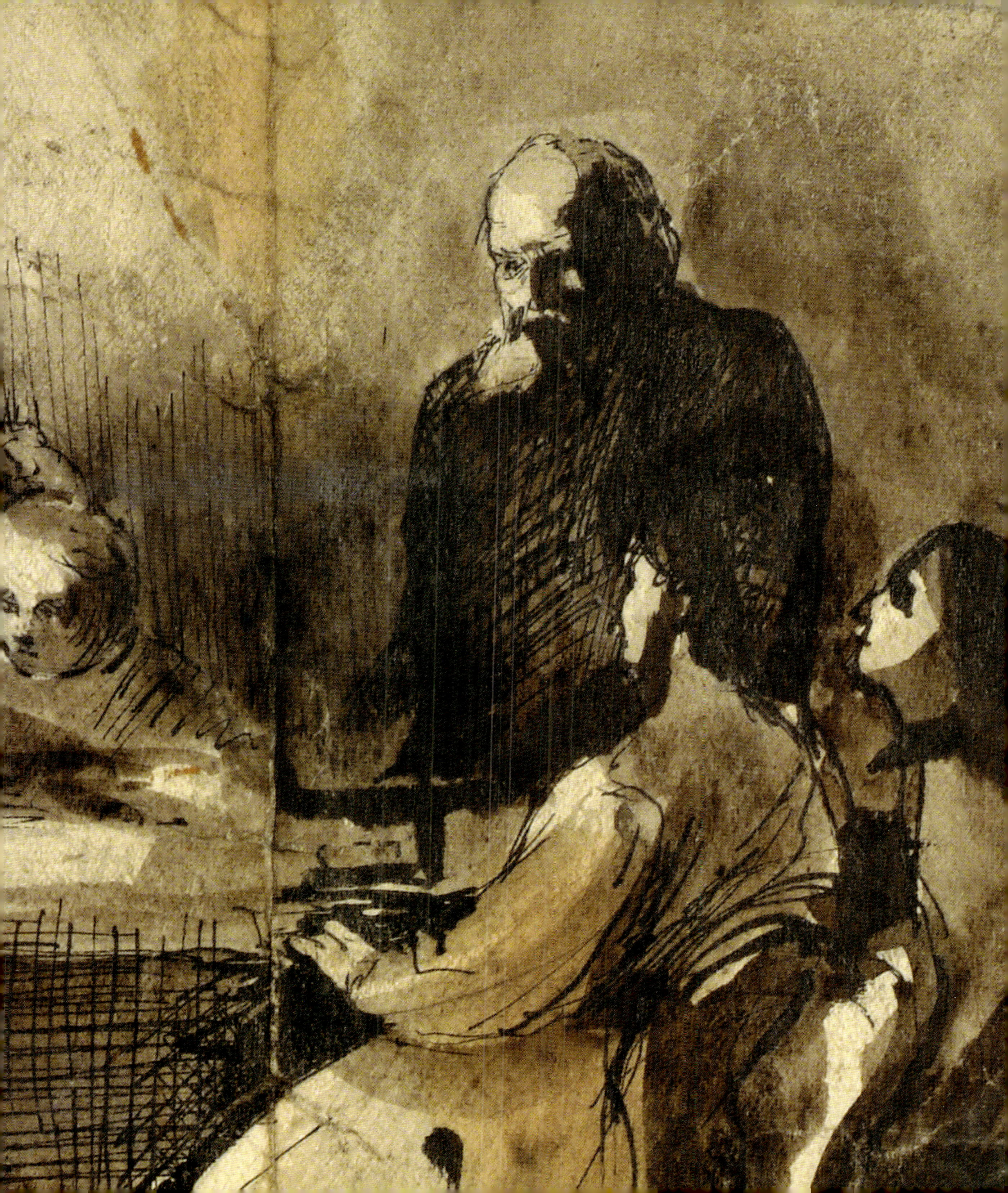

CHRONOLOGICAL SUMMARY OF THE LIFE OF ISAAC ROSENBERG

1890
25 November Isaac Rosenberg born at 5 Adelaide Place Bristol, eldest son and second child of Barnett (or Barnard) and Anna (Hacha) Rosenberg. Their first child, a daughter Minnie, had been born in Lithuania in 1887. In 1887–8 Barnett had emigrated to England from Lithuania, followed by his wife and child. From Leeds in Yorkshire they moved to Bristol.

1892
Sister Annie born in Bristol.

1894
Sister Rachel born in Bristol.

1897
Brother David born in Bristol.

1897
Family moves to 47 Cable Street, Stepney, London E1. Isaac enrols at St Paul's School,Wellclose Square, St George's-in-the-East.

1899
Brother Elkon born.

1899
14 November Isaac enrols at Baker Street School, Stepney East.

1900?
Family move to 58 Jubilee Street, Stepney, becoming acquainted with the family of John H Amshewitz (1882–1942), a professional artist. He encourages Isaac and introduces him to the schoolteacher Winifreda Seaton. She befriends and corresponds with Isaac until his death.

1902
Isaac begins special classes at Stepney Green Art School, sent by his headmaster. About this time his sister Minnie introduces him to Morley Dainow, librarian at Whitechapel Library.

1905
Isaac is apprenticed to Carl Hentschel's, Engravers of Fleet Street. He meets the painter Frank Emanuel and attends his artists' club 'The Limners'.

1907
Family moves to 159 Oxford Street, East London. Isaac starts evening classes at London School of Photo-engraving and Lithography, Bolt Court, Fleet Street. He frequents Whitechapel Art Gallery with fellow artists David Bomberg and Mark Gertler.

At Amshewitz's suggestion Isaac attends evening classes at Birkbeck College and is taught by Alice Wright who discusses poetry and corresponds with him until his death.

1911
Isaac meets young Jewish writers and artists Samuel Winsten, Joseph Leftwich and John Rodker, who form a group centred on the Whitechapel Library and Art Gallery.

17 MARCH Isaac, copying pictures in the National Gallery, meets Lily Delissa Joseph (sister of the artist Solomon J Solomon, RA). Taken on as her son's art tutor, he meets her sister Mrs Henrietta Löwy, and Mrs Herbert Cohen. He paints a three-quarter length *Self-Portrait*, later reworked as the head-and-shoulders *Self-Portrait* now in the National Portrait Gallery.

13 OCTOBER Isaac joins the Slade School of Fine Art, sponsored by Lily Delissa Joseph, Mrs Henrietta Löwy and Mrs Herbert Cohen. Mrs Löwy's daughter Ruth is a fellow student (she later marries the publisher Victor Gollancz). Other students include Bomberg, Gertler, Stanley and Gilbert Spencer, Jacob Kramer and William Roberts.

1912
Isaac writes to and meets Laurence Binyon, poet and a curator in the Prints and Drawings department at the British Museum, who corresponds with him and later writes the 'Introductory Memoir' to *Poems by Isaac Rosenberg* (1922).

SPRING/SUMMER Isaac produces 50 copies of his first 24-page pamphlet of poems *Night and Day*, printed for him by Israel Narodiczky for £2.

WINTER Rosenberg family moves to 87 Dempsey Street, Stepney East.

Isaac has disagreements with his patrons and instead receives funds from Jewish Educational Aid Society until he leaves the Slade in 1914. He exhibits at the New English Art Club.

1913
SUMMER Isaac spends holiday to recover failing health in Sandown, Isle of Wight, accompanied by his friend the artist David Bomberg.

NOVEMBER Mark Gertler introduces Isaac at the Café Royal to the poet T E Hulme and to Edward Marsh, private secretary to Winston Churchill and a patron of the arts, who published five volumes of the popular anthology *Georgian Poetry*. Marsh buys Isaac's pictures, writes regularly to him and encourages his poetry.

1914
MARCH Isaac leaves Slade School of Fine Art

MAY Isaac exhibits at Whitechapel Art Gallery exhibition *Twentieth Century Art: A Review of Modern Movements*.

Unable to find work and in poor health, Isaac sails for South Africa (with a grant from the Jewish Educational Aid Society) to stay with his sister Minnie, who had moved to Cape Town in 1913 with her husband Wolf Horvitch. He completes a number of paintings and gives lectures on art, published with two poems in the magazine *South African Women in Council.*

4 AUGUST Great Britain declares war on Germany.

1915

MARCH Isaac arrives back home in Dempsey Street. April Isaac produces 100 copies of his second pamphlet of poems, *Youth*, printed by Israel Narodiczky for £2.10s, paid for by selling three pictures to Edward Marsh.

MAY Isaac meets the author Sydney Schiff (whose pen name is Stephen Hudson) at the Café Royal. He read Isaac's poems and corresponded with him until his death.

JUNE/JULY/AUGUST *Colour* magazine, edited by T M Wood, prints 'Heart's First Word', 'A Girl's Thoughts' and 'Wedded' (I).[1] The poet Ezra Pound recommends Isaac's work to Harriet Monroe, founding editor of the magazine *Poetry: A Magazine of Verse* in Chicago.

JULY Isaac and the printer, Reuben Cohen, publish the first (and only) edition of *Jewish Standard*, which reprints Isaac's essays on art.

SEPTEMBER Isaac starts evening classes in block-making, but fails to find work.

OCTOBER Isaac enlists and is sent to the Recruiting Depot at Bury St Edmunds, Suffolk, to join Bantam Battalion of 12 Suffolk Regiment 40th Division, as he is too short for other units.

NOVEMBER Isaac is in hospital with cut hands after a fall. Lascelles Abercrombie (1881–1931), poet, critic, and later professor at Leeds and London universities, starts correspondence with Isaac after his friend Marsh shows him Isaac's poems.

1916

16 JANUARY After four days' Christmas home leave Isaac transferred to 12th South Lancashires, Blackdown Camp, Farnborough, Hants.

March Isaac transferred again to 11th Battalion King's Own Royal Lancasters at Blackdown Camp as Private Isaac Rosenberg, no. 22311.

19 MAY During six days' embarkation leave Reuben Cohen of Narodiczky's (under name of Paragon Printing Works) prints Isaac's play *Moses.*

(?)2 JUNE Isaac embarks with his unit for France. He writes 'The Troop Ship'.

JUNE In mid-June Isaac begins a correspondence lasting until his death with two older poets, R C Trevelyan (1872–1951), poet and translator of classical literature, and Gordon Bottomley (1874–1948), Georgian poet and dramatist. Bottomley encouraged Isaac in life and preserved his reputation and many of his manuscripts after his death, editing and selecting the *Poems by Isaac Rosenberg* (Heinemann, 1922), and co-editing with D W Harding *Collected Works* (Chatto & Windus, 1937).

AUGUST Isaac's unit moves into trenches.

SEPTEMBER Isaac sends 'Break of Day in the Trenches' to Harriet Monroe of *Poetry* (Chicago).

25 NOVEMBER Isaac's 26th birthday.

DECEMBER Harriet Monroe prints 'Marching–As Seen From the Left File' (sent in by John Rodker in January 1916) and 'Break of Day in the Trenches' in *Poetry* (Chicago).

1917

JANUARY Isaac's health fails and he is assigned to a Works Battalion behind the lines.

EARLY MAY Isaac's health improves and in a letter to Marsh he mentions his poem 'Dead Man's Dump'.

LATE MAY Isaac writes to Marsh again about 'Dead Man's Dump' and a further poem, almost certainly 'Daughters of War', as well mentioning his play *The Amulet.*

JUNE Isaac reassigned to 229 Field Company Royal Engineers, attached to 11th Battalion KORL.

JULY/AUGUST Isaac writes to Marsh and Bottomley about the drafts of his play, now called *The Unicorn.*

16 SEPTEMBER Isaac at home on leave for ten days and is in contact with Bottomley, Schiff and Trevelyan. Meets scholar and critic Jacob ('Jack') Isaacs at Café Royal. Visits Sonia Cohen.

LATE SEPTEMBER *Georgian Poetry* (third volume, edited by Marsh) published including extract 'Ah! Koelue!' from Isaac's play *Moses.*

LATE OCTOBER Isaac admitted to 51st General Hospital with influenza and remains there until December. In a letter to his boyhood friend Leftwich, refers to his two soldier brothers also being in hospital.

1918

LATE JANUARY Isaac back in the trenches with 4th Platoon A Company 11th KORL.
7 FEBRUARY Isaac transferred to 8th Platoon B Company 1st Battalion KORL in the 4th Division, after 11th Battalion broke up owing to shortage of men.
EARLY MARCH Isaac writes to Marsh that he has requested a transfer to the Jewish Battalion in Mesopotamia. Isaac manages to meet his brother David.

11 MARCH Isaac's battalion, 1st KORL, moves to Arras for training.

19 MARCH Isaac's battalion moves into front line, the Greenland Hill Sector near Arras, until 24 March.

MARCH 28 1st Battalion KORL moves back into front line. Isaac writes his last letter to March enclosing his final poem, 'Through these pale cold days'. The Germans launch full-scale attack and Isaac's battalion loses 70 men.

31 MARCH Isaac detailed for a wiring patrol that night.

1 APRIL Isaac fails to return. His remains are later found with those of his comrades.

Private Isaac Rosenberg no. 22311 is buried in Bailleul Road East British Cemetery, north east of Arras in Northern France.

Compiled by Jean Liddiard, editor of Isaac Rosenberg *Selected Poems and Letters* (2003) and *Isaac Rosenberg: Poetry Out of My Head and Heart: Unpublished Letters and Poem Versions* (2007), both published by Enitharmon Press.

SELECT BIBLIOGRAPHY

SOLO EXHIBITIONS:

LIDDIARD, J (handlist) *Isaac Rosenberg Poet & Painter 1890–1918: The Half Used Life* (London: Imperial War Museum, 22 Nov 1990–2 April 1991)

LIDDIARD, J (foreword) and CLIFFORD SIMMONS *1890–1918: Isaac Rosenberg: A Poet and Painter of the First World War (Word and Image: VI)* (London: the National Book League, 1975)

SILKIN, J & DE SAUSMAREZ, M *Isaac Rosenberg 1890–1918*: a catalogue of an exhibition held at Leeds University May–June 1959, touring to the Slade, University College London together with the text of unpublished material (Leeds: University of Leeds with Partridge Press, 1959)

LEFTWICH, J *Isaac Rosenberg: Catalogue of the Memorial Exhibition of Paintings & Drawings* (London: Whitechapel Art Gallery, 1937)

SELECTED GROUP EXHIBITIONS:

ANON., New English Art Club Exhibition, Winter 1912

ANON., New English Art Club Exhibition, Winter 1915

GOWING, L *British Self-Portraits, from Sickert to Present Day* (Arts Council, 1962: Laing Art Gallery, Newcastle, 10 Feb–3 Mar; Leeds University, 10–23 Mar; Birmingham City Art Gallery, 7–28 April; National Library Wales, Aberystwyth, 5–26 May; Leicester City Art Galleries, 2–23 June; Salford City Art Gallery, 30 June–14 July; Guildford House, Guildford 21 July–11 August; and Bournemouth College of Art, 18 Aug–8 Sep)

GROSE, I (intro) *Jewish Artists of Great Britain 1845–1945* (London: Belgrave Gallery & Bradford: Cartwright Hall Art Gallery & Museum, 1978)

KIMBER, J *Gordon Bottomley and his Circle* (Norwich: University of East Anglia Library, 1974)

RAMSAY, G (introduction) *Twentieth Century Art: A Review of Modern Movements*, Whitechapel Art Gallery, 1914

STALLWORTHY, J *Poets of the First World War* (London: Imperial War Museum, 1974)

STALLWORTHY, J *'Anthem for Doomed Youth'* (London: Constable in association with Imperial War Museum, 2002 – to accompany the exhibition 31 Oct 2002–27 April 2003)

POETRY, PLAYS, REVIEWS AND LETTERS:

ROSENBERG, I *Night and Day* (London: I Narodiczky, 1912)

ROSENBERG, I 'In the Workshop' in eds., Picciotto, C & Kohan, C M *A Piece of Mosaic (being the book of the Palestine exhibition and bazaar)* (London: T Fisher Unwin, 1912)

ROSENBERG, I 'Romance at the Baillie Galleries: The Works of J. H. Amshewitz and the Late H. Ospovat' *Jewish Chronicle* (May 1912) 'Art'; 'Beauty (II)' and 'The Dead Heroes' in *South African Women in Council* (South Africa, December 1914–January 1915), 'Art' republished in eds., Cohen, R and Rosenberg, I, *Jewish Standard* (July, 1915)

ROSENBERG, I *Youth* (London: I Narodiczky, 1915)

ROSENBERG, I 'Heart's First Thoughts', 'A Girl's Thoughts' and 'Wedded' (1) in ed., Wood, T M *Colour*, Vol 3, no. 1 (August 1915)

ROSENBERG, I *Moses: A Play* (London: Paragon Printing Works, 1916)

ROSENBERG, I 'Marching–As Seen from the Left File' and 'Break of Day in the Trenches' in ed., Monroe, H *Poetry: A Magazine of Verse* (Chicago, December 1916)

ROSENBERG, I 'Ah! Koelue!' (from Moses) in ed., Marsh, Sir E H *Georgian Poetry: Volume Three, 1916–1917* (London: Poetry Bookshop, 1917)

POSTHUMOUS EDITIONS:

ed., BOTTOMLEY, G (with an introductory memoir by Laurence Binyon) *Poems by Isaac Rosenberg* (London: William Heinemann, 1922)

eds., BOTTOMLEY, G & HARDING, D W *Collected Works of Isaac Rosenberg. Poetry, Prose, Letters and Some Drawings, including Portraits* (London: Chatto & Windus, 1937; revised 1949 & reprinted 1962)

eds., BOTTOMLEY, G & HARDING, D W *Collected Poems of Isaac Rosenberg* (London: Chatto & Windus, 1974)

HARDING, D W *Poems: Isaac Rosenberg* (London: Chatto and Windus, 1972)

ed., LIDDIARD, J (with introduction) *Isaac Rosenberg: Poetry Out of My Head and Heart – Unpublished Letters & Poem Versions* (London: Enitharmon Press in association with The European Jewish Publications Society, 2007)

ed., LIDDIARD, J *Isaac Rosenberg: Selected Poems and Letters* (London: Enitharmon Press in association with The European Jewish Publications Society, 2003)

ed., NOAKES, V *OXFORD AUTHORS: Isaac Rosenberg* (Oxford: Oxford University Press, 2008)

ed., NOAKES, V *Poems and Plays of Isaac Rosenberg: A Critical Edition* (Oxford: University of Oxford, 2004) ed., PARSONS, I (with introduction; foreword by Siegfried Sassoon) *Collected Works of Isaac Rosenberg: Poetry, Prose, Letters, Paintings and Drawings* (London: Chatto and Windus, 1979)

ROSENBERG, I *Moses: A Play* (London: Imperial War Museum, Department of Printed Books: Arts and literature series; no.2, 1990) Complete facsimile of the Imperial War Museum manuscripts of *Moses*

ed., WILSON, J MOORCROFT *Selected Poems of Isaac Rosenberg* (London: Cecil Woolf, 2003)

SELECTED ANTHOLOGIES:

BLOOM, H *Poets of World War I: Wilfred Owen & Isaac Rosenberg* (Philadelphia: Chelsea House Publishers, 2003)

HUNTER, J *Modern Poets* (London: Faber and Faber, 1968)

HUSSEY, M *Poetry of the First World War: An Anthology* (London: Longmans, 1967)

MARLAND, M *The War Poets* (London: Times Newspapers, 1972)

BIOGRAPHICAL:

COHEN, J *Journey to the Trenches: The Life of Isaac Rosenberg, 1890–1918* (London: Robson Books, 1975)

LIDDIARD, J *Isaac Rosenberg: The Half Used Life* (London: V Gollancz, 1975)

MACCOBY D AND EUROPEAN JEWISH PUBLICATIONS SOCIETY *God Made Blind: Isaac Rosenberg, His Life and Poetry* (Northwood: Symposium in association with the European Jewish Publication Society, 2000)

TOMLINSON, C *Isaac Rosenberg of Bristol* (Bristol: Historical Association, 1982)

WILSON, J MOORCROFT *Isaac Rosenberg: The Making of a Great War Poet: A New Life* (London: Weidenfeld & Nicolson, 2008)

WILSON, J MOORCROFT *Isaac Rosenberg, Poet and Painter: A Biography* (London: Cecil Woolf, 1975)

SELECTED CRITICAL:

BEWLEY, M *Masks & Mirrors: Essays in Criticism* (New York: Athenaeum, 1970)

CHRISTIE, T '"For Isaac Rosenberg": Geoffrey Hill, Michael Longley, Cathal O'Searcaigh' in ed., Kendall, T, *Oxford Handbook of British and Irish War Poetry* (Oxford: Oxford University Press, 2007)

DESMOND, G *The Truth of War: Owen, Blunden, Rosenberg* (Manchester: Carcanet Press, 1984)

JOHNSTON, J *English Poetry of the First World War: A Study in the Evolution of Lyric and Narrative Form* (Princeton: Princeton University Press; Oxford: Oxford University Press, 1964)

LAWSON, P *Anglo-Jewish Poetry from Isaac Rosenberg to Elaine Feinstein* (London: Vallentine Mitchell, 2006)

QUINN, P *Dictionary of Literary Biography: Volume. 216: British Poets of the Great War: Brooke, Rosenberg, Thomas* (Detroit; London: Gale Group, 2000)

SILKIN, J *Out of Battle: The Poetry of the Great War* (Oxford: Oxford University Press, 1972; reprinted 1978)

ed., SILKIN, J *Penguin Book of First World War Poetry* (London: Penguin, 1979)

STALLWORTHY, J *Anthem for Doomed Youth: Twelve Soldier Poets of the First World War* (London: Constable in association with the Imperial War Museum, 2002)

THESES:

AL-JOULAN NAJOUF, A '"Essenced to language": The Margins of Isaac Rosenberg' (Glasgow: Department of English Literature, University of Glasgow, 1999, PhD Thesis)

CHRISTIE, T 'Modernism, the Metaphysical Poets and the First World War' (Atlanta, Georgia: Department of English, Emory University, 2007, PhD Thesis)

DAVIES, E O G 'The Poetry of Isaac Rosenberg' (Nottingham: University of Nottingham, 1954, MA Thesis)

LLOYD, M 'Poets and Patriotism – Three experiences of the Great War' (Southampton: University of Southampton, 2001, MA Thesis)

SAMSON, L 'Isaac Rosenberg: Selected War Poems' (Herts: University of Hertfordshire, dissertation, 2005)

TALLETT, V M R 'Visionary and Revolutionary Impulses in the Work of Isaac Rosenberg (1890–1918)' (Leeds: University of Leeds, School of English, 1992, MA Thesis)

MUSIC:

COOKE, A *Nocturnes: A Cycle of Five songs for Soprano, Horn and Piano* London, Oxford University Press, [1963], including 'Returning we hear the larks' (Isaac Rosenberg)

WEISGALL, H *Soldier Songs: For Baritone* [op.6] (New York: Merrymount Music Press, 1953) [Music score, originally for medium voice and orchestra; acc. arr. for piano Pl. no., 277-32, including 'The dying solder' (Isaac Rosenberg)

OTHER:

ALLENTUCK, M 'Houghton Library, Harvard Library Bulletin, Vol. 13, no 3: Isaac Rosenberg and Gordon Bottomley: unremarked documents', July 1975

DICKINSON, P 'The Real Voice: A Study of Isaac Rosenberg, 1890–1918', written and narrated by PD, transmitted 15 Dec 1954

producers, HARRISON, G AND PANTOLEON, R 'The Half-Used Life: the Story of Isaac Rosenberg, Poet and Painter': script for proposed 1 hour drama documentary for Channel 4; Producer Consultant: Jean Liddiard, c.1990

HILL, G *Geoffrey Hill* (Eynsham, Oxford: Fantasy Press [for the] Oxford University Poetry Society, 1952) [Fantasy Poets, No. 11: 'To William Dunbar — God's little mountain — Genesis: a ballad of Christopher Smart — Holy Thursday of William Blake — For Isaac Rosenberg']

PERIOD CONTEXT:

CORK, R *A Bitter Truth: Avant-Garde Art and The Great War* (New Haven and London: Yale University Press in association with Barbican Art Gallery),1994

TICKNER, L *Modern Life & Modern Subjects: British Art in the Early Twentieth Century* (New Haven and London: Yale University Press), 2000

For an extended bibliography, please also refer to footnotes accompanying catalogue essays.

NOTES

1 ISAAC ROSENBERG THE PAINTER
PART I: 'ART IS NOT A PLAYTHING'

1 Isaac Rosenberg to Mrs Herbert Cohen [no date, presumably October 1912], ed., Parsons, I *Collected Works of Isaac Rosenberg: Poetry, Prose, Letters, Paintings and Drawings* (London: Chatto and Windus, 1979 & 1984), hereafter *CW79*, p.193.

2 ed., Bottomley, G, with an introduction by Laurence Binyon *Isaac Rosenberg Poems* (London: Heinemann, 1922), p.7.

3 National Portrait Gallery: Institutional Records, *Registered Packet 4129*, Maurice de Sausmarez to David Piper, 23 November 1959.

4 Originally Dovber, he changed his name to Barnett (also written Barnard) when he arrived in Britain. His parents had originally intended him for the rabbinate but the introduction of conscription of Jews caused him to flee; he was briefly a Hebrew teacher before his marriage to Anna (Hacha), after which he tried a succession of jobs, eventually becoming a peddler.

5 Annie Rosenberg, 'In memory of my dear brother', in ed., Liddiard, J *Isaac Rosenberg: Poetry Out of My Head and Heart – Unpublished Letters and Poem Versions* (London: Enitharmon Press, 2007), p.133.

6 Isaac Horvitch, foreword in Liddiard, op.cit., p.9.

7 Brodetsky, S *From Ghetto to Israel* (London: Weidenfeld & Nicolson, 1960), p.32.

8 Cork, R *David Bomberg* (New Haven and London: Yale University Press, 1987), p.20.

9 Annie Rosenberg, op.cit.

10 Isaac Horvitch, op.cit., p.9. Rosenberg's most recent biographer, Jean Moorcroft Wilson, notes however, that Rosenberg was still speaking only Yiddish at this age, so perhaps it is not surprising that he chose this means of self-expression.

11 Minnie Horvitch, (unpublished) 'Memoir of Isaac Rosenberg', cited Isaac Horvitch, op.cit., p.9.

12 Annie Rosenberg, op.cit., p.133.

13 Ibid.

14 David Bomberg to Joseph Leftwich, 8 April 1957, Tate Gallery Archive 878.2.1. Bomberg recalled 'Later he [Rosenberg] went to Bolt Court School of Art[,] founded for Teaching Drawing & the process of reproduction by William Richard Lethaby [...]. Lethaby had already perfected the scheme of the Central School of Art which was at that time a small affair opposite the Regent St Polytechnic in 1907. I was Lethaby's Student at the Central School of Art. I stayed from 1908–10. Isaac carried on at Bolt Court and did [?] excellent work there. Its standard was high in relation to the printing trade but not to painting.'

15 Amshewitz spelt his name both Amshewitz and Amschewitz and Rosenberg also spelt it both ways. We have used the former spelling in line with his widow Sarah Briana Amshewitz who published *The Paintings of J H M Amshewitz* RBA (London: B T Batsford Ltd, 1951).

16 Cohen, J *Journey to the Trenches: the life of Isaac Rosenberg, 1890–1918* (London: Robson Books, 1975), p.26.

17 Winsten, S 'Portrait of a Young Poet', *John O'London's Weekly* (10 November 1950), p.589.

18 '*To J. H. Amshewitz*' beginning 'In the wide darkness of the shade of days' (*CW79*, p.43n).

19 Dated 1911, (see ed., Noakes, V *Poems and Plays of Isaac Rosenberg: a Critical Edition* (Oxford: Oxford University Press, 2004), p.14, and commentary, p.305.

20 See *Jewish Chronicle* (10 April 1908 and 26 November 1909). The selection of Amshewitz was controversial because of the choice of a non-local artist. Rosenberg took Bomberg to Amshewitz's backyard to see the lunettes. Bomberg – even then marked out as a rebel – rejected them, but noted that Rosenberg remained loyal to his early mentor. Bomberg told Leftwich that Amshewitz 'had in Isaac a loyal supporter', David Bomberg to Joseph Leftwich, op. cit.

21 There is some confusion over the date of this portrait. Leftwich recalled in his diary in early 1911 that Amshewitz was painting a full-length portrait of Rosenberg, although in Sarah Briana Amshewitz's book, *The Paintings of J H Amshewitz* (London and New York: Batsford, 1951), plate 10, this head-and-shoulders portrait is given the earlier dating of 1909. It is possible Amshewitz painted a second portrait in 1911; but this is certainly the portrait discussed by Rosenberg in his *Jewish Chronicle* review entitled *Isaac Rosenberg – Poet and Painter*, oils 1909, formerly Jew's College, London' (fig. 10).

22 'Romance at the Baillie Galleries: The Works of J. H. Amshewitz and the late H. Ospovat', *Jewish Chronicle* (24 May 1912), *CW79*, pp.286–8.

23 Morley Dainow to Laurence Binyon, 18 December 1920, in Liddiard, op. p.131.

24 Isaac Horvitch, op. cit., p.11.

25 Isaac Rosenberg to Miss Seaton [before 1911], *CW79*, pp.180–81.

26 Frank Emanuel to Laurence Binyon, 28 April 1921, in Liddiard, op. cit., pp.126–8.

27 The Maccabeans were founded in 1881 to represent the 'acknowledged secular, professional and intellectual elite of Anglo-Jewry' (Black, Eugene C *The Social Politics of Anglo-Jewry 1880–1920* (London: Basil Blackwell, 1988), p.155), cited Tickner, L and Gross, P 'The Jewish Education Aid Society and Pre-First World War British Art' in *The Ben Uri Story from Art Society to Museum and the Influence of Anglo-Jewish Artists on the Modern British Movement* (London: The Ben Uri Gallery, 2001), p.65, n.4.

28 *Jewish Chronicle* (28 September 1906), p.23.

29 Frank Emanuel to Laurence Binyon, 28 April 1921, in Liddiard, op. cit., pp.126–8.

30 eds., Picciotto, C and Kohan, C M *A Piece of Mosaic: being the book of the Palestine Exhibition and Bazaar* (London: T Fisher Unwin, 1912). See Essay 5.

31 The drawing and poems were located among some 27, 000 items by Emanuel's brother Charles and sent to Rosenberg's sister Annie in 1959. She later gave them to Rosenberg's biographer Joseph Cohen and they now form part of The Joseph Cohen Collection of World War I Literature/the Joseph M Bruccoli Great War Collection, Thomas Cooper Library, University of South Carolina.

32 Cohen, J, op. cit., p.201. n.6. The portrait is on a piece of cardboard on the front of which is the poem beginning 'In Arts lone paths I wander deep'. It is inscribed, possibly not by Rosenberg 'to F. L. Emanuel'; see Noakes, op. cit., p.301.

33 Hammond's portrait of Rosenberg is inscribed 'This drawing of Isaac Rosenberg was made by H. C. Hammond at Bolt Court Art Schoool in 1914.'

34 Frank Emanuel to Laurence Binyon, op. cit.

35 Ibid.

36 Wilson, J M *Isaac Rosenberg: Poet and Painter* (London: Cecil Woolf, 1975), p.53.

37 See *Jewish Chronicle* (14 May 1948), p.12.

38 *Jewish World* (6 August 1917).

39 Emanuel had a preoccupation with cleanliness, maintaining that 'at the Slade stage scenery was preferred to nature, ugliness, sordidness and disease were preferred in its models – to beauty and health and cleanliness.' (Emanuel to Binyon, op. cit., pp.127–8).

40 Cited Wilson, J M, op. cit., p.52. Paul Nash's autobiography, *Outlook,* makes no mention of Rosenberg either at Bolt Court or at the Slade, though Bomberg later wrote that Nash thought highly of Rosenberg's poetry (letter to Leftwich, op. cit.).

41 Bomberg to Leftwich, ibid.

42 Rosenberg continued to have contact with Bolt Court until at least 1914 as the portrait by H C Hammond shows.

43 Wilson, J M, op. cit., p.52. Amshewitz had studied there himself (1898–1900): see Grose, I *Jewish Artists of Great Britain 1845–1945* (London: Belgrave Gallery, 1978), p.13.

44 Noakes, op. cit., p.xxxviii.

45 Ibid., p.xxxix, has 1910.

46 It is listed as 'cat no. 38, *Birkbeck Art School Study*, Carbon Chalk, 1908' in Rosenberg's memorial exhibition in 1937. The Imperial War Museum give the medium as pencil; Noakes, op. cit., p.xxxviii, gives 1908 and quotes *Birkbeck College Student's Magazine*, who give the medium as charcoal.

47 Noakes, op. cit., pp.xxxviii–xxxix.

48 Joseph Leftwich, Diary: Monday, 2 January 1911, Tower Hamlets Local History Library, no L. 5766 100 LEF.

49 'I met Rosenberg through Mitchel [sic] [.] I met Zadkin [sic], Mitchel was likewise taking his character in pencil – thinking Zadkin speaking little English, spoke to the artist in French. Mitchell introduced me to Zadkin and Rosenberg the same time. Zadkin I presented to Gilbert Bayes.' (David Bomberg to Joseph Leftwich, op.cit.). Ossip Zadkine (1890–1957), an exact contemporary of the two young men, worked mainly in Paris, where he settled in 1909, becoming a French citizen in 1931, but he was in London from 1906. By 1912 he was moving among the leading avant-garde in Paris and may have introduced Bomberg to contemporaries such as Picasso and Brancusi on his trip there in 1913. Bomberg recalled that his friendship with Rosenberg began 'very shortly' after the latter began his apprenticeship at Carl Hentschel's, around 1905–6. However, he also asserted that Rosenberg had already started an 'Evening Student course [sic] at the Birkbeck School of art' under Cecil Ray, which would put the date at 1907. (David Bomberg to Joseph Leftwich, op. cit.)

50 Fluent in several languages and well-read, Mitchell was, according to Bomberg, held in 'high esteem' by Rosenberg. (David Bomberg to Joseph Leftwich, ibid.) Cohen (op. cit., p.64) describes Mitchell as 'half Scottish, half Japanese, an art student living alone in London. Rosenberg took him home and Hacha offered him lodging.' He shared a room with Rosenberg. 'For a time he and Rosenberg were inseparable. After Rosenberg acquired his own studio, and later went off to South Africa and then to the war Mitchell stayed on, reluctantly leaving the Rosenbergs only in 1919 when he realised that part of Hacha's inconsolable grief over Isaac's death was expressing itself in resentment towards him.'

51 *CW79*, op. cit., pp.xv–xvi.

52 Leftwich, J 'Isaac Rosenberg, Poet and Painter', *Jewish Chronicle Supplement* (24 September, 1937), p.6.

53 In his reminiscences of Rosenberg published in *The Zionist Record*, South Africa (23 July 1937), p.15, Amshewitz recalled how 'One day he [Rosenberg] came into my studio. I could see he was labouring under some mental excitement, and said: "Mr. Amschewitz [sic], I have got a poem here," – feeling in his pockets the while – "I think it's a good idea" (the search in his pockets getting more frantic) and then disappointedly, "I must have forgotten it somewhere" – and then he collapsed, shaking with laughter – "Great snakes! But I have forgotten to write it!"' (cited Noakes, op. cit., p.305).

54 Isaac Horvitch, op. cit., p.10.

55 Winsten, S 'Portrait of a Young Poet', op. cit.

56 Rosenberg also drew the poet, Lazarus Aaronson in 1915, 'on [the] back of the last page of text in a volume of *Poems by Francis Thompson*, inscribed "I. R. 1915" (exhibited Leeds, 1959, cat no. 42). Aaronson's Whitechapel circle, as Joseph Leftwich recalled, overlapped with that of the Whitechapel Boys: 'My own group was [Samuel] Winsten, Rodker and Rosenberg. But we often joined with others, [David] Bomberg and [Mark] Gertler, [Jack] Isaacs and [Lazarus] Aaronson.'

57 Leftwich mentions Winsten, Rodker and Rosenberg by name in poems including *Imminence* (1912), written at the height of their friendship in Whitechapel and in *My Friends*, written more than 20 years later in 1933, in which he meditates on the dissolution of the group. He also dedicates the poem *A Prayer* (1915) to *A A Wolmark*. All three poems are published in Joseph Leftwich: *Along the Years Poems 1911–1937* (London: Robert Anscombe and Co Ltd, 1937), p.24, p.42 and p.113.

58 Bomberg to Leftwich, op. cit.

59 ed., Wilson, J M *Selected Poems of Isaac Rosenberg* (London: Cecil Woolf, 2003), p.10.

60 'There is no record of Rosenberg's interest in Yiddish. There is altogether too much inclination to minimize Rosenberg's Jewish feeling. He couldn't get away from it [...]. It was their poetry not the language that drew me to the Yiddish poets I discovered in Whitechapel [...]. I spoke of them to Rosenberg and he discussed poetry with them. He made drawings to some of their poems. Alas, not preserved [...].' Leftwich, J *Along the Years*, op. cit. In 1911, under Rosenberg's influence, all the Whitechapel writers began to experiment with poetry: 'Not that he told me to write, or bothered much about what I wrote', Leftwich recalled, 'I am sure it was his presence in our group, the influence of his example, that led us all three to experiment with verse.'

61 Cohen, J, op. cit., p.67.

62 Photograph of the oil exhibited Leeds University, *Isaac Rosenberg,* 1959, cat.no.28 (photo 2). If, as biographical evidence suggests, this portrait was painted in South Africa it must belong to 1914, although stylistically an earlier date is suggested.

63 Ben Uri Gallery, London.

64 Glynn Vivian Art Gallery, Swansea.

65 Private Collection.

66 City Art Gallery, Leeds.

67 All three in Tate Britain.

68 eds., Picciotto, C and Kohan, C M, op. cit.

69 See Essay 5 for literary context. In his diary for Tuesday, 19 September 1911, op. cit., Leftwich observed: 'There is Revolt abroad. Rebellion everywhere. Strikes, Revolutions, and at the end of them all, things remain as they were. In [?] England there was a general strike of dockers and a larger one of all sections of [?] Passport workers who joined cause with the dockers [...].'

70 'At the time Sickert was demonstrating his manner of approach 1908 to [...] Duncan Grant and Spencer Gore[,] Harold Gilman and others of the Group[.] You mention that Isaac was part of an [sic] he came [to] the Camden Town Group with their first exhibition at the Carfax Gallery (Robert Ross), Redfern St, St. James [,] so it is certain he knew these men and Sickert [...].' David Bomberg to Joseph Leftwich, op.cit. Writing in April 1957, Bomberg evidently remembered the substance of Rosenberg's association with Sickert and the Camden Town Group but misremembered the detail (for example, the Carfax Gallery was in Ryder – not Redfern – Street; and Arthur Clifton, rather than Robert Ross, was managing the Carfax Gallery in 1911 when the first exhibition took place).

71 In 1916 Rosenberg's sister Annie sent Zangwill a copy of Rosenberg's play *Moses.* In reply Zangwill (12 June 1916, cited Cohen, J, op. cit., p.149) had

written, 'You can tell him from me that I think there are a good many beautiful and powerful lines, but that I hope his experiences of war will give his next book the clarity and simplicity which is somewhat lacking in this.' Cohen further comments (ibid., p.207, n.59), 'Years later when Zangwill realised Rosenberg's literary worth he asked Leftwich why Rosenberg's poems had not been called to his attention while the poet was still alive. Leftwich informed Zangwill, to his chagrin, that at the time he had dismissed Rosenberg's poems as both obscure and trivial.'

72 Baron, W *Perfect Moderns: A History of the Camden Town Group* (Aldershot, Hants: Ashgate Publishing Ltd, 2000), p.29.

73 Ibid.

74 Both private collection.

75 The two parts were first published in *South African Women in Council* (December 1914–January 1915); republished in *The Jewish Standard*, 1915; and in *CW79*, pp.289–97.

76 Isaac Rosenberg to Sydney Schiff [July 1915], *CW79*, p.216.

77 Leftwich Diary, Tower Hamlets, entries for 3, 5, 8 and 9 March 1911; cited Tickner, L *Modern Life & Modern Subjects* (New Haven & London: Yale University Press, 2000), p.201 and p.307, n.93.

78 Cohen, J op. cit., p 42.

79 Tickner, L op. cit., p.201.

80 Leftwich diary, Wednesday, 8 March 1911, cited Cohen, op.cit., pp.42–3.

81 See Essay 2.

82 Excerpts from unpublished memoirs by Sonia Joslen (*née* Cohen), courtesy of Joan Rodker.

83 Ibid.

84 Cohen, J, op. cit., p.46.

2 ISAAC ROSENBERG THE PAINTER PART II: 'SHAKEN AND SHIVERED'

1 *CW79*, p.294.

2 'The Slade and its Relations to the Universe' [1911–12], *CW79*, p.300. See also 'The Slade and Modern Culture', ibid., pp.300–301.

3 Isaac Rosenberg to Miss Seaton, [1912 ?September], *CW79*, p.191.

4 Cited Haycock, D B 'A Crisis of Brilliance', in ed., Walsh, M *A Dilemma of English Modernism: Visual and Verbal Politics in the Life and Work of C R W Nevinson (1889–1949)* (Delaware: University of Delaware Press, 2007)., p.36.

5 David Bomberg to Joseph Leftwich, 8 April 1957, op. cit.

6 From 1908–11, Goldstein applied three times to the JEAS for Slade funding, without success, only finally gaining a loan in 1913 after financing his own first year in 1912 and gaining a 2nd prize for Head painting.

7 Tickner, L, op. cit., p.280 n.28.

8 'In the large manner and luxury/Of a giant who guests/In a little world of mortals/He condescends a space/His ears to incline,/But as though listn'ing were a trouble' (Xliv, *CW79*, op. cit., p.127). Although undated, the poem probably originates from 1914 when Rosenberg and Kramer overlapped at the Slade.

9 Isaac Rosenberg to Miss Seaton, op. cit.

10 Alice Mayes, 'The Young Bomberg 1914–1925', cited Cork, R, op. cit., p.29.

11 Although they are given a later date (1915) by the British Museum.

12 Cohen, J, op. cit., p.66.

13 Isaac Rosenberg to Miss Seaton, op. cit.

14 Isaac Rosenberg to Laurence Binyon, [no date but dated 1912] in *CW79*, p.192.

15 C KoeChila to Laurence Binyon, 17 June 1921, in Liddiard, J, op. cit., p.132.

16 Mark Gertler [interview], *Studio*, 104, 1932, p 163, cited MacDougall, S *Mark Gertler*, op. cit., p.75.

17 See Essay 3.

18 'ART', *CW79*, p.294.

19 Ibid.

20 Ibid.

21 The lines in Rosenberg's hand read: 'Sing unto the Lord, for He hath triumphed gloriously/The Horse & its [sic] rider hath He thrown into the Sea.' The painting is in a private collection overseas.

22 In December 1912–January 1913 he wrote to Miss Seaton that 'The Blakes at the Tate show that England has turned out one man second to none who has ever lived. The drawings are finer than his poems, much clearer, though I can't help thinking it was unfortunate that he did not live when a better tradition of drawing ruled. His conventional manner of expressing those astounding conceptions is the fault of his time, not his.' (*CW79*, p.198).

23 Duncan Grant, *Bathing*, 1911, oil on canvas, Tate.

24 Grant was one of a number of young painters asked to decorate the student's dining room at the Borough Polytechnic (Elephant and Castle) on the theme 'London on Holiday'. His *Bathing* canvas and its companion piece *Football* form part of the seven paintings by six artists which Roger Fry assembled for the project. The event received extensive press coverage so it possible that Rosenberg may have seen the works *in situ*. See Shone, R *The Art of Bloomsbury* (London: Tate Gallery Publishing, 1999), pp.147–9; and Watney, S *The Art of Duncan Grant* (London: John Murray, 1990), p.31.

25 Current whereabouts unknown.

26 Hassall, C *Edward Marsh: Patron of the Arts – A Biography* (London: Longmans, 1959; this edition New York: Harcourt, Brace and Company, 1959), p.281. In November 1913 Gertler had introduced Rosenberg to Edward Marsh at the Café Royal. Marsh thereafter bought Rosenberg's paintings and encouraged his poetry. Rosenberg also sold three paintings to Edward Marsh to fund the printing of *Youth* in 1915 and Marsh included an extract from Rosenberg's 'Ah! Koelue!' from his play *Moses* in the third volume of *Georgian Poetry* (published late September 1917).

27 Three Gauguins of Tahitians were shown in *Manet and the Post-Impressionists* at the Grafton Galleries in 1910: (128) *Tahitians* (c. 1891), (86) *Tahitian Women Bathing* (1892) and (120) *Three Tahitians* (1899).

28 A preliminary study (oil on canvas, before 1873) for *Summer* is in the National Gallery, London, bequeathed by Arthur Haythorne Studd 1919. The finished work hangs in the entrance hall of the Musée D'Orsay, Paris. Rosenberg may have seen it in reproduction.

29 See Tickner, L, op. cit., pp.70–74.

30 Shone, R (intro) *The Friday Club 1905–1922* (London: Michael Parkin Gallery, 1996), unpaginated. See also Spalding, F *Duncan Grant* (London: Chatto & Windus, 1997), p.96: 'Duncan went down to Brighton to see the exhibition *Modern French Artists* [1910] organized by Robert Dell, where amid large quantities of Impressionist and academic painting were works by Gauguin, Matisse, Cézanne, Degas and Puvis de Chavannes.'

31 For example, Gertler's *The Return of Jeptha* (current whereabouts unknown) and the work of John Currie (which was also strongly influenced by John).

32 Last exhibited at Rosenberg's Memorial Exhibition at the Whitechapel Art Gallery in 1937, priced at 100 guineas, it was subsequently lost.

33 Isaac Rosenberg to Miss Wright, 15 July 1912, *CW79*, p.187. (Miss Alice Wright had taught Rosenberg painting at Birkbeck in 1907–8.)

34 Ibid., postmarked 6 August 1912, *CW79*, p.188.

35 Isaac Rosenberg [fragment of a letter to Ruth Löwy, 1912, probably July], *CW79*, p.188.

36 There is difficulty over the dating of this work. Stylistically, it belongs to the Slade period, *c.*1912. However, in a letter to Edward Marsh [not dated but believed to be 1915], *CW79*, p.213, Rosenberg wrote 'I'm doing a nice little thing for Meredith's 'Lark ascending': *Their faces raised/ Puts on the light of children praised.* Everybody is in a sort of delirious ecstacy, and all, feeling in the same way express the same feelings in different ways, according to their natures. I think you'll like it.'

37 Cohen, J, op. cit., p.74.

38 Isaac Rosenberg to Miss Wright [postmarked 10 August 1912], *CW79*, p.188.

39 Isaac Rosenberg to Ruth Löwy [1912 ?August], *CW79*, p.189.

40 Isaac Rosenberg to Mrs Cohen [no date. Presumably Sept–Oct 1912], *CW79*, p.192.

41 It went to Stanley Spencer for his *Nativity*.

42 Isaac Rosenberg to Miss Wright [no date, *c.*October 1912], *CW79*, p.194.

43 Cohen, J, op. cit., p.73.

44 Frank Emanuel to Laurence Binyon, 28 April 1921, in Liddiard, op. cit., pp.126–8. Rosenberg wrote to Ruth Löwy [1912 ?October, *CW79*, pp.193–4] that he had had 'a bit of a scuffle with Mrs Cohen lately. She was very disappointed at my picture and said she was sure I could have done better [...]. She said that unless I get into a more healthy style of work she won't help me [...]. God knows what she means by a

more healthy style of work[.] – Do you feel ill when you see my work[?] I know some feel people faint looking at a Michel Angelo[.]'

45 Laurence Binyon in ed., Bottomley, G *Poems by Isaac Rosenberg* (London: William Heinemann, 1922), pp.7–8.

46 Ibid.

47 The painting *Beata Beatrix* (*c.*1864–70, Tate) by the poet and painter Dante Gabriel Rossetti (1828–82) was inspired by the Italian poet Dante's *Vita Nuova* and portrayed 'the beloved at the moment of her transition from earth to heaven'. It was Rossetti's 'mourning tribute to his wife', Elizabeth Siddal, who died in 1862 from an overdose of laudanum. It shows her 'with eyes closed in ecstatic expectation. In the artist's words, it is an ideal image of death, symbolized by "sudden spiritual transformation. Beatrice is rapt visibly into heaven seeing as it were through her shut lids". The "radiant bird, a messenger of death" drops a poppy into her hands. In the background Dante, the lover, gazes towards Love "in whose hand the waning life of his lady flickers as a flame. On the sundial at her side the shadow falls on the hour of nine"' Marsh, J *Pre-Raphaelite Women: Images of Femininity in Pre-Raphaelite Art* (London: Weidenfeld & Nicolson, 1997; this edition, Phoenix Illustrated, 1998), p.141. Birds, particularly larks, and the poppy – a symbol of both life and death – would become important images in Rosenberg's poetry.

48 Isaac Rosenberg to Laurence Binyon, op.cit., pp.62–3.

49 Ibid., no date but dated 1912 in *CW79*, p.192.

50 Isaac Rosenberg to Gordon Bottomley 'France Aug 8 1916', in Liddiard, op. cit., p.80.

51 Isaac Rosenberg to Edward Marsh [October–November 1915] *CW79*, pp.223–4.

52 The verse fragments are from a poem of 1914 entitled 'The Search' (see *CW79*, p.130, xxxvii).

53 David Bomberg to Joseph Leftwich, op.cit. However, Bomberg also fell out with Tonks, bringing his palette down over his head after one dispute. Not surprisingly, the Slade staff later labelled Bomberg 'a disturbing influence'. JEAS Archives (25 June 1913), cited Gross, P 'The Whitechapel Boys', in ed., MacDougall, S *Mark Gertler: A New Perspective* (London: Ben Uri Gallery, 2002), p.27, n.5.

54 It is possible that Amshewitz advised Rosenberg to approach Marion Harry Spielmann. Spielmann was prominently depicted in a pen-and-ink group portrait executed by Amshewitz in 1907, subsequently donated by Spielmann to the National Portrait Gallery.

55 Tickner, L, op. cit., pp.287–8, n.76.

56 Haycock, D B, op. cit., p.x, n.32.

57 Ibid., p.39.

58 Cohen, J op. cit., p.59.

59 JEAS Minute Book, 19 Nov 1910; 18 Jan 1911, cited Tickner, L, op. cit., p.287, n.76.

60 Frank Emanuel to Gordon Bottomley, op. cit., p.128.

61 Cohen, J, op. cit., p.61.

62 The minutes of 18 January 1911 record that 'A vote of thanks was passed to Mr Sefton Sewell for his kind attention to Gertler's teeth'; and on 29 March 1911, when Mrs. Nevinson invited Gertler to spend a week in Paris with her and her son and £3.10. was needed for expenses, Lady Desart had a whip-round there and then to collect the money from committee members who were present.

63 Dickson, R 'Jacob Kramer – the Hare', *William Roberts & Jacob Kramer: The Tortoise and the Hare* (London: Ben Uri, 2003).

64 See Isaac Rosenberg to Mr Lesser [late Dec 1912], *CW79*, p.197. This must have been a particular worry since when his older sister Minnie had earlier developed eye strain, she had developed glaucoma, eventually successfully treated by an operation. (Cohen, J, op. cit., pp.21–2.).

65 Winsten, S 'Portrait of a Young Poet', *John O'London's Weekly* (10 November 1950), p.589.

66 Isaac Rosenberg to Miss Wright [no date but must be Oct 1912], *CW79*, p.194: 'I am sending a drawing and perhaps a painting to the New English Art as the Pro– advised me to.'

67 Parsons, I *CW79*, p.xii and Liddiard, J, op. cit., p.17, record that Rosenberg also exhibited 'another painting' which remained unsold. However, NEAC records record only the *Sanguine Drawing* (no. 6).

68 See Essay 5.

69 *Jewish Chronicle* (15 May 1914).

70 Cited Steyn, J 'Inside Out: Assumptions of "English" Modernism in the Whitechapel Art Gallery, London, 1914', in ed., Pointon, M *Art Apart* (publisher), pp.212–230.

71 Probably cat no 8, *The Artist's Father*, 1911.

72 Tickner, L, op. cit., p.159, believes that 'Rosenberg's *My Father* was presumably one of the two portraits of his father from 1911. Of his other paintings, *Murder of Lorenzo* (Keats) is known, but *The Judgement of Paris, Portrait* and *Head of a Girl* cannot be identified.'

73 Dated 1912, oil on board, 30.4 x 24.8, formerly Ben Uri Art Society, current whereabouts unknown. Last exhibited London: National Book League, 1975 (no. 48).

74 Believed to date from 1914 or earlier, current whereabouts unknown.

75 Tickner, L, op. cit., p.159.

76 *Jewish Chronicle* (15 May 1914), p.10

77 Annie Rosenberg, op. cit., p.134.

78 Cohen, J, op. cit., p.103 maintains that *Portrait* was one of a number of self-portraits completed by 1914, and that *Head of a Girl* was probably the pencil study reproduced in *Art and Letters*, vol 1, no 3, Summer 1919, p.109 with five poems and a memorial note by his sister Annie.'

79 See Sonia Cohen's description in Essay 1.

80 Isaac Rosenberg to Edward Marsh [October–November 1914], *CW79*, p.206. However, Parsons, ibid., n.1, believes it to be 'almost certainly' the NPG one (cat no. 24). A fine second self-portrait, in which Rosenberg appears in a dark suit (rather that the familiar green one), wearing an orange-brown tie and a shirt with rounded collars (cat no. 20) is believed to date from this trip. However it is a much more traditional portrait, more densely painted, with some impasto, which, stylistically, appears to belong to an earlier period, *c.*1910–11.

81 Annie Rosenberg, op. cit. p.135.

82 Isaac Rosenberg to Edward Marsh [postmarked Cape Town, ?July 24, 1914], *CW79*, pp.204–5. Bomberg later commented that Rosenberg had 'a good [?]friend [...] in Edward Rowarth' (Bomberg to Leftwich, op. cit.). Edward Roworth (1880–1964), whom Rosenberg met at Cape Town, was a Dutch-born painter and a major figure in the South African Society of Artists, *c.*1902–50. Trained in Manchester under Hubert von Herkomer and Tom Mostyn, and at the Slade under Tonks, he had also spent time in Florence studying the Italian Renaissance. There are no further references to him in Rosenberg's published letters to test the truth of Bomberg's assertion.

83 Rosenberg articulated his opinions on many of his contemporaries in 'Art II' (*CW79*, p.297): 'Henry Lamb is a shy, a tremulous and ever-shaken life in shadow. Compared to Lamb, John is the broad ocean with the sun on it, and Lamb the sea with the moon. Innes paints landscapes very much like the Chinese and Mantegna. They have the vague beauty of perfumes and luxuriant reverie. Mark Gertler has a deep understanding of nature and sometimes achieves to the intensity we call imagination. John Currie has painted lovely things without being very convincing as a draughtsman. David Bomberg has crude power of a too calculated violence – and is mechanical, but undoubtedly interesting. Roberts, who is yet a boy[,] is a remarkable draughtsman in a stodgy academic way, clear, logical, and fervent. But the finest of all is Stanley Spencer. He is too independent for contemporary influence and goes back to Giotto and Blake as his masters. He strikes even a deeper note than John, and his pictures have that sense of everlastingness[,] of no beginning and no end[,] that we get in all masterpieces.'

84 See Essay 5.

85 Isaac Rosenberg to his family [late 1914], *CW79*, p.207.

86 Margaretha 'Scrappy' van Hulsteyn (1896–1970), known as Marda Vanne, was a South-African born actress who had defied her parents's wishes to go upon the stage. She was briefly married to J G (Hans) Strijdom (he went on to become South Africa's fifth prime minister) and later set up a theatrical company, 'The Good Companions', with the London born actress of Welsh descent Gwen Ffrangçon-Davies (1891–1992), whom she met upon the London stage (Internet Shakespeare Editions, supported by the University of Victoria and the Social Sciences and Humanities Research Council of Canada).

87 Isaac Rosenberg to Edward Marsh [undated letter], *CW79*, p.206.

88 Annie Rosenberg, op. cit., p.135.

89 Their daughter Joan was born in 1916.

90 Parsons, I 'Introduction', *CW79*, p.xxiv.

91 Isaac Rosenberg to Edward Marsh [spring 1915], *CW79*, p.211. Presumably Marsh was not offered, or refused, the portraits of Sonia and Clare.

92 Correggio, *The Madonna of the Basket*, *c.*1524, National Gallery, London.

93 Correggio, *The School of Love/Venus with Mercury and Cupid*, *c.*1525, National Gallery, London.

94 There are also sanguine studies of nude children, *c.*1908 or earlier, Imperial War Museum, London (not illustrated), though no specific picture has been identified as the model for this work.

95 *The Virgin with the Infant Saint John adoring the Infant Christ accompanied by an Angel*, *c.*1491–1508, National Gallery, London.

96 Isaac Rosenberg, 'ART, Part II', *CW79*, p.292.

97 Rosenberg explained that if he had 'a little longer on it it would have been very fine indeed but the model cleared off before I could absolutely finish'; Isaac Rosenberg to Edward Marsh [spring 1915], *CW79*, p.211, 2nd letter. Had Rosenberg not described Sonia's deep blue dress in his first letter, it may have been assumed that he was talking about the portrait of Clare, who had been pursued at the Bomberg by Slade and painted by him as a Michelangelesque 'sibyl' (see Essay 7); then apparently painted later 'in the same blue dress' by Rosenberg (see Tickner, L, op. cit., p.289, n.81.). It is also curious that he should refer to either woman as 'the model' but then they were not known personally by Marsh. Sonia later told her daughter Joan that Rosenberg continued to work on her portrait during his final leave in September 1917 but this may have been merely a pretext for his visit. He described it as 'unfinished'

98 The model for this work has not been identified.

99 NEAC 1915 w, adds: Military Hospital "Bantams", 12th Suffolks, Bury St Edmunds: (62) drawing; (130) *Woman in Grey & Red*; (278) *The Family of Adam.*

100 Ibid., [1915 ?October], *CW79*, p.219.

101 Isaac Rosenberg to Ezra Pound [apparently unfinished letter, 1915], *CW79*, p.214.

102 Isaac Rosenberg to Sydney Schiff [early November 1915], *CW79*, p.221.

103 Isaac Rosenberg to Edward Marsh [Probably May 27, 1916], *CW79*, pp.233–4.

104 Bomberg to Leftwich, op. cit.

105 Isaac Rosenberg to Sydney Schiff [October 1915], *CW79*, p.219.

106 Jacob Kramer to Herbert Read [4 November 1918], Letter HR/JK 30, Herbert Read Archive, Special Collections, University of Victoria, Canada.

107 Isaac Rosenberg to Sydney Schiff [November 1915], *CW79*, pp.221–2.

108 Ibid.

109 Ibid., [early December 1915], *CW79*, pp.224–5.

110 Isaac Rosenberg to Edward Marsh [December 1915], *CW79*, pp.225–6.

111 Isaac Rosenberg to Sydney Schiff [early December 1915], *CW79*, pp. 224–5. This was not, in fact, true: they were correctly listed under Rosenberg's name.

112 Isaac Rosenberg to Miss Winifreda Seaton [December 1915], *CW79*, p.226.

113 Isaac Rosenberg to Edward Marsh [October-November 1915], op. cit., p.225.

114 Isaac Rosenberg to Sydney Schiff [late December 1915], *CW79*, p.227.

115 Ibid [early 1916], *CW79*, pp.229–230.

116 Ibid., [1916, ?March], *CW79*, pp.230–31.

117 Isaac Rosenberg to Lascelles Abercrombie, [11 March 1916], *CW79*, p.230.

118 This took place from July–November 1916.

119 Isaac Rosenberg to Sydney Schiff [late July 1916], *CW79*, pp.238–9.

120 Isaac Rosenberg to Edward Marsh [August 1916], *CW79*, pp 242–3: 'Do you know anything about artists out here to disguise things, landscape sheds etc. Col S J Solomon is their Chief I believe and I know him a bit. I wonder if I'd be any good at it. Who should I have to approach about it.'

121 Annie Rosenberg, op. cit., p.135.

122 Isaac Rosenberg to Laurence Binyon [Autumn 1916], *CW79*, pp.248–9.

123 The Battle of Pozières took place on the Somme from 23 July–3 September 1916. One copy of the poem, written in August 1916 in France, was sent to Gordon Bottomley; and two fair copies were sent to Rodker and Miss Seaton (whose copy has not survived). See Noakes, V, op. cit, commentary, p.362.

124 Isaac Rosenberg to John Rodker [no date, no address], *CW79*, pp.250–1.

125 Noakes, V, op. cit., p.362.

126 Isaac Rosenberg to Gordon Bottomley [February 1917], *CW79*, pp.252–3. See Essay 3.

127 Isaac Rosenberg to Gordon Bottomley [21 September 1917], in Liddiard, J, op. cit., p.106.

128 Isaac Rosenberg to Edward Marsh [postmarked January 26, 1918], *CW79*, p.267.

129 Isaac Rosenberg to Edward Marsh [28 March 1918, postmarked 2 April 1918], *CW79*, p.272.

130 Ibid.

131 Bailleul Road East British Cemetery, St Laurent Blangy, Northern France.

3 ISAAC ROSENBERG
WAR POET AS PAINTER

1 'The Pre-Raphaelites and Imagination in Paint', *CW79*, p.298.

2 See Sassoon's foreword to *Collected Works of Isaac Rosenberg: Poetry, Prose, Letters, Paintings and Drawings* (London: Chatto and Windus, 1979) [*CW79*]; T S Eliot's remark, quoted in Wood, J *The Broken Estate: Essays on Literature and Belief* (London: Pimlico, 2000), p.139; and Leavis, F R *New Bearings in English Poetry* (London: Penguin, 1972), pp.57–8.

3 Isaac Rosenberg to Alice Wright [postmarked August 6, 1912], *CW79*, p.188.

4 Isaac Rosenberg to Ruth Löwy [1912, probably July], *CW79*, p.188.

5 See ed., Noakes, V *Poems and Plays of Isaac Rosenberg: A Critical Edition* (Oxford: Oxford University Press, 2004), p.28.

6 ed., Bottomley, G (with an introductory memoir by Laurence Binyon) *Poems by Isaac Rosenberg* (London: Heinemann, 1922), p.7.

7 Ibid., pp.7–8.

8 'The Pre-Raphaelites and Imagination in Paint', op. cit., p.298.

9 Isaac Rosenberg to Sydney Schiff [November 1915], *CW79*, p.222.

10 Isaac Rosenberg to Edward Marsh [postmarked 1 December 1915], *CW79*, p.223.

11 Ibid.

12 Ibid.

13 Isaac Rosenberg to Lascelles Abercrombie, 11 March 1916, *CW79*, p.230.

14 Isaac Rosenberg to Sydney Schiff [late December 1915], *CW79*, p.227. cf. 'What If I Wear Your Beauty at this Present', lines 11–12: 'I like an insect beautiful wings have gotten/Shed from you [...]' (in ed., Noakes, V, op. cit., p.78).

15 Ibid., pp.123–4.

16 John Rodker to Harriet Monroe, 25 February 1916, Chicago.

17 *CW79*, op. cit., p.227.

18 See Cork, R *David Bomberg* (New Haven and London: Yale University Press, 1987), p.115.

19 See the striking back jacket of Sarah MacDougall's *Mark Gertler* (London: John Murray, 2002).

20 ed., Noakes, V, op. cit., p.127.

21 Letter in Imperial War museum [IWM].

22 Isaac Rosenberg to Gordon Bottomley [postmarked 15 August 1916], in ed., Liddiard, J *Isaac Rosenberg: Poetry Out of My Head and Heart – Unpublished Letters and Poem Versions* (London: Enitharmon Press, 2007), p.81.

23 See ed., Noakes, V, op. cit., pp.133–4.

24 IWM.

25 Isaac Rosenberg to Gordon Bottomley, [postmarked 23 July 1916], in ed., Liddiard, J, op. cit., p.73.

26 ed., Bottomley, G, op. cit., p.40.

27 See ed., Noakes, V, op. cit., pp.134–6.

28 Isaac Rosenberg, 'Joy', from 'Shorter Fragments of Prose', *CW79*, p.303.

29 Isaac Rosenberg to Edward Marsh [postmarked 8 May 1917], *CW79*, p.254.

30 See ed., Noakes, V, op. cit., p.139.

31 Ibid., pp.141–2.

32 Gordon Bottomley to Isaac Rosenberg, 21 December 1916, IWM.

33 Gordon Bottomley to Denys Harding, 20 September 1934, Bristol University Library.

34 Gordon Bottomley's notes to his fellow-editor, Denys Harding, on *Collected Works of Isaac Rosenberg* (London: Chatto & Windus, 1937)

35 Gordon Bottomley to Isaac Rosenberg, 7 September 1916, IWM.

4 WHITECHAPEL AT WAR
THE WHITECHAPEL BOYS AND THE GREAT WAR

1 Leftwich, J *Along the Years Poems 1911–1937*, (London: Robert Anscombe and Co Ltd, 1937), p.24.

2 Isaac Rosenberg to Edward Marsh, [late December 1915], *CW79*, p.227.

3 *Jewish World* (7 October 1914), p.7.

4 Levene, M 'Going against the Grain: Two Jewish Memoirs of War and Anti-War, 1914–18', *Jewish Culture and History*, Volume 2, No. 2, pp.66–7.

5 Jacob Kramer to Herbert Read [9 August 1918], Letter II, Herbert Read Archive, Special Collections, University of Victoria, Canada.

6 *Jewish Chronicle*, 6 October 1916, p.12.

7 Gilbert Cannan to Ottoline Morrell [not dated, *c.*August 1914], cited MacDougall S *Mark Gertler* (London: John Murray, 2002), p.101.

8 Maccoby, D *God Made Blind* (Northwood, Middx: Symposium Press [Science Reviews], 1999), p.76.

9 *Jewish Chronicle* (6 October 1916), p.12.

10 Mark Gertler to Carrington [June 1915] in ed., Carrington, N *Mark Gertler: Selected Letters* (London: Rupert Hart Davies, 1965), pp.95–6. Hereafter *MGSL*.

11 *Voices* (July 1919), Volume 2, Number 1, p.5.

12 *Jewish World* (30 December, 1914), p.1.

13 *Jewish Chronicle*, (November 19, 1915), p.16.

14 *Jewish Chronicle*, (8 February 1918), pp.16–17.

15 Though he was neither born nor raised in the East End and worked outside it, Epstein had strong links to the generation of young artists emerging from it.

16 Michael Sadler, Kramer's patron, Vice-Chancellor of Leeds University and one of the earliest collectors of modern art in England, wrote to Kramer in August 1917: 'I enclose a copy of Colonel Scovell's letter, and urge you to take his advice. It is splendid that Colonel Patterson, the officer in charge of the new Jewish regiment, knows all about you [...].' Michael Sadler to Jacob Kramer [21 August 1917], cited Roberts, J *The Kramer Documents* (Valencia: J Roberts, 1983), p.26.

17 Cork, R 'Bomberg's War Poetry' in Jason, N *Poems and Drawings from the First World War by David Bomberg* (London: Gillian Jason Gallery, 1992), p.7. Cork further suggests that Rodker may have selected Bomberg as the artist to design the cover for *Poems by John Rodker*, privately printed in 1914, because of his empathy towards both word and image.

18 David Bomberg, extract from 'Winter Night', in *Poems and Drawings from the First World War by David Bomberg*, pp.23–5.

19 The first version, *Sappers at Work: A Canadian Tunelling Company* (1918–19), is in the Tate. The second, final version, *Sappers at Work: A Canadian Tunelling Company* (1919), is in the National Gallery of Canada, Ottawa.

20 *Poems and Drawings from the First World War by David Bomberg*, op. cit., p.12.

21 P G Konody (1872–1933), the distinguished writer and art critic

22 Cork, R *A Bitter Truth: Avant Garde Art and the Great War* (Yale University Press: New Haven and London in association with the Barbican Gallery, 1994), p.229.

23 Vols 1–4 are held in the British Library; Vol 6 is held in a private collection. Bomberg's poetry does not appear in any of these volumes but it is possible it was published in vol. 5, which we have not been able to trace. See Essay 5.

24 Mark Gertler to Carrington, August 1914, *MGSL*, p.100.

25 Mark Gertler to Dorothy Brett, 16 September 1914, University of Texas, Austin.

26 Noel Carrington, 'War and New Friends' in *MGSL*, p.76.

27 Ibid.

28 Mark Gertler to Edward Marsh, 19 October 1915, *MGSL*, p.102

29 Rosenberg marked the occasion with the poem 'Lusitania' (see *CW79*, p.99).

30 *Daily Telegraph*, 13 June 1916.

31 Private Collection, London.

32 Mark Gertler to Carrington, Sunday, December 1915, *MGSL*, pp.106–8.

33 Ibid.

34 *Daily Telegraph* (21 November 1915)

35 Cited Woodeson, J *Mark Gertler: Biographer of a Painter 1892–1939* (London: Sidgwick & Jackson, 1972), p.185.

36 Mark Gertler to Brett, 10 February 1916, University of Texas, Austin.

37 Ibid.

38 Mark Gertler to S S Koteliansky, 13 September 1916, British Library.

39 Mark Gertler to Carrington, [*c.*May 1916], University of Texas, Austin.

40 Lytton Strachey to Ottoline Morrell, 3 July 1916, cited Holroyd, M *Lytton Strachey* (London: Chatto & Windus, 1994), p.369.

41 St John Hutchinson to Mark Gertler, [*c.*November 1916], cited *MGSL*., pp.128–9.

42 *Evening News* (27 April 1917), cited Wilcox, D J *The London Group 1913–1939: The Artists and their Works* (Aldershot, Hants: Scolar Press, 1995), p.12.

43 Mark Gertler to Carrington, 2 March 1918, *MGSL*, p.158.

44 Mark Gertler to P G Konody, 23 March 1918, Art Dept., Imperial War Museum.

45 In 1920 Gertler was finally diagnosed with tuberculosis and spent the first of several prolonged periods in a sanatorium.

46 Mark Gertler to Ottine Morrell, 24 April 1918, University of Texas, Austin.

47 P G Konody [letter not signed] to Mark Gertler, 31 May 1918, Dept. of Art, Imperial War Museum, London.

48 Mark Gertler to Ottoline Morrell, 24 April 1918, University of Texas, Austin.

49 Mark Gertler to Ottoline Morrell, 2 October 1917, ibid.

50 David Bomberg's experience with P G Konody shows that this was not entirely without foundation. Bomberg was devastated by Konody's rejection of his commissioned painting of Canadian sappers.

51 Perhaps ironically, the subject of shelterers in the underground was eventually carried out by the artist Walter Bayes (*The Underworld*, 1918), with whom Gertler would come into open conflict in the early thirties, when he was employed under Bayes as a teacher at the Westminster School of Art.

52 Taylor, J R *Meninsky* (London: Redcliffe Press Ltd, 1990), p.39.

53 See Essay 6.

54 See Essay 7.

55 See Essay 5.

56 *Jewish Chronicle* (23 July 1915), p.18.

57 Isaac Rosenberg to Joseph Leftwich, [8 Dec 1917], *CW79*, p.266–7.

58 DNB. This suggests he volunteered as conscription was not introduced until 1916.

59 Cited Dickson, R and MacDougall, S 'Hurrah for the New Art! The Emergence of Wolmark the Colourist' in *Rediscovering Wolmark: a Pioneer of British Modernism* (London: Ben Uri Gallery, 2004), p.41

60 See Essay 5.

61 The curators are grateful to Peter Eisden for the information relating to this painting. Norman Mortimer Joseph Kohnstamm was the eldest son of Rudolph and Emily; born in 1897 and killed in action in France on 22 March 1918. If this work was painted in 1916, as Wolmark recorded, the sitter was then still alive, and presumably Wolmark added 'the late' to the title after his death. The painting is now in the collection of the Jerwood Foundation, London.

62 The painting is in a private collection in London.

63 A number of earlier studies of this work are known. See Dickson, R and MacDougall, S op. cit., p.41.

64 Geoffrey Konstam, son of Wolmark's patrons, recalled Wolmark's frequent visits to his parents house during the war: 'Then in 1919 a fellow medical student and I posed as nudes for a large painting he was doing of an army medical inspection. Wolmark had recently experienced such an examination and was turned down because of his severe myopia. The composition included a self-portrait as one of the examinees.'

65 Jacob Kramer to Herbert Read [27 October 1918], Letter IV, Herbert Read Archive, Special Collections, University of Victoria, Canada.

66 Jacob Kramer to Herbert Read [24 November 1918], Letter VII, ibid.

67 Herbert Read to Jacob Kramer [undated, possibly December 1918] cited J Roberts, op. cit., p.39.

68 Isaac Rosenberg to Laurence Binyon [Autumn 1916], *CW79*, pp.248–9.

69 Ben Uri Gallery/London Jewish Museum of Art.

70 Arts Council Collection, South Bank Centre, London.

71 Leeds Art Gallery.

72 Gross, P 'A Cultural Moment in the Midst of Change' *The Ben Uri Story*, op. cit., p.22.

5 FIRST FRUITS
THE WHITECHAPEL BOYS IN PRINT, C.1912–20

1 Defined as 'a magazine not intending or achieving mass circulation' (ed., Bury, S *Breaking the Rules: The Printed Face of the European Avant Garde 1900–1937* (London: British Library, 2007), p.38.

2 The project is directed by Professor Peter Brooker (University of Nottingham) and Dr Andrew Thacker (De Montfort University) and is supported by the Arts and Humanities Research Council (AHRC) for four years from 2006.

3 Home page from MMR website: http://www.cts.dmu.ac.uk/exist/mod_mag/index.htm

4 Leftwich, J 'Jewish London 50 Years Ago' in ed., Sonntag, J *1915-1965: Fifty Years Achievement in the Arts – Commemorative Volume to mark the fiftieth anniversary of the foundation of the Ben Uri Art Society* (London: Ben Uri, 1966), p.15.

5 Leftwich, ibid., p.14.

6 Including Henri Gaudier-Brzeska and Jessica Dismorr, under the art editorship of J D Fergusson, as well as drawings and woodcuts by Horace Brodkzy (see 'The Life and Times of Horace Brodzky Artist and Etcher' by John Brodkzy, unpublished typescript in Tate Gallery Archive, TGA 931/9 (p. 6). Works by other key modernists, such as Picasso, were also featured. *Rhythm*'s less-celebrated contributors included Laurence Binyon 'Return to Poetry' and Thomas Moult 'Vision' in *Rhythm: Art Music Literature Quarterly* vol. 1, no. 4 (London: The Saint Catherine Press, Stephen Swift & Company, Martin Secker, Spring 1912).

7 Moult, T 'Periodicals: A Survey of Contemporaries, Jan-Feb', *Voices*, vol. 3, no. 2 (March 1920), pp.84–6.

8 *The Jewish Standard*, 1 July 1915, pp.2–3.

9 Advertisement for Good's Cameo Corner, *Voices*, vol. 3, no. 2 (March 1920).

10 Advertisement for Elspeth Phelps 'alluring clothes', ibid.

11 *Art & Letters*, vol. 1, no. 4, (June 1918), unpaginated.

12 The firm's publications reflected the internationalist views that T Fisher Unwin held in line with his liberalism and interest in world politics, and featured such writers as George Bernard Shaw, Henry James, W B Yeats, Joseph Conrad, Rudyard Kipling and Israel Zangwill.

13 Isaac Rosenberg to Ruth Löwy [1912, ?March], *CW79*, pp.185–6.

14 See Essay 1.

15 *Art & Letters*, vol. 1, no. 1, (June 1917), Preface.

16 This work is discussed further in Essay 1

17 *Jewish Chronicle* (10 May 1912), p.24.

18 Ibid.

19 *Jewish Chronicle* (24 May 1912), p.15. See Essay 1.

20 Cohen, op. cit., p.47.

21 ed., Aptroot, M *Jewish Books in Whitechapel: A Bibliography of Narodiczky's Press* (London: Duckworth, 1991), 'Israel Narodiczky and his Whitechapel Press', pp.vi–xii.

22 ibid.

23 The printing cost Rosenberg £2.10s for 100 copies, which Rosenberg sold at 2s 6d or gave away. He funded the venture by selling three life drawings to Edward Marsh (see Noakes, V, op. cit., p.xlii.)

24 For a full account of its birth see Mazower, D 'A cultural moment in the midst of change: background to the times of the establishment of the Ben Uri Society', *The Ben Uri Story from Art Society to Museum and the influence of Anglo-Jewish Artists on the Modern British Movement* (London: The Ben Uri Gallery, 2001), p.38.

25 Part I of the lecture and the poem 'Dead Heroes' appear in the December 1914 edition; Part II and the poem 'Beauty' in that for January 1915 (see Noakes, V, op. cit., p.xlii).

26 Horace Brodzky *The Painter, Wyndham Lewis, Colour,* vol. 1, no. 6 (January 1915), p.224; Mark Wayner *Chief Rabbi, Colour,* vol. 5, no. 2 (September 1916), p.66; David Bomberg *Poster Design, Colour,* vol. 15, no. 2 (Sept 1921), unpaginated; Mark Gertler *Agapanthus, Colour,* vol. 2, no. 2 (March 1915), p.69; Jacob Kramer *Maxim Gorky, Colour,* vol. 5, no. 5 (December 1916), p.174; Bernard Meninsky, *Mother and Child, Colour,* vol. 6, no. 2 (March 1917), p.47; Morris Goldstein, *The Student, Colour,* vol. 6, no. 2 (March 1917), p.50.

27 *Jewish Chronicle* (15 May, 1914), p.10.

28 Brodzky, J, op. cit., p.6.

29 Frank Harris wrote to Brodzky (28 February 1913, TGA 949. 2.7) that he hoped that publication of Brodzky's photo and some of his 'sketches' in that week's issue would 'get your really fine work better known'. In the early twenties in New York, Brodzky renewed his acquaintance with Frank Harris, then editor of *Pearson's Magazine.*

30 Brodzky, J, op. cit., p 10.

31 Ibid., p.9.

32 Cited ibid., p.8.

33 Bomberg also included him in the 'Jewish Section' of *Twentieth Century Art: A Review of Modern Movements* at the Whitechapel Art Gallery in May 1914.

34 Private Collection.

35 Lew, H R *Brodzky* (Melbourne: private publication, 1987), p.18. The Epstein and Kramer drawings are shown courtesy of Michael Parkin Fine Art Ltd, London; the Wolmark drawing is courtesy of the Belgrave Gallery Ltd, London.

36 Brodzky, H *Henri Gaudier-Brzeska* (London: Faber and Faber, 1933), p.118. The book was published in England by Faber and Faber in 1933 upon the recommendation of A R Orage.

37 Portland Stone relief, Kettle's Yard, Cambridge; see Silber, E *Gaudier-Brzeska Life and Art: with a Catalogue Raisonné of the Sculpture* (London: Thames and Hudson, 1996), p.260 (41).

38 There are 6 bronzes, including one at the Southampton City Art Gallery. For full details see Silber, E, op. cit., p.261 (46). For an account of the relationship between Gaudier-Brzeska and Wolmark, see Silber, E 'Three Portraits and a Friendship: Wolmark and Gaudier-Brzeska', in eds., Dickson, R and MacDougall, S *Rediscovering Wolmark: a Pioneer of British Modernism* (London: Ben Uri, 2004), pp.24–31. A bronze version of the bust of Brodzky is in the collection of Tate, London.

39 Plaster bust, probably destroyed; see Silber, E, op. cit., p.261 (45).

40 Edited by the wood engraver H G Webb, *Art Chronicle* was published in London from 1909 to 1914 and eventually incorporated *Art News*, the journal associated with the Allied Artists Association. It published images primarily by more traditional artists, such as Frank Emanuel.

41 *Colour*, vol. 1, no. 1 (August 1914), p.24.

42 cited John Brodzky, op. cit., p.16.

43 Ibid., p.16.

44 Ibid., p.17.

45 Cohen, S, op. cit, p.114.

46 Hannah Berman was listed by Leftwich as one of the founding members of the 'Focussers' (see Essay 4).

47 *Colour*, vol. 6, no. 2 (March 1917), p.50.

48 TIS 'About Naviasky', *Colour*, vol. 12, no. 3 (April 1920), pp.46–9.

49 Lewis, W *Blast* (London: John Lane, The Bodley Head, 1915), pp.78–9.

50 Ibid., p.31.

51 Ibid., p.79.

52 Lewis, W *Blasting and Bombardiering* (London: Eyre & Spottiswode, 1937), p.90.

53 *Art & Letters*, vol. 1, no. 1 (July 1917), pp.1–2.

54 Ibid.

55 Read, H *The Contrary Experience* (London: Faber and Faber, 1963), p.102.

56 Charles Marriott (b. 1869) was an art critic and writer, with a particular interest in modern art.

57 Read, H, op. cit., p.99.

58 *Art & Letters*, vol. 2, no. 2 (Spring 1919), p.iv.

59 Ibid., vol.2, no. 3 (Summer 1919), pp.106–8.

60 Ibid., p.109.

61 eds., Beaumont, C W and Sadler, M T H *New Paths* (London: C W Beaumont, 1918), dedication page.

62 Ibid, pp.7–11.

63 Ibid., pp.85–92.

64 Ibid. pp.112–119. J G Fletcher commented, 'Jacob Kramer is far more essentially hebraic in his outlook than Gertler, whose Jewish outlook seems to me to be over-emphasised. Kramer is a grim, bitter realist' (ibid., p.117.)

65 *Voices* vol. 2, no. 1 (July 1919), pp.1–2

66 Romain Rolland (1866–1944) was a French writer, dramatist and Nobel prizewinner; a pacifist, he was best known as the author of the novel series *Jean-Christophe* (1904–12).

67 *Voices*, vol. 2, no. 5 (November 1919), p.188.

68 Ibid., vol. 5, no. 1 (January 1921), p.1.

69 Ibid., vol. 5, no. 3 (Summer 1921), p.73.

70 Ibid., p.74.

71 Zangwill, I *Voices*, Vol. 1, no. 1(January 1919).

72 *Voices*, vol. 3, no. 1 (February 1920) includes two poems and a prose piece by S Winsten.

73 See Essay 7.

74 Ibid., vol. 2, no. 1 (July 1919), pp.5–17.

75 Ibid., vol. 4, no. 5 (November 1920), unnumbered plate.

76 L G 'Pictures: The London Group', *Voices* vol. 1, no. 5 (May 1919), pp.271–2, praises Gertler's 'profound *Still-Life*'; ibid, vol. 2, no 6 (December 1919), pp.261–2, commends 'the masterful canvases of Bomberg […] the bass harmonies […] of Gertler, once more huge and anguished, Form resolving from jealous Chaos.'

77 S Winsten, *Voices*, vol. 4, no. 1 (July 1920), pp.38–9. This issue also included a plate by Bomberg of a seated Vorticist figure, possibly a writer at a desk or a painter at an easel. (vol. 4, no. 1 (July 1920), pp.38–9).

78 Isaacs, J *Voices* vol. 4, no. 2, (August 1920), pp.75–6.

79 *Rhythm*, vol. 2, nos. 11 and 12.

80 Drey, O R *Voices*, vol. 2, no. 4 (October 1919), pp.174–5. The same issue included an article 'Are the Jews a Nationality?' by Israel Zangwill.

81 Jacob Kramer *Jews at Prayer*, *c.*1919, oil on canvas, 87.6 x 49.8 cms, Tate, purchased 1975, T01973.

82 *Voices*, vol. 1, no. 5 (May 1919), pp.318–9.

83 Ibid., vol. 3, no. 3 (April 1920), pp.127–8.

84 *Renesans*, vol. 2, no. 3 (June 1920), pp.162–168

85 Leftwich, J 'Jewish London 50 Years Ago', op. cit., p.15.

86 *Voices* vol. 3, no. 3 (April 1920), pp.127–8.

87 Ibid.

88 *The New Age* was under A R Orage's influential editorship from 1907–22.

89 Ludovici, A *The New Age*, January 1913, 12:11: 260: 'Building upon his thoroughly conscientious method he ought to do wonderful things', Ludovici predicted. 'He appears to be young. When he has found and appropriated his love, all this painstaking and severe painting of his will stand him in good stead. He will unbend. Let us hope that grace will follow.'

90 Lawson, P 'John Rodker: Minority Modernist' in *Anglo-Jewish Poetry from Isaac Rosenberg to Elaine Feinstein* (London, Portland, Or: Valentine Mitchell, 2006), p.78, fn. 24. The same volume contains the essay 'Isaac Rosenberg: Roots and Regeneration', pp.19–46.

91 *Poetry: A Magazine of Verse* was founded in Chicago by Harriet Monroe in 1912.

92 See Essay 4.

93 Rodker, J 'The Theatre in Whitechapel', *Poetry and Drama*, March 1913, pp.43–4.

94 Ibid., 'The New Movement in Art', *The Dial Monthly*, May 1914

95 Moult, T *Voices*, vol. 3, no. 2 (March 1920), pp.84–5.

96 He published *The Modern Woodcut, a Study of the Evolution of the Craft* in 1924. Furst also started a series of part-publications called *Modern Woodcuts* and went on to found the annual *The Woodcut* in 1927, which lasted for four issues (see Carey, F, op. cit., p.11).

97 Pound, E 'The Curse', *The Apple* vol. 1, no. 1, First Quarter (January 1920), p.22.

98 TIS, 'Picassine Poisoning', *The Apple* vol. 2, no. 1, First Quarter (1921), p.2.

99 Lewis's drawing of Pound appeared in *The Apple*, vol. 1, no. 2. Second Quarter (April 1920), p.97.

100 Peretz, J L 'The Stagnant Pool', translated by Hannah Berman, was published in *The Apple*, vol. 1, no. 4, Fourth Quarter (1920), p.246.

101 *Portrait of Esther Lahr* in *New Coterie* no.2 (Spring 1926), between pp.64–5.

102 Published by the Ovid Press in an edition of 200 copies: 15 copies on Japan vellum numbered 1–15 & not for sale, 20 signed copies numbered 16–35 and 165 unsigned copies numbered 36–200.

103 *Voices*, vol. 3, no. 3 (April 1920) acknowledged a Gaudier-Brzeska reproduction courtesy of Rodker's Ovid Press.

104 First published in March 1914.

6 FIGHTING ON DIFFERENT FRONTS

ISAAC ROSENBERG AND JOHN RODKER

1 John Rodker, typescript of *Memoirs of Other Fronts*, John Rodker Papers, Harry Ransom Center, University of Texas at Austin, 100b. The first paragraph of this passage appears in *Memoirs of Other Fronts* (London: Putnam, 1932), p.142.

2 John Rodker, 'Hymn to Death 1914 and On,' *Hymns* (London: Ovid Press, 1920), p.17. I have kept the eccentric spacing and punctuation as it appears in this volume.

3 Isaac Rosenberg, 'Marching—As Seen from the Left File,' ed. Noakes, V *The Poems and Plays of Isaac Rosenberg*, (Oxford: Oxford University Press, 2004), p.124.

4 Letter from Rodker to Harriet Monroe, 14 March 1916, quoted in Cohen, J, op. cit., pp.134–5.

5 Hartley, L P, 'Novels,' *Week-End Review*, 11 June 1932. Clipping in box 40 folder 7, John Rodker Papers.

6 [John Rodker], *Memoirs of Other Fronts* (London: Putnam, 1932), p.110–111

7 Rodker, J, 'Twenty Years After,' *We Did Not Fight: 1914-1918 Experiences of War Resisters*, ed., Bell, J (London: Cobden-Sanderson, 1935), p.285.

8 Levene, M, 'Going against the Grain: Two Jewish Memoirs of War and Anti-War (1914–18),' *Forging Modern Jewish Identities: Public Faces and Private Struggles*, ed., Berkowitz, M, Tananbaum, S L and Bloom, S W (London: Vallentine Mitchell, 2003), p.83.

9 *Memoirs of Other Fronts*, p.16.

10 Typescript of *An Ape of Genius*.

11 Rosenberg, *Poems and Plays*, p.128.

12 For a discussion of how some of Rosenberg's writing strategies were taken up by other Anglo-Jewish writers, see Cheyette, B, '"Ineffable and Usable": Towards a Diasporic British-Jewish Writing,' *Textual Practice* 10.2 (Summer 1996): pp.295–313.

7 WHITECHAPEL GIRL

CLARE WINSTEN AND ISAAC ROSENBERG

1 'Clare Winsten (1894–1989): A Student at the Slade 1910–1912', The College Art Collections, The Strang Print Room, University College London, Press Release (June 1994).

2 Tickner, L *Modern Life & Modern Subjects* (New Haven & London: Yale University Press, 2000), p.289, n.81.

3 She has work in the British Museum (Print Room); Strang, UCL; Ben Uri Gallery/London Jewish Museum of Art; University of Essex Library; Shaw's Corner (now a National Trust property) at Ayot St Lawrence, nr Welwyn, Hertfordshire; and the Bernard Shaw Collection, Harry Ransom Humanities Research Center, University of Texas at Austin; as well as a number of private collections.

4 I am grateful to Wendy Butler, Slade Records, for providing this information.

5 Born Michel Birnberg, birthdate unknown; died in Tel Aviv in 1928. Feige Zellermayer was born 24 December 1856 in Husyatin. The date of their marriage (on a torn copy) is illegible but it took place in Czernowitz, Galicia, Ukraine. I am grateful to Benedict Birnberg, the artist's nephew, for providing this and subsequent information on the family.

6 Ibid.

7 They do not therefore appear on the 1901 census.

8 Gerty Birnberg went on to become a very able dress designer; Jonas attended the Central Foundation School, then on to Cambridge where he was a Senior Wrangler (gaining a double first in the Maths tripos), followed by a lifetime career as a maths teacher; he was also a brilliant chess player and played for England.

9 See fig. 28, *Portrait of Jonas (the Artist's Brother)*, *c.*1920. Jonas was certainly born in Galatz (or Galati), a city in Eastern Romania on the lower Danube, in 1894. Gerty could also still 'bring to mind Romanian words' in her last years (ibid.).

10 Ibid.

11 Tickner, L, op. cit., p.158, describes Birnberg as 'the daughter of a teacher who had moved into Whitechapel'.

12 'I think of the fathers whom I knew of the new anglo-Jewish 'intellectuals' of Whitechapel – the father of my boyhood friend Samuel Winsten [...] the father of Isaac Rosenberg [...] And [...] the father of Selig and Jack Brodetsky the father of Clara Birnberg, the artist who married Winsten, and did the St. Joan statue in Bernard Shaw's garden, round which he had ordered his ashes to be scattered.' Joseph Leftwich 'Jewish London 50 Years Ago' in ed., Sonntag, J *1915–1965. Fifty Years Achievement in the Arts: Commemorative Volume to mark the fiftieth anniversary of the foundation of the Ben Uri Art Society* (London: Ben Uri, 1966), pp.12–13.

13 This address is given on Clara Birnberg's Slade records.

14 Benedict Birnberg, op. cit.

15 Cited Tickner, L, op. cit., p.158 and n.81.

16 Benedict Birnberg, op. cit.

17 I am grateful to Margaret Haq, Librarian, and Penny Patterson at Central Foundation Girls School, Tower Hamlets, for uncovering this information in the archival records of past students, and to Jonathan Harrison for permission to quote from this file.

18 Central St Martin's history, archival information.

19 Birnberg was one of the few poor, working-class, Jewish students from Whitechapel not to have benefited from JEAS funding.

20 Central Foundation Girls School archive records.

21 Stephen Chaplin, 'Clare Winsten: a student at the Slade 1910–12, an exhibition of her drawings, The Strang Print Room, University College London, 6 June–26 June 1994', [catalogue text comprising folded A4 sheet unpaginated]. I am very grateful to Stephen Chaplin for discussing Clare Winsten's work with me.

22 At some point, whether by accident or design, two years was dropped from Clare Winsten's birth date, which is usually given as 1894. This is the date that appears on most accounts, including the notes to her exhibition at the Slade in 1994: *Clare Winsten (1894–1989): A Student at the Slade 1910–12*; and this is also the birth date given on her death certificate (see Family Records Office).

23 Nash, P *Outline* (London: Faber and Fabert 1949; this edition, London: Columbus Books Ltd, 1988), p.92.

24 Stephen Chaplin, notes for 'Clare Winsten: a student at the Slade 1910–12', Clare Winsten file [unpublished ms.], Strang archive. William Roberts remembered that the students were 'continually exhorted by Professor Tonks and Steer to study Ingres and Degas' (cited Williams, A G *William Roberts: An English Cubist* (Aldershot, Hants: Lund Humphries, 2004), p.12). Roberts also recalled that work by Augustus John and William Orpen was hung in the studios 'as examples of what he and his generation might achieve' (cited, ibid., p.13).

25 Clare Winsten, Unpublished Autobiography, cited Chaplin, S, op. cit. Stephen Chaplin read the autobiography, having been lent in by Theodora Winsten, in preparation for his introduction on Clare Winsten for the exhibition of her drawings. The autobiography is in a private collection and not currently available for public study.

26 Ibid.

27 Cited Cork, R *David Bomberg* (New Haven & London, 1987), p.28.

28 This took Carrington, a great Slade prize-winner, a full year.

29 Abdu'l Bahál (1844–1921) was the son of Bahaulah, the founder of the Bahai faith; he was only briefly in London from August–December 1911, during which time he also visited Bristol and Paris, so the drawing can be dated fairly precisely. He was among those 'blasted' on page 21 of Wyndham Lewis's journal in 1914.

30 Reference is made to her being taught by Steer in notes in Clare Winsten's file in the Slade Archive.

31 Some female students never progressed to painting at all: Barbara Hiles, a Slade contemporary, had previously studied art in Paris but was not allowed to pursue painting until 1914, after she won a second prize in the Slade Summer Competition (Gerzina, G *Carrington: A Life of Dora Carrington 1893–1932* (London: John Murray, 1989), pp.22–3. Tonks was also hard on Hiles but 'when he declared one day that 'if she knew anything about dressmaking she had better go home and do it', she leaped 'up from her donkey and [told] him, in a voice quivering with emotion, what she had in fact made every stitch of clothing she was wearing. Thereafter he treated her with greater respect' (cited, ibid., p.23).

32 Cited Chaplin, S, notes, op. cit..

33 Cited Hill, J *The Art of Dora Carrington* (London: Herbert Press, 1994), p.12, n.4.

34 Tickner, L, op. cit., p.158.

35 Diana Manners, later Lady Diana Cooper, Viscountess Norwich (1891–1986), was an actress, society hostess and author, active pre-war in a circle known as 'the coterie'. She was brought up as the third of the three daughters of the Duke of Rutland but her true father was believed to be the politician and journalist Harry Cust (1861–1917). Iris Tree (1897–1968) was a poet actress and painter and the second daughter of the actor-manager Sir Herbert Beerbohm Tree.

36 Reynolds, M *The Slade: The Story of an Art School, 1871–1971*, unpublished manuscript, pp.184–7, cited Gerzina, op. cit., pp.23–4.

37 Tickner, L, op. cit., p.149.

38 Including Gertler, Bomberg, Rosenberg, Kramer, Wolmark, Wayner, Schloss and Goldstein.

39 I am grateful to Ken Henderson for checking the archival records of the Society of Women Artists on my behalf. He comments: 'We have looked through the old catalogues for the SWA and can find no reference to Clare Winsten or Clara Birnberg so she did not exhibit with the Society of Women Artists.'

40 Chaplin, S 'Clare Winsten: a student at the Slade 1910–12', op. cit.

41 Laughton, B 'The Slade 1871–1971', introduction, Centenary Exhibition Catalogue (London: Royal Academy, 1971).

42 Cited Cork, op. cit., p.18.

43 Ibid.

44 Cork (op. cit., p.33) writes that Kandinsky had exhibited 'an important [...] canvas, *Composition 1*, [...] in London two years before [1910] at the Allied Artists' Association'; the memory of which may have influenced Bomberg's *Island of Joy* (1912). Through both her Slade and Central School connections, Birnberg is also likely to have known of and visited AAA shows.

45 A device famously used to great effect in Bomberg's *Ghetto Theatre* (1920, Ben Uri Gallery).

46 Private Collection.

47 Tate. See also Roberts' *Study for the Return of Ulysses* (1913, Tate) and *The Return of Ulysses* (1913, Nottingham City Museums & Galleries).

48 Oil on canvas, 46 x 81 cms, Ben Uri Gallery, presented by Liss Fine Art, 2007.

49 Private Collection.

50 Tate.

51 Tate.

52 Tate.

53 Paul Liss has suggested that the subject matter is a massacre of the innocents. Birnberg may have studied Rubens's and Mocetto's works of this name in the National Gallery.

54 Tate.

55 She also believed that he 'influenced' Ernest Brown [of Leicester Galleries] not to show her work 'because she was a woman and would not develop', cited Chaplin, S *Diary 70:* 7 March 1994. Stephen Chaplin noted these comments in his diary after reading Clare Winsten's Unpublished Autobiography. I am grateful to him for sharing them with me.

56 Records for the Women's Freedom League (1907–61; ref 2/WFL Box FL054–FL059) are housed at the Women's Library, London.

57 Central School records have not survived for this period.

58 Work was anonymous so it has not been possible to trace Birnberg's involvement with Omega.

59 Tickner, L, op. cit., p.289, n.81.

60 Chaplin, S, notes for 'Clare Winsten: a student at the Slade 1910–12', op. cit.

61 Chaplin, S, 'Clare Winsten: a student at the Slade 1910–12', op. cit.

62 The 'Jewish Section' has been discussed in detail in a number of essays, notably Steyn, J 'Inside Out:

Assumptions of "English" Modernism in the Whitechapel Art Gallery, London, 1914', in ed., Pointon, M *Art Apart: Art Institutions and Ideology across England and North America* (Manchester: Manchester University Press, 1994), pp.212–230. See also Tickner, L 'David Bomberg: In the Hold, Jews and Cubism' in Tickner, L, op. cit., pp.142–183; and Tickner, L and Gross, P 'The Jewish Education Aid Society and Pre-First World War British Art', in *The Ben Uri Story from Art Society to Museum and the influence of Anglo-Jewish Artists on the Modern British Movement* (London: The Ben Uri Gallery, 2001). For an overview of the Whitechapel Boys, see MacDougall, S 'Something is Happening There: Early British Modernism, The Great War and the Whitechapel Boys, in ed. Walsh, M *Avant-Garde and Avant-Guerre: London, Modernism and 1914* (Cambridge: Cambridge University Press, 2008). For a short summary, see Dickson, R and MacDougall, S 'The Whitechapel Boys', *Jewish Quarterly* (Autumn 2004, Number 195).

63 Tickner, L, op. cit., p.146.

64 Current whereabouts unknown.

65 (No. 30): *Rocks (black & white)*. Helen Saunders (1885–1963), studied at the Central School and The Slade (1906–7), exhibited with the Friday Club in 1912, the Allied Artists' Association in 1912–13 and joined Wyndham Lewis's Rebel Arts Centre in 194. She was one of the signatories to the Vorticist manifesto, *Blast*. Like Birnberg and Saunders' fellow female Vorticist, Jessica Dismorr, she was also involved with the Suffragette movement.

66 (No. 32) *Colour Emotion*. Amy Drucker (1873–1951) studied in Lambeth and had a studio in Bloomsbury. Of Jewish descent, she travelled widely in the Far East, South America, Abyssinia and Palestine.

67 (No. 33) *Washerwomen*. Thérèse Lessore (1884–1945) studied at the Slade (1904–9) and exhibited at the AAA in 1912 and was a founder member of the London Group. She married Walter Sickert in 1926.

68 The Omega Workshops were established by Roger Fry in 1913 (until 1919) with the support of Vanessa Bell and Duncan Grant. Artists worked no more than three and a half days a week and all work was sold anonymously. Objects included furniture, textiles and painted objects.

69 L K [probably Leo Koenig] *Jewish Chronicle* (15 May 1914), p.10.

70 Tickner, L, ibid., p.159 and n.89.

71 Birnberg believed that someone 'she knew [...] [had] removed her work from the 'accepted pile' to the rejects of the London Group', cited Chaplin, Diary 70, op. cit.

72 *Voices* (Volume 3, March 1920) included reproductions of two drawings by 'C. B. Winsten', a female head (opposite p.43) and a seated female Vorticist figure (opposite p.78).

73 Winsten's involvement – if any – with the Vorticist movement is unclear. Although 'the oddest collection of rapins in black hats, girls from the Slade, poets and journalists' (Heard, A *William Roberts (1895–1980)* (Newcastle: Hatton Gallery, University of Newcastle, 2004), p.36.) gathered together at Wyndham Lewis's Fitzroy Street studio prior to the birth of *Blast*, Birnberg's name has never been mentioned in connection with the movement.

74 A breakaway group formed in 1907 by 'dissenting members of the Women's Social and Political Union' in a dispute over 'a lack of constitutional democracy', founding members of the Women's Freedom League included Charlotte Despard, Edith How Martyn, Teresa Billington-Greig, Octavia Lewin, Anna Munro, Alice Schofield and Caroline Hodgeson. 'They classed themselves as a militant organisation, but refused to attack persons or property other than ballot papers, unlike the WSPU. Their actions included protests in and around the House of Commons and other acts of passive civil disobedience.' Like many other suffrage organisations, the League suspended its practical militant political action during the First World War and started voluntary work, 'though not the 'war work' of the type advocated by other suffrage groups'. They formed 'a number of women's police services and a Woman Suffrage National Aid Corps that provided some help to women in financial difficulties and limited day care for children. Furthermore, in 1915, the WFL founded a National Service Organisation to place women in jobs. However, the following year, political activity began again when they joined the WSPU in a picket of the Electoral Reform Conference. When women were granted suffrage after the war, they continued their activities with a change of emphasis. The organisation now called for equality of suffrage between the sexes, women as commissioners of prisons, the opening of all professions to women, equal pay, right of a woman to retain her own nationality on marriage, equal moral standards and representation of female peers in the House of Lords and they continued with this programme of social equality until the dissolution of the group in 1961.' Women's Freedom League Records (1907–61) introduction (ref 2/WFL Box FL054–FL059), the Women's Library, London.

75 The Goupil Winter Salon, Dec 1934–Jan 1935 (London: Goupil Galleries) includes an oil (no. 101) by 'C. Winsten', presumably a landscape, entitled *Chanctonbury Ring*, priced £50.

76 Her son's name (according to his obituary in *Transportation Science* (Vol 1, Feburary 2006), p.1: was Christopher Blake Winsten. 'Known for his work with statistics [...] he also worked at the Universities of Oxford and London (Imperial College), arriving at the University of Essex in 1968.

77 Blake, C *Modern English Art: A Visual Broadcast* (London: George Allen & Unwin Ltd), 1937, includes three works by 'C. Winsten': *Christopher* (frontispiece (verso)), *Lamplight* (p. 27) and *May* (p. 29) in the collection of W. N. Edwards. A note on p.26 states: 'C. Winsten. Trained at Slade School. Works shown at the Goupil Salon, the Leicester Galleries, Modern British, and the French Gallery'; and p.28: 'C. Winsten. The work is strong, personal, and rich in colour, with ability worthy of a penetrating vision. Works as eagerly to seize a scene in the open spaces, fighting against wind and rain, as sitting silently in the studio gathering the subtle changes in the sitters.'

78 See Chaplin, S 'Clare Winsten: a student at the Slade 1910–12', op. cit.

79 Leftwich uses 'Samuel'; the Birnberg family use 'Simon'.

80 'Many of the immigrants had been members of the Bund in Russia, including the entire family of Samuel Winsten, a close friend of Joseph Leftwich and Isaac Rosenberg. The eldest Winsten had been a Bund leader. The Bund in Russia was the Jewish Social Democratic Party and had Marxist sympathies. The Bundists in England joined the Social Democratic Federation which had it own party newspaper, *Die Neue Zeit* until 1908, when its editor Morris Myer having joined Poale-Zion (workers for Zion) founded the most successful non-political Yiddish daily *Die Zeit* or *Di Tsayt*, which lasted for nearly forty years.' See Lloyd, M 'Poets and Patriotism – Three experiences of the Great War' (Southampton: University of Southampton, 2001, MA Thesis).

81 Leftwich, op. cit., p.12.

82 Joseph Leftwich Diary: 1 Jan 1911–24 Jan 1912, Tower Hamlets Libraries, local history library, no L. 5766 100 LEF (Monday, 2 January 1911): '[...] While on the subject of Jimy [Rodker], I told Simy [Winsten] abut the fire-side discussion in the S[ocial] D[emocratic] P[arty] Club, when the Y[oung] S[ocialist] L[eague] clique was referred to as a 'band of snobs': of Simy they had said then, these staunch Socialists, that he is a thin, tall overgrown fellow, very self-conceited and desirous of showing his little public-school knowledge at all times. Thus it is impossible to mention in his presence the word "coal" for example, without him immediately saying "Coal?" – What is the scientific formula of coal, do you know?'.

83 Joseph Leftwich, 'Autobiographical Note' in ed., Goldsmith, S J *Joseph Leftwich at Eighty-Five: A Collective Evaluation* (London: The Federation of Jewish Relief Organisations, The Association of Jewish Writers and Journalists, The World Jewish Congress Yiddish Committee, 1978), p.6.

84 See Essay 1.

85 Wilson, J M *Isaac Rosenberg: Poet and Painter* (London: Cecil Woolf, 1975), p.42.

86 Winsten, S 'Portrait of a Young Poet', *John O' London's Weekly* (10 November 1950), p.589.

87 I have been unable to verify a date, having checked the marriage registers at the Family Records Centre at Farringdon for 1914–18 under Weinstein, Winsten, Winston, Winstone and Birnberg. However, Clara was signing herself Birnberg in May 1914 and Winsten by November 1919, so it is reasonable to assume that the marriage took place between these dates.

88 See Essay 2

89 'It was a group of intellectuals, writers and artists,' recalled Leftwich 'including Selig and Jack Brodetsky, Isaac Rosenberg, Alfred Wolmark, David Bomberg, Samuel Winsten, John Rodker, Lazarus Aaronson, Jack Isaacs, Emanuel Miller, Jacques Spira, Alec Sarner, Hannah Berman, Gertrude Azulay, Gabriel Costa, Charles Landstone, Harry Samuel, William

Chadwick, Ruth Löwy (Mrs. Victor Gollancz), David Hillman, Mark Wayner, and in the Yiddish field Abraham Vieviorka, who went to the Soviet Union and died there in 1935, and Abraham Teitelbaum who became a leading actor in Maurice Schwartz's Yiddish Art Theatre in New York. We became friends – many of us –' Leftwich also points out, 'for the rest of our lives' (Leftwich, '"Jewish London" Fifty Years Ago', op. cit., p.14). Leftwich also claims that when Wolmark was active in the Ben Uri served on the Ben Uri Art Committee (1946–56) and Israel Zangwill was President, Leftwich also claims that Winsten was Secretary at the same time. But he may have muddled the dates for Wolmark served on the BU Art Committee from 1946–56, Israel Zangwill having died in 1926. Winsten would have been living out of London during Wolmark's time at the Ben Uri, but may have served alongside Zangwill at an earlier date. It is also unlikely that Rosenberg was there, given Leftwich's later invitation to him to join (see Essay 4, p.13).

90 'Conscientious Objection in Britain during the First World War', the Peace Pledge Union website, 2008.

91 See Essay 4

92 'Conscientious Objection in Britain during the First World War', op. cit.

93 Ibid.

94 Ibid.

95 All titles and quotations from Winsten, S *Chains* (London: C W Daniel, 1920).

96 *Voices* (Vol 2, no. 5, March 1920) includes two drawings by C B Winsten opposite. p.43 and opposite p.78.

97 *Voices* (Vol 3, no. 1, Feb 1920) includes two poems and a prose piece by S Winsten.

98 See Essay 5.

99 Winsten, S 'Notes on Present-Day Art' includes a review of 'The New Art Salon, 160 Shaftesbury Avenue and X Group (Mansard Galleries) – European Art', in *Voices* (Vol 3, no 4, May 1920), pp.165–6.

100 'Conscientious Objection in Britain during the First World War', op. cit.

101 The copies of this magazine held by the British Library have been destroyed.

102 J Leftwich, ibid., p.15, names an article from 1933 which has not been traced. See also S Winsten, 'Portrait of a Young Poet', op. cit.

103 Jayne Addams (1860–1935), pacifist social work pioneer, author and friend of Canon and Mrs Samuel A Barnett. She established Hull House, a settlement house for immigrants and workers, modelled on Toynbee Hall, in Chicago in 1889.

104 Holroyd, M, op. cit., p.760, writes that 'Winsten was to fashion a career out of being Shaw's neighbour at Ayot [St. Lawrence] […] In their imaginations the Winstens lived through famous people, soliciting politenesses which, in the abundant retelling, swelled into exotic compliments. Shaw enjoyed playing with their cat Fuzia (a tortoiseshell […]), sitting for Clare Winsten ([…] a sculptress and painter) and chatting to her husband (who had been imprisoned as a youthful pacifist in the Great War). Now that Apsley Cherry-Garrard had left Larmar Park, the Winstens were 'the only people in the village I can talk to or can talk to me'. However, Stephen Winsten was disliked by Shaw's loyal secretary, Miss Patch, and was described by Lady Astor as a 'Polish Jew' (cited, ibid., p.763).

105 Shaw also sat for the following artists: Rodin, William Strang, Troubtetzkry, Jacob Epstein, Sara Botzaris, Kathleen Bruce (Lady Scott), Joseph Coplans, Jo Davidson and Sigismund de Strobl (Holroyd, M, ibid., p.354).

106 One of her portraits of Shaw is in the British Museum Print Room, another (together with other work) is in the Art Collection, Harry Ransom Humanities Research Center: Clare Winsten / Bernard Shaw Collection, University of Texas at Austin, ref. 65.527.1–19

107 One, formerly in the Shaw theatre, is now in Camden Town Hall, the others are in private collections. Clare made numerous drawings and paintings of Shaw. I am grateful to Jonathan Harrison for supplying this information.

108 Oil on canvas, 43_ x 32_", signed 'Winsten 1945', private collection. Exhibited *The Faces of Authorship: An Exhibition of Twentieth Century Literary Portraits From The Humanities Research Center Collections, The University of Texas at Austin, November 24, 1968–January 4, 1969* (88); The Art Museum of The University of Texas at Austin, Twenty-third and San Jacinto.

109 Winsten, S *Days with Bernard Shaw* (London: Hutchinson, 1948), p.241. At least two casts were made in bronze from the head of this piece, cast by the Morris Singer Foundry, one is in England; another is at the University of Texas at Austin. Weintraub, S 'George Bernard Shaw', *Dictionary of National Biography* (Oxford: Oxford University Press, 2004)..

110 Talk by Sir Ernst Gombrich at the Private View of the *Exhibition of Clare Winsten's Drawings* at the Strang print Room, University College, London on the 6th June 1994, courtesy of Geoff Hassell. I am grateful to Geoff Hassell for sharing information with me on Clare Winsten.

111 *Buoyant Billions: a comedy of no manners in prose by Bernard Shaw and in pictures by Clare Winsten* (London: Constable, 1949), published in an edition of 1025 copies. Artwork from this project is held in the Art Collection, HRHRC, Winsten/Shaw Collection, University of Texas at Austin, ref. 65.34.1-24; see also 65.527.20-169.

112 Holroyd, M, op. cit., p.761.

113 Ryder, R D 'Ruth Harrison (1920–2000)' *Dictionary of National Biography* (Oxford: Oxford University Press, 2004).

114 London: Phoenix House, 1956. Artwork from this project is held in the Art Collection, HRHRC: Winsten/ Shaw Collection, University of Texas at Austin, ref. 65.540.1–21.

115 There were three Round Table conferences to discuss India's move towards dominion status: November 1930 – January 1931; September – December 1931; and November – December 1932. Gandhi was the congress representative at the Second Round Table Conference.

116 I am grateful to Jonathan Harrison for this information.

117 Jacob Kramer also sketched Gandhi in 1931.

118 Current whereabouts unknown. According to her grandson, Jonathan Harrison, she painted a number of portraits of Gandhi.

119 Gombrich, E, op. cit.

120 Private Collection.

121 Not dated, pencil, British Museum Print Room.

122 1960, work on paper, British Museum Print Room.

123 All current whereabouts unknown.

124 Chaplin, S, op. cit.

CHRONOLOGY

1 Rosenberg also wrote a second poem with this title, 'Wedded' (2).

Ben Uri

The London Jewish Museum of Art

A Museum for Everyone Bridging Communities through Art

INTERNATIONAL ADVISORY BOARD

UK

Prof. Brian Allen
The Paul Mellon Centre for Studies in British Art
Sir Anthony Caro
Sculptor
Ms. Gill Hedley
Independent Curator
Prof. Griselda Pollock
University of Leeds
Dr. Andrew Renton
Writer and Curator
Sir Norman Rosenthal
Royal Academy of Arts
Sir Nicholas Serota
Tate
Dr. Evelyn Silber
Glasgow University

EUROPE

Mr. Joel Cahen
Jewish Historical Museum Amsterdam
Mr. Georg Heuberger
Jewish Museum, Frankfurt
Dr. Felicitas Heimann-Jelinek
Jewish Museum, Vienna
Dr. Leo Pavlat
Jewish Museum, Prague
Ms. Laurence Sigal
Jewish Museum, Paris
Mr. Edward van Voolen
Jewish Historical Museum Amsterdam

AMERICA

Prof. Bruce Boucher
Art Institute of Chicago
Mr. Tom L. Freudenheim
Curator and Writer
Prof. Sander Gilman
Emory University Atlanta
Ms. Susan Tumarkin Goodman
Jewish Museum, New York
Mr. Daniel Libeskind
Architect

ISRAEL

Prof. Mordechai Omer
Tel Aviv Museum of Art
Ms. Shlomit Steinberg
Israel Museum

PATRONS

THE BERSON CIRCLE

Greta & Victor Arwas
Pauline & Daniel Auerbach
Esther & Simon Bentley
Miriam & Richard Borchard
Barry Cann
Clydesdale Bank
Marion & David Cohen
Nikki & Mel Corin
Beryl & Neil Davis
Suzanne & Henry Davis
Rachel & Mike Dickson
Wendy Fisher
Sue & David Glasser
Lindy & Geoffrey Goldkorn
Madelaine & Craig Gottlieb
Averil & Irving Grose
Tresnia & Gideon Harbour
Peter Held
Morven & Michael Heller
Sandra & Stephen Joffe
Sandra & John Joseph
Annely Juda Fine Art
Kessler Foundation
Tamar Kollek
Agnes & Edward Lee
Pamela & Michael Lester
Hannah & David Lewis
Hannah Lowy & Lord Mitchell
Alastair McEwan
Hugh Merrell
Robin & Edward Milstein
Diana & Allan Morgenthau
Mischon de Reya
Susan and Leo Noe
Susan & Martin Paisner
Shoshana & Benjamin Perl
Ingrid & Mike Posen
Simon Posen
Janice & Barry Prince
Ashley Rogoff
Marilyn & Anthony Rosenfelder
Ann & David Susman
Esther & Romie Tager
Myra Waiman
Alma & Leslie Wolfson
Sylvie & Saul Woodrow
Della & Fred Worms
Matt Yeoman

ACKNOWLEDGEMENTS

LENDERS TO THE EXHIBITION

The authors, editors and trustees would like to thank the private owners, named and anonymous, and the directors and staff of the following museums and galleries for generously lending their works to the exhibition.

Ben Uri Gallery, The London Jewish Museum of Art: *Attack; Portrait of Mrs Herbert Cohen*

British Library: *Moses; A Merry Xmas from the 40th: Design for a Christmas Card*

British Museum, London: *Head of a Male Figure; Study of Nude Woman (seated with Knee Raised); Study of Nude Woman (Seen from Behind Walking); Portrait of Horace Brodzky; Portrait of Isaac Rosenberg* (1913)

The Joseph Cohen Collection of World War I Literature/the Joseph M Bruccoli Great War Collection, Thomas Cooper Library, University of South Carolina: *Self-Portrait* (1906); *Head of a Barrister; Self-Portrait* (1912); *Hark, Hark, the Lark; Three Rough Sketches: 39 Rosenau Road; Letter to Sydney Schiff c July 1917*

Imperial War Museum, London: *Head of a Monk; The Fountain; Trees; Head of a Woman 'Grey and Red'; Self-Portrait in a Pink Tie; Portrait of Marda Vanne; Sketch of Soldiers Arriving on Leave; On the Departure Platform Victoria Station*

Imperial War Museum, Department of Documents: *Isaac Rosenberg, Letter to R C Trevelyan* c 1916; *Isaac Rosenberg: Untitled Letter, 1917; Isaac Rosenberg: Untitled Letter, 1916 or after*

National Portrait Gallery: *Self-Portrait* (1915); *Isaac Rosenberg; Sir Edward Marsh*

The Parkes Library, University of Southampton: *A Piece of Mosaic being the book of the Palestine Exhibition and Bazaar*

Private collections: *Head of a Woman in Profile; Self-Portrait in a Steel Helmet; Gunner Loading Shell; Soldier Patrolling Tunnel*

Private collection, courtesy of Christie's: *Study for Merry-Go-Round* (aka *Studies of Heads*); *Study for Merry-Go-Round* (aka *The Straw Hat*); *Portrait of Gaudier-Brzeska*

Private collection, courtesy of Sotheby's: *Self-Portrait with Trilby*

Private collection (Luke Gertler): *Youth*

Private collection (Raymond Francis): *Morris Goldstein; LCC School Bolt Court Medal*

Private collection (Mrs Gerda Horvitch): *Caxton and Edward IV; Copy of Correggio's Venus, Cupid and Mercury; Self-portrait with Trilby (facing left)*

Private collection (Joan Rodker): *Portrait of Sonia*

Private collection (Jonathan Rosenthall): *Military Portrait; Military Portrait (with cap)*

Private collection (Mrs Betty Silver): *The Artist's Father* (1911); *The Artist's Mother; Self-Portrait* (1912); *Self-Portrait in a Red Tie*

Private collection (Doron D Swade): *Self-Portrait* (1914)

Private collection (Bernard Wynick): *Night and Day;* Slade certificate; Letter from Israel Zangwill; *Art & Letters*, Summer 1919

Strang Collection, University College London: *Portrait of Isaac Rosenberg* (1914); *Clare Winsten* (1915)

Tate: *Self-Portrait* (1911)

Tullie House Museum and Art Gallery, Carlisle: *Family Group at a Meal; The First Meeting of Adam and Eve:*

Victoria and Albert Museum: *The Billet*

COPYRIGHT CREDITS

PICTURE CREDITS:

Ben Uri Gallery, The London Jewish Museum of Art: *Attack*; *Portrait of Mrs Herbert Cohen*

Berg Collection, New York Public Library: *Untitled Landscape*

British Library, Department of Manuscripts: *A Merry Xmas from the 40th*: *Design for a Christmas Card*

British Museum, London: *Head of a Male Figure*; *Study of Nude Woman (seated with Knee Raised)*; *Study of Nude Woman (Seen from Behind Walking)*; *Portrait of Horace Brodzky*; *Portrait of Isaac Rosenberg* (1913); *Portrait of Abdhul Baha; Portrait of Ezra Pound*

Imperial War Museum, London: *Head of a Monk*; *The Fountain*; *Trees*; *Head of a Woman 'Grey and Red'*; *Self-Portrait in a Pink Tie*; *Portrait of Marda Vanne*; *Sketch of Soldiers Arriving on Leave*; *On the Departure Platform Victoria Station; Isaac Rosenberg in the 'family' suit; Bantam Regiment poster*

Imperial War Museum, Department of Documents: *Isaac Rosenberg, Letter to R C Trevelyan c.*1916; *Isaac Rosenberg, Untitled Letter, 1917; Isaac Rosenberg, Untitled Letter, 1916 or after*

Jerwood Foundation: *Portrait of Norman Kohnstamm*

Jewish Museum, London: *Israel Narodiczky outside his print works*

The Joseph Cohen Collection of World War I Literature/the Joseph M Bruccoli Great War Collection, Thomas Cooper Library, University of South Carolina: *Self-Portrait* (1906); *Head of a Barrister*; *Self-Portrait* (1912); *Hark, Hark, the Lark*; *Three Rough Sketches: 39 Rosenau Road; Letter to Sydney Schiff c July 1917*

Liss Fine Art: *Untitled Figure Study*

National Portrait Gallery, London: *Self-Portrait* (1915); *Isaac Rosenberg* (bromide print); *Marda Vanne* (1921); *Edward Marsh*

The Parkes Library, University of Southampton: *A Piece of Mosaic being the book of the Palestine Exhibition and Bazaar, cover design; 'The Wharf'*

Private collections: *Head of a Woman in Profile*; *Self-Portrait in a Steel Helmet*; *Gunner Loading Shell*; *Soldier Patrolling Tunnel; Sacred Love; Stephen ('Inca') and Clare Winsten in Clare's studio; Family group with Clare and Stephen ('Inca') Winsten and their daughters Theo and Ruth; 'Inca'*

Private collection, courtesy of Christie's: *Study for the Merry-go-Round (aka Studies of Heads)*; *Study for Merry-go-Round (aka The Straw Hat)*; *Portrait of Gaudier-Brzeska; Portrait of John Rodker; The Medical Inspection*

Private collection, courtesy of Sotheby's: *Self-Portrait with Trilby*

Private collection, courtesy of David Stern: *Portrait of the Artist's Father c.*1914

Private collection (Benedict Birnberg): *Portrait of Jonas*

Private collection (Raymond Francis): *Morris Goldstein*

Private collection (Mrs Ruth Garson): *Sing Unto the Lord*

Private collection (Mrs Gerda Horvitch): *Caxton and Edward IV*; *Copy of Correggio's Venus, Cupid and Mercury*; *Self-portrait with Trilby (facing left)*

Private collection (Joan Rodker): *Portrait of Sonia*; *Portrait of John Rodker*; *Sonia Cohen*; *John Rodker and David Bomberg*; *Whitechapel scene with Ruderman's store*

Private collection (Jonathan Rosenthall): *Military Portrait*; *Military Portrait (with cap)*

Private collection (David Routledge): *Potrait of Isaac Rosenberg* (1915)

Private collection (Mrs Betty Silver): *The Artist's Father* (1911); *The Artist's Mother*; *Self-Portrait (with raised hand)* (1912); *Self-Portrait in a Red Tie*

Private collection (Doron D Swade): *Self-Portrait* (1914)

Private collection (Bernard Wynick): *Barnett, Anna and Minnie Rosenberg; Isaac Rosenberg and his siblings; The Slade picnic*; *Isaac Rosenberg in uniform; Isaac Rosenberg and his brother Elkon in uniform; Studio portrait of Isaac Rosenberg*

Slade Archive, University College, London: *Clara Birnberg (Clare Winsten) in the life-modelling room ? at the Slade; Female Head (?Self-Portrait)*

Strang Collection, University College London: *Portrait of Isaac Rosenberg* (1914); *Clare Winsten* (1915)

Tate: *Self-Portrait* (1911); *Merry-go-round; Vision of Ezekiel*

Tullie House Museum and Art Gallery, Carlisle: *Family Group at a Meal*; *The First Meeting of Adam and Eve*:

Turner Bennett: *Dawn* (aka *Morning*)

Victoria and Albert Museum: *The Billet*

Additional images of works whose current whereabouts are unknown:

Fig. 2: *Self-Portrait (in profile facing left)*, formerly David Burton; Fig. 5: *The Murder of Lorenzo*; Fig. 6: *Ruth Löwy as the Sleeping Beauty*; Fig. 9: *Minnie Horvitch, the Artist's Sister*, all reproduced in ed., Parsons, I *Collected Works of Isaac Rosenberg: Poetry, Prose, Letters, Paintings and Drawings* (London: Chatto and Windus, 1979 & 1984); Fig. 10: *Portrait of Isaac Rosenberg*, 1909, reproduced in Amshewitz, S B *The Paintings of J H M Amshewitz RBA* (London: B T Batsford Ltd, 1951), Plate 10; Fig. 13: *Head of a Poet (Isaac Rosenberg)*, reproduced in Cork, R *David Bomberg* (New Haven and London: Yale University Press, 1987), p. 44, fig. 50; Fig. 17: H C Hammond *Portrait of Isaac Rosenberg*, courtesy of Jean Moorcroft Wilson and Weidenfeld & Nicolson; Fig. 18: 'Types of the Russian Army', reproduced in Wyndham Lewis, *Blast*, Vol 2 (London: John Lane, The Bodley Head, 1915), p.31; Fig. 20: *Major L Rothschild*, reproduced in *Colour*, Vol 4, July 1916, p. 214; Fig. 26: *Portrait of Joseph Leftwich c.*1915, reproduced in ed., Goldsmith, S J, *Joseph Leftwich at Eighty-Five: A Collective Evaluation* (London: The Federation of Jewish Relief Organisations, The Association of Jewish Writers and Journalists, The World Jewish Congress Yiddish Committee, 1978), p. 5; Fig. 29: *Seated Female Vorticist Figure c.*1920, reproduced in *Voices*, Vol 3 (March 1920), opp. p.78; Fig. 31: *Soldier c.*1917, reproduced in *Colour*, Vol 6, May 1917, p.117.

With special thanks to Patrick Gorman, Stuart Bunce and Douglas Atfield for photography; Ed Maggs (Maggs Bros), Tom Graves (Weidenfeld & Nicolson) and David Stern for assistance with images; Isambard Thomas for catalogue design.

The Ben Uri Gallery expresses its appreciation to the Paul Mellon Centre for the Study of British Art, the Dorset Foundation and Michael Lazarus for their generous sponsorship of this catalogue.

This catalogue is published to coincide with the exhibition
Whitechapel at War: Isaac Rosenberg and his Circle at
Ben Uri Gallery,
The London Jewish Museum of Art,
2 April – 8 June 2008,
touring to
The Stanley & Audrey Burton Gallery,
Leeds University,
16 June – 5 September 2008.

British Library Cataloguing-in-Publication Data
A catalogue record for this book is available
from the British Library

ISBN 978-0-900157-09-7

Edited by Sarah MacDougall and Rachel Dickson

Copy-edited by Huw Molseed and Harriet Powney

Catalogue designed by Isambard Thomas, London

Printed by Graphicom, Verona